Roads

to

Rome

by

Cameron Stansfield

Roads to Rome: Copyright Cameron Stansfield 1995.

Edited and written by Cameron Stansfield.
Design and typsetting by Cameron and Polly Stansfield.

Published by: Cameron Stansfield
9 Finedon Road
Burton Latimer
Northants
NN15 5QB
Tel: 01536-722 297
Fax: 01536-722 302

ISBN 0 9527016 0 X

This book is dedicated to
Stan Witts.

Introduction

As pigeon fanciers, we are all familiar with the many and varied methods which can lead to success. Indeed, there can surely be few other competitive pastimes in which there are so many different roads to the top. Hence the title of this book.

Roads to Rome provides a platform for fanciers right across the spectrum to voice in detail all aspects of their management and their own particular philosophy on the sport. There are sprint men, distance enthusiasts and all rounders, club and fed flyers and national specialists, north roaders and south roaders. And as you will see, no two fanciers agree on everything or do everything exactly the same.

They all do, however, have at least three things in common. They all have many years of success behind them, they all follow a system which is within the means of just about any British fancier and, of course, they all have some good pigeons. This last point cannot be overstated so due emphasis has been placed on the bloodlines they fly.

The final part of the book is given over to something altogether different. It is a close-up look at the Pau National, a race which holds a special fascination not just for some of the fanciers in this book but for fanciers far and wide. It begins with an interview with former National Flying Club chief convoyer, John Goodwin, and goes on to highlight the fanciers and birds who have been to the fore in recent seasons.

You are sure not to agree with everything which is said in the following pages, but that is the beauty of our sport.

Contents

ROY SEATON

It took Roy Seaton four years to win his first card. That was back in the 1950s and it gave no indication of what was to follow. From that humble start, he went from strength to strength. So much so that between 1968 and 1979 he was the top prizewinner in two different clubs in Dumfries. Then came a move to Annan, one of the true hotbeds of the British Isles, and things took a turn for the worse. He was still managing to win prizes but not with his former consistency, as his pigeons continually suffered from wet droppings. He emulsioned over the paintwork in his loft, tried antibiotics and even had post-mortems carried out on a couple of birds - all to no avail. Then, in 1984, he had some seed which he found on the grass outside his loft analysed. It had the appearance of pink-coloured wheat and turned out to be poison ivy seed which had blown over from some nearby trees. He cut the ivy off the trees and within a month the watery droppings ceased. However, most of his birds had been so badly damaged that he decided they would have to go. That summer, he went to Belgium and struck up a friendship with Jean-Pierre Baert of Blankenberg. The stock he brought back was to bring about a change in his fortunes. Within five years, he was to win a national himself and, these pigeons, both for Roy and others, have left a lasting mark on the sport in Scotland.

Which clubs are you a member of?
My wife and my son and I fly in the Annan & District Homing Club, the Annan 2B Club, the Annan Burgh Single Bird Club, the Scottish National Flying Club and, last year, hoping to get birds to come on a better line, we joined a newly formed club called the Annan & District Premier Club which is convoyed by the South Lanarkshire Fed. Flying in the single and two-bird clubs creates extra interest in the club racing, with each member competing on equal terms. It is a very competitive area and in club racing we can send up to 800 birds some weeks. However, from the inland races the club does not do very well in the federation. This is possibly due to geographical layout as we have the Cumbrian hills and the Solway Firth to our south and we all have to train off the line of flight. Most of the birds come in from the north-east side of the town, having followed the A74 up through Carlisle and Gretna, and then break off for their lofts. When it comes to national racing, however, the Annan Club has a record second to none, past or present, and if you are fortunate enough to have the first bird home in the club you are usually well placed in the national.

Give me a brief outline of the family of birds you now race.
The base of our present family of pigeons originated from Jean-Pierre Baert of

Blankenberg in Belgium. These are based on a pigeon called 'Supercrack', which won three firsts national, bred eight national winners and is grandsire to at least sixteen national winners. I was introduced to Jean-Pierre when I went to Belgium on holiday in 1984 and was very impressed with his family of pigeons. When I was leaving he presented me with six squeakers about six days old and I brought them back and reared them under my own pigeons. One of them turned out to be an exceptional breeder, being the dam of our Sartilly National winner, 'Jean-Pierre', and also of my brother's 2nd open SNFC Sartilly winner, which in turn bred his 6th open Rennes pigeon. Her nestmate bred a pigeon which won the Dewar Trophy for best performances into Scotland, scoring from Sartilly, Rennes and Sartilly II in the same year and her half-sister bred the 1st International Barcelona winner for Bohm of Germany in 1989. In 1986 Jean-Pierre reared me twenty late-breds and I went to Belgium in the December and brought them home. These pigeons have been responsible for a lot of prizewinners for myself and others from 100 to 611 miles, notably two hens that won the two-bird average from Niort with the SNFC, winning 9th open Niort on the day and 14th open Niort, and two birds I gave to my friend, Billy Jamieson, a chequer hen which was 2nd and 14th open Rennes and a blue hen which also scored twice from Rennes. This latter pigeon of Billy's is now at stock, having bred his 9th open Sartilly winner.

What is the breeding behind 'Supercrack'?
No one knows. The fancier who bred him died before 'Supercrack' had established himself and when Jean-Pierre went back and had a look in his old loft book there was no reference to his ring number. When people say they have a brother to 'Supercrack' they are guessing.

Do you think it takes pigeons time to acclimatise to new surroundings, particularly distance pigeons?
I can only speak from a personal point of view, but over the years the pigeons I've introduced have acclimatised quickly. The Jean-Pierre Baert pigeons, for example, scored the first year I sent them to the nationals. Mind you, I took it easy with them and they only went over the channel when they'd reached two years of age. Perhaps more significant than acclimatisation is the system you use. When you bring pigeons in you must follow the methods of the fancier you get them from.

Do you fly natural or widowhood?
Mostly natural, although last year I also tried twelve cocks on widowhood with some success. Working twelve-hour shifts, I found it difficult to work both systems so I intend to go entirely over to widowhood in the future. Having had a lot of success with hens in the past, I will try to race both sexes on it, perhaps re-pairing the hens for the longer races if I think they need that little extra motivation.

Which races are you most interested in?

The nationals, although I concentrate on each old bird race as it comes along and always try to make sure I have a bird entered which has a chance of winning.

So not all your birds are sent fit enough to win?
No. If I send a team of forty to one of the earlier races I'd expect only about eight of them to be going with a real chance. The others will be going as part of their preparation for the nationals and if they were fit I'd be very upset.

Typically, how many such prep races do your national birds have?
Usually four, with the last one being four weeks before the national race they are going to. Hopefully they will have had a six or seven-hour fly in one of these races. They then have 'open hole' and exercise when they want to, up until ten days before basketing when they get four or five single tosses from 26 miles, finishing on the Saturday before basketing. However, if a pigeon comes into top condition which is not intended for the race I will take the opportunity and send it. This has happened a number of times. One pigeon I had flew 300 miles on the Saturday and when it landed, it looked as if it had never been away. I sent it back on the Tuesday to Rennes and it was my first pigeon, winning 27th open when there were only twenty-nine birds on the day. When a pigeon comes into super form, grab the opportunity with both hands.

Are you a good judge of a pigeon?
You really put a fancier on the spot with a question like that. I would have to say I know what I'm looking for, but it takes me three years to prove whether I'm right or not. It is very easy to describe the type of bird you like but very difficult to say whether or not it will win in national competition, so you must race them to sort out the good from the bad.

So would you describe yourself as a patient man?
Very patient. That's why when I buy pigeons I ask only for the best. And if the best aren't available at the time I'll wait until they are, as it's no use my waiting three years for a pigeon if I don't think I've got the right stuff to begin with. If you have the correct tools to work with it makes the job much easier and what Van Hee said is very true: 'The apples don't fall far from the tree'.

What qualities do you look for in a pigeon?
When I handle a pigeon, I like it to be balanced, and have silky feathering, a nice throat, a bright eye with a small pupil and vent bones as tight as they can be. I won't have a pigeon in my loft with bad vents and some of my hens have vents as tight as the cock birds. For distance racing, I also think the wing is of the utmost importance. By looking at it you may not be able to say for certain that the pigeon will fly fourteen to fifteen hours on the wing, as you obviously need more than just a good wing for that, but you should be able to say if it won't. It is essential that you have plenty of ventilation

between the four end primaries. I once had a pigeon with a poor wing but the heart of a lion. He would try so hard but would come back tired after only eight hours. I was confident he had the determination but was sure that his broad flights were holding him back. I trimmed the outside webbing of his last three flights to make it like a normal good wing, having first tried the same on a stock pigeon to see if it might work, and after that he took two good positions, one after doing fourteen and a half hours on the wing. I would make the point, though, that whilst all the good national prizewinners I have handled have had the attributes I have mentioned, I have also handled many birds like this that could not home in race time.

Have you tried trimming the flights of any others since?
No because I now breed for the wing. And by that I mean, if a pigeon hasn't got the wing I want, I don't give it a chance to breed.

What do you mean by a nice throat?
A small throat. Having travelled to Belgium a lot over a number of years it has become apparent that all the top lofts I have visited pay a great deal of attention to the throat of the pigeon. Having been shown what to look for and having checked my own pigeons, I found that the best all had one thing in common. They all had a small throat.

Is a strong back something you also look for?
Not so much as the other things, though having said that, I've only ever had one pigeon score in the nationals that really stuck it's tail up in the air. One of the things I've also noticed in Belgium is they don't seem to bother about backs either, as long as a pigeon is good in the vents and has the right breeding. Jean-Pierre Baert once asked me to go through some of his pigeons because he wanted to get his numbers down. I picked one out and told him I thought it was weak in the back. He looked in his loft book and said he couldn't kill it because it was out of one of his best pigeons.

If you were to go into another fancier's loft, could you pick out his best birds?
If I went at feeding time. All good pigeons are moderate eaters. Watch the pigeons skirting the trough and you won't be far off picking the best ones.

Why is form easier to achieve some years than others?
I believe it's down to the position of one's loft in relation to the prevailing weather conditions, particularly if you have a traditional open-fronted loft which you can't control. Most of the Belgians nowadays are having their lofts closed in, with no air coming in at ground level. Instead, it comes in through the soffits at the front of the loft, drops, rises and leaves again through the soffits at the rear. You don't need to go to those lengths, but it is essential that you have a good, dry and draught-free loft. When I was going to start racing on my own in 1965 I realised the importance of having correct loft design. When looking at the club and national results in our area the loft of JT Jamieson

& Son stood out from the rest. I reasoned that their loft design must be correct so I copied it. I'm sure also that food has got a lot to do with how good a season you have. In my exceptional years I've had a good batch of dog-tooth maize. I've spoken to others who have found the same and who would agree with me on this. Unfortunately, good dog-tooth maize is hard to get now so one or two of us are considering approaching Kellogs.

Would you say that maize is the most important grain for racing?
No, a balance of good quality grains is the important thing.

Would you like to see a late liberation for the Scottish National races?
No. To time a pigeon on the day of liberation from a 500-mile race, sometimes after fifteen to sixteen hours on the wing, gives me a tremendous thrill. It means that all the planning and hard work over the year has been rewarded. I do not think a 500-mile race over two days can compare with it. It is too much of a lottery because it makes pigeons go down to roost when they are still fit to fly and some probably continue in failing light and finish up injuring themselves. If we had two-day races maybe we would have to look for a different type of pigeon. It is not so much the distance that beats most, but time on the wing. Compare your pigeons with athletes. If Linford Christie raced Roger Black over 400 metres you would expect Roger Black to win every time. But if you had two races over 200 metres you would expect Linford Christie to win.

Are you in a good position for the nationals?
Better than the Ayrshire boys, anyway. It's sixty-five miles from Annan to Ayr, but from Rennes they're only getting thirty-five miles overfly. They would do better, I feel, if they trained from Millom in Cumbria rather than Annan and taught their birds to cross the Solway. Those of our pigeons which were liberated with the South Lanarkshire Fed last year came on an excellent line. It was as if they were coming up over Morecambe Bay and we had no problem getting them to cross the Solway. The best position to be in for the nationals last year, however, was Eyemouth over on the east coast. In future, it will be a challenge to try and beat the eastern fanciers, as I believe they have an easier route. Their pigeons have no hills to face, unlike ours which have to come through the Cumbrian fells, and theirs are also favoured by the prevailing westerly winds.

You suggested you might need a different type of pigeon if the Scottish National opted for a mid-day liberation. As it stands, with an early liberation, would you, yourself, need different pigeons if you lived further north?
No. The family I have at the moment is quite capable of winning up to 600 miles. They have won from Niort for myself and they have won for people I have given them to in the Edinburgh area as well.

What velocity are your pigeons best suited to?
I used to think about forty miles an hour, but when I won the national they were going much faster.

How do you account for the poor racing suffered by the Scottish National in recent years?
There are a number of reasons. To pick out one, I don't think our birds should be liberated with pigeons flying to lofts further down the country. Our pigeons are effectively flying against sprinters and they burn themselves out.

Can sprinters be turned into distance pigeons?
You'd find one or two in any sprint family - the slower ones. Having said that, it's hours on the wing which is the deciding factor. Given a tail wind from Rennes the sprinters would stand a chance. I think you're more likely to get a distance pigeon to win at a shorter point than the other way round.

Do you think some pigeons fail from the distance not because they can't do the hours on the wing but because they just don't know at the outset which way home is?
Yes. I heard a fancier recently likening the way the homing instinct works to a wireless. The point he made was that when the batteries are fully charged it is able to pick the signal up more easily so you get a good reception and I think you might be able to apply that to pigeons in top condition.

What do you give your birds on their return from a race?
They get glucose in their water and are fed on a depurative mixture for twenty-four hours. If they have had a hard fly I try to encourage them to go back on the nest and confine them to the loft. I also give them some groats and, if it is not too late in the evening, I may hand bath them in warm water to help relax them.

At what age is your family at its best?
Three or four, or even five.

Are you a good young bird flyer?
No. I have never been very successful with youngsters. Maybe this is due to my working shifts. One day they're exercised in the afternoon, the next day they're not out until 7 pm when I finish work, so there is no routine, which I think is essential.

What do you ask of youngsters?
They are trained to 26 miles then I take my pick of them and leave these to mature. The rest are raced and the aim is to give them some experience without straining them. All of my best pigeons never raced as youngsters. It's similar to training racehorses. A top

trainer will never push a young horse too far.

What about yearlings and older birds?
As yearlings I like them to fly as many races as possible up to Cheltenham, 200 miles, then I stop the pick of them and the others fly to the south coast. I train late-breds with the following year's youngsters before putting them on the road at two - with some good results. I expect two-year-olds and above to fly one of the channel races, and the pick of them will be for Rennes, our main SNFC race. If they give me one good performance a season I'm happy.

Having had the chance to observe how the Belgians operate, would you say they are ahead of us in any respects?
I'm not convinced they're so much ahead in terms of feeding - we're being a bit brain-washed with that one - but I'd say they are in terms of stock-sense. They are more severe in their culling. They see winning as being down to type, so, for example, if a youngster doesn't have the wing they want, they don't wait for it to reach the basket. Consequently, they have much more uniformity of type. It amazes me the similarity in the pigeons from top lofts there. Also, if they have a champion they don't limit themselves to four youngsters a year off it as we do. All the Belgian fanciers I know practise the Bull system. I went to the loft of one well-known fancier who had bred seventy eight youngsters in one season out of the same pigeon.

Is there a down side to using the Bull system, in so much as one is going against nature?
I couldn't speak from a personal viewpoint, as I've never really had the room to try it, but if there is, they don't mention it.

Do you favour line-breeding, inbreeding or crossing?
Breeding is one of the most interesting aspects to pigeon racing and one I look forward to every year. I have tried most methods and now have a tendency towards line-breeding to different birds in my loft and then crossing the different lines. When a new top racer emerges, I start line-breeding to it, my favourite pairing being grandparent to grandchild and uncle to niece, providing they complement each other, aiming all the time to produce a medium-sized, well-balanced racer. I have found, in the past, when I practised inbreeding the performances suffered and found the opposite when trying a cross. Do not think your pigeons are the best and you can't find anything good enough to bring in as a cross or your results will surely suffer over time. The Belgians cross all the time - crossing out and then bringing the progeny back in.

Do you take the eye into account?
I don't worry about eye-sign as such, but I never mate together two pale-eyed pigeons or pigeons with the same type of eye. I'm always looking to improve and, to me, greater

depth of colour in the eye, as indeed with feather, is a step in the right direction.

How many good pigeons do you expect to breed in a season?
When you have the right stock it should not be difficult to breed a number of good ones, but the number of really top birds produced each season is very small. In fact, if I get one or two, I think I have done really well. For some unknown reason, though, some seasons turn out to be exceptional and I produce a higher percentage of top pigeons, even though I may have retained the same matings as in previous years.

Do you sell youngsters?
Yes, but except for youngsters which have been promised for sales, I keep the first round off the stock birds for myself.

How many birds do you house?
I normally winter a team of one hundred and twenty, which is comprised of forty pairs of racers and twenty pairs of stock birds.

Most of your original stock birds from Belgium are now getting on in years. Has that had any effect on the quality of their youngsters?
No, as I float their eggs under healthy feeders. It is the rearing of youngsters by old pigeons that is the problem and not the actual age of the bird, so if they are reared under something else they should be as good as any other youngster.

Does being kept prisoner have any effect on a pigeon's ability to breed winners?
There seems to be a difference of opinion about this amongst various fanciers. I have found that numerous well-known lofts in Belgium and Holland keep their stock pigeons prisoner. Some born in 1987 have never flown out in their lives and look none the worse for it. If prisoners have access to an aviary and are supplied with the correct food, vitamins and such like, there should not be a problem. With the hawk trouble we have now perhaps they are better locked away.

What causes the first two primaries to be fretted on a squeaker?
Being double-reared and not being covered as tightly as ones that are single-reared. It makes no difference to the pigeon, though. The original pigeons I brought back from Belgium were covered in frets where the feathers had been checked as they were bursting but it did them no long-term damage.

Is a dropped tail feather a sign of strain or even constitutional weakness?
No. Dropped tail feathers are caused simply by the follicle of the flight being caught on something. If you cut the feather and leave the quill it will grow okay again.

Do you flag your birds?

No, never. If you can, it saves a lot of training by car, but my loft is situated two metres from my house and also has a large building directly behind it. If I started to chase them they may be tempted to start landing on roofs. I don't want to start throwing stones and falling out with neighbours. Because my naturals are on 'open hole', they keep pretty active anyway, flying quite a lot on and off all day, and I find two or three tosses a week from 26 miles is enough to keep them fit.

Have you tried working your birds harder?
I have yes, but it didn't work for me. Back in 1978 we had five on the result from Rennes, having worked them as I do now. The following year I thought, right, I'll improve them even more, so I took them to Shap every day. The result was they didn't perform as well. After that I reverted to my old way and the better they came again. The lesson I learnt is that a pigeon often comes into form not from continuous exercise, but from rest.

Which comes first, mental or physical condition?
Physical condition. After seven or eight hours on the road they have the muscle they need and then mine tend to rest in the last few days before basketing which puts them right mentally. One of the final bits of preparation I do before a national comes five days before basketing. I put a pinch of *Sliepsanol* in the throat, leave the bird for three or four minutes and then squeeze the wattle. Any yellow mucus that is there will come out. I did this with my blue cock who was 2nd open Niort and also with my 9th open pigeon.

Do you think they would have done as well without the *Sliepsanol*?
Not the one which was 2nd open. The slit in his mouth was always kind of closed and he was struggling to reach top form.

How many times a season can it be used effectively?
I wouldn't know. My birds only have one channel race a season and so I only use it once.

How much weight do your distance birds carry?
I reason that you won't see a fat marathon runner and so I send them on the light side. Having said that, I'm sure there are some pigeons which actually come on for being in the basket for a few days and put on more weight.

How do you choose your pool pigeons?
Recognising form is very difficult, as it can show itself differently with different pigeons. Most pigeons in form have a tendency to eat and drink less. Not only that, but they also tend to leave the peas and beans and eat more of the cereal grains. With widowhood pigeons a bird that's in form tends to strike out on his own, keen to fly, but

with natural pigeons it can be quite different. When we were 1st SNFC Sartilly and again when we were 2nd SNFC Niort, 611 miles, we could not get those two birds to exercise around the loft for more than five minutes and had to give them a few training tosses from 26 miles.

Why do you think it was they wouldn't exercise?
I know why. One of them was jealous of a cock in an adjoining box and I'd given the other a youngster which he wouldn't leave alone for any length of time. What they also had in common was a darkening of the eye-ceres as if someone had put mascara on them and, when single-tossed in training, they never circled but headed straight for home. The only other time I've had pigeons do that was in 1978 when I singled up my Rennes team. They went straight home and it was as if they were chasing each other. When choosing a pool pigeon for a race I am looking for all these things plus past performance from the forthcoming racepoint, if possible.

Are these final training tosses given more for mental or physical tuning?
More mental.

If a pigeon does hang about from these final training tosses will you ever decide it's not ready and withdraw it from your team?
No. I wish I could say I was like that, but I'm afraid they go anyway.

Which contributes more to success, the fancier or the pigeon?
I think in sprint to middle distance racing it is fifty per cent pigeon and fifty per cent man, but in distance racing I think it is seventy per cent pigeon and thirty per cent fancier.

Which is the most important motivating factor in a long race?
The loft. A lot of people probably kid themselves that it is the man, but I don't think it is.

Take me through your feeding system.
Correct feeding is the difference between winning and just making up the numbers at the races. Over the years I have tried many different methods and have found the main thing is not to overfeed. Having to work twelve-hour shifts, I cannot feed as I would like to, so have had to adapt accordingly. My birds are fed in their boxes on 25 per cent barley and 75 per cent *Premium Gold* which I get from *JA Swainston & Son* of Durham. This is a good quality mixture made up of beans, maples, green peas, dun peas, maize, dari and tares. Barley is a key ingredient as the pigeons will not eat it unless they are really hungry and I will not give them any more until the last grain is eaten. This way my birds are never overweight. I also go round each box and give them a pinch of linseed every day. When the racing is finished I change to *Versele-Laga Moulting Mix*

and only feed once a day, one ounce per bird. This year I've added extra beans to it, as I used to when I lived in Dumfries. When the last flight is fully grown the feeding changes to 75 per cent barley and 25 per cent *Premium Gold* plus linseed and I feed only six days a week. The birds always have a good fall of down feathers the day after they have missed a feed and handle better for it. I change back to 25 per cent barley, 75 per cent *Premium Gold* two weeks before mating when I also start feeding *Hormoform*. I use it as a colour feed for the eggs, continue with it until I wean the youngsters and then cut it out again when racing begins because I think it makes them moult more quickly. I am not fussy if the corn is polished or not. In the past I used to buy my tic beans and barley from the farm, to which I added dog-tooth maize which was all powdery, and the birds raced well on it.

How would you feed if you had more time available?
I'd do as I did when I lived in Dumfries - feed each grain separately. That way each pigeon would be guaranteed a balanced diet. I'd start with beans, then so many peas, then dog-tooth maize and finish with barley - making sure not to overfeed. If you let them, pigeons will eat what they like and not necessarily what's best for them.

Do you put anything on your corn?
Yes. I use cod liver oil, freshly mixed for the days on which I feed it.

Do you treat sick pigeons?
Yes. I hear people saying once they have been sick they will never be any good, but I cannot agree. When I had just started on my own, my birds were full of the cold, bringing up yellow phlegm which stuck to the walls of the loft, and I was told by experienced fanciers to kill them. Instead, I treated them with *Rovamycin* and they made a full recovery, winning from 50 miles to 554 miles. I altered my loft ventilation after that and did not have any more trouble.

What do you treat against?
Worms, canker, coccidiosis and respiratory disease.

When do you treat?
I start four weeks before mating, beginning with treatment for worms for which I use *Levamisol*. I then miss a week and treat for cocci using *Sulphamethazine*. The birds are treated for canker when they are on their first nest of eggs and every month during racing. For this I use *Ridzol S*, which I get from Belgium. I think many losses can be put down to respiratory problems, particularly young birds losses, so I give the old birds a course of *Tylan* once the youngsters are away and treat the young birds also two weeks before they start racing. The pigeons get multivitamins after each treatment but they do not get any grit during the treatment period itself, as the calcium can reduce the effectiveness of some medications. Nowadays, you've got to be on top of everything. Last

year, for example, we in the Annan area had a lot of trouble with young bird losses, but it wasn't caused by respiratory problems. We had them tested and it turned out to be candida, which is a fungal growth, in their crop. The youngsters retained the food in their crop and then when they were sick in the basket the condition quickly spread. I used *Nystan* and it cleared up within five days. I now believe that is the reason I lost a lot of old birds in the nationals. They looked all right, just a little tired at times, and I was at a loss to know what was preventing them from coming into condition. I gave them more training but it did them no good. From now on I will have them tested regularly.

Why treat for canker so often?
If I don't, I find I can't maintain the same level of condition.

Does treating regularly affect a pigeon's fertility?
No, not at all. I had one pigeon which filled his eggs up to twenty-two years of age.

Have you had any other experiences with sick pigeons?
One in particular. I've vaccinated against paramyxo every year but in 1990 my pigeons contracted what looked very much like it. It started in the young bird section with wet droppings and then they had difficulty pecking their food and were unable to fly straight. It spread through the hut, section by section, and I lost thirty-two pigeons, mostly year-lings and two-year-olds. The older pigeons that had been vaccinated with *Harkers'* vaccine in 1986 were not affected, however. I think the vaccine I had used on the younger birds must have been from a bad batch, as two other well-known fanciers that I am friendly with had the same problem after using the same vaccine. The MAFF was called in, did all their tests and said it was a virus similar to paramyxo! Whatever it was, I hope I never see it again as it is a struggle to get back to strength when you lose so many birds.

What else goes in your drinkers?
A multivitamin product for babies called *Abidec*, which I give to all pigeons twice a week throughout the year at the rate of 2 mls to a five-pint drinker. And I also use garlic, twice a week when racing, and three or four times a week during the winter. I don't think you need to use it if you feed a continental mixture, but if you feed beans, it's essential in order to thin the blood. I take the skin off the clove and slice it twice to let the juice out and use two cloves in a fountain, using the same cloves for a week. Inci-dentally, I'm actually allergic to onions, so I have to wear rubber gloves.

What other products do you use in your day-to-day management?
As far as supplements go, *Fabry White Salt,* a cattle lick and pink minerals. I don't, however, use any minerals outside of the racing season and neither do I ever leave grit in the loft where it attracts dust. I give it immediately after they've eaten and then take

it away again. As for hygiene measures, I spray the loft with *Virkon S* and to keep my pigeons clear of lice I use a *Vapona Bar* and creosote my nest boxes regularly. I also grow lavender in the garden and hang bunches of it inside the loft.

Why can so few British fanciers race successfully from 600 and 700 miles compared to the Dutch and the Belgians?
Not enough over here send, whereas over there just about all of them have a go. If we did the same our losses would be heavy at first because at that distance I believe a lot of pigeons are beaten before they come out of the basket, but eventually we'd be left with pigeons that would do it.

How do you account for the heavy losses the fancy is experiencing?
I think it is a combination of various things, with transporters, hawks and clashing contributing the most. There has also been a change in the fancy in general. Whereas in the past we kept small teams of pigeons and gave the youngsters more individual work, today we breed larger teams of youngsters and overcrowd. Also, we used to make do with just good clean food and water and any sick bird was disposed of, but today there are a variety of potions and pills which are supposed to help you win or cure sick pigeons. Likewise, when we wanted new stock we saved up and wrote to a top flyer, whereas today, stock is purchased from a variety of commercial breeding studs with pedigrees as long as your arm. Pedigree is a good thing as long as it is not just a piece of paper. Breeders must breed birds to win and racers must win, otherwise they have to go.

Why is the fancy in decline?
It is a real problem with many causes. Unemployment must figure high on the list for the number of fanciers leaving the sport and it is hard to attract new members due to the expense of starting from scratch. With the cost of a loft, clock, some reasonable stock plus membership fees for club, fed and union, who can afford it? The Annan & District Premier Club, of which I am a member, gives free membership for any fancier under eighteen years of age, supplies them with a clock, and each member gives them two youngsters.

What advice would you give to a new starter looking to purchase his initial stock?
It must be very difficult, but wherever they choose to go I think late-breds would be ideal. They are reared when the weather is good, are often of a nicer type than earlier-breds, and can usually be purchased off a fancier's best pigeons as he has already bred what he requires for himself. Another bonus with late-breds is that the youngsters bred from them tend to be slower moulters, which is good for distance racing.

How would you describe your approach to pigeon racing? Are you laid-back?
No, very dedicated.

Fanatical?
Yes. In so much as if my birds are not winning, I will go out and get some that will.

Do you still get the same enjoyment out of the sport today?
No. There is too much ill-feeling, too much politics and too much commercialism nowadays. After all, pigeon racing should be a hobby.

Which of the Belgian fanciers have most impressed you?
There have been so many that have impressed me for different reasons. Robert Venus, for example, has some tremendous stock pigeons, while Silvere Toye has a marvellous set-up. However, the pigeons that impressed me the most were those of Jean-Pierre Baert's. When I saw them, I thought, I need look no further. In this country, the finest team of pigeons I've seen are Tom Gilbertson's of Carlisle. They have all the qualities I mentioned that I look for and the performances to go with it.

R. & M. SEATON & SON.
ANNAN.

SARTILLY 438 miles.
RENNES 480 miles.
NIORT 611 miles.

53rd NAT SARTILLY (89)
121st NAT SARTILLY (89)
77th NAT RENNES (91)
135th NAT SARTILLY (91)
SU.87S.8865.
BLUE HEN

64th NAT RENNES (91)
SU.88.S.10214.
BLUE HEN

71st NAT RENNES (89)
14th NAT NIORT (91)
SU.87S.8876
DARK HEN

12th NAT SARTILLY (91)
SU.88.S.10183
BLUE COCK.

48th NAT SARTILLY (91)
SU.87S.8837
CHEQUER HEN

"MONIQUE".
60th NAT RENNES (89)
8th NAT NIORT (91)
SU.87S.8858
CHEQUER HEN

'Kleine Blauwe'
An excellent stock cock. Double grandson of 'Supercrack'.

R&M Seaton & Son's **'Golden Hen'** SU84S10370

Dam of 1st SNFC Sartilly, 2nd SNFC Sartilly, 1st Sartilly for G Bainbridge of Carlisle. A son was runner-up for the Dewar Trophy, whilst her nestmate bred the bird which won the trophy, both raced by my brother. Grandam of 1st Sartilly, 6th & 20th Open SNFC Rennes. Half-sister to the dam of 1st International Barcelona for Bohm of Germany.

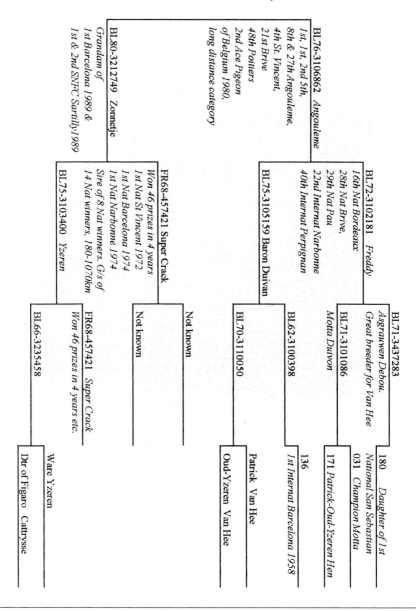

Graham Groom (right) with Jimmy Angus.

GRAHAM GROOM

Graham Groom flies to the town of Burton Latimer just outside Kettering. Highly successful over many years as both a racer and shower of pigeons, he epitomises the back garden, dyed-in-the-wool pigeon fancier, one who has thought and worked his way to success. He approaches the sport in a quiet, unassuming manner, leaves nothing to chance and, whether he wins or loses, usually knows the reason why. Had he lived in an area receiving greater publicity then, with pigeons like 'Barmy' and 'Eleven', who have won thirty-eight races between them, he would have been known far and wide. Not that this bothers him unduly. He is more preoccupied with what lies down the end of the garden and how to get the best out of each pigeon.

Graham, as you're just as keen on the showing as on the racing side of the sport, perhaps you could begin by telling me how you prepare a bird for the show pen?
My preparation begins once young bird racing is over. I'm not a professional, otherwise I'd part my old birds once they'd finished racing. As it is, I don't have the room to part earlier.

Why would you part earlier if you could?
I find that, as things stand, I have to rush the birds through the moult.

How do you do this?
I feed a high carbohydrate diet, plus a lot of oil seeds, and also try to keep the loft as warm as possible without compromising on ventilation. I should point out that I do not have any artificial heating.

Do you restrict their liberty?
Yes, otherwise they'd burn off the energy I want them to use to grow their flights and I'd have a situation where they weren't growing their end flight until January. To show successfully, you have to bring forward the moulting of the end flight by a month to six weeks.

How do you condition your birds for a show?
Well, as I mentioned, I keep them in and then, two weeks prior to the show, I give them a day's liberty in order to tone up their muscles. They are still on a high carbohydrate diet with oil seeds every other day. About eighteen hours before the show I place them in a distinctly warmer environment, usually the house, and that way they tighten up and lose any puppy fat they may have.

After a show, how long does it take to bring a bird back into condition?
Although the weight loss is tremendous after a show I've found that, providing you keep them shut up and get them back into a routine as soon as possible, it takes about a week. I never put them back into the loft on the night of the show, but the next day I get them to bath inside the loft. I'm a great believer in the bath. As with human beings, it relieves the stress and the strain and it's the best way I know of relaxing them.

Do you put anything in the bath?
Potassium permanganate. It doesn't get rid of lice if they're already there, but it helps keep them away.

By getting your birds back into this cycle as soon as possible, how many shows can you get out of them in a season?
Three or four. Last season I managed to get four best in shows out of one Krauth cock.

How do you know which birds will show successfully?
You've got to have a feel for the right type and I think I've actually got a better feel for showing than racing. In my younger days I always kept my eyes open and came to realise that judges usually go by first impressions.

What do you look for when judging?
I look in general for a pigeon with a good appearance, profile and overall stance. The right pigeon in peak condition stands out in the pen. It has a presence about it. In the hand I favour strong-backed, apple-bodied pigeons with a nice taper towards the keel to give the right balance. I forgive minor flaws in flights, 'honesty marks' as I call them, but I never forgive lice. If I'm judging a class of thirty, I pick out six through the wires and then go by first impressions in the hand. Usually, you'll find that the first, second and third in a class are clean, clear of lice, but when you reach the minor cards, it's often a problem to choose between type and condition. I favour fret marks over lice, working on the assumption that a lousy bird cannot be in the peak of condition.

Do you think a racing man can adequately judge a class of show racers?
Not unless he's into showing himself. I'm totally behind the showmen on this. Obviously he still has an opinion but you must remember that whereas good racing pigeons come in all shapes and sizes, show racers conform more to a type.

Would you house a team of pigeons that excelled on the road, but were no good in the show pen?
No. I enjoy showing as much as racing so my pigeons have to be able to do both. One of my ambitions is to compete in the major shows.

Are you tempted to try your hand with show racers?

I'd like to if I had the facilities.

Would you know what to look for?
There would only be one way to find out.

Do you go easy, racing wise, on birds that will score in the pen?
I used to, but not now. They all have to toe the line. For example, I lost the cock that won four best in shows on a training toss three races into last season.

To avoid fret marks, how do you help your birds recover from a hard fly?
Firstly, you must send them fit and in the right condition in the wing. I like to see a flight half to three-quarters of an inch through for the distance. When they home I use *Red Band* and then, depending on the length of the fly and the time in the basket, I put them on depurative, garlic and brewer's yeast for between twenty-four and forty-eight hours. Having said that, if a bird is two days late and has tried, you can't avoid fret marks. As I mentioned earlier, I also think a bath is the greatest thing of all when it comes to relaxation.

Some fanciers say that a tired bird won't gorge itself if fed a normal mix after a hard fly. Do you agree?
I accept that as a rule a tired pigeon won't gorge itself, but some do, and at the end of the day I'm in control of the pigeon so I don't give it the opportunity.

Do you force a bird to rest by restricting its liberty?
Yes. In a situation where I've only sent one of a pair to a race the natural tendency of the mate that has stayed at home can be detrimental. For example, if a cock has been away for a week, the hen will be looking to go to nest again. You must remember, though, that each is an individual, so what applies to one, doesn't necessarily apply to another.

After a few days in the basket and a long fly some pigeons aren't inclined to go back on the nest. How do you overcome this reluctance?
I try to create a situation where the partner, if it has stayed at home, is removed from the loft until the day of liberation. Before the mate arrives home, I warm both the nest and the eggs and return the mate. That way the one that has stayed at home is conned into thinking that, as its nest is warm, its mate can't be too far away. Hopefully the pigeon will then encourage its mate to sit when it arrives back. I've had pigeons held over for a few days that had been sitting a week, yet a fortnight later I've put them back into Thurso on the same pair of eggs.

Given that some pigeons are reluctant to go back on eggs after a long, hard fly, what is it that motivates them to race home?

It's a combination of a love of the partner, the owner and the environment.

Which is the strongest?
I'd put the loft environment above the man.

After a particularly hard fly, at what point can you tell that a bird won't recover sufficiently to score again?
When it's still in a terrible condition after forty-eight hours. By that time it should have started to pull back into shape and resemble its old self.

How do you prepare pigeons for the distance?
When I find out the date of the race, I count back fourteen to fifteen weeks. They rear one youngster in the first nest and then follow the natural cycle all the way through. A month before Thurso I like some to have a 300-mile race, whereas others go to Berwick and are then kept at Northallerton, which is 140 miles, this last race being three weeks before the big one. In the three weeks before Thurso, I give them a couple of thirty mile tosses. Alternatively, I stop some a month before Thurso, get them down on eggs and then give them a Pontefract or Northallerton seven days prior to Thurso. Two seasons ago, I was 2nd fed Thurso with a pigeon that went to Berwick and then had only one more race in the five weeks before, but you can only do that by restricting the diet. I should also add that I never let my birds out on the day of basketing.

How many birds do you send to the longer races?
About six or eight in a variety of conditions because you never know what sort of race might turn up. Perhaps one or two will hit it right and the others will struggle to get home, even though they may have been way out in front after 300 miles. I totally subscribe to the view that you need to send birds in a variety of conditions.

Aren't you afraid of losing good pigeons this way?
To be competitive you can't afford to be. I can't remember pulling a pigeon out of a race unless there was an obvious reason for it not to go, such as a minor health problem, injury or the casting of two flights in one wing almost simultaneously.

Are fanciers who don't take into account the state of the wing being hit and miss in their approach?
I don't know. I suppose they don't really consider what they're asking the pigeon to do and aren't looking at the pigeon as an individual. Some exceptionally fit pigeons will come through, but if everything else is equal and the velocity is down to 900 to 1250ypm, a pigeon with nine plus flights will prevail over one carrying only eight.

Do you map out a programme for all your pigeons?
Yes, and I don't normally deviate from it. Of course, after a hard race you need to have

a rethink, but otherwise they go where intended because I'm in control. Having said that, I was kicking myself this year when I couldn't send a cock that was previously successful from Lerwick back again because he was wrong in the wing, having dropped two flights together.

How come he caught you out?
I wasn't thinking and he was too fit too soon. That's one of the problems with feeding a high carbohydrate mix, the pigeons glow with health and get ahead of themselves.

Would you explain your training and feeding methods?
Prior to racing, the old birds are trained on line about six times and during the season they get a thirty mile chuck once a week. If they only fly round home for ten minutes some nights, so be it. By correct feeding I know how much flying they'll do, so if they don't fly for longer when I expect them to, I want to know why.

And feeding?
The basic diet I took out of the *Squills* column in *The Racing Pigeon* about twenty years ago. I modify it slightly depending on the forthcoming race. Maize is the most important grain for racing, as it is for moulting and showing. The mix prior to the distance races has plenty of protein but after Berwick it consists of 55 per cent maize, 20 per cent dari and milo, 15 per cent peas, 5 per cent wheat or groats and 5 per cent safflower. Before Berwick I feed 40 per cent maize and adjust the other grains accordingly.

Have you tried feeding a higher protein diet?
When I tried my hand on the south road for two or three years I did, but it wouldn't work for me on the north without my having to change my methods. I used to feed the old birds an ounce and a quarter of a heavier mix but now I feed only an ounce throughout the season.

How does your approach differ with young birds?
I feed more protein. I mix my own squeaker mix, one that contains no maize, and then I have a fad whereby they get nothing but peas and beans for a month, by which time training has begun. Then I switch to a breeding mix for a few weeks before putting them on a high carbohydrate diet.

Why do you not put them on a high carbohydrate mix earlier?
I find I lose too many youngsters. I've tried it and the pigeons became too fit before they were ready. I exercise them twice a day for six days before the first race, but through the diet I'm able to hold them back.

Six days a week implies that you don't let them out on a Saturday?
If I did I'd lose too many pigeons.

So I take it you don't believe that allowing your youngsters to get mixed up with batches of race birds helps to sort the good ones from the bad?
No. Pigeons have different maturity rates. When you have pigeons of various ages and from different families and you turn them all out together, you run the risk of losing two-thirds of the slower-maturing ones, so why chance it?

What do you expect of your young birds?
I know a lot of people say they don't take young bird racing seriously, but I have two fast-maturing families so I like to see a youngster pick up two or three cards. I also like them to have a minimum of four races. The slower-maturing young birds must be consistent.

How does your training differ with young birds?
I'm not particular about training them on the line of flight to begin with, as long as they home from a northerly point. The early tosses are aimed at giving them confidence. When I'm happy that they're running freely, I try to get them to come as fast as possible on the best line and that means repetitive training. I'm fortunate in that my wife, who helps me considerably, is at the home end, so it's a case of once round and in. There are only two places for a young bird, in the air or in the loft. I'm totally against giving them their freedom in the garden, they must toe the line, although I take the opposite view with old birds.

What about late-breds?
I've never done any good with late-breds that haven't been trained. I've lost them as yearlings even when I've waited till June. Now I train them, sometimes single tossing from work which is seven or eight miles to the north. It doesn't matter how cold the weather gets as long as it's a clear day.

Why is it necessary to train them?
I don't know really but it could be because they get set in their ways and somehow object to the basket later in life. Or it could be that a pigeon's capacity to learn lessens with age.

You obviously attach importance to young bird performances, so presumably you breed off the best ones the following year?
I have one guideline that I work to and it's simply that, irrespective of pedigree, I won't breed from a pigeon until it has scored. This year I've got seven or eight youngsters as good as anything else I have, so I'll breed from them accordingly and the others will act as feeders.

Using your system, how many years will a pigeon go on winning?
With the winds that we get on the north road pigeons are having to sprint 450 miles, so,

consequently, the edge is going off them once they are three to four years old. They're also getting a bit crafty by then whereas the younger birds are keener.

Would you say the same applies on the south road?
Racing on the south into Northamptonshire is different. For a start it's very erratic. One or two pigeons do the velocity you expect and the rest are an hour or more behind. I changed my feeding system when I raced south - less small stuff and more protein - because the birds were taking longer to do the same distance, either because of the wind or clashing. Consequently, an experienced older pigeon can be an asset on the south road.

Did your best north roaders make your best south roaders?
Some, especially those that were my best middle to long distance birds on the north.

Going back to the north road, do you subscribe to the view that a good club pigeon will also be a good championship pigeon?
Basically they're the same pigeon as long as you compete in the open races and don't mollycoddle them. My 2nd section, 11th open Midlands Championship Fraserburgh last year was achieved with a bird you might term a 'normal' club pigeon. Having said that, successful birds in the Northampton Town & District Fed have to be individuals anyway because lofts are spread over quite a large radius. The same may not be true if your birds are used to corridor flying.

Moving on, do you mind prisoners?
I have one or two but the answer is, not really, I prefer to have all birds flying out. I think it's detrimental from a mental point of view if not a physical one. I think a prisoner starts going downhill after three seasons.

What are your views on the eye?
I like to see an eye strong in colour, one where there's plenty of 'activity'. A gravel eye lacks depth but it often looks as though there is something going on in it. I don't like flat, hard eyes. As far as sign is concerned, for breeding I like a full, dark circle with a serrated edge. These I pair to 'neutral' eyes, those strong in colour but with little or no actual breeding circle.

So you don't pair two similar eyes together?
About two years ago I put two together as an experiment and the result was that the eye lost all its definition.

What about the eye for racing?
I do not like wild eyes that glare at you, but are very weak in colour. It's not that I've got rid of such birds, it's just that I've lost them on the road. I've never successfully raced

a pigeon with a washed-out eye either, but I have won with pigeons that lacked sign to varying degrees.

What strains do you fly?
For the middle to long distance, mostly Krauths crossed with Kirkpatricks, both of which originated predominantly from F Parkinson. I also have a few Busschaerts from Mr & Mrs Dave Boxford, but I don't know the exact lines as they don't concern me. For sprint to middle distance, I fly Beverdam and Pickering Janssens, and one or two of Alf Jones' 'Dark Uns', which are Busschaerts.

I know you've raced many excellent pigeons but two in particular stand out, 'Barmy', who won twenty-four separate races, and one you simply refer to as 'Eleven' which, although he's only four, has now won fourteen different races. Could you compare them for me?
There is a big difference between the two. I never flew 'Barmy', he conditioned and flew himself. He wanted to be competitive. I called him 'Barmy' because the more difficult he was to catch when basketing for a race, the further in front he was on race day, even up to 300 miles on a hard day. The first race I sent him to was a comeback after Berwick and he finished 3rd club. In his only other race as a youngster, Brixworth Open three weeks later, he finished 3rd open. That winter I said to my good friend Pete Chamberlain, whom I have to thank for breeding him, that this pigeon was different from all the others and that I thought he was going to be something special. Anyway, in his first race as a yearling he was ninety minutes behind, which I put down to lack of experience. The following week, after no training, he was a last-minute entry for Pontefract, from where he topped the section and finished 3rd fed. The next week, after one fifteen mile toss, he was 1st section and 1st fed from Northallerton. Then he did the same again from Morpeth, missed Berwick, and then won 1st section and fed from the next Northallerton. In the only other short race of the season he was 2nd club, beaten by a loftmate.

Presumably he carried on in the same vein as a two-year-old?
Sort of, except he wouldn't trap. Ridiculous as it may sound, I'd changed the roofing felt on my loft and he took exception to it. When he came he would land on the Fire Station look-out tower at the back of my garden. Fortunately it didn't affect my other birds and when they came, down he'd come. Anyway, I changed the felt back again and the following season he won four more firsts. For the next couple of seasons I raced him on widowhood and he won just the same. He won his last race at seven. I gave him a couple of races as an eight-year-old but by then it was clear he couldn't cope.

So most of his wins were gained on natural?
Yes. He just went through the cycle and conditioned himself.

Did you ever show him?
Once, through the wires and he came second. He doesn't come to hand as he might, although he's always been a bird that caught the eye in the loft.

How does 'Eleven' differ?
I simply used to enter 'Barmy' and bask in the glory, whereas I have an association with 'Eleven'. I can have a conversation and reason things out with him and I'd like to think that, although it's he who has had to do the work, I have contributed as much to his success as he has. With 'Eleven' I have a sense of achievement. He won his first ever young bird race from Worksop and was then 2nd from Pontefract the week after. After three more races, he was given two thirty mile tosses and, calling a hen to nest, was then 1st section and fed from Berwick, after which I stopped him for the season. As a yearling he won three separate Northallertons and a Morpeth. At two, he won three firsts including 1st fed Berwick again, followed by two wins the next season. Last season he won another three races, although, in truth, it should have been more. One week he messed about and I was so angry with him I timed my next bird instead, which happened to win the race. If I'd been the sort of fancier who tried to boost a pigeon's number of firsts I suppose I would have forgiven him.

What birdage do you compete against?
'Barmy' topped the fed four or five times and the section seven times, competing against an average of 1,800 to 2,000 birds, although the most he beat was approximately 2,500.

How do 'Barmy' and 'Eleven' compare as breeders?
Over two generations they're about level, although, of course, 'Eleven' is still young whereas 'Barmy' has now stopped filling his eggs. 'Barmy' only ever bred one bird to win as a youngster and oddly enough that was for Pete, the chap who bred him, whereas several sons and daughters of 'Eleven' have won as youngsters, including one that won Raunds Open from Northallerton last season.

Are the two cocks related?
No. 'Eleven' is a Janssen whereas 'Barmy' is a Busschaert cross.

Busschaert crossed with what?
You'll laugh when I tell you. A Fuller-Isaacson hen.

Do you have any gripes about the sport?
On the whole, I've made plenty of friends through the sport and enjoy it immensely, although I do now feel that some of the enjoyment is being lost because it's everything at a price. This year I've given away four youngsters off 'Eleven' because I'm in the sport purely and simply for enjoyment and not financial reward.

ROBERT O JONES

Good distance fanciers are constantly walking a tightrope, caught between the need for progeny testing, whilst always having to be careful not to over-commit themselves and court disaster. One bad race can undo years of work. Robert O Jones of Resolven has performed this balancing act better than most for over twenty-five years. Despite taking on the often hazardous route from Scotland into the heart of South Wales, he has managed to create and maintain a family of true long distance pigeons. In recent years he has begun the process all over again with the introduction of a number of Jan Aardens. These he has mixed with his old family, bringing together the best of the old and the new.

How difficult a racepoint is Lerwick?
In my opinion, it is the hardest 600-mile race into the United Kingdom. Why? Because it's an island in the upper North Sea, 120 miles off the mainland, the weather is often very cold, changeable and windy and the birds have no option but to fly the water first. Then they have the Scottish mountains to cross before reaching the Western Hills. Where I live in West Wales, just to make things more difficult, they have the Brecon Beacons, which are 2,900 feet high, directly in their line of flight at the home end. In the last eight years, only ten per cent of the convoy has come home in race time.

Is Lerwick a lottery when it becomes a two-day race?
No, the best birds still come through. Some people send plodders, thinking they'll stick at it, but it takes them even longer.

Why do you think so few have made it?
When pigeons are liberated they don't know how far they've got to fly so they keep going at their natural speed. A lot of sprint to middle distance types drop after 300 or 400 miles, having given everything they've got. There are a lot of Lerwick birds found flown-out in North Wales, for example. Meanwhile, the distance pigeon keeps going at its own pace. I'm sure they're well behind after 400 miles but they keep going and eventually reach the front. My 'Lerwick Hen' was a typical distance pigeon. If the velocity was over 1200ypm she would be behind the main flock, but she would keep going all day at her own pace. She won races from 700 to 1000ypm.

This would seem to disprove the theory that a good pigeon can win at any distance?
Up to a point. The Jan Aardens win from 60 to 600 miles.

Have you noticed any common characteristics in your best distance pigeons?

In my opinion they have been birds that have been a bit special, having put up many good performances before. Invariably they have also been intelligent birds. 'Lady of Darkness' and the 'Lerwick Hen' were very similar. Both were medium to small, apple-bodied pigeons, specially bred from a long line of proven long distance blood. Incidentally, 'Lady of Darkness' beat 10,000 birds from Thurso, arriving at 10.25 pm, but because it was completely dark she would not land on the loft. I used my car lights to light up the loft. She was clocked at 10.43 pm but was beaten by a bird clocked at 11.20 pm flying two miles further. She was outside the hours of darkness and her time counted as 4.30 am next morning. This archaic rule is still in existence in the Welsh Grand National!

Do you lose many at Lerwick?
No, not many. But as I only send my best, the ones I have lost have all been excellent pigeons. For example, I lost 'Shetland Leader' on his third attempt when he was a six-year-old. It is a graveyard for good pigeons.

How many do you send?
Between one and three, and so far I've managed to score every time. I don't send every year, only when I think I've birds that will do it. For example, I didn't send in 1993 because, out of the three I'd earmarked, one was hawked, one was injured and the other wasn't in quite the condition I look for.

How often do you send them?
'Trotty' and my 1967-bred 'Lerwick Hen', the mother of my loft, did it three times, but these days I'm of the opinion that twice is enough. I now put them in the stock shed.

Do you give them any special attention after a distance race?
On return from a normal race they are fed a light mixture of chicken corn, but if it has been a marathon, like Lerwick, I sometimes give them the egg-white of a chicken egg, cooked and placed down the throat. I wash it down using a pipette. They also get a glucose solution in the water.

What does the egg-white do?
It provides a wealth of goodness, such as protein, immediately, although the droppings aren't too clever. An old miner friend, Jack Smith, started me on it years ago.

What keeps them on the wing?
To begin with, they must be extra special and supremely fit. And it is of paramount importance that they are really contented in the loft. I think they are motivated by a bit of everything, the fancier, the nest and the environment. I believe that a lot of pigeons have the physique for Lerwick, but it's what's in their heads that counts, and whether they have the guts and will to get home. I regularly time birds in after 10 o'clock and it

can get very dark down here in the valleys.

Have you found any difference in the type needed for Thurso as opposed to Lerwick?
No. The same pigeons normally do well at both. I fly in a very competitive club, so for a bird to win at either it has to be very good.

How much does Lerwick take out of them?
Two years ago I had a bird die from its exertions. The 'Lerwick Hen' would spend two or three days in her box after a trip, and it was a week before the 'Lerwick Cock' even flew again. They are very sore, and their wings must ache like hell. There is no such thing as an easy Lerwick, so don't listen to fanciers who tell you their birds were up and jumping next day.

Is it wise to confine them to their boxes even once they are inclined to be out and about?
I think enforced rest is the best policy. In the case of a cock who wants to start driving again, too much activity can do him more harm than good.

Have your results been achieved on natural or widowhood?
Up to the present I've flown natural with old birds and raced young birds to the perch. However, with my being out from 8.00 am until 4.00 pm (I'm a lecturer at a local Further Education college) I think I will eventually turn over to widowhood. I won't try to fly both!

How fit are your birds early in the season?
As the 300 to 600-mile races are my only interest at present, in the early races my birds are only going through the motions. I make sure they are fit enough to home, not to win, and it's only as the distance increases that I try to wind them up. I usually start to come into my own from the 250-mile stage.

What are your favoured nesting conditions?
I like cocks flying Lerwick either at the end of driving or with a big youngster. Hens always go sitting twelve to sixteen days.

What do you feed and why?
I don't feed any particular brand. I've always had livestock around me - my grandfather was a poultry farmer and I helped him from an early age until he died when I was sixteen. I think I'm a good stockman and I select food with experience behind me. I favour plenty of protein when breeding and in the early part of the week when racing, and I increase the amount of carbohydrates as the distance gets longer. I've almost always fed a bean-based main feed, but in 1988 I fed no beans and still won 1st fed

Lerwick. I've also got a lot of time for 'chicken corn' - crushed maize, wheat and some barley.

Which is the single most important grain?
For rearing, peas, and for racing, beans. But I don't feed too many beans too early in the season as it takes the pigeons longer to get fit.

Do you hand or hopper feed?
Hopper because I'm lazy. I don't fill the hopper, but give just enough and a little pinch extra.

How do you make sure the hens get a balanced diet, as the cocks will take their pick first?
I'm usually able to arrange for someone to replenish the hopper at about half-past two. The hens usually eat more after they've exercised so, by feeding at that time, they get the same as the cocks.

Do you flag your birds?
Because of hawks I keep my birds locked up from the end of September to 1st March when I pair up. They are often sluggish to begin with but after they've had a couple of weeks of regular exercise, I will then 'encourage' them to fly for half an hour. It takes about three weeks before they will fly freely, but mine never exercise a lot. They do perhaps twenty minutes, but never as much as an hour.

Do your pigeons put on more weight through being captive all winter?
Yes, but it doesn't worry me as I can easily get it off by feeding depurative (not barley). Winter fat is a natural thing. Wild animals and birds carry it.

What is the ideal weight for the distance?
Obviously I know what it is when I'm handling a pigeon, but it is very hard to put into words. I would say mine tend to be a little bit heavy.

Do they lose that extra weight in the basket or the race?
They work it off in the race. Pigeons don't lose much weight in the basket. 'Whitewings' was in the basket at Lerwick for twelve days and he still had the weight on him.

Do your birds field?
They are allowed to field around our bungalow on Sundays after a bath, and also when feeding their first round in March. They pick up grubs, slugs and the like, all of which provide protein for the growing youngsters.

How do you prepare your Lerwick and Thurso candidates?

The main objective is to get the bird extra-fit and contented. The general rule I follow is to stop them four weeks before the intended race. I then put them down in their favourite nesting condition and train them regularly up to the night of basketing. I don't keep racing them as I think a bird has only so much energy. They are fed a high carbohydrate mixture and a few peanuts too. They wouldn't eat peanuts at first, but after I starved them for two days they did. Now they'll eat them first and one good hen I have could find a peanut in the bottom of a sack.

At what age does your old family reach its peak?
If I can hang onto them until they are three they are always excellent. Some of my best performances have been achieved with three and four-year-old cocks. By then they have gained plenty of experience and I can begin to play around with them.

How do you mean?
A lot of my best performances from Thurso and Lerwick have been put up with driving cocks. Every time I've sent driving cocks to Lerwick they've scored. I take the hen away until five days before basketing so that by the time the cocks are sent they are well into driving. 'Shetland Leader' won two firsts from Lerwick like this.

I imagine they are birds with a good temperament and not mad drivers likely to throw away their chance by fretting in the basket?
They have a good temperament, yes, but as they haven't seen their hen for a while they become very possessive when driving. 'Shetland Leader' would drive his hen onto the roof of the house over the road, but only because he hadn't seen her. He wouldn't have done it normally.

Are your birds tame?
Yes. People can't get over how tame. Last year, I inadvertently stepped on one and killed it.

How big a jump do you give your Thurso and Lerwick birds?
Very often their last race is from 300 miles, but my first bird home from Thurso the year before last, a three-year-old hen, was having her first race of the season.

What's the shortest amount of time it would take you to prepare a bird for Lerwick?
Two months. I can't do it more quickly than that because it takes me three weeks to get them to fly properly. There are no short cuts.

How can you tell when a bird is coming into condition?
Recognising form comes from knowing your own birds. For example, 'Shetland Leader' was always at his best when his hen was on the point of laying. Generally, the hens tend

to sit that bit extra in the mornings when they have been sitting fourteen days. It's often the quiet pigeons that are on form and not those that are clapping off everywhere, which is different to widowhood pigeons!

Do you favour hens or cocks?
I've had success with both, but perhaps my preference is for cock birds.

Are you a good judge of a pigeon?
I'd say I have a fair idea as nearly all my pigeons have been hand-picked by myself.

What do you look for?
I tend to go for those which are similar to ones I've won with in the past.

Which is more important, the man or the pigeon?
In distance flying the contribution of the pigeon is the greater. It has to be bred for the job. No sprinter will win from 600 miles. In short distance flying, the position of the loft is often the governing factor!

How hard do you work your youngsters?
They are all expected to fly the programme through to 287 miles if fit and healthy. Almost all my best racers flew the whole programme as youngsters. What is becoming a constant problem now, though, is the predation of falcons and hawks which often disrupts the training of young birds. Some lose confidence due to constant falcon strikes and have to be left until the yearling stage before serious training can resume.

Do you flag youngsters?
Never.

How many of your youngsters come through the programme?
Most. And because I don't lose many, the surplus are sold off at the end of the season to enable me to get down to my required number. I am always having good reports of winners from these.

What causes clashing and losses in general?
Too many young birds clash because federations use the motorways to reach race points, north and south, and invariably they clash on their returning journeys. Losses, I think, are sometimes caused by the pigeons failing to 'lock on'. Speaking as a geologist, I know that where you find a concentration of iron, such as in the iron ore fields off the coast of Lancashire, it can cause a magnetic anomaly which affects the homing instinct.

Do you train on the line of flight?
Young birds are initially trained on the line of flight, afterwards they go anywhere. For

instance, if there's a strong north wind then I'll train from the south. Old birds will go anywhere training.

Do you breed late-breds?
Only rarely do I breed any for stock, and never for racing.

How far do you send yearlings?
They are expected to fly the Yearling National from Crieff, 324 miles. Some are sent on to New Pitsligo, 411 miles, and Thurso, 476 miles.

Do your two-year-olds go to Lerwick?
No, but they are expected to fly Thurso. I never send birds younger than three-years-old to Lerwick, and then only the exceptional ones.

Has a pigeon to score before you'll breed off it?
Yes. I only breed from my proven racers.

Do your winning pigeons invariably breed winners themselves?
Not all have been successful at stock. However, brothers and sisters of the actual big winners often turn out to be good breeders. Indeed, I have found that the nestmate of a champion is often better at stock. I have also found that the actual youngsters off great birds may not be as good a racers themselves, but their children in turn, and therefore the grandchildren of the originals, are. In other words, the winning stock may be a generation away from the champion bird.

Do you breed off old pigeons and prisoners?
Yes. I put very old birds, ten years and above, to yearlings, with very good results. Prisoners present no problem, although I have very few.

Which strains do you race?
I fly two families, one that I've built up myself since 1966 on Thurso and Lerwick winners, and the other is the Jan Aardens which originated from *Clwyd Lofts* in 1986. I'm at present also introducing a sprint to middle distance family based on Janssens. These are yet to be tried out, but I've got the best from Alan Maull, Rhigos, three times 1st Welsh Combine, and Brian Clayburn of Yorkshire.

On which pigeons are your old family based?
They are bred down from a cheq pied cock WHU68C621, a Krauth that cost me £4, and a cheq hen WHU67S7309, a Vandevelde from Dodger Matthews of Cadoxton. She was later to be called the 'Lerwick Hen', having won from there three times. Scores of 500 and 600-mile winners have come down from this pairing to win and score in nationals from Thurso and Lerwick.

How have you maintained a family?
By inbreeding in the first instance, and latterly through crossing. My old family were very inbred over the years and needed fresh blood. I now don't breed too near, perhaps only going as near as grandsire to granddaughter.

Do you place much store in a bird's pedigree?
I only use pedigrees when mating up my own family of pigeons. If I use an introduction it can be bred from a Rhode Island Red for all I care, as long as the lineage has been proven to be successful. I'd never buy a bird just because it was a Jan Aarden, for example. I would have to examine the bird first. I never introduce blindly!

What led you to bring in the Jan Aardens?
Michael Johnston of *Clwyd Lofts* phoned me in the autumn of 1985. He wanted me to try out his Jan Aardens because I was so successful at the distance. He sent down three pairs in 1986, free of charge! These six pigeons were numbered WHU86B9541-9546 and did as follows:

9541 Cheq hen (dam of 1st Lerwick)
9542 Cheq cock (2nd Thurso and sire of 1st Thurso)
9543 Cheq hen (3rd open Welsh Combine and grandam of 1st Welsh National)
9544 Cheq hen (1st Welsh Combine over 16,000 birds and grandam of 1st Thurso)
9545 Cheq Pied hen (lost off loft)
9546 Dark Cheq cock (sire of 1st Lerwick)

Did you treat them just the same as your own team?
I raced them harder, if anything, sending them to every race as young birds. I thought it had to be more than just coincidence that all five scored so I stopped two, '41' and '43', and put them in the stock shed.

Are the Jan Aardens of a similar type to your old family?
No. My old family are long cast and not particularly pretty pigeons, whereas the Jan Aardens are shorter and more rounded, with better feather quality and richer eyes.

Being of a different type, have they crossed well?
They've blended in very well. The Jan Aardens brought a touch of class into my family, which had always done well for others when used as a cross. Rather than produce a different type, though, the youngsters have tended to take after either one family or the other, even those off the same pairs. The feather of my birds is also better now. It feels like silk and gives off a lot of white sheen.

Which line dominates in your loft today?
If I was to put a percentage on it I'd say the Jan Aardens dominate about 70:30 per cent. Whether pure or crossed, they win from 60 to 600 miles.

Do you not find it a little sad that the links with your old family are diminishing?
Not really. Things have to go on. The cross has proved so successful that I tend to concentrate on it.

Why have many of the old families died out?
Probably because they take longer to mature. My old family is a good example. If you were to take a photo of one as a youngster and again as a two-year-old you would hardly recognise it.

Would you say you were a good breeder of pigeons?
I'm still having to cull, so I haven't cracked it yet.

Are hens that have been raced hard spoilt for breeding in any way?
I think they can be. I find that of my two Jan Aarden hens, '43', who only raced as a young bird, breeds a higher percentage of good birds than '44', who was 1st combine. They are now both seven years old and '44' is becoming loose in the vents.

Do you try to keep breeding hens going as long as possible?
I don't aid them. I try to keep things as simple as possible being of the view that what happens, happens. I think that by the time they are nine or ten they have usually had it.

Do you follow any theories?
Recently my cousin, Graham Harris, introduced me to the wing theory and it was fascinating, but I tend to use my own knowledge as a stockman when mating up or selecting new stock.

What are your thoughts on eye-sign?
All good birds have good eyes, but so do some poor ones!

How many birds do you keep?
I keep fifteen pairs of racers, ten pairs of stock pigeons and breed approximately forty to fifty young birds.

Would you describe your loft?
It is designed to be dry and well ventilated. It has a very open frontage which faces south-east and therefore out of direct rain and wind. Many of the lofts I've been to are too dusty and damp.

What do you use on the loft floor?
I always use a deep litter of clean straw. Also shavings are put in nest boxes and on the perches. The straw provides warmth to youngsters just parted, nest material for old birds and stock pigeons and keeps the loft very clean, cosy and dry. I clean out the floor

twice a week and it takes no time at all.

How do you control parasites?
I spray the loft twice a year, and put lice powder in the base of the nest pans and on the perches. I never have time to delouse each bird individually. They seem to remain lice-free with this treatment.

What do you treat for?
My father is the local pharmacist and therefore I've access to anything. Basically I administer paediatric dosages of worming treatments before and after rearing young-sters. No one product in particular, as they all have very similar properties. I treat for canker with *Harkers Spartrix* tablets at the beginning of the season and also for cocci, using a *Harkers* treatment. I don't normally treat more often than that, but last year I treated for canker again because there was an epidemic in the West Wales area and one or two of mine had it in the mouth.

Do you treat for anything else?
I don't use any other medicines unless absolutely necessary, and then only individually. I think it is a mistake to treat continually as disease becomes resistant. A vet told me that in the pig industry, because of continuous treatment, they are now hard-pressed to find a product to which strains haven't become immune.

Do you try to save sick pigeons?
I don't get many sick pigeons, but if one is ill I tend to isolate it and let it get over the illness itself. They usually recover.

Do they go on to win?
'Lady of Darkness's' nestmate, the 'Thurso Cock', had double one-eyed cold as a young-ster. Although normally I use paediatric eye-drops for one-eyed cold I left him alone and he cured himself.

Do you treat for respiratory problems?
No, as I've never needed to. However, I do sterilise the bath water and the drinking water on Saturday and Sunday after a race. I use *Unichem's* sterilising liquid. If I had the time I'd still do what was the common practice years ago, which was to leave the drinkers out to dry in the sun. Canker and other diseases won't live without water.

What else do you put in your drinking fountains?
The only other thing I use is a paediatric vitamin and iron compound when they are rearing.

Did you vaccinate before it became compulsory?

I always did the young birds, at six weeks old, but hadn't ever vaccinated the old birds.

Is vaccination necessary?
I think it is essential for youngsters, but not the old birds. Do we humans continue to vaccinate our children? I have friends who are vets, my father is a pharmacist, I'm an honours graduate in science, and I know that the pigeon fancier is exploited with all sorts of cures, pills and the like.

Which local club do you belong to?
I'm secretary of Glynneath RPC, the most successful club in the West Wales Federation and South-West Wales Amalgamation.

What is the general approach to racing in your area?
On the north route, flying in South Wales is mainly geared towards winning the Welsh Grand National. There is south road flying with its own national, but with having a smaller membership, it is far less attractive. The main type of flying is still with the natural system, but more and more are turning to widowhood. The reason why natural flying has been prevalent is that the main 'races to win', Thurso and Lerwick, have traditionally been suited to natural pigeons, particularly hens.

Why are you considering widowhood?
One of the reasons is that I'm finding it increasingly difficult to do my hens properly.

Do you think you'll be as successful if you turn to widowhood?
I will persevere until I crack it.

Would you still race hens?
Yes, as I would probably re-pair everything at the 300-mile stage.

Are you tempted to compete on the south road?
I have already, but I found I couldn't be in two places at once as the nearest south road club was seven miles away. If everybody turned south I would have a go, although I think it would be very difficult to do well with the National Flying Club. From my experience, young bird racing, in particular, would be a complete waste of time. They won't come across the Bristol Channel and I found that my youngsters always homed from the north. You know what youngsters are like, they'll follow anything.

What are your views on the political side of the sport?
At the moment in Wales, pigeon politics are ruining the sport. I'm directly involved in trying to iron-out the 'politicians', which last year meant that we had no combine racing as such. However, this year I put forward a race programme, and got it passed, which meant that *all* the federations competed from the same Scottish racepoints *at the*

same time.

Why are there so few people coming into the sport?
Pigeon flying is a 365-days-a-year sport and with people having so many other leisure activities now, it's not attractive. In our club we have been lucky to have six new members in the last year. This is unusual.

What are your views on the books you have read and the videos you have seen?
There are good and bad videos and books. I hate reading a list of the racing performances of an individual fancier because it often means nothing to me. Some videos are very amateurish and really no more than a con!

Are you as keen today as you've always been?
As I now have a young family, pigeons have tended to take a little bit of a back seat of late. I'm not fanatical about them anymore, although I do still keep meticulous records. Pigeons are second nature to me now and I'm more easy about things. Before I used to be a bit paranoid. However, the 'high' you get from seeing a bird home late at night after fifteen plus hours on the wing is something I wish all fanciers could experience.

'Lady of Darkness'
1st fed, 3rd open Welsh National, 5th combine Thurso, 10,155 birds.
(Only bird on the day in fed - timed at 10.43 pm.)

The 'Combine Hen' Blue hen, Wales86B9544

1st Welsh Combine Roslin Park, 16,000 + birds. Dam of 1st Thurso. The 'Combine Hen' is nestmate to the 'Jan Aarden 43' - g.dam of 1st National 1992. Bred by Clwyd Lofts & raced by Robert O Jones.

Blue Cheq cock GB85N11423
A g/son of Super Stud x Madam Hollandaise. This pairing produced 15 x 1st prize winners, also 3rd, 4th, 5th, 6th & 9th sect Carteret National. Also 15th, 42nd & 52nd open from Rennes & Nantes

Blue Cheq w/f hen GB83N04121
Bred for stock. A winner herself & dam of winners. A full-sister to Champion 650

Blue Cheq hen GB82N05271
A son of Clwyd Lofts Number One stock cock Champion Super Stud

Blue Cheq hen GB83N86454

Blue w/f cock GB78Z22160
Sire of Champion 650 & other winners in the Clwyd Lofts race team. 160 is half-brother to Champion Roundhead

Cheq w/f hen GB79N56269
Dam of winners, including Champion 650. Winner of 5 x 2nd,fed & over 50 club, fed & open positions

NL75000099
Champion Super Stud

BELGE76- 656698
Madam Hollandaise Dam of many winners

NL75-2000099
Champion Super Stud

GB76B89113
The Spencer Hen, Dam of birds to win 18 prizes

HOL.75-281927
Sire & g/sire of Amal winners

HOL74-11633311

GB78J00282
Sire of winners. Bred from direct Ko Nipius stock

GB78J00284
Dam of winners. Bred from direct Ko Nipius stock

'Jan Aarden 43 Hen'
3rd Welsh Combine Morpeth.
Nestmate to 1st Welsh Combine
Roslin Park, 16,000 birds. Grandam
of 1st Welsh National 1992.

'The Corridor Cock'
Winner of seven firsts, including
1st Thurso. Grandsire of 1st Welsh
National Lerwick.

'Shetland Leader'
1st club, 1st fed, 4th section,
29th National Lerwick 1988.
1st club, 2nd fed, 4th section, 25th
National Lerwick 1989.

Pedigree of one of Robert O Jones's Top Stock Cocks

Number One Stock Cock
The Corridor Cock
Blue cock 77M4118
Won from Craven Arms to Thurso. 1st Thurso 1980. Sire & g/sire of numerous birds to score from Thurso & Lerwick. G/sire of Folly Girl 1st & 3rd open Lerwick

Cheq Pied cock 68C6210
The Krauth Cock. Sire of the loft. Bred winners in almost every nest. G/son of the Flying Dutchman. 1st International Barcelona

Direct Krauth
Son of The Flying Dutchman

Direct Krauth
Direct Krauth

Blue Tic hen 75F3413
Always stock

Blue w/f cock 73F3938
Sire of 500 & 600 mile winners

Cheq hen
1st Elgin

The brilliant stock hen
Faithful Lady
Blue hen 79L3189
1st Thurso, 2nd sect 1981 Dam of Lady of Darkness, 1st sect (only bird on day), 3rd open Thurso 1982 Also dam of the Thurso Cock 1st Thurso, 3rd fed, 7th sect Welsh Grand National

Cheq w/f cock 78P2052
4th Thurso. Full brother to White-Wings, ace racer & stock bird. Winner of 6 x 1st, 2nd Thurso & 2nd Lerwick

Cheq Pied cock 74H8987
Stock. Brother to Northern Flight, 1st & 2nd sect Thurso

The Lerwick Hen 67D7309
3rd, 3rd & 5th fed Lerwick

Northern Flight

The Krauth Cock

Cheq hen 73E3274
1st Thurso, 3rd Elgin etc

Cheq Pd hen 72J156

Dark Cheq Pd hen 73E3263
Scored from Thurso & Lerwick 1985. Proved outstanding stock hen

The Marsh Hen
1st & 2nd sect, 10th & 16th open Welsh. G.Nat.Thurso

Northern Flight

The Lerwick Hen 67D7309
Vandevelde

Perth Hen 71K6658
1st fed Perth etc.

Young Patsy
Channing bloodlines
The Lerwick Hen 67D7309
3 x 1st Lerwick

JOE E SHORE

If there was an election tomorrow to ask fanciers who they thought were the best five channel flyers in Cheshire, Joe E Shore of Comberbach would not lose his deposit. He has been clocking distance birds with almost monotonous regularity for many, many years, first with what he terms his 'old family' and latterly with new additions. These, either crossed with his old blood or kept separately, have seen him move with the times. His is a no nonsense approach, based on the 'toe the line' principle and 'first feet on the landing board' theory. This approach yields an average of twenty firsts a season at all distances.

Joe, in a piece written on you in 1985, you said that 365 days of your year were geared towards one day in July, namely Pau National day. Does that still hold true?
No. To be honest I've lost interest in Pau a little bit. I now believe Pau to be one of the easier racepoints to fly, providing that you're able to operate 'open hole' and you have a family of 'homing pigeons'. I can't operate 'open hole' now because of the hawk problems.

What has led you to think it is one of the easier racepoints?
Well, my old family put up some excellent performances from there, but I've since brought other pigeons in and done just as well. Don't get me wrong, they've got to be the right sort of birds for the job, birds that will stick at it, but depending on what sort of race it is, not necessarily 'racing pigeons'.

Define what you mean by 'racing pigeons'?
Five hundred milers. By that I mean 500 miles on the day pigeons. They're alright if you're flying to the coast, but there is absolutely no way you will get them up here. I know from experience that those aren't the pigeons to fly Pau with. The pigeons you want for 700 miles are the sort that come next day looking as though they haven't been out of the loft. You won't get the 500 milers that race their hearts out on the first day.

Won't get them in good time, or won't get them full stop?
There are lots of good 500 milers lost at Pau.

Can you breed for Pau, for near 700 milers?
I'd say not. You need to know which birds from your family will face it, pedigree alone is useless.

Can you give me an example?
A very good example, my cheq hen '51416' who was well up three times from Pau, including 2nd section, 33rd open. She had a list of wins in hard races. From one channel race I timed her at 4.34 in the morning to be 2nd fed and she was later 3rd open in one of the biggest smashes the Great Northern ever had out of Saintes, but she was too slow to win from Nantes. She was an exceptional pigeon at Pau, but she was too slow to win from 420 miles.

What about your cock who was 2nd section, 12th open?
He was four years old when he took 12th open. He won nothing before that, and he won nothing after that.

He must have been a good pigeon all the same, so why do you think he never matched that effort?
Too slow. I couldn't fly Pau as I used to anymore, waiting four years for a pigeon who was too slow to win from anywhere else. I don't keep a pigeon above two years old now if it hasn't scored. That's how my attitude has changed.

Typically, what preparation do you give your Pau candidates?
I nearly always send them to the Nantes National.

And what do you look for in the way of performance from Nantes?
Nearly all my best 700 milers have been pigeons that had a night out at Nantes.

So Nantes is an ideal stepping stone?
Yes, although not this year. My first bird, a mealy cock, who was just off the result, didn't see Nantes.

Can you explain?
I'd taken him off the road, but he wasn't filling all his eggs, so on the Wednesday a friend of mine gave him a 25-mile toss from Prees. On the Saturday he raced from 129 miles and on the following Tuesday he was in the basket for Pau.

How old is he?
Seven, so at least you could say he was experienced. That was the only preparation he had though and it has certainly made me think.

Let's return to the distinction you made between 500 milers and 700 milers. Recently a number of the longer flying members of the Scottish National Flying Club have expressed the opinion that if they were to move down to the Annan area they might as well get rid of their 'distance' pigeons. Can you see their point?
Yes, it's not as daft as it might sound. They have a point. They are two different sorts

of pigeon.

So you're more careful these days not to send your best 500 milers to Pau?
Yes, and I take it further than that. If they are winning up to the coast I keep them there, and if they are winning from Nantes, then I don't send them to 500 miles. It's not that the birds winning up to the coast won't channel, most birds today will do Rennes which is 360 miles, but when pigeons do well from a particular racepoint it's not worth the risk of sending them further. It can blunt their speed a little as well.

You said you no longer have the patience to wait four years for a bird. Have you changed your approach in other ways?
Yes, I'm now all widowhood.

Why the change?
Because I thought I'd try some yearling cocks on widowhood to see how they raced against my natural birds.

What happened?
They beat all my natural birds out of Niort, 490 miles, on what was a good, hard, honest racing day.

Would they have beaten your natural birds, say, fifteen years earlier?
If I'd known as much then as I think I know now then, yes, they probably would have. I'm not saying from Pau, but up to 500 miles.

So you switched completely?
It's so easy now. I used to strive for weeks to get pigeons as near to sitting ten days as possible. I don't have to do that now. Widowhood has revived my interest. I must have raced it thirty odd years ago, but it was only about 1985-86 that I went back to it proper.

Ten days was always the condition that suited your family?
Yes. I never had any success with pigeons feeding youngsters. Where they originated from they raced well to youngsters, but not for me.

Why the difference, do you think?
Don't know, perhaps I wasn't good enough. It's so much easier flying pigeons dry.

Now you're all widowhood, do you miss that striving, as you termed it?
Like heck I do! That's what gave me ulcers.

In the early eighties you brought in a new family. Why?
My old family were becoming too slow. They were wonderful homers, and when it was

hard I knew I'd get them, but you've got to move with the times. I've coined an expression that I use in my adverts - 'these birds are strain makers not heartbreakers'. Well, my old family were heartbreakers, so I brought in other birds, some of which I crossed, and now I have a family that can race all distances. And it's the new family that is gradually taking over.

Where did you bring pigeons in from?
The pigeons that have had the most impact came from a Mrs A Bowyer of Northwich.

Why did you go there?
A young bird stray of hers came in here and when I took it back I liked what I saw. At the time she was making racing in the South Lancashire Combine look easy. They were raced natural, and on straw, and I'd never seen pigeons look so happy.

You tried the birds, what about the straw?
I tried that too, but it got everywhere.

What strain were these Bowyer pigeons?
Vanhee/Stichelbaut.

Was the actual strain important?
No. It was the pigeons themselves and the person's integrity.

So you don't attach much importance to pedigree and strain?
No. Obviously where they come from is important, but it's the integrity of the person that I'm after. I'm always telling people that a pedigree is just a piece of paper and sometimes it's not worth the paper it's written on. I know of pigeons that are meant to be this or that breed, which are in fact bred off birds that are an entirely different strain altogether, and of several youngsters supposedly off a particular pair all of the same age. The integrity of the seller is the most important thing to consider when buying pigeons. People think pedigrees are too good to fly, whereas if they kept on sending they would end up with the best.

You wouldn't go to auctions then?
I get sick looking at the auctions advertised today. People should remember that there's nothing fair in business. I don't like what is happening in the pigeon world.

Where did your old family originate from?
A poultry pen.

Can you enlarge on that?
Yes. There were about eight or ten youngsters without rings in a poultry pen at Chelford

market. You had to buy the lot of them for 1' 6d each, so I culled all except two gay pieds and paired them together.

Where did those birds come from?
Eddie Stanier of Chelford. In those days he was winning out of turn in the Manchester Flying Club. He flew all his birds to youngsters which, as I said earlier, is something I could never do, and those same youngsters were put into the market to be sold for meat.

What breed were the two pieds?
The old Hansenne family of Bob Dunne. I said to Eddie months later that the only two I'd kept were the two pieds and he told me that Bob Dunne preferred not to sell his pieds as they were the ones he wanted for himself.

What made you keep just the two pieds?
Whether it was stock sense or because my wife, Marion, liked them I can't remember.

And these two pieds founded your old family?
Yes, and when the cock stopped filling his eggs I gave the hen to Bill Mather of Warrington and she filled his loft with winners too.

You sell quite a few birds yourself. How have you managed to stay at the top, when others sell and end up with declining performances?
I don't have a number one pair. In fact it's unusual for me to keep a pair together for any length of time, and I've plenty of birds capable of producing winners. I'd like to think I've sold plenty of good pigeons. I was quite thrilled last year when two pigeons I gave to the Cheshire Combine Breeder/Buyer sale were 1st and 3rd in the longest young bird race, flown by two different fanciers. One thing I would say about selling pigeons is this, I thoroughly dislike writing out pedigrees. I've got records as good as anyone and I can trace all my pigeons back if needs be, but I just don't like writing out pedigrees.

I imagine selling a few pigeons also helps you to unearth breeders you might otherwise miss?
Actually there are a lot of good pigeons here that I've nothing off myself. People come and I open the door of the loft and say there are the youngsters, take your pick. The mealies and pieds for example, stand out, so they get taken, and when I look, I find I've got nothing off certain pairs left for myself. My old family used to have lots of pieds and whites, but I've only the one white pigeon now. Having said that, the white ones are funny things. They lie dormant for generations and then pop up again.

How much of your old family have you got left?
Less and less all the time. I still get inundated with requests for the old stuff, but most

are now crossed.

I notice you keep quite a sizeable team. Why?
I couldn't fly the programme I do with, say, just twelve widowhood cocks. I need plenty of pigeons and consequently I'm able to keep up with the demand for youngsters.

Why wouldn't twelve widowhood cocks suffice?
I haven't counted but I fly perhaps as many as fifteen channel races a year. These are all with different clubs and there's no duplication.

Now that you only race hens as youngsters, and they don't have to toe the line like your cock birds, how do you choose which hens to breed from?
Stock sense. I know, as a stockman, that I can see sense in a pigeon. Knowing the family is important as well and the hens must have been consistent. They don't need to be big winners, but they mustn't have made many mistakes either.

What about the idea that some pigeons race well but can't breed to type?
I'm only after those that can do both.

Do you like old stock pigeons?
Not really, nor prisoners, although I do have one or two. Having said that, my three-times Pau hen bred some of her best children when ten years old, although even then she was paired to a yearling cock.

I can understand that age might matter in a hen, after all it is she who produces the egg, but should it be of consequence in a cock bird?
I know what you're saying, that as far as we understand genetics, age shouldn't matter, but it does.

So you like to breed off young stock?
I'll tell you what happens time and time again. The best pair of youngsters are the first two a pair of yearlings produces. They still breed winners after that, even if separated, but seldom anything as good as the first two. I don't know why, but it's what I've found to be true.

Do you visit many lofts?
I used to when I was a young lad. Every Sunday we used to jump in the car and go and visit good local fanciers.

What made you stop?
I came to realise that what made them good fanciers was the fact that they were at home with their birds and not at somebody else's. I realised that was where I should be, at

home with my birds. I'm just the same now, when the clocks have been read I like to get back. There's always something that can be done, like giving a latecomer some special attention.

I notice, looking at your lofts, that you've got no ventilation at floor level. Why is that?
I experimented and thought the birds were healthier with it closed off. I used to get snotty wattles, but now I get very little trouble. While we're on the subject of snotty wattles, everything out of my three-times Pau hen used to get them come autumn.

Yet they were sound pigeons?
They were. One year I timed seven pigeons on the winning day in the section from Pau and six were out of the old hen, by four different cocks, bred in three different seasons.

What other measures do you take to keep your birds healthy?
I put *Milton* in the water every day at the rate of 2mls to a gallon. In fact the only time they don't have *Milton* is when I'm treating for canker and coccidiosis. I also spray for red mite twice a year because one of my lofts is an old poultry hut and once there's been red mite in a place you'll never get rid of it, so I spray to keep it under control. One word of warning about using *Milton*, whatever you do, don't exceed 2mls.

What about vaccination?
I inject the young birds in June and then the whole lot in December.

So the young birds see the needle twice in six months and therefore three times in eighteen months?
Yes. I've worked with livestock all my life and you get used to a needle. I get annoyed when people moan about vaccinating.

Do you treat sick pigeons?
Yes. Nobody would knock you on the head if you had a cold, would they? Look at Sebastian Coe and all these other top athletes, they've often got some ailment or other.

And the birds are of value after they've been treated?
Yes, providing you catch them in time. Don't get me wrong, I cull if they don't respond to treatment, but I'm not the first to cull.

How do you feed during the close season?
I give them a light mix in the morning and for the evening feed they get beans only, thrown on the floor.

Do you use beans in the racing season?

When I was on the road years ago they used to be hopper fed beans with a bit of wheat thrown in when I had the time and they used to win out of turn, but now I feed a widowhood mix and they hardly see a bean when racing.

What about when breeding?
Beans and wheat. I feed them in their boxes. If I used a mixture they'd throw it about, so I use beans. The youngsters stay on beans and wheat until about a week before racing starts.

So you put some store in beans?
Yes, although one thing I did notice when I raced on beans was that in hot weather they made the birds thirstier.

What do you feed your widowhood cocks in the racing season?
A Belgian brand called *Marimans Super M,* which I get from Ruabon. I've used all the other brands and there always seems to be a difference in the quality. I've never had a poor bag of *Marimans.* It's heavier than your typical widowhood mix and probably the best food I've used to date.

What else do you feed?
I'm a great believer in peanuts. I don't give them ad lib, what I do is go round morning and night and feed all my cocks in their boxes. On a Monday they get perhaps only one peanut at each end of the day, but by Thursday they get three or four at a time. This system helps you to give individual attention to each bird. I keep them in a glass coffee jar and the pigeons go mad when they see them. Some cocks even chase me from box to box, and of course this helps to create jealousy.

I suppose the only drawback of feeding peanuts like that is you can't afford to miss a feed?
You don't miss a feed if you're on top of your job.

What have you learnt after forty-odd years as a fancier?
That it's crackers to send young birds over the channel at this distance in the condition they're usually in.

If you had your time again, would you race pigeons?
Yes, pigeons have been very good to me. Through selling pigeons I've made friends countrywide.

Billy Jamieson holding the Scotland's Own Fancier of the Year trophy.

BILLY JAMIESON

Prior to setting up on his own in 1982, Billy Jamieson was the junior member of one of Scotland's most successful ever lofts, that of JT Jamieson & Son of Annan, eight times winners of the south section in national competition, including 1st open from Nantes. He therefore had a hard act to follow, but follow it he has, for in 1991 he was voted Scotland's Own Fancier of the Year and he has continued since then to go from strength to strength. He keeps a relatively small working loft and sets his season out for the four Scottish National races.

Which clubs do you compete in?
Apart from the Scottish Nationals, I fly with the Annan and District Homing Club and, sporadically, the Scottish Border Amalgamation. Racing into the Annan area is mainly geared up for Scottish National racing. It has been this way for many years now and the incentive is to live up to the performances of outstanding national flyers, both past and present. I've stopped flying in specialist races with two and three-year-olds as they're too tempting and I want my pigeons to keep their reserves.

What is the makeup of your current team?
My present day birds are based on pigeons going back to the days when I flew in partnership with my father, JT Jamieson. They were based on a John Kirkpatrick pied hen which produced many winners. These were later crossed with a mealy cock bred by DJ Murray of Brydekirk and a grizzle cock from JR Naylor of Ormskirk in Lancashire. The grizzle cock was purchased in 1958 and was a Procter-Smith. The DJ Murray cock was a Kirkpatrick x Sion. The blood of these birds won out of turn at Scottish National level in the sixties and seventies. In fact every grizzle my father and I breed today goes back to the Procter-Smith cock. Other birds which made an impact at this time included a pied cock bred by Thomson Brothers of Annan, direct from their champion, 'Cloggy's Choice', three times Nantes, 543 miles, on the day. This blood was Kirkpatrick x Lulham. Later birds included an outstanding blue hen from Pat McGrath of Sheffield and a mealy cock from Dave Angus of Symington, Lanarkshire, which was inbred to 'Townfoot Goodboy', the SNFC Rennes winner of 1962. This was the base I used when, in 1982, I went on my own. However, always on the look-out for something good to try, I introduced birds from Eric Fox & Son of Bakewell. These blended well with the old blood, producing some outstanding national performers. A red cock from my uncle, Matt Jamieson's, 1st open SNFC Nantes 1986, 543 miles on the day, is also doing well for me at present, as is a cheq cock I purchased at a local clearance sale. He contains the blood of Matt's 'Border Star', crossed with lines of the late Tommy Little of Creca.

Do birds have to acclimatise to new surroundings?
Acclimatisation could be a factor with some strains, perhaps longer distance ones.

When did you introduce the birds from Eric Fox & Son?
I sent for four pigeons in 1984. I put one to stock and she has been responsible for some good birds. She is a daughter of their 1st section, 15th open Pau cheq w/f cock when paired to their 1st section, 7th open Pau, Billy Erwin hen. Believing that you have to try a fair number in order to get a true reflection of their ability, I sent for four more the following year. This time a red hen stood out and she, too, is leaving her mark. She is off their red cock that took 46th open Pau and her dam was 1st section NFC Nantes. They have bred some good direct pigeons, but it is their grandchildren in particular that have started to come through, and I haven't bred many.

How have you managed to bring these different lines together?
I use a combination of line-breeding and cross-breeding. I also try some close inbreeding, but I have a dislike for half-brother and half-sister pairings, certainly for producing good racers. I rarely pair the same birds together for two successive years.

How important is pedigree?
The pedigree is made up by the pigeon's performances. By that I mean look at the pigeon first, then the pedigree, if there is one. When I go to clearance sales I always study the bird first and, if I like it, it doesn't bother me if no pedigree exists as long as the loft was a good winning one from the channel competitions.

Having blended these pigeons over the years and tested them out to the distance, what size of bird has evolved?
Medium-sized pigeons, with the hens just a shade above medium.

Would you say that pigeons of this size are more suited to the route you fly?
Possibly, but having said that, I've known plenty of small channel hens over the years.

Have your performances at the distance been achieved on widowhood or natural?
I fly natural. Having had great success at national level with hens, I've not given any other method a thought. A system will not in itself give success without pigeon know-how, at least not years of continued success.

Do you try to win all races or lean towards the channel events?
I concentrate on the four SNFC races, which are two from 443 miles, one from 480 miles and one from 543 miles. I do not believe that nowadays a fancier can succeed at all distances with the same pigeons, as the game is too specialised, with young bird specialists, widowhood sprint birds and the like.

How important is feeding in your management?
Feeding is an art and many good pigeons are wasted because fanciers are 'too good' to their pigeons. My feeding is very basic and I'm not bothered either way whether the corn is polished or not. For breeding and racing I use a mixture called *Prince* which comes from *JA Swainston & Son* of Durham. It is made up of beans, peas and maize. At this point I must say that, although I give the birds plenty of the mixture, I like to see it all eaten. Fanciers who have a mixture in pots or hoppers all day are not giving the bird a full mixture. Two weeks before the first national I introduce peanuts. This only entails going round each nest box after feeding and giving each bird two or three peanuts from my hand. In the winter months, after the moult is complete, I introduce barley, gradually building up to ninety per cent in mid-January. I no longer use seeds.

When did you stop feeding seeds and why?
I stopped feeding seeds, apart from the little bit of linseed which is in my moulting mix, in 1988 because I thought it was a case of being 'too good' to the pigeons.

Why do you favour feeding mostly barley after the moult?
Because the pigeons hold their form better for later in the year and it also keeps them in better condition for pairing up. Some people say barley dries the feathers, but I've never found that to be true. I wouldn't be without barley again for winter feeding as my least successful seasons on my own came when I didn't use it.

What do you treat for?
I treat for canker once a year with a *Fabry* product called *Tricoxine*. I usually do this when the birds are down on their first round of eggs. I have, over the years, tried other products, including a very popular Belgian brand, but I am happiest with *Tricoxine*. I also treat for worms prior to pairing up, using *Spartakon* tablets. I'm happiest with *Spartakon*, although the pigeons do 'drop' a bit. I give the tablets in an empty crop as I've seen pigeons throw up otherwise. I should add, at this point, that I give them a vitamin course in the water for three or four days after any treatment. I don't treat for cocci and, apart from paramyxo vaccination at Christmas-time, my birds receive no other treatments.

Why do you treat at all?
I don't know why, other than to keep my mind at rest. I don't have my droppings analysed.

Are you in favour of vaccination?
Yes, I believe fanciers must take every step to ensure their birds' safety from this disease. In all the years since vaccination began, I have encountered no problems.

How do you control parasites?

I spray the loft with *Ectofen* pre-season and in high summer, and I occasionally powder. I use *Fabry Bath Salts* and they also keep the birds clean. No good fancier should be troubled with lice.

When do you give your birds a bath?
I've no fads about the timing of baths and don't believe it has any effect on performance.

Some people say that silky-feathered pigeons will do better than coarse-feathered ones on a certain type of day. Is that so?
I can't say I've ever really noticed.

What do you feed your youngsters when they're weaned?
I wean youngsters on 100 per cent New Zealand maples, adding a touch of maize and barley as they start to perch.

Can you explain how you stop your channel birds coming into form too early?
Feeding barley helps and also I don't pair up until mid-March. I also hold them back by the way I train. If you train too much too soon, you are not entirely successful in holding them back and they come into form too early. I train pre-season and then drop off.

How do you make sure your birds get sufficient exercise?
By flagging, which I believe is an indispensable method. Where I live in the town, it's a must, even if only to get the birds reasonably fit. Once in the swing of it, my birds go really well at home, although I have found that the better they exercise, the slower they are in the inland races.

Do you take the hens off the nest?
Never, as they pull the others down. Because I don't flag as much as most, I make up for it with heavy training as the nationals approach.

Do you flag the stock pigeons as well?
I flag the younger stock pigeons, but lock the older ones in their boxes as they, too, pull the others down.

How do you bring your channel birds to their peak?
They are usually given three to four races before their selected event, but to start with, none of my channel birds are raced before the third or fourth race on the programme, which is 92 or 117 miles, although they are given some pre-season training to Appleby, which is 45 miles. After the youngsters have been weaned, the cocks are flagged around the loft for thirty minutes in the morning and the hens thirty minutes in the late after-

noon, building up to one hour. Ten days before the first national race, the birds selected for this event are then tossed daily from Appleby up until marking. The birds for Sartilly 1 usually have a 200-mile race from Worcester as their last outing. For Rennes birds it's usually Cheltenham, which is 220 miles. I have sent the odd one to Mangotsfield, 242 miles, a week later, but this is risky as it does not allow time for a holdover or a bad race. My Nantes birds fly Cheltenham or Mangotsfield as their final prep race.

Have you tried sending them further than Mangotsfield to get more time on the wing?
Yes. In 1993 I tried my Nantes team from Weymouth, 300 miles. A very hard race ensued and, although I later timed a very good pigeon from a very difficult Nantes race, I view the decision to fly Weymouth as a mistake.

At which point do you decide which pigeons are going to which race?
The birds for the first three national races are selected for their individual national race early in the season. Birds for Sartilly 2 are usually doubled back from Sartilly 1, along with one or two fresh two-year-olds. These also receive daily tosses from Appleby in the ten to fourteen days before marking.

How big is your average channel team per race?
I send six to eight to Sartilly and Rennes and three to five to Nantes.

Can you tell me a little more about the pigeons that you clocked in last year's nationals?
The red pied hen that was 58th open Sartilly was off the old family crossed with a Stichelbaut obtained from *Louella Lofts* in 1989, and, being a two-year-old, it was her first time across. The blue pied hen who was 18th open Rennes is a very plain pigeon I bought at the Raffles Club Sale in Carlisle. The auctioneer announced that the next lot was a Tommy Gilbertson, so I put my hand up and bought her without seeing her. She cost me £31, but to be honest I wasn't very taken with her when I saw her. However, she's never stopped improving and has only ever made one mistake, taking four or five days from a Mangotsfield smash. She is a granddaughter of Tom's 'Treble Five'. The parents of the red cock that was 70th open Rennes are a cock that scored three times over the channel (and which I later lost at Nantes) and a half Stichelbaut blue hen that came in 68th open Sartilly 2 in 1993. The blue hen's sire is directly off 'Border Princess'. The grizzle cock who was 27th open Nantes traces back to the Procter-Smiths with a Fox of Bakewell cross. Like the year before, the Nantes National was a very hard race and I dropped two of the four I sent. Previously he had scored at Sartilly 1 as a two-year-old and followed up with 27th open Sartilly 2. At three he missed the result at Sartilly 1, but made amends with 114th open in the second Sartilly.

What education do you give your young birds?
I don't expect a lot from them. How far I race them depends on circumstances. Youngsters that have a long fly in a training toss and then encounter a bad race are usually put by for the year. In 1989 my youngsters only had one race, from 66 miles, after an horrendous training toss. From that 1989 crop some of my best channel birds appeared. On the other hand, many of my good channel birds have flown right through to the Young Bird National, but this is usually only if their pre-race training has been good. I think the main thing is to make sure youngsters are not over-taxed. A good fancier will know when to call a halt.

And yearlings?
I like all my yearlings to compete in as many races up to 300 miles as possible. I don't send yearlings any further than this as they are still developing. I should also add that my yearlings never win many prizes. In fact fast yearlings have, in my experience, never made good channel birds.

Aren't you tempted to send some over the channel?
No. I won't put yearlings over the water any longer. When I flew with my father, we had yearlings which put up some excellent performances, but they never did as well again.

The first time your pigeons go over the channel, therefore, is at two years of age?
Yes, and I expect everything from my two and three-year-olds, although I never condemn a two-year-old for disappointing on its first channel crossing. All racers in my loft must have won a national certificate by the time they complete their three-year-old stage or else they are out. I should point out that, apart from selected birds that compete from Sartilly 1, my birds only fly one channel race per year.

What kind of bird do you need in order to do well in the nationals?
It is difficult to describe a type of pigeon that will win in national competition, although I do try to breed a type. I like a pigeon that pleases in the hand and looks the part, but if that was all it took, it would be simple. I must say that the vast majority of the good channel birds that I have had experience of are good handling pigeons, although not always good lookers. For example, the hen that I timed from the Rennes National in 1993 to win 18th open, has excellent handling qualities but a very plain head and eye, which gives her a rather common look. I never condemn a bird for its size, although I prefer it not to be too big. Obviously I am looking for a bird that, regardless of looks and size, will battle from dawn till dusk.

Does it take a different type of pigeon to win from Sartilly than from Nantes or Niort?
I've never really thought about it. It may just be down to maturity and, for that reason,

I'm not keen on sending two-year-olds to Nantes. I prefer three and four-year-olds. However, it's no use sending old plodders that have done nothing all their lives.

How important is after-race care?
I don't give my birds any special feeding or treatment after a hard race. Good pigeons from a well-proven line generally have a quick natural recovery rate. Allowing them to rest should be the most sensible course, but again it is up to the fancier to read the signs.

Are hens that are raced hard spoilt for breeding?
No, hard races don't affect hens when it comes to breeding, but then I don't put them over the channel two or three times in a season as some people do. When racing, I've found that my best channel hens have been good, consistent layers. I've also been successful with barren hens - you can put them down in whatever nesting condition you want - and indeed my father won the Scottish National from Nantes with one.

It may take you two or three years to find out if a pigeon is good or bad, but do you wait that long before breeding off it?
No. To begin with I always breed from selected pairs of yearlings. I like to think that all my birds are well-bred and worth breeding from, although it does not really work like that.

What do you take into account when matching pairs?
Well, one thing I am not averse to is 'compromise pairings'. By this I mean I will pair a bird which is longish cast to one that fits nicely in the hand, or a biggish bird to a small to medium one, but not extremes in any direction. I have only one loft, with a maximum of twenty-eight pairs including stock birds, and in many ways my pairings are guided by channel plans. I always try to pair my more fancied channel birds to stock pigeons, that way there is no danger of losing a fancied candidate's mate. Also, yearlings are rarely paired to channel birds, as their racing would be restricted to only two or three races. I pair up in the middle of March and take one round off the racers. Thereafter, they nearly always race dry. I can't get many off my stock pigeons when they are paired to racers. I shouldn't have to, mind, if the stock's any good.

How many good birds do you produce?
I think a good fancier will tell you the percentage of good birds from a season's breeding is very small. You just need to look at the number of proven three and four-year-olds in almost any loft and it tells its own story. Most good fanciers, however, will agree that there are what I call 'plum' seasons, when a higher than usual percentage of good birds appear. I have had previous experience of these and hopefully will do every year from now on! Among the years that stand out for me in terms of breeding success are 1965, 1973, 1975, 1989 when flying on my own, plus one or two others. I don't know the reason for these 'plum' seasons, other than that you get more matings which click.

Do you sell many pigeons?
Only the odd one, mostly late-breds.

Are old pigeons and prisoners worth breeding from?
Breeding from old pigeons is fine but I always give them a youngish mate, say a two or three-year-old. Under no circumstances, however, would I even keep a prisoner, let alone breed from one. I am convinced that pigeons which are shut in all the time lose their vitality quickly. Any birds I purchase at clearance sales have to be relocated to my loft.

What are your views on pigeon politics and commercialism?
I leave pigeon politics to people more suited to it. Commercialism is, in my opinion, killing the sport.

What are your thoughts on late-breds from a racing point of view?
I have done very well with them. They are always trained in the year of their birth, with about five or six tosses to thirty or forty miles. Much of this is done after the last young bird race. The following year they go to 300 miles along with the rest of the yearlings. I have found one or two good channel birds like this, the best being a pied hen bred in 1983. She scored five times over the channel, including 5th section, 10th open SNFC Rennes, 1988 - a very hard race.

There has been talk recently of the Scottish National birds being liberated later so that no one can time on the day. Where do you stand on this?
I believe that, to get true results from a pigeon race, early liberations are a must. It's important that the birds have a full crack at a long distance race on the day.

What do you think about eye-sign?
I never pair up birds with similar coloured eyes, but, apart from that, I don't worry about it as long as the eye is bright and healthy looking. However, I do like a small pupil, though care should be taken with the type of light when studying this.

What do you look for in the wing?
One thing I do like to see is good space between the last three flights but, as with eye-sign, I have no real fads. Many fanciers swear by the so called 'step' but I have owned some outstanding channel racers that never had this. The pied hen that won 10th open Rennes in 1988 had the 'step', as did her daughter who was three times a prizewinner over the channel, but others haven't had it.

What about the throat?
The throat is one of the main points I take care to check on. All my best breeders and racers have a nice pink throat with an open slit in the roof of the mouth. When I select

pigeons this is one of the main points I look for. Definitely.

Why do some lofts disappear from the scene almost as quickly as they arrive?
Many good ones tend to slip into oblivion after a few years of great results because of the narrow-mindedness of the fancier, who thinks nothing is good enough to introduce in. I think that fanciers should keep an open mind on the breeding side of the game. By this I mean you should be looking for or trying new blood every season. Many introductions will fall by the wayside, but every once in a while one will click. Crossing is so important to maintain good performances.

Why are losses so high?
My own firm opinion on this, and many will disagree, is that there are too many untried continental so-called 'super strains' in this country. Birds are now too far removed from the actual winning ones to be of any use at all. These birds may flatter to deceive up to 200 to 300 miles on easy days. Clashing may account for some young bird losses, but not as many as fancy press articles would have us believe.

Would training from different points of the compass give birds more experience and so reduce losses?
I don't know. I have always concentrated on giving my birds, both old and young alike, line of flight training.

Do your birds field?
No, I never have any problems with fielding.

Do you use deep litter?
No. I acknowledge some excellent fanciers do, but I prefer to scrape out daily.

How do you recognise form?
Recognising form is very difficult. I try all year to get my birds to peak in June and early July, and I would therefore expect the whole loft to be on song at that time. I like to think, when I send a team to a channel race, I have a lot of them right. When I select my poolers I tend to look at that particular bird's record from being a young bird right through to the present. I have also found that my best birds, past and present, are self-motivated pigeons. By this I mean that once away from their eggs two or three nights, they are raring for a 'crack' at the race.

You say that your best birds are self-motivated. Can I assume you don't play tricks?
I certainly don't believe in messing with pigeons to 'motivate' them. Good keen pigeons will motivate themselves.

What nesting condition do you aim for?

I prefer the vast majority of my birds to be sitting six to fourteen days. We constantly read of Belgian fanciers who tell us the only way to race long distance hens is to send them on eight to twelve-day youngsters. I personally can never race hens like this, as I don't think any hen is at her best in this condition.

Will you treat sick pigeons?
To a limit. However, if a pigeon stops eating for a few days because of illness and its body starts to fall away, I no longer have any confidence in it. I think you will find, though, that the really good birds never have a day's illness in their lives.

Can you recommend any good books or videos?
I think there are many good books and videos on the market. They're probably being overrun a little with Belgian widowhood methods, but each to his own. Two books I would recommend to anyone who is interested are *Win With Olympic* and *Pigeon Lore*, both by Major A Neilson Hutton. They are very old books, but there is a lot of good common sense in them.

Why is the sport declining?
A lot of ink has flowed over this one, giving all sorts of reasons. I honestly think that young people today are being brought up in a different culture, with different values in life; cars, foreign holidays, cash in the bank, mortgages and so on are now more important. The hard fact is that pigeons are low on the list of people's priorities nowadays.

What are your thoughts on loft design?
Definitely none of your closed-in lofts with pantiled roofs for me. I believe in a small back garden loft with a good working team of birds in it. My own loft is twenty feet long with one third of the front open and the birds keep very healthy in it. It doesn't matter how fancy the loft is or how much it costs, it means nothing if the birds are second rate or the fancier gives less than one hundred per cent.

Which contributes more to success, the fancier or the pigeon?
I think it is fifty-fifty. Put simply, a mediocre fancier with good birds will get bad results, and a good fancier with mediocre birds will also get bad results.

Do you have faith in your ability to judge the merits of a pigeon?
You've got to have confidence in your own ability to select pigeons, no doubt about it.

Have you noticed anything which your best birds have in common?
I'm a better hen fancier, as are my father and uncle, and I've noticed that the best pigeons I've raced on my own or with my father have been hens that were suspicious of me in the winter. They were cagey. I could name you a whole list. They change completely when on eggs, though, and I can't get my hand under them. Cock or hen,

my best pigeons sit more keenly when fit.

Cagey hens have proved better than flirty hens that incline towards showing to you?
Yes. I'm not a believer in flirty hens, but, having said that, I wouldn't condemn them either.

What keeps a bird going after twelve to fifteen hours on the wing?
Fitness keeps it up, but you would have to ask the pigeon if it was the eggs or something else that keeps it going.

Some pigeons show little inclination to go back on eggs after a long race. How do you encourage them?
A returning hen will sit if you take her cock away after twenty minutes and keep him away overnight. Cocks, though, are a different ball game.

Would you say there are fewer or more good channel birds about today?
I think there are now fewer because of the influx of sprinters and the fact that fanciers send good pigeons too often and ask too much of them by sending them across two and three times in a season. I think the best thing the Scottish National could do is scrap the Gold Award.

When do you know the time has come to retire a bird?
You could ask yourself that question a thousand times, and yet you'd still send it once too often. I lost my 2nd open Rennes hen in a Mangotsfield smash the next season, and I lost my good '83 hen at Niort as a seven-year-old. I told myself that she was getting on, but she was coming so well in the shorter races that I chanced her.

Living in the Annan area, I imagine news of early arrivals travels quite fast. Do you keep yourself to yourself, preferring not to know who's timed in?
No, I like to hear of times as it creates atmosphere. Hopefully I'll be in front.

What are your ambitions?
Just to keep clocking good pigeons regularly. It means more than if you happen to win a national but nothing else.

Grizzle Hen
3rd section, 3rd open National Sartilly II 1991
206th open National Sartilly I 1992

Grizzle Cock
167th open National Sartilly I 1991
11th section, 27th open National Sartilly II 1991
33rd section, 114th open National Sartilly II 1992
7th section, 27th open National Nantes 1993

Billy Jamieson's Grizzle Cock (see opposite page)

Red Grizzle cock 86S10244
28th sect Sartilly 1, 1988. Flew Sartilly 2 same year. Injured on wires in winter of 88/89 & never raced again. A full-brother to 10244, winner of 22nd sect, 78th open SNFC Niort 1989 & 7th sect, 29th open SNFC Niort 1990 for JT Jamieson

Cheq hen 84S09406
226th open SNFC Rennes 1987 (only 299 birds in race time). 29th sect, 174th open SNFC Rennes 1988. Also won good prizes in Annan & District HC

Grizzle cock SU84S09299
Stock. Outstanding producer. Sire of birds to score from Sartilly, Rennes, Nantes & Niort. Also g/sire of 3rd open Sartilly 1991

Cheq Pied hen 31160
Bred by Mitchelhill & Fell, Carlisle. Outstanding breeder. Dam of winners with every cock she was paired with, including my 7th sect, 46th open Sartilly 2, 1987 (only 168 in race time). This hen was gifted to me by the widow of my uncle, Bob Thompson of Annan. No pedigree was found for her.

Red hen GB85N53628
Bred by Eric Fox & Son of Bakewell. Dam & g.dam of many club & channel prize winners.

Mealy cock 9096
Stock only. Sire & grandsire of many winners

Grizzle hen 82S9050
12th sect 36th open Rennes

Red cock 82J57986
1st sect, 46th open Pau, 2nd sect, 7th open MNFC Angouleme

Red cock 83S01646
Dam won 1st fed Appleton

Cheq w/f 87143069
1st sect 25th open Nantes, 6th sect 64th open MNFC Nantes

Mealy cock 8075
Dam won 1st sect, 4th open Falaise, 15th sect, 115th open Rennes

Red hen 8090
25th sect, 82nd open Rennes. Dam & g.dam of many good channel birds

Red Pd cock 8968
Stock. G/son of 10th sect, 37th open Rennes 1977

Red cock 7068
G/son of Border Star, 1st open SNFC Nantes

Grizzle hen 3368

Red cock 72E91313
4th & 6th fed Rennes

77Z59242 2nd & 3rd sect, 106th & 323rd open Pau

Cheq w/f cock 75Z15477
1st Sect, 15th open Pau

Blue w/f hen 77137272
1st sect, 7th open NFC Pau

Mealy Pd 4894 Also 24th sect, 229th, open Avranches

Mealy cock 7052
Son of 4894, see above

Cheq hen 4053 50th sect Rennes. Sister to 7068

Cheq Pied Hen
41st section, 168th open National Sartilly
26th section, 59th open National Sartilly
9th open Solway Fed Sartilly (22 birds on
the day), 5th section, 10th open National
Rennes (7 birds in section on the day).

Blue Hen
8th section, 30th open National Falaise
1st section, 10th open National Avranches
29th section, 196th open National Rennes
20th section, 96th open National Nantes
Bred by Pat McGrath of Sheffield.

Barry Crisp.

BARRY CRISP

Barry Crisp of Desborough still retains today the enthusiasm he had when he first started with pigeons back in the late 1950s. He is an all rounder, as was amply demonstrated in the space of just eight days last summer. Racing from Saintes, he timed the only bird on the day in his club and also topped the Mid Shires Federation. The following Saturday, on a mile-a-minute day, he took the first six club positions from Salisbury. These six pigeons were all two year olds, all late-breds and all were having the first race of their lives. He has raced both north and south routes with success, but since his restart in the sport after a short break, he has raced exclusively on the south.

When you came back into the sport in 1988, after a five-year break, did you carry on where you left off?
I thought I would, but no, it didn't work out that way. The sport had moved on so far that I found my old values, the pigeons I had and the methods I had been successful with previously were suddenly nowhere near good enough. For example, I used to feed beans, but in today's racing you don't need to. I couldn't believe how much things had changed in such a short space of time and I was amazed at the speeds pigeons were making. Whereas in the past two and a quarter hours was a decent time on a good racing day from Salisbury, which is 108 miles, they need to be home in one hour fifty minutes to be good now.

What did you do?
I sat down and talked to my friend, Jim Hales of Kettering, and he suggested I try some modern-day pigeons. The birds I had would plod home and I could always be sure of getting them, but they couldn't compete at today's racing pace because they were too big and bulky. Consequently I got rid of most of them - I asked Jim to do it for me because I find it very difficult to pick up a healthy pigeon and kill it - and brought in new stock. I could see the difference straight away and thereafter I was flying Salisbury in one hour fifty minutes

Where did you go for pigeons?
Jim gave me a good pair of Janssen stock pigeons to start me off and he also introduced me to a fancier by the name of Roy Thompson of Cannock, from whom he had had pigeons himself. These were Janssens imported directly from Madame B de Bruyn of Belgium. I have about twenty-five of these which I race up to Nantes, 350 miles. I wouldn't say they wouldn't do further but as yet I haven't got round to sending them to the distance because for the longer races I introduced some Con Conings and De Weerdts.

My hope is to cross these with the Janssens to put some speed into them for 500 and 600 miles. The other family I have is my old dark Gurnays. I have always had the Gurnays and when I was a dedicated north road flyer they won through to Lerwick for me. My present ones came from Michael Stalker of Bradford, whom I have known for more than twenty years, in 1988. Michael was very friendly with both Eric Craven and Arthur Mellor of Manchester, and he gave me a pair out of 'Dark Supreme'. Both did a lot of winning and produced winners and I have tried since to form a family around them, crossing some with Logans of the 'Aberdonian' line from Percy Cornell of Chiswick. These fly ever so well on good, hard days.

Do they win from 200 miles when the velocities are up round the 1500ypm mark?
No.

Do you think pigeons are now faster over 450 miles plus?
Yes, I'm convinced they are, all the way down the line. I'm sure today's distance pigeons would beat the old ones.

Do you think you will succeed in speeding up your Con Conings and De Weerdts when you cross them with the Janssens?
I think so, but not at the first cross. I'll have to go further than that. You've actually caught me in the middle of experimenting and I should be able to tell you next year or within two years at the latest whether it works or not.

How many birds have you in total?
At present, about seventy, including prisoner stock which has access to an aviary.

Would you rather they flew out?
Yes, I would really, but I daren't risk it because they cost me too much money.

And is this the best team you've had?
Yes, definitely. I've some good pigeons now. The type is right and the quality is there.

How do you determine your matings?
Some decide for me because if one or both of a pair race well, I keep them together until such time as I might lose one. Many times I've split them up and paid the penalty - some have sulked that much they wouldn't race. Apart from those, I use the old tried and tested method of pairing best to best. The only thing I won't do is pair two big ones or two little ones together, but I will pair big to small, as I've found over many years that you can reach a happy medium that way.

What do you look for in a pigeon?
I haven't got a real type. If they win and can breed pigeons to fly well, they'll do for me.

The only thing I don't like is henny cocks. Cocks should look like cocks. As far as the eye goes, I don't attach much importance to it and the only sort I don't really like is a pale pearl. I've studied eye-sign for many years and it's something I'm interested in, but I've come to the conclusion that it's overrated. As for the wing, I look for a longer forearm for distance pigeons as opposed to sprinters and also for a step between the secondaries and primaries and big gaps between the end flights.

Could an eye-sign man come into your loft and pick out your best pigeon?
If he could I'd make a £20 donation to charity straight away.

Could you go into another fancier's loft and pick out his best pigeon. Not by eye, but on type?
No, I don't think so. I can pick you a good pigeon out - one I like - but as to the best, I wouldn't say yes to that. I wouldn't be frightened to try, though.

How often do you choose the right pool bird?
Nine times out of ten. I know which are the consistent ones and I can tell from their general well-being how they will perform. I always sit in the garden with a note-book and record the weather and arrival times, whilst when they are over the channel I predict the time I think each pigeon will do. I look at the day and think this will be a 44 mph race or whatever and I then work out when I think each pigeon will come based on what speed I think or know it is capable of. And I'm often right.

Do you sometimes get it badly wrong?
Yes, only the other week when I prepared a good Janssen cock for Sartilly. I took his hen away, hand fed his youngster for him to conserve his energy and then put his hen back at dinner time on the day of basketing. He loved the youngster so much he wouldn't take his eyes off it and followed it everywhere and when I put his hen back he went potty. I fully expected to win the race with him, but he was my last pigeon. He was full of fly when he came back after nine hours - as good as when I'd sent him - so I don't know if I'd overdone it and he was sent too well.

Do you handle your racers much?
Yes, those I'm sending the coming weekend I pick up every night to see how they are progressing.

What are you looking for?
Nice, clean, warm feet, rapid eye movement and wattles that are a lovely snowy or chalky white. I've done well also when the wattles have had a pink hue to them but basically I prefer them to be chalky white. And if I see a chalky white 'beard' - two skin-like pieces about a quarter of an inch long either side of the beak - then it's time for maximum pools.

Do you look at the skin around the keel?
I do yes, yes, but I take no notice of it. The skin on most of my winners is purple and some don't lose their scale all season, but they still win. I do take notice of the blood spot on the keel, though. The darker it gets the more confident I am they will perform better.

Is there anything else you look for?
Yes. I hate to hear what I call the whistle of the wings. When a pigeon is on form you shouldn't be able to hear it when it's in flight.

Will you withdraw a channel candidate at the last minute if it's likely to cast in the basket?
No. I've had winners with gaps in the wing so the only time I worry about it is when young birds are up on their last two flights.

How does the management of your Janssens differ to that of your other birds?
To be honest, with having only the one racing loft, they are all treated more or less the same. The only difference is that I don't send distance pigeons as often because I believe the least you can take out of them, the better chance you have. Having said that, it all depends on how their year's gone on. I've sent pigeons that have had plenty of races still in perfect condition. They hadn't gone hard at all. Generally, though, they lead a leisurely life to begin with and I don't start them off until late May. They may have a minimum of two or three races then they rest and have no racing for a fortnight or preferably three weeks before the long one. I've missed chances of winning by not sending them within a fortnight but I believe you can't always see what they've taken out of themselves and I don't want to take the chance. During this rest period they have three twenty mile tosses a week, but in the last week they have no training at all. It's a free and easy week when they can do exactly as they like. If it's a nice day I may even let them out again on a form of 'open hole', but they are just as happy inside the loft as they are out of it.

How much weight do they carry?
I don't bump them up as I do sprinters. Some would say they are too light for the job, but distance is not about putting bull effort into it as a sprinter does. They want strength but not excessive weight, and they don't have to be big pigeons to be strong. Although I do like big pigeons for sprinting, I've always done better with small to medium birds for the distance.

Do they carry more muscle than your sprinters?
No, a different type of muscle. Whereas the muscle on my sprinters feels quite solid, on my distance pigeons, when they are right, it has more of an elastic feel. I don't know the reason why.

What are the first signs that a pigeon is going off form?
That's the difficult part and I couldn't honestly give an answer which applies to all birds. You often only know they've gone past their best when you send them and they don't do what you think they will do. With being on natural I find that I can't keep any pigeon, cock or hen, motivated for more than three or four weeks at a time so it's best to give them three weeks or a month off. Contrary to what a lot of people say, I know my sprinters have already gone off, as opposed to being just about to go off, when the body feels hard.

Is that true also of distance pigeons?
Yes, definitely. I wouldn't even put a distance pigeon in a basket if it was like that.

What are your favoured nesting conditions?
I like sprinters driving, which to me is almost widowhood, and distance pigeons I like to be sitting eight days at the time of basketing. I've not really had much success racing to a youngster in the nest. I used to practise it but I found that only the odd pigeon would respond.

How much importance do you attach to feeding?
Perhaps not as much as I should. I do know the value of grains but, being an older fancier, modern feeding is all new to me. Basically I'm one for variety. I like choice myself and I know the pigeons do, too. They have amazingly different preferences and I let them take what they want. Some will gulp all peas and others maize.

Do you feed heavily?
I have done this year, and I think it may have been a mistake. To be honest, I've been influenced by what I've read whereas I should have just read it, digested it, put it to one side and done my own thing.

Would you take me through your yearly feeding cycle?
All my corn, which I keep in an air-tight plastic barrel to guard against moisture and vermin, comes from *Manor Farm Granaries* of Brington near Huntingdon. It is ever so good. I hand feed twice a day throughout the year but I like them to be tight in the winter so from 1st January I feed 50 per cent barley, 25 per cent beans, 25 per cent peas plus a little linseed - an eggcup per twenty birds. I pair up towards the end of February and put them on a breeding mix called *Racing & Rearing (No 2 Pigeon)* which consists of 44 per cent beans, 18 per cent maples, 18 per cent wheat, 15 per cent maize and 5 per cent tares. Though still hand fed, there is always this mixture in gallipots in their boxes so they are never without food when rearing. For racing I like maize and I'm going off beans more and more, so at the beginning of April they go onto a racing mix called *Racing Classic*, made up of 40 per cent maize, 17.5 per cent wheat, 10 per cent maples, 10 per cent small blue peas, 7.5 per cent small white peas, 5 per cent dari, 5 per cent

milo, 2.5 per cent tares and 2.5 per cent safflower. Meanwhile the youngsters are weaned onto a young bird mix containing 47.5 per cent maples, 25 per cent wheat, 10 per cent milo, 10 per cent popcorn and 7.5 per cent tares. Young birds race on the same racing mixture as the old birds and all are on this through to the autumn. Then, whilst still moulting, all birds have 25 per cent barley and an equal measure of peas and beans.

Do you clean your corn?
Yes, always, as I believe dust on corn is harmful to pigeons. That view is based on an experience I had once with some yellow peas that were as dusty as anything. I didn't bother to clean them and as a result the pigeons really lost the colour and sheen on their necks. I borrowed a couple of my mum's stockings to polish them and after that the colour returned to my pigeons straight away.

What do they have in addition to the staple diet?
Throughout the racing season only I give them a few peanuts - a handful to twenty pigeons daily - as a treat. And I'm a big believer in linseed for distance pigeons, although I know a lot of people are just the opposite. The only other thing I give, now and again, is *Hormoform*, a cupful per twenty pigeons. I haven't used it this year and I haven't done as well - yet! But whether that's the reason or it's because I've had problems with my health and haven't spent so much time with the birds, I don't know. Now I'm retired I normally spend five or six hours a day with them but this year I've spent only half that.

With feeding a high carbohydrate diet throughout the racing season, have you every confidence in getting your birds from the distance?
If the day's okay - a good racing day - I certainly expect to see them, yes. I'm less confident if there's a holdover, though. I hate them because I don't think pigeons eat much in the basket and they use up carbohydrates quickly.

How much work do your birds do during the week?
I'm not a big trainer because I don't think they need it. I give them a twenty mile toss now and again and the rest of the time they exercise for fifteen to twenty minutes at each end of the day. They used to exercise more freely than that so to encourage them I've tried mixing them with the youngsters and it's worked to a certain degree.

What do you put in the drinkers after a race?
Sugared water, two dessertspoons to half a pint of water, always followed on a Sunday by Epsom Salts to purge them, a dessertspoon to five pints dissolved first in warm water. I purge them communally, so any that might be shattered are done as well, and by about Tuesday the old wattles clean up and they begin to get quite bouncy again.

Do you break them down?

I used to feed 50 per cent depurative and 50 per cent racing mix through to Monday morning, but not any more.

Do you use anything for potential respiratory problems?
Yes, this year I've suddenly gone onto *Mycoform-T*, which I give on a Wednesday when racing. Before that I never used anything.

What else goes in your drinkers?
On Tuesdays and Thursdays, a teaspoon of *Milton* to five pints of water. I should point out that I never give water straight from the tap, but let it stand for twenty-four hours first.

When do you wean your youngsters?
I very much like to keep things as natural as possible so I don't like taking youngsters away until they are thirty days old or more. It can be a bit of a drain on the old birds, but as for the youngsters I find the older they are the better. They learn from the old birds how to drink so I've no need to dip beaks and they have no setbacks or checks whatsoever. I pick them off the perches in the old bird loft, spray them very finely with *Johnson's Insect Powder* and then wean them onto a bed of straw treated with *Harkers Loft Compound*, which is a very good disinfectant. I change this fortnighly and in addition I wipe the young bird perches with a cloth dampened with *Jeyes' Fluid*. This is the only time I use straw because I think it can only encourage parasites. At all other times I scrape out twice a day and for nesting material I use tobacco stalks. To keep on top of parasites I also spray the loft twice a year using *Vykil*, which is perhaps not as regularly as I should, and I always brush *Duramitex* under the nest bowls. Consequently I've never had red mite and I see very few lice. A couple on thirty young birds is as many as there will be.

Is it necessary to wipe the youngsters perches?
I don't know if it is really, but I want to give them the best possible start I can. Perhaps I'm too fussy. I know my wife, Kath, thinks so. She says I always check up on her when she's cleaning out, but that's the way I am. If I think she's not doing it right I will go in and scrape out behind her.

What other measures do you take to keep your birds healthy?
I spray the gravel and the grass around my garden with *Jeyes' Fluid*. I'm sure I can't eliminate everything even then, though, as I have a dog and with the best will in the world you can't stop them picking around the salty areas where the dog has been.

When do you first let your youngsters out?
Normally as soon as they're weaned and unless it's foggy they go out twice a day. Having said that, this year they were strong on the wing before I let them out for the first

time, but it made no difference. I only lost one out of thirty.

Do you restrict their food in any way?
No. I like to see them grow and develop so they are hand fed as much as they want twice a day. Except those that mess about and won't come in. They don't get fed.

When and where do you start your youngsters off?
Their first toss is from ten miles and comes three weeks before the first race, by which time they've stopped roaming. I've been told I should train at two miles and five miles until they are coming straight off but I don't. I think they could actually go further than ten miles, but they mean a lot to me, my youngsters, and I don't want to risk throwing them away. In all, they have three or four tosses at ten miles, two or three at fifteen miles, two or three at twenty-five miles, two or three at forty miles and thereafter two or three twenty to twenty-five mile tosses a week.

What causes young bird losses?
I don't really know now. Before I would have said lack of training, but nowadays I think clashing and things like radar have a lot to do with it. We used to take a flask and some sandwiches and train from a spot near RAF Croughton. The birds used to fly around for ages and I put it down to being so close to so many transmitters and radar balls. It was the same when we trained at RAF Willington near Rutland Water. When we moved our pigeons a few miles down the road they cleared much more quickly so I'm convinced there is something in it.

How much racing do your youngsters have?
If I have a fault it's that I ask too much of them. I stop the big gawky ones after two races but the rest, including all the hens, race the complete programme through to Plymouth, which is 200 miles (or to Perth, 300 miles, when I was on the north road).

Has it been worth stopping the gawky ones?
Yes, it's paid dividends time after time.

Do you let your young hens lay?
If that's what they want to do, yes, but I don't encourage it.

Have any such hens made good old birds?
One once. She was a dark cheq Gurnay hen I called 'Penny' because she used to win the pools every week and she went on to be one of the best Gurnay hens I've ever had.

Have you had any success with pigeons that have made mistakes?
Yes, plenty. I once dropped a cheq cock in his third race as a young bird and he was lost for three weeks. Then as a yearling he went to Walsall from a channel race. The fancier

tossed him on the Monday and he was back here within seventy-five minutes. Two years later, from another channel race, the same fancier rang to say he was there again. This time he was back an hour later. In all he did that three times, but in between he scored on several occasions, including 2nd Royan. I don't condemn a pigeon for making a mistake. I've had them back in boxes, tried them again and had some good results.

When do you separate?
I don't as I've found them happier if left together. I've never had much problem with hens laying because I keep them short. Indeed there are virtually no eggs until I increase the feed.

What do you treat for?
Worms, canker and cocci, in that order, before pairing up. I use *Hoechst Panacur* tablets for worms and, as I use most of *Harkers'* products, *Spartakon* for canker and *Coxoid* for coccidiosis. I never treat during racing although I used to use a worming and vitamin powder on the grains and they could race next day.

Do you have your birds tested?
Usually, although I didn't this year. I normally take enough droppings for the vet to get a fair idea and I also ask him to look for enteritis.

Does he normally find anything?
They're never too bad - I sometimes have acceptable levels of canker and cocci but nothing serious. I did, however, once have a very high worm count when I thought the birds looked really well and I didn't think I had a problem.

Is routine important?
I find it is, yes. I like to keep everything the same and do things at the same time of the day. Not only that, but Kath and I always wear the same coat when around the birds.

Is that necessary?
Yes, I'm sure it is. I attach a lot of importance to it. If I haven't got it on my birds grunt at me and, likewise, if I walk through the gate into the garden and I have my coat on they will fly straight to me, but if I'm not wearing it they won't bother. Even on race days, when it's hot and I might be waiting for channel birds, I still wear it all the time. Incidentally, I don't mind having people in the garden during the racing season, but I won't allow anyone in the loft.

Is tameness something you encourage?
Yes, although I've had wild pigeons win just the same. It's perhaps better to describe my pigeons as self-composed rather than tame. I will spend afternoons in the loft with

my youngsters in an effort just to make or keep them as much like this as possible.

What has been your biggest mistake?
Flogging consistent pigeons and expecting too much of them. When I was younger I used to see distance racing as just points A and B covered in the shortest possible time. I never realised what it took. Nowadays I know it takes all they've got, even when they are sent really well. I remember one race from Lerwick, 537 miles on the day into a head wind and no holdover. When they returned they didn't weigh above half what they did when sent.

What else have you learnt after all your years in the fancy?
That there's always a bit more to learn. You think you've seen every situation and know all there is to know but really you've only scratched the surface. I'm always finding something new.

Do you still get the same thrill out of racing today as you've always done?
I think I'm even worse now than when I was younger. Whatever the race, as soon as I know they are up I can't keep still.

Is the average fancier better now?
As far as stockmanship goes, no. Fanciers breed far more than they need. But racing-wise, definitely. The sport is much more competitive today and if I was starting up now I'd find it harder to break my novice status. It took me ages as it was.

NRCC LERWICK

Average position of first bird for those fanciers who have
recorded at least one open position between 1992 & 1994

	Member	Location	Dist	Sect	Average
1	K Bush	Cossall	496	A	9
2	R Foxall	Pilsley	484	A	14
3	J Lovell	Lincoln	480	B	24
4	Hovell & Roberts	Sutton-in-Ashfield	486	A	37
5	M/M Findon	Watnall	495	A	42
6	A Patzer	Huntingdon	542	E	57
7	M/M Dixon	Sutton Bridge	510	C	61
8	D Lee	New Houghton	482	A	64
9	G&W Britton	Newborough	521	E	70
10	J Mcdowell	Huntingdon	542	E	75
11	JW Smith	Hucknall	492	A	75
12	J Leivers	Selston	490	A	77
13	E Gregory	Eastwood	493	A	88
14	A Hallsworth	South Normanton	488	A	92
15	M/M Sedgwick	Pinxton	488	A	105
16	E Bond & Son	Sutton-in-Ashfield	486	A	107
17	H Taylor & Sons	Eastwood	493	A	108
18	P Wraight	Earith	541	F	110
19	Chambers & Smith	Newthorpe	494	A	127
20	M/M Mitchley	Lincoln	483	B	131

...And between 1992 & 1995

	Member	Location	Dist	Sect	Average
1	J Lovell	Lincoln	480	B	21
2	K Bush	Cossall	496	A	23
3	Hovell & Roberts	Sutton-in-Ashfield	486	A	44
4	M/M Dixon	Sutton Bridge	510	C	47
5	G&W Britton	Newborough	521	E	·62
6	A Patzer	Huntingdon	542	E	90
7	A Hallsworth	South Normanton	488	A	125
8	E Bond & Son	Sutton-in-Ashfield	486	A	144
9	M/M Mitchley	Lincoln	483	B	151

KEITH BUSH

'I don't have any theories. Good racers win. Good breeders breed good pigeons. Breed from good stock and let the basket be the judge.' Such is the philosophy of Keith Bush of Cossall, who, over the past six years, has won thirty-nine positions in the first one hundred open of the North Road Championship Club from Lerwick as well as two Gold Medals from Thurso for twice first federation.

Which races are you interested in?
Lerwick with the NRCC. I gear everything to this one race, although when the Midlands Championship Club flew Lerwick I competed very successfully in that from Lerwick and Thurso as well. To this end, I fly natural only and use my local club, Kimberly Miners Welfare, to give my distance pigeons some 'match practice'. Most of the races are below 300 miles and you really need sprint or middle distance pigeons prepared for that distance, so I have little or no interest in nine-tenths of the programme. In my area, there aren't many fanciers who are interested in distance flying and fewer still who manage to fly it consistently well. Many will not put up with the disappointments.

Do you live in a good location for the NRCC?
Yes I do, being about twelve or fifteen miles from first drop, but when flying 500 miles on a hard day location is not so important and a good pigeon will give a good account of itself regardless.

How fit are your birds early in the season?
Not very, especially for the first race. It doesn't seem to make a lot of difference to how they perform, though, as I find that if I train them they'll be about ten minutes behind and if I don't they'll still only be fifteen minutes adrift.

How do you stop your team coming into form too soon?
I don't do anything apart from pair up late. They don't go together until around March 20th so they shouldn't come into form until the end of May. If they do it's hard luck. One year I did pair up earlier - in mid-February - to have them ready for Perth. I was 2nd open but I thought that by Lerwick they were past their best so I've never repeated it.

How much exercise do they take round home?
Not a lot - perhaps half an hour at the most. If it's very hot when the hens come out at mid-day they sometimes turn around and go straight back in again.

You don't flag them, then?
No. I want my pigeons to be happy, not frightened to death. They would only drop in the fields anyway. I wouldn't mind if it was on my land but they drop in the garden centre next door.

How many prep races do your distance candidates have?
Two or three to either 200 or 250 miles, then they are put down to nest.

How much training do they get after this?
In the two weeks before Lerwick I try for a cumulative total of six to eight hours' training so they have four or five tosses from 40 or 50 miles. Then they have four or five days' rest before basketing.

Do you train in any weather?
Yes, all sorts. I've seen them make little tiny circles when I've released them in fog, but they've still come home once it's cleared. I wouldn't do this at the beginning of the season, but later on, when they start coming, nothing will stop them. Living close to the M1, I train mainly on the line of flight, although I usually give at least one toss from the opposite direction. It makes them think!

How much weight do your Lerwick birds carry?
When I have just finished training they are fairly light, but they blow up through being rested and are heavy by basketing time.

Are you confident you will get them right for the day?
Yes, always. All pigeons should be in reasonably good condition in June and July, so anyone should be able to get them ninety per cent right. Beyond that it is luck.

Could you rush your birds' preparation and still do as well?
No. It is time that they need, not anything I could give them.

Do you prepare some for an easy Lerwick and some for a hard one?
I prepare them so that they are fit so, fast or slow, it doesn't matter. Having said that, I do dread it being a fast race because your chances are not so good when they come in batches. And fast from Lerwick means fast - perhaps only eight or nine hours. If we get one of those then that's a season gone for me.

How many do you send to Lerwick?
Twenty to thirty. All that can stand. In 1993 I sent thirty, had nine in the first 100 and timed eighteen by 9.00 am next morning. I had twenty-eight back by the end of the second day and the other two have never come. One of them was going for the fifth time and had never had a night out, but that's pigeons. If you get frightened to lose

them you might as well pack up distance racing.

How many have you lost over the years?
Very few.

With sending a large team, aren't you mindful that a disaster could set you back?
I don't think disasters are very likely at Lerwick. I've only experienced one, and that was when I sent a second-rate team. As far as I'm concerned, the harder it is, the better. That way only the best will come. I may lose one or two, but the best ones will work their way back.

So you normally send your best?
Yes. What is the point of keeping them otherwise?

Why send so many?
To keep the family strong by testing. It's not in the hope of just getting one.

Is your present team the best you've had?
I would say the overall quality has not altered over the last five years.

Do you become anxious waiting for your Lerwick birds?
It's not anxiety I feel but pressure, brought about by people expecting me to do well because of my past record. I must admit that on race day the phone ringing gets on my nerves.

Do you send any back to Thurso a month later?
I only keep the best so I'll tell you what I do. All those that come back after a certain time, depending on the type of day, go back to Thurso. It doesn't matter that they have done Lerwick on the day, if they then don't score at Thurso they are culled. All except those which have bred good pigeons. It would be silly to cull them.

What do you feed on return from a race?
I'm not particular. They eat what they want from the mixture. One year I came out of the house and found a cock who had just done fifteen hours with a cropful of corn. As to the water, I put nothing in it. I've tried glucose and sugar but they hardly drank anything. I couldn't see the point in that, as, after a long race, you want to re-hydrate them.

How long does it take them to pull round after a hard Lerwick?
I like to see them out flying next morning. If not, I throw them out and let them have a few laps. It stops them stiffening up. In 1993 I timed five on the day flying between fifteen and a half and sixteen and a half hours and all were out flying next morning.

How many times can you ask a pigeon to fly Lerwick before it takes its toll?
Two or three. You can tell it's had enough when it starts coming late.

If one of a pair races particularly well, will you keep it with the same mate the following season?
No, I always split them up. If you leave them together for too long and their youngsters turn out to be no good you have wasted a year.

Do you send both of a pair?
Quite often. In 1994, my 3rd and 6th open Lerwick pigeons were paired together.

Are you able to get your birds back on the same nest after a distance race?
When they have been away for any length of time it is very rare they will go back on the nest. Usually it's a waste of time trying and with cocks it's hopeless.

What is your favoured nesting condition?
I usually send my birds sitting up to time or on a small youngster.

How do you select your pool birds?
Well, all the team will look special just before basketing for Lerwick, the good and the not so good, so you have to pool on ability and also on current form, not just on condition. I have noticed one or two act a bit strange when in top condition. They will drop on the house and act a bit daft. Both my award winners from Lerwick (three times in the first one hundred) did this. In 1993 I had four hens and a cock on the day. My first bird was my pool bird, but I hadn't been happy with her. I had lost her cock and she wouldn't pair to anything else but in the end I got her sitting about ten days. I would have preferred her sitting up to time, but I knew she had the ability so I stuck with her. My second bird, a hen sitting up to time, was my second choice. That's luck.

Do you take any notice of the skin on the keel, or mascara on the eye-cere?
That's a new one on me - mascara. As for the skin, no, I don't look at that either. I don't handle my pigeons much once they've completed their training as I think you can tell they are right by watching them.

Do you take any notice of the wing?
No, I don't bother with it as I don't think it makes any difference to how a bird will perform. In the last couple of years I've even sent pigeons with broken flights and done well. One won 5th open MCC and another one had grown a short next-to-end flight after banging it the previous winter but it still came to take 4th section.

Which flight are your Lerwick birds normally on?
Usually their second, although when 'Octavia Gale' took 2nd open she went on her first.

What keeps a pigeon going for fifteen or sixteen hours?
I think it is an inborn will to win.

Have you done better with cocks or hens?
Hens, although I have had some decent cocks, too. I think this is partly because I concentrate more on getting my hens into their best nesting condition and cocks aren't as suited to sitting up to time or feeding a small youngster.

What are your hens like physically?
They are on the small side, with plenty of length in the vent bones. I like hens with plenty of capacity in the vents.

Is there any place for sentiment in your loft?
Only to a certain extent. I tend to keep them going as I've not got the room to keep too many old pigeons.

Could your birds win at shorter distances if that was your aim?
Yes, if I worked them hard early on. Certainly from Perth, from where I have won some decent fed and open prizes.

Do you think sprinters can be made into distance pigeons?
It depends what you get to start with. Just because they haven't won at the distance doesn't mean they can't. It may be that they've never been sent. How long it would take you depends on whether you are lucky to get the odd one with staying power at the outset.

What strain do you race?
The Keith Bush family, originating from my father and developed by me over the past fifteen to twenty years. I can't give you much background on them as I don't know too much about them myself, but I can tell you there is a bit of Trueman Dicken blood in them. This line stems from a son of a cock out of 'Barcy Boy' which I bought in from R&M Venner of Street in Somerset and a hen of Fred Griffin's. There is also a good hen of George Bruninger's in the background. She was a half-sister to a King's Cup winner out of a pigeon called the 'Lloyd's Cock'.

How have you maintained your family?
Through inbreeding and line-breeding and always being on the lookout for a good cross. I breed from the best and others bred from the best, but I don't think there is any way of knowing which will breed the best. It is mainly down to luck. The best often come from where you don't expect it, perhaps two late-breds albeit from good parentage. The only difference between inbreeding and line-breeding is that if you are successful you put it down to line-breeding, but if you fail you blame it on inbreeding.

What do you look for when bringing in a cross?
I go to someone with a family of distance pigeons and keep my fingers crossed. For example, I've just introduced one or two from Robert Jones of Resolven, out of his old family. Crosses usually don't turn out to be any good but then if I picked out two of my own for someone else they probably wouldn't turn out any good either. The cross which is doing best for me at the moment came from Michael Spencer of Barnoldswick, prior to his winning the Nantes National, out of his 'Scottish Lady' blood. One hen scored at Lerwick in 1993 and another was my first bird at Thurso and 6th open Lerwick 1994. I haven't had a another cross in the last five years which has made any impact yet, but if it was that simple it wouldn't be so much fun.

Do you need to see before you buy?
No. Breeding is the only thing that matters so if introductions are from good long distance winning stock they will be something like as far as type is concerned. Good distance pigeons invariably come from good distance stock and, providing you don't go back beyond grandparents, that's all you need to know.

Would you bring in any of the more fashionable modern strains?
No. I prefer pigeons which have been tested and sorted over time, preferably in national competition, not feds.

Are all introductions given their liberty?
Yes, as I don't keep prisoners. I think they deteriorate quickly and I don't like to see them locked up either.

Do you spend hour upon hour in the winter evenings planning your pairings on paper?
No. I don't get much time nowadays so I tend to carry plans for my main pairs in my head, and after that I pair two that take my fancy. When I go down to the loft I don't take a piece of paper with me, I just shove a couple in a nest box and if I like the look of them I will decide there and then to give them a try.

Do you take any particular factors into consideration?
Well, I try and pair older birds to younger mates as I favour youth in my matings, but apart from that I don't look at anything. Except, perhaps, the wing. I like a good length of wing so if I think one's wing is shorter than I like, I may pair it to one with a longer wing to compensate. I'm not interested in the eye at all, though. It doesn't bother me if I pair two of the same colour together or two with pale eyes. I hear people say that pale-eyed pigeons are no good, yet in my family some of my best pigeons have been pale eyed.

You are quite happy to breed off old pigeons, then?

Yes, as I see no reason why age should affect the genes. Plenty of old pigeons have bred good performers.

What's the size of your team?
I have approximately sixty for racing and breed about sixty youngsters.

How many good pigeons do you breed?
It varies from year to year. For example, 1990 was a good year as I produced six or seven 400 to 500-mile winning pigeons, or approximately ten per cent of what I'd bred. In other years I may get only one or two.

Do you sell any?
A few late-breds if anybody contacts me, but otherwise not many. I am very fond of late-breds. They are bred when pigeons and weather are at their best. I often re-mate one or two of my best birds to try new matings and give me more scope when breeding. I usually don't train these late-breds until they are yearlings, but it doesn't worry the best, only the duffers.

Turning to feeding, what and how do you feed?
I hopper feed beans from hatching until the end of the moult and, at the same time, hand feed a mix of peas, maize and wheat twice daily. I don't hopper feed the mix for two reasons. First, because they would throw it about, and secondly, by feeding it twice daily it enables me to exercise control over them. In the winter months I feed a mix of the above building up to eighty or ninety per cent barley in January.

Do you feed a commercial mix?
No. All my corn is purchased from the farm or directly from the mill at a cost of about £9 per 50kg. I can't afford polished corn, especially when I can buy the same thing unpolished at a much lower price. Too much fuss is made of corn. I feed mine as it comes from the farm. It's all dusty but it does them no harm.

How much of the mix do they get?
Whatever they want. To fly the distance you can't afford to be keeping your birds hungry.

How do you ensure your hens get as much of the mix as your cocks?
I try to make sure they are fed at mid-day, especially when they are getting a lot of training.

Do you prefer new crop beans?
Definitely. If you're a gardener you'll notice that if you keep seeds for a year before planting them the germination is terrible.

What sort of pigeon do you need for national competition?
A good one. A pigeon bred for the job. An individual, not a flock-follower. There are plenty that will fly the distance, but not so many that can think it out.

Have you found any difference in the birds that do well at local level and those that do well with the NRCC?
No, because I've never done very well at local level.

Why do you think it is that on the north road the shorter flying members dominate the Lerwick result, yet in the south road nationals there is a much more even spread?
I don't know. It's something I've never understood. If we time after twelve and a half hours, it gives other birds another two hours to fly at least another fifty or sixty miles but they seem to hit a brick wall after they leave us. Perhaps a late liberation would help them.

Have you thought of turning south and having a go at Pau?
Yes, and it's probably something I will do in time.

Do you think your birds would get the extra 200 miles?
Yes. Good distance pigeons are good whether it's a one or two-day race. The best will still win. My brother Neil has had several direct from me which have scored well at 700 miles.

Would you favour an early or late lib?
I think if you're flying Pau to the north you have to have a late lib in order to have a chance of winning. Added to that, with a late lib one could expect pigeons to do it several times, whereas I think flying 500 miles on the day, then up to 200 miles next day would take too much out of them.

Would you race both routes?
No, I would switch the lot. It would be impossible for me to fly both routes, as I have little time to fly pigeons as it is.

Do you think they would cope with the transition?
I'm sure the best ones would, certainly, although perhaps not straight away.

What do you regard as your best performance?
Being 2nd open Lerwick when all the other leading pigeons were on the other side of the country. Drag and wind make a lot of difference even at Lerwick.

Which is the best pigeon you have raced?
'Octavia Gale', bred in 1987. She is now in retirement, having deserved it.

What was her best nesting condition?
All her performances were achieved on her first youngster of the year. Incidentally, in 1990, when she was 12th open, the birds were ten days in the basket, but two out of my first three were hens sent on small youngsters, so that blows another myth.

How was she bred?
From two late-breds. Her sire was a blue cock from a half-brother and half-sister mating, his dam being 2nd open Perth NRCC and winner of the FG Wilson Trophy for best average Perth and Lerwick. She was from 'Rocky', five times Lerwick, four times in the prizes when paired to a slatey hen, 20th open Lerwick, sixteen and a half hours on the wing, timed at 10.02 pm. She was bred by my brother Neil from the 'Nantes Hen'. This 'cross' is working well for Neil, too, his 'Saintes Hen' being out of the 'Nantes Hen' when paired to a son of 'Rocky'. This gives you an idea of how I breed. I concentrate on one pigeon, then 'cross' it with another line of the family. Incidentally, the two late-breds which produced 'Octavia Gale' were sent back to Scunthorpe with Neil for their first training toss - never to be seen again. He's probably kept them and that's why he's flying so well!

Has 'Octavia Gale' bred anything of note?
I haven't that many out of her as she only lays the odd egg, but her grandchildren are doing well, yes.

Does she only lay the odd egg because she's been raced hard?
No. I don't think that makes any difference to a hen's ability to breed at all. It's probably because she had paramyxo as a youngster.

Really! The full symptoms?
No, just wet droppings, although I did have one or two with the shakes. Obviously it didn't impair her racing ability so I think it only has a long-term effect if a pigeon is affected when it is still growing its reproductive organs. For about five years before it became compulsory, I vaccinated my young birds and this gave complete control. I would be much happier if I could continue to do just this as I don't think it is necessary to vaccinate old birds. With human flu it is only the old and weak who are vaccinated.

Where do you stand on general preventive treatments?
Being a pharmacist I am well acquainted with many of the drugs and treatments used on pigeons and for that reason I now don't treat for anything unless I find something amiss. Even then I only treat individuals as opposed to the flock, except in the case of worms - and I haven't treated for them either for at least the last two or three years. All birds have a sub-clinical level of canker and cocci so all you do by treating is destroy the balance. The treatment may only last a week and then you're back where you started. Not only that, but antibiotics can make things worse. You can get all sorts of things,

such as fungal infections, after using them.

Do you treat sick pigeons generally?
Maybe once. But only once.

Do you use anything in the drinker to combat infections they may pick up in the transporter?
No, nothing at all because I don't think my pigeons need it. I think it's more likely your birds will pick something up in the basket if you keep things too clean at home.

How do you control mite and lice?
I spray the loft to keep down mite, using malathion from the garden centre, or sheep dip, usually alternately. As for lice, I haven't used anything directly on the old pigeons for at least the last five years and I find that they carry very few - a balance is reached. The young birds carry a lot of lice - I can see them crawling up my shirt when I basket for training - until they go through their first moult then, like the old birds, they are pretty clean.

Does this not knock the condition off them?
No. It doesn't do them any harm at all as lice only live on the feather dust. Mite, of course, are a different matter.

How far do you race your youngsters?
Usually through to 200 miles, but this is to sort out the bad ones not to judge how they will perform in later life, since I have found it doesn't matter. Although I don't set out to win young bird races I do educate them to race and trap. I like to have control over them and don't want them developing bad habits as you can't afford to have birds sitting out, even from Lerwick.

And the rest of your birds?
Yearlings get the works. Some go through to Lerwick - often successfully - and if they haven't shown some sort of ability by the end of their yearling stage they're out. My family is at its best at two years of age - as I think all pigeons are - so all my two-year-olds and above go to 500 miles unless injured. I don't hold any back because if they're not fit in June and July then they shouldn't be here.

Do you think it would make any difference to your results if you took a gentler approach with your youngsters and yearlings?
No. None at all. It does pigeons no lasting harm if they are raced hard and if they are not right when young then they won't be right when they are two or three. 'Octavia Gale' flew thirteen hours from Thurso as a yearling, carrying nest flights, and I have also won Thurso by twenty minutes with a yearling hen who was at Lerwick a month

before. She later went on to score from the Faroes as well.

Have any of your best birds made mistakes in earlier life?
Yes, quite a lot of them. 'Octavia Gale' often made mistakes, and I've had plenty of others that have nighted-out. I think it wakes them up. I've never had any good ones that had been out all winter, though, nor have I ever had one turn out any good that had gone in someone else's loft. Last year, for example, I had two that went in locally and I lost them both racing.

Do you think inferior stock is the major cause of losses?
That or illness in youngsters. Clashing may be a problem too, but it doesn't bother me as I believe pigeons should be able to clash with others and still find their way home.

Are there any aspects of the sport you have no time for?
Yes. I don't like all the bickering that goes on and would sooner keep out of it. Otherwise it could make keeping pigeons not worthwhile. I keep pigeons purely as a hobby - a recreation. I also think the sport has become too commercialised and is no longer a hobby for many. Too many people are after a quick buck and this has made it too expensive. People will try anything to win, and if they don't, they can't afford to stay in the sport. I think some of the larger studs have done a lot of damage and have put up the cost of pigeons and of the sport in general. They are only in it for one thing - money - the very thing which is ruining the sport.

Do you enjoy books and videos about the sport?
I like reading books, yes, but I've only seen the odd video. One that I had loaned to me was more like a cookery programme and it put me off.

From your own experience, which is more important, the fancier or the pigeon?
For long distance races it is at least ninety per cent pigeon. Good pigeons win *in spite of* what we do, not because of what we do. Shorter distance racing is more down to system and management. What ratio? I don't know as I've never tried it.

You really believe it is as high as ninety per cent?
It might even be higher than that. My part is minuscule. For example, in 1989 I flew to a ramshackle old loft built by myself from any bits of old wood I could lay my hands on. That year I was 2nd open Lerwick and had five in the first thirty-one in the open - on deep litter. In 1990 I had moved house (only next door) and had a brand-new pantiled loft made. That year I was 3rd open and had five in the first twenty-seven in the open. This time the loft was scraped out. The only thing the same was the pigeons and at the end of the day this is the only thing that matters. Not loft, corn, eye-sign or anything else. Good pigeons prepared for the task. I'm sure if I raced a team of duffers alongside my own and treated them just the same, I wouldn't get them from the distance.

Are you a good judge of a pigeon?
I can tell you one I like but, in all honesty, I've no idea whether a pigeon is any good until it wins.

Have you any fads?
None, nor prejudices. I let the basket be the judge. I think that is the problem with most fanciers. They won't accept that you just need good pigeons, bred and prepared for the job. All fanciers would fly better if they sorted them out by the basket. The rest is pure luck.

'Octavia Gale'
2nd club, 4th fed Fraserburgh
1st club, 1st fed Thurso
2nd open Lerwick
12th open Lerwick
18th open Lerwick

'Octavia Gale'

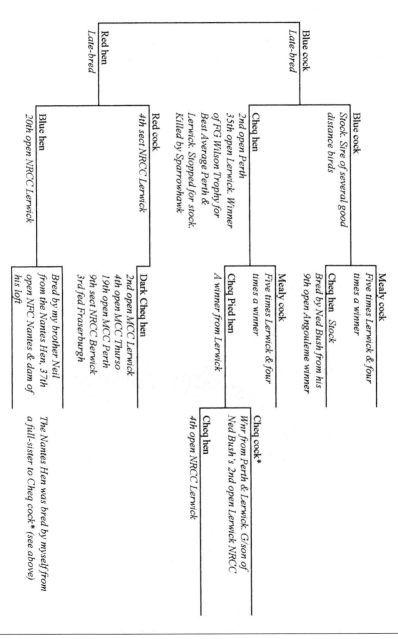

North Road Championship Club
Lerwick 1994

Liberated at 5.50 am on Sunday, 26th June, in a light north-west wind after a one-day holdover. 753 sent 3,663 birds. Only 180 birds clocked in race time.

Pos	Sect	Name	Location	Dist	Vel
1	D1	A Chamberlain & Son	Kirby Muxloe	519	868
2	E1	A Patzer	Huntingdon	542	823
3	A1	K Bush	Cossall	496	821
4	C1	R Todd	Boston	498	804
5	F1	P Dale	Norwich	540	788
6	A2	K Bush	Cossall	496	785
7	E2	Miss M Taylor	Ramsey	534	772
8	I1	Johnson & Son	Ipswich	566	737
9	A3	S&M&J Ellis	Sutton in Ashfield	485	731
10	A4	K Bush	Cossall	496	715
11	C2	Procter, Son & Juby	King's Lynn	514	713
12	A5	Rick & Spiers	Wollaton	497	712
13	A6	R Foxall	Pilsley	484	708
14	A7	F Salt Bros & Son	Kimberley	495	707
15	A8	R Jepson	Underwood	491	700
16	B1	M/M Nix	Spalding	508	687
17	B2	R Geldard	Lincoln	483	685
18	E3	I Bellamy	Paston	523	675
19	A9	E Jephcote	Ilkeston	496	669
20	E4	Miss M Taylor	Ramsey	534	668
21	I2	M/M Fahie	Colchester	577	661
22	A10	K Bush	Cossall	496	659
23	A11	R Hallsworth	Selston	489	651
24	C3	G Knight & Sons	King's Lynn	515	647
25	A12	H Taylor & Sons	Eastwood	493	634
26	F2	M/M Kaschener	Scole	545	632
27	D2	P Stokes	Leicester	527	627
28	B3	Bullers & Buckley	East Bridgford	496	627
29	B4	R Marshall	Lincoln	478	624
30	A13	J Smith	Hucknall	492	624
31	A14	Middleton & Hellen	Carlton	497	622
32	A15	E Bond & Son	Sutton in Ashfield	486	622
33	B5	M/M T Sheriff	Spalding	514	621
34	A16	M/M Boot	Alfreton	485	619
35	A17	D Whelbourne & Son	Nottingham	496	618

36	B6	Collishaw & Johnson	Leasingham	493	617
37	A18	A Barker	Heanor	494	616
38	A19	M/M Sedgwick	Pinxton	488	615
39	A20	K Bush	Cossall	496	615
40	C4	Hawes & Winterton	King's Lynn	515	613
41	H1	M/M Peachy & Son	London	605	606
42	B7	J Lovell	Lincoln	480	605
43	C5	L Manning	Boston	497	603
44	E5	J McDowell	Huntingdon	542	602
45	F3	R Harding	Cambridge	550	602
46	A21	P Elliott	Huthwaite	486	601
47	B8	M/M Mann	Grantham	500	600
48	A22	K Bush	Cossall	496	598
49	A23	M/M Findon	Watnall	495	597
50	B9	M/M Mitchley	Lincoln	483	595
51	A24	R Hallsworth	Selston	489	595
52	H2	L Mardell	Ware	572	594
53	E6	M/M Jarvis	Yaxley	529	593
54	F4	P Wraight	Earith	541	592
55	A25	K Bush	Cossall	496	590
56	A26	K Bush	Cossall	496	590
57	A27	B Prime	Chesterfield	482	587
58	B10	D Marshall	Lincoln	481	586
59	F5	R Wilson	Ely	537	585
60	A28	K Bush	Cossall	496	585
61	C6	R Brocklesby	Boston	497	585
62	F6	Barry & Griffiths	Haddiscoe	538	584
63	F7	M/M Gannon	Norwich	533	583
64	C7	Naughton & Bunton	King's Lynn	515	583
65	E7	A Barnes & Son	Whittlesey	526	583
66	A29	M/M Groom	South Normanton	488	583
67	B11	D Plummer & Son	North Hykeham	482	582
68	A30	K Bush	Cossall	496	581
69	D3	J Cave & Sons	Stoke Bruerne	554	581
70	E8	M/M Spinks	Peterborough	523	581
71	C8	G Knight & Sons	King's Lynn	515	580
72	A31	K Bush	Cossall	496	580
73	C9	Lee Bros	Mablethorpe	475	578
74	B12	J Lovell	Lincoln	480	577
75	E9	GV&W Britton	Newborough	521	574
76	E10	GV&W Britton	Newborough	521	574
77	C10	Hawes & Winterton	King's Lynn	515	573
78	B13	D Clare	Baston	515	573
79	A32	K Bush	Cossall	496	573

John Wheatcroft's

Open/Classic Show Results 1984/85-1993/94

69 1st Prizes

6 x winner Gardner Cup - East Coast Show
5 x winner R Emrys Jones Trophy - BHW Show of the Year
4 x winner R Boden Challenge Trophy - BHW Show of the Year
4 x winner Mitchell Points Trophy - East Coast Show
4 x winner Hilton Thomas Trophy NEHU Show
2 x winner Mitchell Shield - Show of the North
Winter Gardens Rose Bowl - East Coast Show
King's Trophy - East Coast Show
WHU Welsh Centre Trophy - Best Racing Pigeon - Monmouth Open Show
West Midlands Centre Trophy - BOS Racer Midland Show

JOHN WHEATCROFT

Though a racing man also, John Wheatcroft's primary interest lies in showing at the classic and open shows held each winter. In the last ten years he has won sixty-nine firsts through to the highest level, with the majority of these wins coming in eye-sign classes. Not surprisingly, he speaks as someone all too aware of the scepticism with which eye-sign is viewed, but he doesn't regard it as a personal crusade to convince people of its merits. Rather, he sees eye-sign simply as a fascinating topic to set alongside other aspects of the sport.

How much racing do you do?
It depends on the time I have available. I'm a member of a number of clubs - the Sun Inn Flying Club in Pinxton, the Somercotes & District Homing Society, and the Midlands and National Flying Clubs, but for the past few years I have not flown a complete programme. I usually get my birds flown to the distance I require for them to be eligible for the flown classes in the classic shows, youngsters to 100 miles at least and old birds to 150 miles or over.

Just as a matter of interest, what are losses like in your area?
Generally the racing we get is not too bad for land racing. It's usually the channel races where losses can be experienced. Like anywhere else, a good convoyer and race-controller are a big asset to any organisation.

Why are you attracted to showing?
I don't really know. I suppose I'd have say it's mainly because of the many friends I've made through travelling about and meeting people, and because of the chance it's given me to see and handle champions, both racers and show pigeons.

How much preparation do you put in before a big show?
Before the show season starts I usually book my holidays from work for two or three days before each show I have decided to enter, and during those days I spend a lot of time with the pigeons. I clean them up if necessary, check for marks, prepare the baskets and so on. And I always give them a warm bath, using *Bosmolen Bath Salts*. Warm water is better than cold because it soaks into the feather a bit better.

I know some showmen bring their candidates indoors into the warmth the night before a show and this puts an edge on them. Do you?
No, not usually unless I have to be away very early in the morning to get to a show. Most of the shows I attend are quite a distance away so the birds spend enough time in

the basket.

Do you feed differently in the days prior to a show?
My feeding programme starts in the weeks leading up to a show, rather than in the days before. I like a balanced diet so I work with a standard moulting mix, which I hand feed, and then I modify it as the show gets nearer if I think I need to. For example, I sometimes add up to fifty per cent peas if they need more body, whereas if they are not corky enough the day before the show I feed one hundred per cent moulting mix. There again, if they are handling too light I increase the maize, always being careful not to overdo it because too much can make them too fat in the vents.

Which brand of corn do you feed?
It depends on what I can get, really. As long as it's clean and not polished too much I'm not too bothered. For the last few years I've used a couple of different brands, *Bosmolen* and *Hall Farm*, whilst at present I am using *Flying Dutchman* grains, which I'm pleased with.

What do you feed during the rest of the year?
After the show season I mix a breeding mix with depurative (usually fifty-fifty) and they have this until two or three weeks before pairing. I then hopper feed a breeding mix whilst they're rearing, and hand feed a widowhood mix for racing. I never really measure the feed, they usually have as much as they want twice a day.

Do your birds get any specifics?
Yes. For several years I've used *Vetrepharm* products, either *Vetreplex* or *Vitamix* mid-week and, after the shows and races, *Vitalyte Plus*. I thought it might help eliminate stress, which could only be a good thing. I also use garlic oil and brewer's yeast on return from a race and I like to use *Bosmolen* woodash grit and also quite a few pickstones when breeding. There are more and more products on the market for pigeons and, of course, it's the fancier's choice what he gives his birds, but I think a lot of these products are not needed to keep healthy birds.

When and what do you treat for?
I see no point in treating if there's nothing wrong so for the last few years I've treated according to the advice of the vet. I send dropping samples for analysis before breeding and after racing and treat accordingly. Sometimes one section has a high cocci count and another doesn't. During the season I usually take samples to my friend, Gilbert Harrison, who has a microscope for checking for worms and cocci and this, too, has proved useful. I always try to prevent rather than cure. Thankfully I don't have too many problems, but if a bird does get sick I will try and cure it, unless it's always falling ill. Experience is a great help with sick pigeons and there are a few good vets about who can help. I can also recommend a good video, *Keep 'em Healthy* by Armand Scheers.

Which products do you use?
Usually *Amprol* for coccidiosis, *Harkanker Soluble* (or *Ridzol S* if available) for canker and *Hoechst Panacur* tablets for worms, which I've found to be good even though they're not as convenient as wormers added to the water.

Where do you stand on paramyxo vaccination?
It would be nice if research was done to see if a vaccine could be produced to use on youngsters and yearlings only, as the cases I've heard of seem to affect the younger pigeons worst, but as it stands I believe every fancier should vaccinate against it. Having talked to fanciers who've had the problem, I wouldn't like it in my birds. I use *Nobi-vac,* doing the youngsters as soon as they are old enough and again when I do all the old birds in early February. I don't like to vaccinate during the moult.

What have you found to be the best method for keeping your birds clean and healthy inside the loft?
I spray the loft twice a year and for the last few years I've brushed floor white into the floor and tried to clean out twice per day. I had a wire-grid floor at one time but it made the loft very cold, and I've tried most deep litters (straw, sand, granules, peat, sawdust and so on), but I've found that cleaning out is the method to suit me.

How many shows can you get out of a pigeon in the course of a season?
Four or five, it really depends on the pigeon. Some actually like going in the pen, whilst others don't. For example, I've an old hen who shows off to people and I could enter her every week, whereas another old cock I had didn't like going at all. He would sulk if I showed him more than twice.

Does it affect a pigeon as a racer if it is shown in the winter?
I've found it has no effect at all. Several pigeons in my race team have been shown in the winter for several years and have still had prizes racing.

Do your birds exercise in the winter?
No. It's dark when I go to work and again when I come home so they don't go out from September until they are paired and sitting the next season. I don't think it makes any difference to their condition as far as the shows go, though. I know Dicky Graham, a top showman of recent years, only used to let his out for a bath. And nor does it make any difference to their racing prospects. My late friend, Billy Parkes, never used to let his pigeons out much in the winter.

With eye-sign being such a subjective discipline, how do you know which sort of eye will do well in the pen?
Experience really. When you've shown a few times you get an idea of the type needed to win. Most shows publish the list of judges, in which case I try to enter a type of bird

to suit the judge. If I've already had a prize under the judge published I try to put a pigeon in with similar qualities.

Has the type of eye which generally does well in eye-sign classes changed at all over the years?
I would say so, yes. Today judges tend to look for a more evenly-balanced eye. I entered my first show in 1974 and for years and years after that a lot of the pigeons I saw which were winning had a thick eye-sign circle and not much in the iris itself, whereas nowadays there is a bit more in the iris and not such thick eye-sign.

Do you do any judging yourself?
Yes. I've been fortunate to be asked to judge at several top-class shows and many club shows. I find your opinions change the more you get into it and it's something which I've always enjoyed.

When you're judging eye-sign, are you allowed to handle the actual pigeons?
It depends on the show. Normally yes, but at some shows, particularly in Scotland, there is a steward to hold the bird for you.

And are judges swayed by what they feel in the hand?
I'd like to think not, but it must be very difficult when it's a close decision between two pigeons.

Are you ever taken to task?
Occasionally. There was an instance once where a chap complained that I knew a particular pigeon and that's why I'd given it first prize. I admit I did know the pigeon, but when you do a bit of showing that's unavoidable. The point was it was the best pigeon in the class in my opinion.

What do you look for in the eye?
I like to see a nice balanced eye with a rich iris and a quality circle (sphincter muscle) that is pretty strong. I also like to see a clearly defined eye-sign but I don't think it needs to be very wide, just in balance with the rest of the eye. Quite a few good pigeons I have seen have also had a distinct circle between the eye-sign circle and the actual iris, giving the impression there is room for expansion.

At what age can you assess the merits of an eye?
You can see the basics as soon as you wean them but it depends on the family of pigeon. I've seen families where the eye is well developed in youngsters and then it doesn't get any better, whereas my own have only matured by the time they are eighteen months old and sometimes older. Sometimes the change can be quite striking. For example, I have a hen at the moment who had only a reasonable eye as a youngster but, just past the

yearling stage, it changed into a very good one indeed.

What do you make of the so called 'clusters' in the pupil?
You mean the yellow speckled spots right in or near enough in the middle of the pupil itself. I've seen them from time to time and the pigeons with them have all been good breeders.

Have these 'clusters' not got something to do with the deterioration of the retina as a pigeon gets older?
I couldn't say. All the pigeons I've seen with them were oldish, but whether that's coincidence or not I don't know.

What about the 'heart' line around the edge of the iris?
I like to see it present but it is only one part of the eye.

And the size of the pupil?
Yes, I take note of the pupil size because, in good light, I've never seen a really outstanding pigeon with a big pupil.

Isn't the size of the pupil simply dependent on the amount of light reaching the eye?
No. I've seen plenty of pigeons with big pupils and it had nothing to do with the light.

Alf Baker wrote in his book, *Winning Naturally*, that many of his best pigeons had egg-shaped pupils. Is that your experience too?
All I can say is, I've seen good pigeons with them, but I've never actually had any myself. As you've mentioned Alf Baker, I must say I think he was a brilliant judge of a pigeon. I remember he was judging one of the first times I entered birds at the Old Comrades. He gave first prize to my best stock hen.

I recently saw a hen with a split pupil. It looked like an inkpot that had spilt over and the pupil stretched right across the eye. Is that degenerate?
I wouldn't like to see it myself.

Some people might say that show racers have tremendous eyes, yet because they can't race eye-sign is nonsense. What do you say to that?
Show racers have different eyes to racing pigeons. Although they are rich coloured, they don't usually have as much character in the eye as a racer.

What does your team number?
I usually have approximately fifty pairs and a few old pigeons which I don't pair up any more due to their age.

I imagine, with your consistency in shows over the years, you must have a true family of birds. Is that so?
Actually, I have a few birds from a number of families. The main one, and the one which has been responsible for most of my wins, originated from the late Billy Parkes of Killyleagh. I had my first birds from Billy in 1976 and some of these pigeons were still breeding at fourteen and fifteen. In fact, I've still got an original cock here which is a 1975 pigeon. These were from his old Fabry/Locke family and they have suited me because they will race and also show in the winter. I also bought a dark chequer cock, which was bred by Billy, from D Watkins & Son of Tonypandy. This cock had bred good birds in South Wales and continued to do so for me. He was also a good winner for me in the show pen, winning firsts at the Black Country Show, the Old Comrades, Blackpool and others.

How important is the strain name of a pigeon to you?
It doesn't really bother me too much, so long as I like the pigeon and it has a good background, because being a good fancier is more important than having pure this and pure that. But having said that, when I'm wanting a cross for my old family I do try to bring in birds of a Fabry, Hansenne or Gurnay base. I have crossed a few of these in over time and two hens in particular have bred some decent birds. One was a dark chequer Gurnay hen from Sid Collins of Northern Ireland. She was a good winner in the pen and her granddaughter won the Emrys Jones Trophy at Blackpool in 1993, and the other was a blue Fabry hen from Mike Szabo of Chelmsford. She was a winner in the pen and is also a good breeder, being the other grandmother of the 1993 Emrys Jones Trophy winner.

You mentioned some of the old Parkes pigeons were still breeding into their teens. Did their age affect the quality of their youngsters?
No. Age doesn't matter so long as pigeons are healthy and their youngsters are well reared. I've had some very good pigeons out of old hens that have been well looked after. Pairing them to younger birds seems to help. I think longevity is something which is inherent in a family, and dependent also on how you use a pigeon. Whether or not you let it breed, rear, breed, rear and so on.

How important is the actual pedigree of a pigeon?
When it comes to the selection of breeding stock it's a valuable aid, but you must have the pigeon to go with it. I do think, however, that national pigeons are bred from pigeons with a national racing background and to some extent pigeons for showing at the classic/open shows are bred from similar such pigeons.

Which other families are you working with?
I have a few Van den Bosche from D Watkins & Son and also from Mr & Mrs Litherland, some Kirkpatrick-based birds from JM Dalgliesh and Mr & Mrs Gardner and more

recently I have had birds from Alan Darragh of Northern Ireland. These have crossed well into the old family and I have had several winners reported from friends. Because I don't race much I usually let friends have pigeons to try. I also have the odd bird from exchanges with friends. We sometimes loan each other breeding birds and this practice has produced some good results. I have had some good pigeons from racing fanciers, bred from good stock and at a reasonable price, particularly late-breds. I think they are ideal for stock. Usually you can obtain late-breds from good pigeons where you would not get early-breds and all that is needed is the patience to let them develop. I must say that when I first had pigeons from Billy Parkes he sent me some really good pigeons including some proven breeders of winners which gave me a first class start. He and his wife, Jean, made me very welcome on the times I was fortunate to be able to visit their home to see their birds, and not only that, he also gave me some good advice about breeding, eye-sign, feeding and so on.

What was that advice?
On the eye, basically he told me not to worry about pairing two pigeons with the same colour eye together. On loft design, it was to shut my loft in. At that time, I had an open loft and the pigeons only used to come into form when the weather warmed up. Nowadays, my loft is closed in at the front with shutters over the windows to keep out rain but let the air in. It has a few louvres at floor level, an apex roof and windows on all four walls so whilst I still have ample air coming in there's no longer a gale blowing through. Incidentally, most of my nest boxes are quite dark, which the pigeons seem to like. And on feeding, he said don't hopper feed beans, get on a mix with plenty of maize in it. Back then I and nearly everyone else was feeding beans, peas, tares and maize.

What are the eyes of your Van den Bosche like?
Compared with the old distance families, not as strong, but as sprinters go, very good. There doesn't seem to be so much character in the eyes of sprint pigeons, racers or breeders, so the Van den Bosche are unusual in that respect.

Are the eyes of your pigeons as good today as the original Parkes pigeons?
Some of them.

Did you ever see the Parkes Busschaerts?
Yes, in fact he was just switching over to them when I visited.

What was your impression of them, particularly 'Mr Busschaert' and the 'Larkin's Blue'?
I thought they were fantastic pigeons.

How did their eyes compare with his old Fabry/Lockes?
On the whole his original Busschaerts weren't as good, but they *threw* some tremen-

dous-eyed pigeons. I think Billy actually improved their eyes, as I had pigeons out of the originals and their eyes were always a bit better. In particular, he sent me a couple of daughters of the 'Big Man' which could both win in the shows.

What do you take into account when matching pairs?
I inbreed and line-breed quite a lot to try and keep the family and, where possible, I go by eye-sign and type. My other matings usually consist of an inbred cock of my old family crossed with a well-bred hen of another family. When I match eyes I go more on balance and make up than on colour because I think the make up of the eye is more important. I don't like pairing two very light eyed birds together, however.

Nevertheless, will you pair two similar-eyed pigeons together on occasions?
I know people say not to but yes, I will sometimes. Billy Parkes once said to me just try it and see what happens. At that time I had two strong violet-eyed birds from him, so I paired them together and they bred a fantastic chequer cock. He was lost when I lent him to a friend but not before I'd bred a very good hen from him which bred race and show winners, including at Blackpool. If you pair two strong violet-eyed birds together, you may only get one with an eye equally as good as its parents - you may get none at all - but all the ones I have bred this way have had violet/pearl eyes. Whatever the quality of the eyes you match together, though, you will not get outstanding eyes every nest, just now and again.

Is the loss of good eye-sign in a family irreversible?
Not necessarily but it would take a long time to get the quality back. For that reason, if I pair really close, I pick out the one I want and dispose of the others.

How many good birds do you breed in a season?
I've never really kept statistics on it. All I know is some years seem better than others, even when the same birds are paired together.

Have you seen pigeons with no sign at all?
Only ferals, never a racing pigeon. Sometimes you might think one has none, like with very light yellow-eyed pigeons, but it's because it blends into the rest of the eye. I have seen some families, though, particularly extreme distance ones, which don't carry what you would call good eye-sign for showing. I read a piece about this written by Tony Mardon in *Pigeon Sport*. He was basically saying that some extreme distance families have fishy eyes and suggested this may be because many of them have been so inbred they have developed endurance at the expense of speed. I would agree that it seems to be a factor. Certainly, if you get a chance to look through the old *Racing Pigeon Pictorial* eye shots you will see that, although not wishy-washy, many of the extreme distance pigeons do have very light eyes.

Which is the best-eyed pigeon you've come across?
Billy Parkes' old blue 1965 cock, a son of the old 'Fabry Blue'. He must have been twenty when I saw him but even so he still had a really good, strong violet eye.

Which is the best-eyed team of birds you've seen?
Again, Billy's Fabry/Locke family. They were all different colours and all had plenty of character. Even his out-and-out racers, like his six-times France hen, had good eyes, though they were a bit lighter. *(These eyes can be seen in the June 1973 edition of the Pigeon Racing News and Gazette.)*

What about more recently?
Mike Szabo had a very good family before he left the sport. Other than that, I don't know to be honest as I've been to several lofts with good-eyed pigeons. A few years ago I visited the late Bob Harkness and Harry Stockman in Northern Ireland and saw some really good pigeons. My friend, Dicky Graham from Scotland, had some very good birds, too. I bought my 1994 Blackpool winner from his entire clearance sale.

Have you ever come across a top-class pigeon without an eye to match?
I don't know about sprinters because I've not been to enough sprint lofts, but as far as distance pigeons are concerned, I haven't really, to be honest. And I've seen a lot of good distance pigeons, including a number of Gold Award winners in Scotland. I don't say they would necessarily have won in eye-sign shows, but they all had good quality eye-sign to my way of thinking.

Does the true value of eye-sign lie in applying the discipline within the context of a family?
Yes it does really, particularly as an aid to breeding within a family of pigeons. In my own family, for example, all my good hens have good eyes, but I find my cocks can be very deceptive. Because of this I try to mate a really good-eyed hen with a proven racing cock and I've found this a better way of producing good birds.

Can you pick out other people's best birds by the eye?
Not all the time, but the eye does help to pick out a fair percentage of the good birds. There is more to a bird than just its eye.

Even the best racers?
I don't look at the eye much for racing, but again the eye does help.

Who do you regard as the best judge of an eye?
There are quite a few good judges but I think Brian May is as good as anyone.

Do you agree with his views on eye-sign?

Yes. I bought the video of his, *Thru' the Looking Glass*, and I found it very informative, especially as the slides used were of champion pigeons.

To sum up, how would you describe your philosophy on eye-sign?
A lot of fanciers take it too seriously. I go my own way and I'm not one for arguing and falling out with people. It's not worth it. Similarly, I would never go into someone's loft and say, 'kill that'. All the fun in pigeon racing is doing it your own way.

Cheq Cock
Winner of several prizes through to federation level and also a
winner of handling and eye-sign classes through to classic show level.
Sire and grandsire of winners both racing and showing, including the
R Emrys Jones Trophy winner at Blackpool in 1993.
He is a son of 83X10575, see pedigree opposite.

John Wheatcroft's **Blue Cheq Cock GB83X10575**

Raced as young bird and then put to stock, this Fabry-Locke pigeon has bred some really good birds, both racing & showing. He has also been a good winner in the show pen, including 1st Old Comrades & 3rd Blackpool.

Pedigree

Sire — Dark Cheq cock GB76K16064
Purchased from D Watkins & Son. Bred by W Parkes. Sire, g.sire & g.g.sire of winners inc. 2nd sect, 3rd open WGNFC Penicuik, 2nd sect, 7th open fed, 8th sect, 8th open fed Lancaster, 14,000 birds. Won several shows inc. eyesign. e.g. 1st Old Comrades, 1st Blackpool & Emrys Jones Trophy

- **The Fabry Blue NU60B9436** — Sire & g.sire of 10x1st open NIPA, 14,000-27,000 birds & also of many winners from France
  - **Red cock IUUF6312898** — Sire & Dam of 3x1st NIPA & Six Times France Hen
    - Blue cock 58-13218 — Bred by SR Bloomfield
    - Blue hen 57-6716 — Bred by SR Bloomfield
  - **Blue hen NU63C54093** — Bred by SR Bloomfield
    - W Locke's Elizabeth
    - The Fabry Blue
- **Blue Chequer hen NU72A68746** — Dam of winners, including 3rd open Penzance Young Bird National
  - **The Fabry Blue NU60B9436**
    - Blue cock 58-13218
    - Blue hen 57-6716
  - **Dark Cheq hen NU65A73204** — Bred winners in every nest
    - The Fabry Blue
    - W Locke's Elizabeth

Dam — Blue Cheq hen GB76K16192
Bred by W Parkes. Dam, g.dam & g.g.dam of winners up to Pau. Won several shows including 2x1st Old Comrades

- **Dark Cheq cock NU75Z95599** — Sire & g.sire of winners Bred 2nd fed winner at 12 years old
  - **Red cock IUUF63-12898** — Sire & g.sire of 10x1st NIPA & Six Times France Hen
    - The Fabry Blue
  - **Dark Cheq hen NU65A73204**
- **Blue Cheq hen NU72A68746** — Dam of winners inc. 3rd YB National Penzance
  - **Blue hen NU63C54093**
  - The Fabry Blue

JIMMY HAMPSON

Jimmy Hampson lives in the village of Banks, just outside the seaside resort of Southport. This is an area which has often been termed 'Little Belgium', a description which reflects the level of local competition. He has always flown a good pigeon, as witnessed by his winning of 1st North West Combine Nantes some years ago, but for the last ten or so years he has been indisputably one of the area's top flyers. This has much to do with the decision he made in 1983 to try some Busschaerts from the late Billy Parkes of Killyleagh in Northern Ireland. He sent for four squeakers, two cocks and two hens. These he paired together and their offspring were to set his club and federation alight in sprint to middle distance events.

Have you a good eye for a pigeon?
I've an idea what a decent pigeon is, but today there are so many winning that are of a mediocre type, even over the channel, that it's getting harder to judge.

What is your ideal type?
I don't like the vents to be high up over the top of the keel, preferring a bit of space between the keel and the vents. I like pigeons to be shaped like a boat, meaning plenty of depth in front but not too deep in the keel. I like a nice round body with wings that drop down around the side, and a nice, round head. The sort you could put a penny on top of if it were to be photographed. I'm also keen to see the cere at the front of the eye from nine o'clock to twelve o'clock, but not all the way round. And it is also important that the eye is well up in the head. If it is set above beak level I can guarantee it will win. If it doesn't there's something wrong with the fancier.

Apart from a well-set eye, are there any other guarantees of success?
Aye. If you've timed in and no one else has got one.

Do you believe in any theories?
You can't win with bad pigeons.

Apart from that?
I've always looked at eyes. I try and remember the eyes of the best racers and breeders within my family so that when I see a similar eye again, I can try it at stock. I've had the Billy Parkes pigeons for ten years now, though, and I've yet to see another one with an eye like the 'Palmer Hen'. Still, I'll keep looking.

What about the wing?
Personally, I like a wing with a step in it, but what I find now in the birds that I handle is that there are different types of wings winning at all distances.

And the throat?
I have no theories on the throat as long as it is a good colour and has an open cleft.

Is there anything else you look for?
I like to see a pigeon drop straight down on the board from a race. At least that way if it's behind you know where you stand with it. You don't know where you're working at all with those that clap round and you can wait for them to come good forever. That's why good pigeons win Niort. Most fanciers send those that clap round thinking they can fly forever, but the good pigeon beats them hands down.

If you were allowed the pick of a fellow fancier's loft, could you choose his best pigeons?
I'd choose those I liked.

How important is pedigree?
Very, if you want to start and maintain a family.

'Parkes Producer'

'Parkes Producer'

Original pedigree

GB77K17718

Sire: The Larkins Blue Pencil cock **GB77V75881**
Champion breeder of racers & stock birds alike. Sire & g.sire of many winners inland & over channel, including the great Champion 32. Every bird raced from this great cock has won 1st prizes. Winners all over the country from him

- BELGE70-3204164 — *Direct Busschaert, Champion breeder*
  - Schiavon BELGE69-3209043 — *Champion racer*
    - Pied Crayonne
  - Bent Beak BELGE68-3214649 — *Champion breeder*
    - From DE 505 - Sire of Tracy YB National winner
- The Coppi Hen BELGE72-3327722 — *One of the greatest Busschaert hens*
  - BELGE67-3137350 — *Coppi blood*
    - Coppi blood
  - BELGE66-3310940 — *Coppi & DE 85 blood*
    - DE Zitter from Crayonne

Dam: *Dam of the above winners. One of the best pairs of stock birds I have ever owned. Their offspring have won on the north or south*

- Mr Busschaert BELGE75-3101986 — *Sire & g/sire of hundreds of winners, including NIPA, East Down Combine & Ulster Fed*
  - Schicht BELGE72-3216659
    - DE 505
  - BELGE73-3154319
    - Dtr of DE Professor
- The Palmer Hen NU75A16481 — *Dam of the above winners*
  - BELGE70-3204165 — *Palmer's No1 Pair*
    - Tito & Crack blood
  - NU71D17333 — *Champion racer & breeder*
    - BELGE66-3346365
    - BELGE69-3209051

How many winners have your original four Parkes pigeons been responsible for?
They are in virtually everything I have topped the fed with, and plenty of others besides.
Nearly all of the children of 'Parkes Producer' and 'Queen Jean' have won, some in the
teens of times, and nearly all of their children are breeding winners, cocks and hens
alike, land and channel. 'Parkes Producer', either with 'Queen Jean' or other hens is
the sire of at least twelve different cocks that have bred fed toppers for me alone. One of
his sons, 'Alberto', has bred six fed toppers. My other main pair, 'Parkes Toye' and
'Quality', are also sire and dam of many winners, including 'Allen', who won fifteen
times, including three times 1st Southport Fed and, the only time he was sent across the
channel, 2nd Southport Fed, 8th NW Combine Sartilly. Seven days later he won 1st
Banks Open Hereford. 'Allen' is also the sire and grandsire of winners. When I took
the first eighteen positions in Southport Fed's Dorchester race, one of the two in the
first thimble was his daughter. In that race there were approximately 3,500 birds competing from the same liberation. I had the first seven best velocities and finished with
eighteen pigeons in the first twenty-one of the liberation. 'Parkes Toye' and 'Quality'
have also bred many top stock hens. For whoever they have been let go to, they have
bred fed winners. I'll say this, though: no matter how good a pair is at breeding, you
only have to look through your loft to see that the number of pigeons still there off them
is small. For example, I have an old cock which has sired six fed winners, but I've only
got one pigeon in the loft off him at the moment.

'Queen Jean'

'Queen Jean'

Original pedigree

Blue cock IHU79A18474
*Always stock. Sire of many
winners for myself & others.
Full brother to the
outstanding racer
Champion 32 and many
other top racers*

- Blue cock GB77V75881
  *Every bird raced from
  this pair has won 1st prizes*
  - The Larkins Blue
    - BELGE70-3204164
      - *Schiavon* 69-3209043
      - BELGE68-3214649
    - Direct Busschaert
  - Coppi Hen BELGE72-3322722
    Ace breeder
    - 66-3310940 *Coppi 85*
    - BELGE67-3137350

- Cheq hen GB77K17718
  Outstanding breeder
  - Mr Busschaert
    - BELGE75-3101986
      - 72-3216659 *son of De Zitter*
      - BELGE73-3154319
  - NU75A16481
    - *Palmer's No 1 Pair*
    - The Palmer Hen
      - 70-3204165
      - 71D17333

Cheq w/f hen IHU8182061
*Daughter of
Champion Barney*

- Champion Barney
  GB77K16958
  *Winner of 19 1st prizes,
  including 2B club. Sire
  & g/sire of many winners
  with up to 28,000 birds
  Now at Louella Lofts*
  - Cheq cock GB76K16229
    *This pair have bred over
    50 winners*
    - Mr Busschaert
    - The Palmer Hen
  - Dark Cheq Pied hen
    - NU75K61552
    - The Henson Hen

- Smart Bird
  GB79K17298
  *A great racer as a young
  bird & dam of winners
  Now at Louella Lofts*
  - Cheq cock GB78K19832
    *1st, 2nd, 5th & 7th open
    NIPA, 5,000-7,000 birds etc.*
    - Dtr of Mr Busschaert
    - The Larkins Blue
  - Cheq w/f hen 77K19842
    - NU74T61553 *from
      73-3154092 & 73-3154011*
    - NU75K16329 *from
      61552 & The Henson Hen*

Which are the best breeders in your loft now?
I would say that the two original cocks are still my best. Both have bred fed winners in the last two years.

Do they fly out?
No, they have been prisoners all their lives.

What were your first impressions of the Busschaerts when they came from Ireland? After all, they marked a departure in type from the old-fashioned channel team you flew.
I knew from what I'd seen in Billy's loft that they were the right stuff. As for type, I thought they were alright, being pigeons that you could easily get fit, yet with plenty of strength in them. At the time, though, I had no idea what distance they'd get.

Is the type still the same today?
Very similar, particularly in so much as they are still light-framed.

When I saw the Billy Parkes pigeons myself I was struck by the size and boldness of many of his best racing hens. Have such hens proven to be your best?
Actually, no. Many of my best hens have been the smaller ones.

'Parkes Toye'

'Parkes Toye'

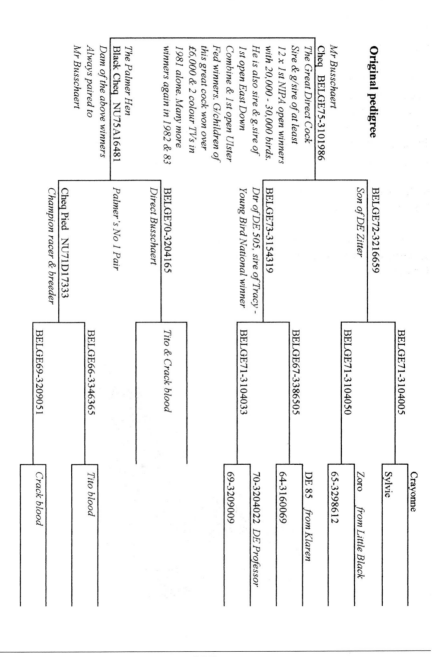

Are your Busschaerts generally on the small side?
It depends. My racers are about half the size of my stock pigeons, even though I always feed them well. If you just breed from them they grow and grow.

How have you maintained the performances of your Busschaerts over a decade?
I inbreed and line-breed to keep the line of a good bird. Over the years, I've practised half-brother and half-sister, uncle to niece and grandparent to grandchild matings quite a lot. However, in the last couple of seasons, because the originals are getting on a bit, I've inbred more closely than ever before, going as close as brother and sister or father and daughter.

Which matings have proved the most successful?
I've found uncle to niece best.

Which other direct Parkes pigeons have had the greatest influence on your loft?
It's difficult to say as I've good pigeons popping up all over the place, but two children of '011', also known as the 'Belgian Hen', have proved particularly good.

Do you have any other Busschaert lines?
Yes, I have a very good pigeon I call the 'Robson Cock'. He is out of a daughter of 'Parkside Superman' and originated from Billy Robson of Sunderland. One cock off him has scored ten times, and a daughter has won five races for Steve Wright of Hesketh Bank.

'Quality'

'Quality'

Original pedigree

Cheq cock GB81K19124 — *Sire of winners*

- **Champion Barney GB77K16958** — *Champion racer & breeder. Now at Louella Lofts*
  - **Cheq cock GB76K16229** — *Sire & dam of at least fifty 1st prize winners*
    - Mr Busschaert
    - Number One Pair
    - Palmer Hen
  - **Cheq Pied hen**
    - 74T61552 *Pearl Eyes*
    - 72N74546 *The Henson Hen*
- **Smart Bird Cheq hen GB79K17298** — *4th open & 18th open NIP4, 26,000-27,000 birds as a young bird. Daughter of Champion 32*
  - **Cheq cock GB78K19832** — *Champion racer & breeder*
    - The Larkins Blue
    - dtr of Mr Busschaert
  - **Ace Breeder GB78K19842**
    - 74T61553 *from*
    - 3154092 & 3154011

Blue w/f hen GB82K06964 — *Dam of young bird winners in 1983*

- **The Henson Cock Blue cock NU74T18193** — *Sire & g/sire of many winners*
  - **Stock. Sire of winners NU73N75476**
    - BELGE70-3204149
    - BELGE70-3204151
  - **Dam of many winners NU72N74545**
    - BELGE66-3346365
    - BELGE69-3209051
- **Blue BELGE73-3154011** — *Direct Busschaert. Dam & g.dam of many winners, inland & channel. A son won 10 1sts for J White, Belfast*
  - **BELGE72-3154145**
    - DE-45 *Champion Racer*
    - DE-85 breed
  - **Champion breeder BELGE71-3104072**
    - 70-343171 *Den Invalide*
    - 70-3204018 *Feitite II*

Have you tried any crosses?
Yes, but I've found it very hard to find one which does not alter the qualities of the original stock and which keeps up the same performances.

Have you thought of bringing in another family and keeping them separate?
To be honest I can't get off the Busschaerts. The nicest family I've seen for a while is the Andre Desmets. I tried one or two and they did okay, but I wouldn't try a dozen as that's not the direction I want to go in.

Have you gained your success on natural or widowhood?
I've raced mainly natural up to now. However, because of the amount of work you need to put in with natural pigeons, I've started to fly a few on widowhood for the channel races.

Which races do you concentrate on?
Mainly sprint to middle distance.

In sprint to middle distance racing, is the fancier more important than the pigeon?
I would say it is fifty-fifty. Just as a bad fancier can ruin a good pigeon, so can a greedy one.

When do you pair up your stock pigeons and what do you rear on?
The stock birds are fed a normal breeding mix all year round and I pair up at the end of January or beginning of February.

As they are prisoners and always on a breeding mix, don't they get a little fat?
Yes, but it makes no difference. They hardly eat anything anyway when you first pair up so the weight soon comes off them.

What does the breeding mix consist of?
20 per cent maize, 20 per cent peas, 15 per cent beans, 15 per cent wheat, 10 per cent milo, 10 per cent dari and 10 per cent safflower.

So you're a bean feeder?
Oh yes.

You haven't found that beans 'poison' your birds, then, as some fanciers believe?
If they do, they haven't made a very good job of it. I've still got too many.

When do you pair your racers?
In early February so that I can get the youngsters away and give my old birds a couple of weeks' training before the first race. If I didn't, I'd always be trying to catch up.

What do you feed for racing?
At the start of the season they race on the breeding mix, but as they get further down the road I increase the maize up to 60 per cent. I still feed 20 per cent peas and virtually halve all the other grains. I should temper this by pointing out, though, that I take notice of what they are eating and also the weather, and feed accordingly.

How important is correct feeding?
Very. I've never really tried feeding any differently because how and what I feed works for me, but at the same time I don't religiously stick with this diet if I can't get hold of grains of the right quality. There's no point feeding anything that isn't up to standard. I always take notice if they leave a certain grain as it means there's something up with it.

Do you feed anything else when racing?
A bit of linseed and *Haith's Red Band*, and just a touch of *Hormoform*. They also have access to as many different kinds of grit and minerals as I can get hold of. I like *Kilpatrick's* grit the best but at present I'm struggling to find somewhere that stocks it.

Which brand of corn do you feed?
I don't. I mix my own food, using as much local corn as I can find.

Do you polish it?
Yes, using a hessian sack. Too much dust on corn breeds disease.

Do you break your racers down at the beginning of the week?
No, I try to keep everything as natural as possible. If they're right, they're right.

Do you measure the feed?
No. I feed twice a day, with them having as much as they want once a day. The old birds, who don't eat as much as the youngsters, get approximately an ounce and a quarter. The youngsters are fed very nearly an ounce and a half although, taking tit-bits into account, I should think they shift near enough two ounces a day when they're really working.

What would happen if you restricted them to a straight ounce?
I'd have more money in my pocket for a start. I have tried it, and I found it was alright for about four weeks but then they were beggared. I'm sure that in some areas, such as the Midlands, where they start off at, say, 70 miles, fanciers have to restrict the food to stand a chance. If that was the case here, I'd do it, but our programme starts off at 100 miles and the distance soon increases. For the first few races, I'm afraid of those fanciers who starve their pigeons, but as we get further down the line I expect mine to overtake theirs.

As you're a generous feeder, how much work do you give your team?
I train regularly and, when I'm not training, I flag young and old alike for at least half an hour, morning and night.

Do your birds field?
Not any more. Fielding today, with all the spraying that goes on on farm land can be no help to keeping a bird fit. In 1983, I culled all the birds I had which were fielding and ended up with only three old birds. Since then I have stopped giving them a 'free hole' and I now only let them out when I am with them.

Do you train from all points of the compass?
No. I always train on the line of flight.

Can you get even a bad pigeon to win?
No. A pigeon has to be decent to begin with, or it would have no chance against the fanciers around here.

Do lice prevent a bird reaching peak condition?
Well, they have not stopped my birds winning. Obviously I dust my pigeons if they get too bad, but I don't worry too much about lice.

How can you tell when a bird is on form?
It will tell you. When it's fit, its eye will get brighter, its feather colour will change and it will appear longer in the leg. You'll also notice that it can't keep still, moving faster around the garden or clapping off on its own. I also like a bird which becomes keener in its box. For a pooler, I choose a bird which feels like a piece of cork and just as light.

Do you ever use a cake?
I used to, but I stopped it when I got the Parkes pigeons. They didn't need it.

What do you feed on arrival from a race?
I give them those small seeds which I have noticed they like best.

Do you make sure they don't eat too much if they're particularly tired?
There's no need, as a tired bird will only eat what it wants. I have never had one yet that has topped itself up.

Do you ever use garlic?
Yes, but not in the water. I have wild garlic growing in the garden and just let them eat it. Although they always eat its flowers, some years they never touch the rest of the plant. I also grow chives, and these I periodically chop up for them.

What does go into your drinking fountains, and when?
After a race, whether inland or channel, they home to glucose. On Saturday evening they are back on fresh water. On Sunday morning I add a tablespoon of molasses to a three-pint drinker, before giving them clean water again in the afternoon. A good vet once told me never to top the drinkers up or stir the molasses again once the drinkers are in front of the pigeons, as once disturbed molasses can act as a poison. I also use multivitamins twice a week.

Do you use any other products?
If I'm not satisfied with my results, I'll try anything, providing it's natural. I think any good fancier will.

Of all the products you've experimented with, which have you found to give the best results?
I think the old iron tonic still takes some beating.

When do you give it?
On a Thursday, during the racing season.

When and what do you treat for?
I treat when needed with what is the best product at the time. Price rules a lot. I'm not a great believer in antibiotics, although having spoken to one or two experts recently I'm now inclining more towards treating. Up to now I've only occasionally treated for canker, using *Emtryl*, and only for cocci when needed, using *Amprol*. Last year I had my birds tested for the first time. They were showing just a touch of canker and also had hairworm, for which I used *Hoechst Panacur* tablets. Prior to that, if I said I'd wormed them as many as half a dozen times in the twenty-four years I've been racing, I'd be lying.

Do you try to cure sick pigeons?
I treat a bird once if it is an isolated case, but if it gets the same illness again I cull it no matter what it has won or bred. I tried keeping the odd one years back, but found that the illness came out again somewhere along the line.

Where do you stand on vaccination?
I'm in agreement with it. One year, I had watery droppings in my youngsters, brought about by a touch of paramyxo they'd caught in the basket. I had to kill a young cock who had topped the fed, and another one who had won three times and who was out of this world.

Did this contact with paramyxo have any effect on your other youngsters?
Yes, it shortened their end flights, so whilst they were still moulting I left the lights on

in the loft until 9 o'clock every night.

Where I race, I've heard one or two rumours of fanciers actually injecting their birds against paramyxo just before a race, as they believe it acts like a booster. Does that surprise you?
No, not at all. There are daft beggars all over, not just in Southport.

Do you treat for respiratory problems?
Yes, if I think something is not quite right. You always have the odd respiratory problem if you keep a few, as I do. I use the best product at the time, be it *Eromycin*, *Erythromycin*, *Tylan* or something else and treat the whole flock. There's no point just treating the odd one as it will have already passed the problem on and you won't get rid of it.

Do you give a respiratory treatment prior to or during the racing season as a matter of course?
No, never.

How many birds do you house?
When I'm approaching young bird racing, between one hundred and fifty and two hundred.

Which is the most important factor in loft design?
Ventilation. It has got to be right for the birds. I think the best design for a loft is one based on the old hen cabins, as they have the correct ventilation. I have flown out of mine for twenty-four years.

What proportion of the youngsters you breed are successful?
Roughly one in six.

You have plenty of multiple scorers, but none that have won a hatful of first prizes. Why do you think that is?
Competition. To my mind, if a pigeon can win twenty-odd firsts there must have been a lot of duffers about.

Do you expect your youngsters to show ability right from the start?
Yes. I like those young birds that show an interest in wanting to get home, and keep only those which score in the first twenty of the fed.

What must a yearling do to earn a perch?
Win.

I take it your Busschaerts are a fast-maturing family?
Yes, but I would have to say that they are at their best as two-year-olds.

Do you think the precocity of the Busschaerts and other sprint-based families has accounted for the demise of so many of the older distance strains?
Partly. I do think birds are now getting much faster but, to add to this, many fanciers have also become too greedy. In the old days the channel flyer used to give his birds a couple of land races and then pick his race to send to. Nowadays, he works them hard and keeps them going.

When do you decide it's time to retire a pigeon?
When it starts breeding winners. If they're showing any sign of turning out good winners, then the three-year-old stage is their last year of racing, as I think their speed goes when they get to four, perhaps for hereditary reasons. Anyway, I think that if you have to keep a pigeon going beyond four, things are getting desperate. You should have yearlings taking their place.

Does such early retirement account for the number of stock pigeons you keep?
Yes. I've never had a good pigeon that didn't also breed good pigeons, so I retire all my best racers to stock. Good racers which can't breed winners are usually flukes themselves. It's the same with horse racing. Occasionally you get a good horse out of poor parents, but no matter what it's mated with it won't breed anything itself. Because mine is a family, I'm confident none of my winners are flukes.

Do you only breed off the winners?
No, because even if they don't win they can still be good breeders. Some of the children off my best pairs have been absolutely useless as racers, but it has made no difference when it comes to breeding the goods. Whether they win or not, they must have a winning pedigree and be birds which, in my judgement, look the part and have not lost the body and shape of the original stock birds.

As you have such a strong team of stock pigeons, how do you ensure they are all given a fair try, as you haven't the room to keep everything they breed?
I breed hard and cull hard. I like to feel vibes coming through a young bird's body since this shows strength, so if a youngster's physique is not making up into something like a body I will cull it before it ever gets raced and replace it with another one. I'm constantly replenishing my young bird team.

Aren't you running the risk of culling decent pigeons?
I'm sure I am, but anybody can be wise after the event. It's not going to prove you wrong, though, if it's gone, is it?

How many do you cull before racing starts?
Anywhere between twenty and thirty.

Do you lose many off the loft?
Quite a few. Perhaps as many as thirty a season.

What causes these losses?
It's down to the type of pigeon they are. They are fiery, highly-strung birds.

How many youngsters have you left after racing?
I breed about one hundred for myself and I'm usually left with about fifty. I think I've done alright if twenty of those have taken fed positions.

What is responsible for the number of birds lost in general?
People who send pigeons which are not one hundred per cent fit and healthy. These spread illness to the rest in the basket. Feds and combines are also at fault for changing racepoints instead of stopping where they are. They should be made to stop with the same race programme for five years so that other organisations know where they're racing from.

What do you see as the main problems with the sport?
There are too many greedy pigeon flyers with only one interest in mind - money. Added to that, the people at the top, the RPRA, are not looking after the new starter. To begin with, a pigeon clock should only cost £50 at the most and the RPRA should be running the sale of them. Also, we have had paramyxo for a number of years and yet we are still no closer to finding a cure than when we first started vaccinating. The way things are going, you'll have to be a vet before you can fly pigeons. It boils down to this: there are too many people making money who are not interested in the fancy in general.

How would you solve these problems?
Firstly, I would make sure that the money made by us was used for us. Charity should begin at home. Secondly, officials should be voted in by the fancy, not by their friends.

Why is membership falling?
Because the people in charge are not helping to keep costs down, and because of clubs not letting good fanciers in. People are always looking for a way to stop a good fancier winning, proposing things to benefit only themselves. Recently I played hell with some fanciers after they voted for a no-bean mix to be fed in the baskets. As far as I was concerned, this was done just to suit the widowhood flyers.

What's the best way a new starter can learn about pigeons?
If he wants to know anything, he should talk to a good old fancier. Most videos are a

complete waste of money and the novice learns nothing from them. Of all the loft videos I have seen, including the ones which top fanciers have made, I have not seen a good one yet. The only ones worth buying are those about the treatment of illness.

Which clubs do you fly in?
I focus on club racing with Banks Homing Society, which is affiliated to the Southport Federation. For the six channel races the birds are duplicated into the North West Combine. Apart from the odd open race, the only other organisations I fly in are St Helens 3 Bird Club and the North West Classic Club.

Do you compete in the nationals?
No. I've never really been interested in national racing. If you want to fly in the nationals you need to keep a lot of birds to find those that will do it, and a big pocket. Nearly all the national flyers in our district have gone backwards over time as far as club and fed racing is concerned.

The village of Banks has witnessed some fine Pau performances over the years, with the Pimlott Brothers topping section L in the very hard national of 1992, Tom Ryding clocking a number of good birds over the years and, indeed, Jimmy Warren winning it with 'Lancashire Rose'. As there is less glory in club and fed racing than national racing, aren't you tempted to give it a go?
No. People who say it is harder to win in the nationals should try getting onto the fed sheet for twenty-one weeks a season.

I recently spoke to a good fancier from your area who thought your birds would do well from Pau if you were to send them. Would you agree?
To be honest, I don't know. I'm not likely to find out either, as I think 500 miles is far enough for any bird you think much of. Anything that does 500 miles on the day in a north-west wind is a class bird, whereas two-day racing is down to luck. As a point of interest, a lot of national flyers from around here, and the late Tom Ryding was among them, used to prepare a pigeon for an enforced night out at Pau by sending it to Sartilly. Then, first thing next morning, they'd put it back in the basket and give it a fifty mile toss.

Did it work?
They invariably seemed to time a good one. Tom Ryding, in particular, did very well.

Which pigeons stand out in your memory?
My own 'Combine Cock', which topped the North West Combine from Nantes, because he is the best-balanced pigeon I've ever seen in my life. He was bred by Micky Bridge of Burscough. Of the Parkes pigeons, 'Mr Busschaert', the 'Larkin's Blue', '228', and his last NIPA winner stand out particularly. As for hens, the 'Palmer Hen' was as good

a hen as I've ever seen.

Which fanciers do you have the highest regard for?
I've great respect for Joe Dorning of Preston. He would win wherever you stuck him. Locally, George Lloyd of Birkdale is a fancier who doesn't keep many yet always does well. Jack Cropper of Banks is still one of the best and has seen off many an up and coming rival. John Blundell is another in the same mould. Of the older fanciers, Dick Baldwin of Rufford has flown many a good pigeon, whilst I regard a former clubmate, Dicky Aughton, as the finest handler of a pigeon you'll ever find.

Where would you place yourself amongst these fanciers?
I wouldn't like to say. It's up to other people to rate you.

JIM HANNAH

Recently I spoke to a fancier from the south of England who had made a point of visting successful lofts the length and breadth of the British Isles. I asked him which pigeons had most impressed him and he answered Jim Hannah's. After over thirty years in the sport, Jim Hannah's star is still in the ascendent. In 1993, competing in the biggest federation in Scotland, he won not only the old bird average, but also the combined average and the best average from the four longest old bird races. Over the years, his birds have also peppered the Scottish National results. This, despite competing in the often disadvantaged west section and only sending a small team - sometimes just the one pigeon. He has adapted a system to suit his long working hours, flies natural and his birds come into their own from the middle distances onwards.

How long have you been flying pigeons and which clubs do you presently compete in?
I have raced pigeons since 1960, competing in the Livingstone Memorial Flying Club since its formation in 1974. The club was named after Dr David Livingstone, who also came from Blantyre, and is affiliated to Lanarkshire Fed which is the biggest in Scotland, with twenty-eight clubs sending twelve to thirteen thousand pigeons in the early races. I also compete in the Scottish National Flying Club.

Could you describe the nature of racing in your area?
Most fanciers fly natural, although some do practise widowhood. Unlike some specialist fanciers down south, who only compete in sprint races, Scottish fanciers tend to compete right out to 500 miles. Some, of course, keep several pairs of Busschaerts or other sprint-type birds for the early part of the programme and race through to the last channel race with their own 500 milers.

Which bloodlines form the basis of your present day family?
At the moment, I think I can claim to have my own family of birds. The base of the loft came from the late Arthur Hill of St Just and is basically Kirkpatrick x MacGillivray. I also had a son and daughter of Jock MacGillivray's 'Dream Girl', 1st open SNFC Nantes 1956, and 'Glory Girl', 1st open SNFC 1958, as well as various other Kirkpatrick-based birds. To these, I added pigeons from W Wilson of Larkhall in 1969, Newcombe Brothers of Macmerry in 1974, and John Feenie of Hamilton in 1975, with the last named proving perhaps the best when crossed into mine. The latest introductions have come from George Rankin & Son of Blantyre. George and I have been exchanging birds these last three seasons and we have also been mating our best birds together and

sharing the youngsters. Another introduction to have crossed well also came from an arranged mating, this time with Douglas Telfer of Motherwell. This one was out of Douglas's blue hen, the only pigeon ever to have won the west section of the SNFC twice, taking 7th and 11th open. She originated from Brownlee Brothers of Carnwath and was bought at their entire clearance sale.

Which pigeon has had the most influence on your loft?
In more recent times, my good hen 'Bonnie Lass', who was 13th open SNFC Rennes in 1987 when only a handful of pigeons made it on the day. She is now leaving her mark as a breeder.

Have you tried any sprint families?
I have tried several in the last few years, in particular Janssens and various Busschaert lines, only to find them wanting. They have not survived in the loft at all.

Why do you think they failed to last the course?
They didn't adapt to my management for some reason, possibly because they didn't acclimatise. Three years ago I won the young bird average and points cup with a team of sixty youngsters, twenty-five of which were Busschaerts, and only two of the Busschaerts contributed.

Did you try any of them at the distance?
Only one of them got that far. I've had better luck with Wildemeersch pigeons, but then only when used as a cross.

Which distances do you prefer?
I prefer the 500 mile plus races but I find that my birds excel from 250 miles onwards. I fly natural only and in the last few seasons my hens have been my best distance birds.

Why do you think that is?
I don't know. Prior to having my birds stolen I had an equal number of good channel pigeons of either sex. One reason might be because recently many of my best pigeons have been grandchildren of 'Bonnie Lass' and all of these have been hens.

What do you feed?
I feed *Spillers Breeding Mix* twelve months of the year. It is an all round mixture which contains good quality grains. I alter the diet slightly in June and July for the distance races and also hand feed the birds in their boxes instead of by hopper. I also increase the maize content slightly - to about fifteen per cent - and for the distance races only I add peanuts. How much I give depends on the needs of each individual bird. I prefer light, buoyant birds, not solid, heavy-muscled ones because birds have to *race* 500 miles. Heavy pigeons will not keep up. I have to feed my pigeons at 6.15 am and 6.45 pm to fit

in with work, which means the hens are sitting both times, so I feed in the boxes to control their intake, making sure that the hens get what they need, which sometimes means having to lift them off the nest, and that the cocks don't get too much. I believe that fanciers in general grossly overfeed. I sometimes buy a bag of *Red Band* and feed a little every day in June and July, but generally I don't feed seeds at any other time of the year. The young birds are raced on *Spillers Breeding Mix* as well. I do not like my birds to get too fat during the winter as I think it is unhealthy, especially for hens, so I do not feed too heavily, although if it is really cold I give extra. I use grit all year round, red stone grit and oyster shell mixed fifty-fifty, and also *Kilpatrick's* minerals.

Have you tried feeding a less rich diet in the winter?
I have sometimes included barley and oats up to seventy per cent, but I don't think it really matters much as my birds have gone on to perform the same each year.

Do you favour polished corn?
No, it is an expense which is not really necessary. I prefer to feed a quality brand name which is consistent in quality grains.

What do you treat for?
I treat for canker when they are sitting their first round of eggs, using the white tablets called *Flagel*. I give each bird half a tablet one night and the other half the next night, starting from box number one, doing cock and hen, and proceeding in numerical order. That way I do not miss any. I do this about an hour before dark. The hens are, of course, on their nest and usually I don't have to lift them off. I wet the tablet slightly so that it goes down their throats more easily. Usually I only treat the birds once a year; it's very seldom that I treat them later in the season. The young birds reared are free from canker. I do not treat for coccidiosis or worms because I clean my loft regularly twice a day, or more in the racing season, and I believe this keeps cocci and worms at bay. I inject my birds annually with *Colombovac PMV*. I haven't had respiratory disease for years so I don't treat for it.

Why do you favour using *Flagel* tablets for canker?
Because a couple of years ago I went to an Armand Scheers lecture and had my eyes opened to the fact that the product I was using was only effective against a limited number of canker strains.

Are you happy about vaccinating?
It's a must and does the birds no harm at all.

Do you treat sick pigeons?
Yes, but I dispose of them if they don't respond reasonably quickly.

Do you use any other specifics?
I only use treatments for other ailments if and when I think it necessary. The best treatment you can give your birds is good management. It costs nothing.

How do you combat lice?
I dip my old birds in January or February with *Clorcarb*, using one sachet to a gallon and a half of water and I do not get anything on them that would cause a problem for the remainder of the year. I don't get lice on my young birds either. I used to powder my birds weekly but found I got more on myself than the pigeons. When I dip them I choose a sunny, warm day or bring them inside in a basket where it's warmer.

What do you expect of your pigeons, from being youngsters to two years of age?
My young birds fly most of the programme, depending on feather condition, of course. About five races, up to 160 miles, is the norm. Yearlings fly to the coast, which is approximately 360 miles, and one or two may be sent to 500 miles, but not often. Again, I give them about five races. I like to jump them as I find I have fewer losses this way. Two-year-olds fly the channel. They get two or three races to the 260-mile stage, which comes about four weeks before their main channel race.

Do you flag your pigeons?
Yes, and I'm convinced that flagging contributes to my success in a big way. It's the oldest form of training and still one of the best. I start my training programme a month before the bird is due to fly its channel race. It consists of three weeks' flagging for up to an hour or an hour and a quarter, and one week's tossing. When tossed, the birds should be on the wing for approximately an hour so I adjust the mileage depending on the wind and general weather conditions. My pigeons have 'open hole' unless the weather is particularly bad, but I can only flag them in the evening. I always lift the hens off the nest. Indeed, I flag hens up to the night they lay their first egg and then I flag them again the night after and also on the evening of the day they lay their second egg. Although I don't leave them on 'open hole' if the weather is bad, I flag them whatever the weather, including in heavy rain.

Which nesting and wing conditions do you favour for the distance?
My birds usually go to their national race with their first or second flight half-way up. I have also done well with birds that, for some reason or other, were on their first flight in one wing and second flight in the other. I prefer my birds to be sitting eleven to twelve days for the distance, although lately I've been just as successful with birds sitting six to seven days, hens included.

How many channel races do your birds have in a season?
Just one for the past couple of years. I should explain that in 1989 I had all my best birds stolen and, feeling a bit down, I sold a further sixty, only keeping six or seven

pairs of late-breds off my best. Five of those stolen came back but it meant I virtually had to restart in 1990. As my team becomes stronger I shall revert to sending some over the water twice in a season, which is common practice around here.

What do you give the birds on arrival from a race, particularly after a hard fly?
I give a little sugar or glucose in the water, and a little *Red Band* or the smaller seeds or grains from the general mixture, which I sieve out for the purpose. I never overfeed birds at this time, preferring them to have several light meals.

How frequently do you allow your birds to bath?
I give my birds a bath twice a week during the racing season, on a Sunday and either Wednesday or Thursday. On Sunday mornings, the cocks get a bath first and then I refill the bath with clean water for the hens. I don't leave the water after they have finished bathing as it becomes contaminated. Sometimes I even bath my birds on a Friday morning. It does no harm to let them bath so close to a race. In fact I think it's beneficial, helping to relax them.

Do your birds exercise in winter?
They don't go out much at all from November until I pair up, due partly to the fact that I am troubled by hawks.

How do you determine your matings and when do you pair up?
I usually pair up the first week in March and my old birds rear two nests, usually a double first nest and then a single youngster in the second round. Generally I line-breed to winning lines of particular birds within my family, pairing a good hen to a son of another good hen or vice versa, and I also cross some, of course. My first two birds over the channel last year were Arie Visser crosses. I rarely inbreed myself but in 1990 I purchased a Visser hen from *Top Lofts* which is inbred to Visser's top breeding hen '702', dam of 2nd National Barcelona and 2nd National Bergerac. I paired her to an inbred cock of my own and produced three youngsters in 1991, two hens and a cock. Last year one hen took 33rd open Rennes, and the other hen 4th fed Sartilly. The interesting thing about these two performances is that they were both put up on very hard days. The 33rd open hen took 4th section, with only nine birds on the day, and in the fed race there were only ten birds on the day.

What percentage of the birds you breed make the grade?
That's a hard question to answer as percentages can vary from year to year. Actual prizewinners may amount to fifty per cent, 500 milers ten per cent. Some years, like last year, I breed a lot of useful birds. I departed from my normal practice and mated the birds off the top of my head the day I paired them up and I believe they are the best crop of yearlings I've ever had. Time will tell!

How many birds do you winter?
Usually thirty-odd pairs, but due to having an excellent team of young birds last year, I have ninety odd birds at present, and that's after I reluctantly parted with some.

I assume, therefore, that you sell a few pigeons?
Yes, young birds and late-breds.

Do you breed many late-breds?
Yes, because they make ideal stock birds. All my best pigeons are bred from late-breds.

Do you breed from old pigeons and prisoners?
Yes, as long as they are healthy. I endeavour to mate them with yearlings or late-breds.

What do you think of wet feeders?
Usually it means something is wrong, so I investigate and treat as necessary.

What are your views on pigeon politics and commercialism?
Politics are sometimes detrimental, especially when voiced by the really old-type fanciers who are unwilling to change their views for the betterment of the sport, and I also think there is too much commercialism, but then it keeps people in a job. My main complaint is that it adds to the cost of pigeon keeping, which is unnecessary.

Do you believe in eye-sign?
No. As with all theories, eye-sign is illogical.

What is the main cause of losses?
Heavy losses are usually due to bad weather and clashing, which are both brought about by bad race controlling. Human error is, I think, the main cause of losses. Race controllers rely on weather forecasts to make their judgements, but these are often inaccurate and of no use to fanciers. Line of flight information from fellow fanciers takes more time but is the best way. The information can be pooled by several race controllers, whether racing north or south, and fed controllers up and down the country can use this information so that a Scottish fed controller, for example, knows the weather on the south coast at 5.00 am. Sometimes weather conditions change so quickly it's a difficult operation, but more co-operation is needed. I also believe there should be fewer birds put into the transporter baskets because it would help to cut down stress and lead to better races. Pigeon fanciers do not help each other enough at times.

Do you always train on the line of flight?
No. Training is training no matter what the direction.

Do your birds field?

Yes, and I think it's okay as long as everything else is in order. A local fancier once went to the spot where my birds were going one year and brought home a bucket of the same grit and ash that mine were taking. He said all his birds were sick when they ate it!

Would you use a deep-litter system?
Not on your life! Apart from the fact that it houses parasites, it's a very lazy way of keeping birds.

How do you assess form and pick your pool pigeons?
Sometimes a bird picks itself. Mostly I look for tightness of body, shining feathers and clear wattles and ceres. I do not handle my birds as often as I used to. Condition can be seen and your eyes tell you that all is well in the loft.

What are your views on books and videos?
Books provide knowledge, as do videos, but I disagree with the high cost of many. I also disagree with those that are a form of advertising.

Why is the sport declining?
Many sports and hobbies are faced with the same problem. If a census were taken to see what percentage of pigeon fanciers would be racing pigeons in fifty years' time then we would be in for a big shock. The reason for the decline is, I'm sure, because the younger generation are inhibited about keeping livestock either by parents, housing departments or local authorities. I think that modern interests generated in young people perhaps contribute as well. I also believe that far too much money leaves the sport. I know of no other sport that gives as much to charitable causes as ours, and yet no one thinks any less of them for it. The Budgerigar Society thrives and carries out medical research from its funds. They must think pigeon men are mad, especially when the fancy is in decline.

What are your thoughts on loft design?
The design should, of course, be decided by the circumstances required, whether you're flying widowhood or whatever. The ventilation should be determined by the location of the loft. Mine faces north and as such I have very little ventilation, but my loft is always fresh and dry. It's a case of trial and error and perhaps experience. Birds do not like draughts and these make it very difficult to get birds into form. The modern continental lofts are certainly pleasing to the eye, especially those with tiled roofs.

Are you in favour of a later liberation for national races?
As for Rennes, 539 miles, and Sartilly 498 miles, these racepoints can be flown on the day from early liberations so I'm happy with an early lib. However, I'm absolutely in favour of a later liberation for such races as Nantes and Niort. Niort is 672 miles and

Nantes 600 miles to me and these races, following early liberations, have been very hard of late, going into the third day. To clear the prizes, I'm of the opinion that a late afternoon liberation, say 2.00 pm, would be better. Then I think the overall velocities would be greatly improved, resulting in a better race all round. I'm sure the Pau National would, if liberated at say 4.00 pm, result in a far more even result to all competitors at all distances. All competition within the sport must be shown to be fair to all competitors and not favour only the 'Golden Mile' fanciers who get their cake and eat it every year. I think the same fanciers and pigeons would come to the fore because the consideration is time on the wing irrespective of whether it's over two days or one. The Dutch have proved that the system works, sending pigeons back to the distance a fortnight after a 600-mile race.

Why does the Scottish National Flying Club not attract more fanciers?
Political reasons. At present one has to pay full dues to fly the entire programme, but the average fancier does not have the birds to compete in all the races. Most have only enough to fly the fed programme. The Young Bird National is open to all fanciers and it has proved an outstanding success, with record birds away. The way forward is to allow fanciers to pay only for those races in which they wish to compete.

What type of pigeon have you found to do best in national competition?
I have seen and handled many national winners and Gold Award winners over the years in my capacity as a National photographer and they come in various shapes and sizes, but generally medium to small.

Which contributes more to success, the pigeon or the man?
Management is the key to success and you need good birds as well. They go hand in hand no matter what your goals are. Keep your management simple. I'm sometimes amused by the latest products designed to make birds succeed and wonder why I win regularly without using such things as tonics. Novices must exercise extreme patience if they intend to succeed with pigeons. I believe this is why a lot of older fanciers are not successful at the distance.

'Bonnie Lass'
13th open Scottish National Rennes and Jim Hannah's top stock hen.

ALAN BULLEN

The first thing you notice when you visit the home of Alan Bullen is how much loft space he has, the second is how few pigeons he keeps. Lofts which could house well over a hundred contain rarely more than half that. This is because he neither enjoys having nor feels you need to keep large numbers to be successful and, accordingly, he has for many years adopted a system which roots out the poorest birds early on. Those that are left can be worked on with confidence and this is important to him, as he leaves nothing to chance in his preparation of individual pigeons for the tasks he sets them. The family he races has a name synonymous with his home town of Croston, the Croston Barkers, and these he has flown for over forty years.

You have maintained a family of Barkers for many years. What were the base birds and which introductions have you used?
The base of my family is the old Jimmy Nolan Barkers and the Reuben Eastham Barkers, which go back to the early 1900s. They came from Tom Blackstone and Reuben Eastham himself in 1954. The key pigeons were grandchildren of 'Chimney Jack', which traced back to the old Blampeyn Bovyn blood, and grandchildren of Eastham's 'Dol Hen' and a cock named 'Wild Blue'. I can't give you any more background on the Eastham pigeons than that, as he was a man who played his cards very close to his chest.

When did you add to this base?
I introduced my next pigeons in 1979, through Ronnie Wilson. The base of these was also Reuben Eastham Barker. I thought my pigeons were in need of a 'cross' so I brought in the same family but from a different environment. I believe that just being fed and treated in a way different to your own makes the blood run differently and gives your pigeons the boost that they need. The Wilson pigeon which made the biggest impact was a blue pied son of his 2nd section, 98th open Pau hen of the mid-seventies. He is now the sire or grandsire of everything in the loft.

Are your present-day birds as good as the originals?
No, they are better. Physically, they aren't as big because of the influence of the Blackstones on the Easthams. The two families were originally the same in size and shape, but they changed when crossed. Dr Rigg was the first to prove that the cross worked. Today, the Eastham line dominates the Blackstones by 75 per cent to 25 per cent. I have brought nothing else in since 1979.

Are you planning to bring in another cross?
Not at the moment as I don't need one yet, although in the future I might look towards the Van Bruaenes or Cattrysse.

Why those two breeds in particular?
Because of their performances at the distance into this country and because I think they are of a type which would hit with mine. I would only bring in a hen, though, as I prefer daughters of good performance cocks. Hens put tenacity into a family for the distance.

How would you use a cross?
I would bring it in and then breed it out, first pairing the sire back to his daughter. From these I would mate brother and sister, before then putting the Blackstone blood in at the fourth generation.

Would you still test them at every generation?
Rigorously. The only way to keep them winning is by ruthless elimination.

With having an inbred family, do you get many throwbacks to good pigeons of the past?
Occasionally. For example, last year I bred a blue hen with flecks on her eyes just the same as the hen I won 12th open NFC Nantes with in 1969. Whether this means she will also turn out to be good, though, I don't know.

Is there any difference in the breeding or racing capabilities of your silver cocks compared with your silver hens?
I've had plenty of silvers of either sex and they have been equally good, whether racing or breeding. Whatever the colour, my good racers turn out to be good breeders nearly every time.

Do you only breed from pigeons that score?
No. Providing a pigeon is bred right and I think it is going to be good, I will breed off it.

What is your ideal type?
For my needs I want a pigeon with a strong back and a dipped tail and its last four flights must be narrow and long. There should be hardly any webbing on the leading edge of the end flight and the amount should increase slightly on each consecutive flight in. If you can imagine the beginnings of an s-shape, that is what I want the end flight to be like. I also reject a lot of pigeons because they aren't long enough in the wing. I like tight tails, but although the cover feathers on the tails of mine do come well down that is not something I actually look for. And the vents must be tight, like a pair of pincers, on both cock and hen.

Do you condemn a pigeon with open vents?
Yes. I won't even keep one.

Why?
Because in the early days, when I flew with Tom Blackstone, we had one or two and they never did anything. I resolved then never to keep another.

Do the vents not get looser with age?
Not normally. If they do I cull.

Do you take note of the throat?
Not overly, although I can't stand pigeons with wide throats. I lose them before they ever get to the distance.

Do you think there is anything in eye-sign theories?
I'm sure, although I don't spend time on them. I wouldn't let an eye man I respected come in my loft and take away what he thought was my best pigeon.

But I presume you do look for something in the eye?
Primarily I regard the eye as an indicator of health. Apart from that, I like it to be rich and broken up with strong colours, as I've never seen a pigeon with a wishy-washy eye win at the distance on a hard day. My family is basically orange or brown-eyed, but I do have the odd gravel. I need to have these because if I'm not careful the eyes get too rich.

Apart from health, can the eye tell you anything else?
I can tell if a pigeon is inbred by its eye. I don't base this on eye theory but on what I've seen in families.

Do you breed off old pigeons?
Yes, but they've got to have been really good racers, especially the hens.

What about prisoners?
Only for a season. Prisoners deteriorate after the first year and I wouldn't breed off them beyond that.

When do hens start to decline?
I think they get past their best when they're eight or nine. I have bred off hens that were twelve-years-old, but they were exceptions.

Do you ever try artificially to extend the breeding life of old pigeons?
Once they start to 'go' I cull them. I won't prop them up or aid their fertility. Hens have an egg bed. If you open up a Rhode Island Red you will see all its eggs in a bed, from

the one it is about to lay all the way down in size to the last one it will ever lay. They are all there.

Are hens that have been raced hard spoilt for breeding?
Providing they've always returned to a natural environment it doesn't make any difference to their ability to breed good, sound youngsters.

How do you select your matings?
Actually, I very rarely mate pigeons together. I tend to let them pair the way they want, even the stock birds. I know, though, which birds go into which cabin so my pairings are more controlled than you might think. This is one of the reasons why I keep no more than six pairs in any one loft.

Would you describe your lofts?
My lofts get plenty of air, although there are no draughts, and I have lofts facing different angles. The loft facing east is better for young birds and distance pigeons as they come into form later than those in the lofts facing south. I keep only twenty-five pairs, and have between three and six pairs in a loft.

How important is loft location?
On land, very, but over the channel you're not going to win every race no matter where you live.

When do you pair up?
I always pair up on a full moon and my birds are only together from March until I part them immediately after the last old bird race.

Why do you pair up on a full moon?
Because the pigeons seem to have more of a sex drive and the cocks settle better with their hens.

Why part them so early?
They moult better and you preserve your pigeons. They get used to the system and are keener the year after to get on with the cycle.

How many youngsters do you take off each pair?
I normally take only the first round. The dog takes the rest of the eggs. Occasionally I take four off certain stock pigeons, floating their first round after ten days.

How many good pigeons do you produce in an average year?
Out of the thirty to thirty-five youngsters I breed, I expect to make about five or six of them into 500 to 700 milers by the time they are three years old. There aren't many

good pigeons when it comes to the distance and nobody gets more than ten per cent of pigeons which will do it year in, year out.

What do you feed for rearing?
When the eggs are due to hatch, they go on 100 per cent Tasmanian or New Zealand peas. As you can see, I'm a protein man. The only other things they get, apart from clean water, are grit, pickstones, coal dust and whatever they pick up in the fields.

When do you wean your youngsters?
Either at eighteen days or before the hen lays again. The hens go with the youngsters and are given a hopperful of peas. They will feed any youngster that comes to them, and after four days the youngsters are feeding themselves. After a week, the hens are moved to another compartment and go on a mix of 25 per cent beans, 25 per cent peas and 50 per cent maize. They then have no wheat. The cocks are given this mix as soon as the hens are taken away. The hens are flown odd for most of the land races. My best yearling hens never see another youngster until they go to the race I've mapped out for them.

Does it matter if the hens lay after going with the youngsters?
No, although I'd rather they didn't.

Why do you feed only peas for rearing?
I've tried all sorts of food for rearing youngsters, and have found maple peas are best. Why they should be better than beans, I don't know. I wouldn't feed a pellet because I like my pigeons to use their gizzard to grind food. This is one of the reasons I don't feed my racing cake at this time.

At what point do you begin to vary the youngsters' diet?
After eight weeks when they go on the same mix as the race team. The sooner I can get them on beans the better.

Why?
Because, rearing aside, beans are the best food for pigeons. I've certainly never poisoned mine.

Would just peas be sufficient for their nutritional needs if your birds didn't pick up extra in the fields?
I don't know, but I encourage mine to field so I don't worry about it.

Do you feed a commercial mix?
No, I get my peas and beans from the farm and my maize from *Bamfords* of Bretherton. I don't clean any of it, I just feed it as it comes out of the driers. My only indulgence as

far as food is concerned is peanuts. I spend more on them than my basic diet. When the channel races arrive I fill a pint jug daily to feed forty pigeons and just throw them on the grass. They come off the nest for them and are allowed as many as they want. I use human consumption peanuts called *Golden Glow*, which are the ones you see mixed with raisins.

Why do you feed peanuts?
Because they put the correct sort of weight on a pigeon and help build up its stamina and muscle.

Do you give them greens?
My pigeons get no greens from me. They get what they need from the fields.

Why do you move the hens?
So that they'll hold their flights. My pigeons always have a good wing for the channel races. Normally I get them on their second flight, preferring it to be a quarter to a third up. I like the flight to be like a paint brush. Sometimes they are sent still on their first flight and they do well, but I think they come into form more once they've cast their second.

Does it matter if they're on their third or fourth flight?
They are still alright when on their third, but I wouldn't send them on their fourth because I've never seen them do much in that condition. Mine also start to throw their cover flights when they reach their fourth flight.

Which races do you concentrate on?
I gear all my pigeons up for 500 to 700-mile races, but they go to at least one earlier channel race. Assuming a pigeon has a straightforward race at 350 miles, it is then given three weeks' rest before the long one, but if they race from 400 miles I give them four weeks' rest.

What is the key to distance racing?
Long distance pigeon racing is about rest, not training, and about getting the birds into the right humour. I use the land races for training and then set about getting a bird's mind right during the resting period. I expect any bird in the loft, if got right, to do the job I ask of it. I don't keep many going beyond five years of age, though, because I think you've got to have young stuff.

How quickly can one get a pigeon into race condition?
Six weeks is the shortest amount of time it would take me to get a bird from winter condition into the form needed to fly 500 miles. It is better to build up slowly to a peak.

When does a pigeon's preparation begin?
Eight weeks before the chosen channel race. If I intend to send a hen to Angouleme, for example, then I will first give her two 200-mile races and one 150-mile race in the space of eight days, eight weeks before. I then prepare her for a 350 or 390-mile race, either Sartilly or Rennes. This preparation involves working on her condition so that she will be in the same state physically as she will be for Angouleme. At this point the crucial, missing ingredient that will be needed for the big race four weeks later is the proper mental condition. Although she will try, in my opinion she will not do as well as from Angouleme, by which time I will have her in the proper condition both mentally and physically. I prepare her mentally through a combination of things, including the work I give her, the rest she has and by talking to her.

Can a poor pigeon be made fit?
I can get any pigeon fit after it's twelve months old and it's gone through my system - even bad ones - but fitness alone is not enough. You must get it into the right humour. If I do, I know when I'm waiting that I'll get it. To give you an example, I've got a cheq w/f hen who I could tell was enjoying her racing as a young bird. I was watching her. As a yearling she came steadily, but a friend who saw her said she wasn't sound. As a two-year-old I sent her to Rennes and this time my friend said I'd lose her. However, she was perfect when I sent her and she won the club by twenty minutes, finishing 17th combine. Now she'll go to Pau.

Do you play any tricks?
Never with distance pigeons. By distance I mean over 400 miles, as anything less I consider a sprint nowadays. I don't bother with the land races but I do try one or two tricks for the shorter channel races, such as having a hen sitting anything up to seven eggs by the day of basketing, or leaving a cock to feed a three-week-old hen youngster for a week before basketing. By then he is on the floor calling the youngster and he won't let anything else near his box.

What nesting condition do you aim at?
When it comes to the longer races, I mainly like my hens to be chipping or feeding a two-day-old youngster. I was told by a good fancier that when a pigeon is feeding soft food it takes twenty-five per cent more air into its lungs, which can only help in a long race. Having said that, a pigeon has got to want to come home.

What does make it want to come?
I think at 500 miles the environment's got to be right and the pigeon fit, but most of all, it's got to be in the right humour. In the last few hours of flying, it's the love of the home and master that keeps it going, not the nest, as I'm sure that after three days away a pigeon has forgotten what it was doing in the nest box.

Do you have any problem getting a pigeon to go back on its nest after a channel race?
Not usually because I only send one of a pair, and that one is taken away until its mate returns.

What body shape do you aim at?
A fit, well-muscled pigeon should be the shape of a dimpled turkey.

Skin, blood-spot, eye-cere: what do these tell you about the fitness of a bird?
Forget the skin on the keel. I don't take any notice of it because a pigeon sitting eggs doesn't have scaly skin. I don't take any notice of the blood-spot on the keel either. In my family, the eye-cere goes a dark bluey colour and this I do like to see.

Do you train during the final days before basketing?
I will give some a 50-mile toss during the resting period if I think they need it, but only if I can take them myself or guarantee they won't be away from the loft more than two or three hours. It is vital that you eliminate stress and keep them in the right humour.

Do you always choose a fine day for training?
No, I train in all weathers except fog.

Do you do anything else in the lead up to a pigeon's main channel race of the year?
I worm it eight days before basketing, using half a *Piperazine* tablet from the vet.

How does the amount of muscle differ come the intended race?
From their prep channel race to a month later when they go to the long one, they carry an extra two to three ounces of muscle.

In what way does a pigeon's condition need to be different for Pau than for 500 miles?
A pigeon needs more muscle for 700 miles. Therein lies the problem with a mid-day liberation from Pau. The weight we need on pigeons if we are to get them at 700 miles is not conducive to success if they are liberated in the heat of the day. An early morning lib would be better for the further flying pigeons. The good ones would fly over 500 miles on the day and, if well muscled, we would get them well up country next morning.

How to you put on the extra muscle?
By feeding a cake.

What are its ingredients?
Half a packet of *Scotch Porridge Oats*, 3 eggs, 2 tablespoons of glucose, 2 tablespoons of *Cytacon*, 3 tablespoons of *Bemax* (a health food), 2 dessertspoons of honey (any

kind), 1 teaspoon of table salt and 2 dessertspoons of *Complan*. I used to add 2 tea-spoons of *Vionate* (vitamins) and 1 teaspoon of brewer's yeast, but I took it out as I didn't think it was necessary. I mix all this with the fat from a pig's kidney and make it into a meal. I dry it on a tray, not in the oven. Therefore it isn't cooked. If it's still too moist I dry it off with ordinary flour.

How much do you give?
In the early part of the season, as much as they'll eat once a week. A fortnight before Sartilly, our first channel race, I then give each bird a couple of tablespoons daily, and for the long races they get as much as they want in the five days before basketing.

Would your performances drop off if you didn't use this cake?
Definitely. Everything is in the cake. It is the booster.

Can't pigeons win regularly on just clean water and the basic diet?
Not in my experience and I don't agree with those who say they can.

Do you ever use cod liver oil?
No. Pigeons don't need it if the sun's shining.

How can you tell when a pigeon has peaked and is just beginning to go off form?
That's something that I can't comment on. You have to know your own pigeons.

Does a bird in top condition carry bloom?
Bloom means fatness not fitness. Of course, you will see a little on the surface of the bath, but you shouldn't see too much.

Do you add anything to the pigeons' bath water?
No, nothing.

When do you give a bath?
It is always full and always in front of them. I leave the water in for a week at a time. They drink it and it does them no harm at all.

Do you send a big team to channel races?
No. When they are three or four I know when they'll win, so I don't need to send a basketful if one pigeon is right. I can go in my loft, pick one out, get it ready and score. People make the mistake of sending a basketful in the hope of getting one, instead of just sending one that is right.

How many do you lose over the channel?
Years of using the same system has left me with a type and, consequently, after the

yearling stage when they go across three times, I don't lose many. If you get them right when they are young and try and lose them you will be left with birds you can rely on.

When you were 2nd section, 18th open Pau with 'Another Rose' what nesting condition was she in?
She was sent sitting two-day-old eggs and trying to feed a two-day-old youngster. I found out she flew to that condition the season before when she was 3rd West Lancs Two-Bird from Avranches. I can't tell you why I came to try her like that in the first place, though, and I haven't tried it on any others since. She went to Pau twice after, scoring both times in the section.

When you said you get a pigeon right by talking to it, what did you mean exactly?
I talk to them a lot. When they are over the channel, I go to them every night in the dark and feed them peanuts by torchlight whilst they're sitting. They start to roar and go mad when they hear me coming out of the back door, so I'm sure they think more about me for doing it. I think into their minds and I believe that when it's getting late and they're nearing home they'll keep going because they know I'll be there. Pigeons do think. They are clever.

Would you say yours were tame pigeons?
Yes and no. Some years I've timed them as they've dropped to the ground in front of me, and they'll also climb all over me if I fall asleep in the garden, but on the other hand they don't like me getting hold of them. I believe in getting close to them, without becoming too familiar. They don't want you to be catching them all the time, but then again, they should think that you are protecting them. When I'm basketing for the channel I wait for a pigeon to go back on the nest, I won't catch it in the loft. It's just a quirk that I have.

What do you feed them on return from a race?
I feed depurative for two days before putting them back on their normal mix.

Do you put anything in the water?
Yes, two things, one of which is a bottle I mix myself. It is a four-way mix made up of 4oz Epsom Salts, 2oz Glauber's Salts, °oz Sulphate of Iron and a teaspoon of medicinal creosote mixed in three pints of boiling water. I give them this every Sunday at the rate of 1 tablespoon to a five-pint drinker and it certainly does them good. It works on the principle of the old-fashioned electrolytes, clearing the system of lactic acid. It won't cure anything but it will keep things away. The channel birds are also given glucose in their boxes on their return. If they have the constitution, they'll have picked up within twenty-four hours.

If you turned your mind to the shorter races, do you think your family would have

the speed to do well?
They can win on land given the right system. I used to fly widowhood in partnership with Tom Blackstone back in the early sixties and we were practically unbeatable on land. However, because they were fed differently and we trained daily, we couldn't get them from across the channel.

Is there any difference between 500 milers and 700 milers?
It definitely takes different condition to fly one compared to the other, though not necessarily a different type of bird.

Brian Denney maintains that one could turn a sprint family into a distance one within five years. Do you agree?
He is exactly right. He must use the same system as me. I would expect to lose a lot in the process, but after five years I would be left with a nucleus of two and three-year-olds. You would have to get your youngsters into tip-top condition and try to lose them.

What do you treat for?
I don't treat for canker but do occasionally treat for coccidiosis with *Coxoid*. And, as I said earlier, I also worm them eight days before their main channel race.

Can't all your work be undone in the basket if they come into contact with others that aren't entirely healthy?
If pigeons are fed by hopper or directly on a floor of deep litter, and have 'open hole', they build up a resistance to almost any sort of disease. By picking through muck at home, they will have resistance to things they might otherwise pick up in the basket. Whilst on the subject of being in the basket, I love to hear of other people who refuse to feed beans. If their pigeons are fed beans in the basket they won't eat them to begin with because they're not used to them, whereas mine will have a cropful.

What does your deep litter consist of?
Sand, sawdust and droppings. I use washed sand because it has had all the dust taken out of it. I riddle it every three months or so and change it every two or three years. I prefer deep litter because I am certain that pigeons fed in pots or on a clean floor are more susceptible to picking up disease.

Do you get many sick pigeons?
No. You won't get much disease if you look for something to cull every time you go in the loft. I don't treat sick pigeons.

How common is respiratory disease?
Ninety-five per cent of pigeons will suffer from it at some stage if their loft is not properly ventilated. All livestock needs fresh air, and what's more, fresh air also sorts

the wheat from the chaff by exposing those with a suspect constitution.

A pigeon may have mycoplasma without it being visible, so how can you tell if it's affected?
Put your ear to its back and give a good press on its keel. If you hear a crackling sound as the bird breathes, it has got mycoplasma.

Can you cure a pigeon of this naturally?
Yes, but it takes a long time. It is better to treat as you can clear it up in three days using a bottle.

How do you control lice and other parasites?
I dip my birds once a year before racing starts, likewise the youngsters, using *Ectofen* as per the manufacturer's instructions. I also spray the loft every month with industrial bleach, mixing it half and half with water. It froths on the walls and I come out with my eyes streaming. Additionally, I spray the lawn in front of the loft with *Jeyes' Fluid* to guard against anything that wild birds might bring in. Mind you, with having an open loft and my birds fielding, I think they have developed a natural resistance to most things. To keep away vermin, I always have mouse poison down and take the hoppers out at night.

Do you ever use garlic?
No. Instead, I chop some onions and sprinkle glucose powder on them. I throw them on the grass ad lib once or twice a week, but only for channel racing. I reckon it does a similar thing to garlic in that it helps to keep the blood 'clean'.

As your birds are on 'open hole' how do you keep cats at bay?
I have a dog which I leave in the pen all day with the pigeons. She lies in the nest boxes and even takes eggs or youngsters out of the nest. I don't know how she can tell the difference, but if the eggs are newly laid, she'll eat them, whereas if they've started to be turned, she won't. She takes the youngsters into her shed, licking them and keeping them warm.

Does the dog not unsettle the pigeons?
I always try to get the dog to do it whilst I'm there, so they see it as 'normal' and therefore don't become stressed. They also know that if I'm not there, I'll return their youngsters when I get home. They belt the dog when it goes in their box, but the dog usually wins and I've seen hens chasing the dog across the garden to get their eggs or youngsters back. I have now put a gate in the loft just for when I want the eggs to hatch. Before this dog goes I'll get another one and train it up.

Would you prefer your birds not to field?

No, I want them to field. If they don't go, there is something wrong with them.

Are they ever troubled by hawks?
Sometimes. They will stop going for a couple of days if they've been struck at, but they will soon go back again. Pigeons on 'open hole' get used to hawks.

Does a pigeon's feather wear out, as some suggest, if exposed to the elements all winter?
That's a load of rubbish! Feathers don't wear out. Feather condition is brought about by feeding. The feather of widowhood pigeons is not as good as the feather of birds that are out all the time because they are not getting the oil feed they should.

Do you ever get birds with wing stiffness?
No, never. If you have any then you'd better watch out for paratyphoid.

What training do you give your youngsters?
Their initial toss is from thirty miles. After the first race, I always single them up, from any direction. Years ago I used to take them to Leyland and let them go with the Scottish pigeons.

Do you race them to the perch?
Yes. Mine don't pair as they are bred too late.

What do you ask of youngsters?
I'm very hard on them. They go every week unless their cover flights are missing or they're bear round the ears and I always place a question mark over any that make two mistakes.

Do you send youngsters over the channel?
Not at the moment, but only because there are no channel races on the programme. If there were I would rear ten early youngsters, as I think they need age, and set about making them individuals. I would operate a jealousy system, so although they'd be paired up they wouldn't be sitting.

Does sending them over the water spoil them?
No, they go on to be good old birds, but I modify my system slightly so that they only get two channel races as yearlings and no 500-mile race.

Taking it a stage further, if a youngster is completely flown out for whatever reason, is it ever likely to make up into a winning distance bird?
There is no point at which an exhausted pigeon can't be saved and go on to win. I make sure they don't have any heavy food for three or four days. They are given dari, saf-

flower, milo and other small grains, which is what I call depurative. Depurative, to me, is not barley.

How many of your young birds come through?
After the treatment I give my youngsters, I'm satisfied if I'm left with fifty per cent. More often than not I'm left with seventy-five per cent.

When do you separate your youngsters?
Straight after the last young bird race. I use up the food they've been racing on, adding a little wheat, and then I buy new crop tic beans.

Why new tic beans?
Because the old crop gets too dry. I reason that as a farmer always uses new beans to grow his next crop they must be better for pigeons.

What do you feed after racing?
In the winter they are fed 50 per cent beans, 25 per cent protein white peas and 25 per cent maize with a little wheat.

Because you race youngsters hard, do you go easy on them as yearlings?
No. All my yearlings cross the channel three times, with the best ones going to 500 miles. They fly harder than my older pigeons.

Why so severe?
Because if a yearling can't fly 500 miles it is not going to get 700 miles as a three-year-old.

Do you carry on in the same vein with two-year-olds?
No. I regard the two-year-old stage as a resting period, although they do still go to 500 miles. I have been successful with them at 600 miles but I think it probably takes too much out of them. I now think 500 miles is far enough.

How do you know when the time has come to stop a pigeon?
When it slows itself down and doesn't try as hard as it did. Knowing when comes from experience and knowing each individual pigeon. If I'm in any doubt at all they stay at home.

Would you say you have a good eye for a pigeon?
I could pick anybody's best pigeon out off the perch by the way it looked at me. There is just something about them that tells you, especially hens. It might not be the best racer, but if it isn't, it will be the best breeder.

Can you pick out your own best pigeons before they prove themselves?
No.

Would you say you were a better fancier with cocks or hens?
I'm a hen man. I trust them more.

Why are there so few of the old families left?
Because the fanciers who had them didn't have faith in them. I've seen so many good families over the years, but hardly any have been preserved.

Has the standard of pigeons improved over the years?
Today, I think there are more pigeons capable of flying the distance, but there are fewer outstanding pigeons.

Why are their fewer outstanding pigeons?
It's possibly because people treat pigeons differently and expect more of them nowadays.

Are there any problems with the sport as you see it?
Yes. Today there is no compromise. For example, if a fancier forgets to transfer a bird, he should be given a rap on the knuckles, not be suspended. I think, to a degree, widowhood has also spoilt the sport, with fanciers being too greedy and timing in a clockful. Many fanciers who keep sprinters can't get them over the channel, so they get more sprinters to replace them and, at the same time, want to do away with channel races. The sooner we get back to pigeon racing as a sport, the better. We may then encourage more youngsters to take an interest.

Have you tried any other methods?
I've been using my methods a long time and I don't think I've ever done things much differently. When you hit on a system that works, don't change it.

What mark out of ten would you give yourself as a stockman?
Now there's a question. I would say nine.

And as a racing man?
Nine again. One always makes a mistake somewhere along the line. It's human error.

Does any particular mistake you've made stand out in your memory?
Probably the biggest one was asking too much of a hen who was very good up to Nantes by sending her further. I now know by a bird's condition on return from 450 miles whether or not it will get further.

Which is more important, the fancier or the pigeon?
For the distance, the contribution between pigeon and fancier is fifty-fifty. The pigeon has got to be as good as you and you've got to be as good as the pigeon. You've got to know how it thinks, its moods and, most importantly of all, how and when it will win for you.

Would equally good pigeons from elsewhere adapt to your system?
Most introductions wouldn't stick my programme in the first couple of generations, but eventually one or two would adapt.

If you had to restart with just a couple of your own pairs, would you know which ones to take?
To begin with, I don't think I could restart with only four of my birds because I would need more than that to maintain a family. If I was allowed to choose eight, however, I could go in the loft right now and pick them out.

Is there anything in the sport which you read or hear that irritates you?
Yes, people telling me how to feed pigeons.

Which fanciers do you have the highest regard for?
The late Bill Martland of Mawdesley I rated the highest of all. He never kept above twelve pairs and his performances in two-bird races up to Nantes, especially with yearlings, were fantastic. Present day, I think R&B Smith of Burtonwood are as good as anybody in the country.

Are there any golden rules with distance pigeons?
Never disappoint a pigeon when you ask it to do a good hard day's work. I never send both of a pair to the same race, because I want one to be at home when the other gets back. Keep them happy and content.

The Croston Barkers

A typical example of the inbreeding practised by Alan Bullen to maintain his unique family of Croston Barkers. This mating of half-brother & sister was used to intensify the lines of 89575 of the Reuben Easthams & 9884 of the Blackstone & Bullen.

Cheq cock 86N3762
Flew Niort 517 miles as a yearling. 1st Lune Valley 2 Bird Rennes, 5th Ormskirk Amal open Bergerac 626 mls

Silver hen 87N7329
Three prizes as a young bird. Not raced as a yearling. 1st club, 2nd amal, 3rd combine Niort 517 miles as a two-year-old. Since stock

Blue Pied cock 79E89575
No 1 Stock Cock
Best of the Reuben Eastham Barkers

Cheq hen 76E9884
Another Rose
2nd sect, 18th open NFC Pau 1979, 719 miles & numerous other channel prizes

Blue Pied cock 79E89575
No 1 Stock Cock
Best of the Reuben Eastham Barkers

Silver hen 82J50179
1st Niort 517 miles 1986
Sold to T Nelson of Northern Ireland

Blue cock 75X14335
2 x 1st Weymouth then stock

Blue hen 73T85196
2nd sect, 98th open Pau

Cheq cock 75A7658
The Pau Cock
Good open positions plus many other prizes

Blue hen 74A6430
Stock

Blue cock 75X14335
2 x 1st Weymouth then stock

Blue hen 73T85196
2nd sect, 98th open Pau

Cheq hen 76E9884
Another Rose
2nd sect, 18th open NFC Pau

Blue cock 75X14335
74A6430 Stock

72Z83198 1st Niort 500 miles
Silver hen 68M Stock
72Z83198 1st Niort 500 miles
71D3519 Stock
68D47738 Son of 1st N.W Combine
69N54471 The Broken Wing Hen
67R660 Stock
69N54471 Stock
72Z83198 1st Niort 500 miles
Silver hen 68M Stock
72Z83198 1st Niort 500 miles
71D3519 Stock
73T85196 2nd sect, 98th open Pau
75A7658 The Pau Cock
2 x 1st Weymouth then stock

Pete Chamberlain (right) with Tony Cowan.

PETE CHAMBERLAIN

We are all familiar with the scenario. It's clock reading time and you think you are in with a shout. One or two members advance congratulations in your direction, somewhat prematurely, but you think it wise not to accept. After all, there are still a couple of clocks to check and one of them belongs to the chap who always seems to get a good one. This occasion turns out to be no different, the chap's gone and pipped you again and all you can do is turn your thoughts to the next race. Here we turn the spotlight on somebody who has clocked a good one more often than his fellow clubmates would care to remember, Pete Chamberlain of Burton Latimer, Northants.

I know you give a lot of thought to keeping your birds healthy so perhaps you could begin by telling me which of the common diseases you treat for?
Canker, coccidiosis and worms, in no particular order. Treatment for one is followed by clear water for a day and then multivitamins. A fortnight later I treat for another, again with clear water the day after, then multivitamins, and likewise again after the last treatment. I've noticed that treating for canker knocks the birds back the most.

When do you treat?
The time for treating is in the winter, although not when the weather is severely cold. A pigeon needs all its reserves to stand the cold, so I prefer not to knock them back with any treatments until the weather is milder.

As you've competed only on the north road, have you always vaccinated against paramyxo?
Yes, although I missed doing the young birds one year because the club bought the vaccine in bulk and it ran out. I'm not happy about doing it because I've had a couple of bad experiences. The worst one was last winter. It was too cold, so cold, in fact, that after we'd done half the birds we popped inside for a cup of tea, leaving the vaccine on the windowsill. Anyway, I didn't realise it at the time, but the vaccine had almost frozen. It congealed in their necks, giving rise to lumps of varying sizes where the needle had gone in. I dug out the scabs with a pen-knife and fortunately, though some bled, the pigeons were none the worse for the experience.

If you don't like vaccinating, why did you always choose to vaccinate before it became compulsory?
Because I've had the disease in my loft and I wouldn't want it again.

What happened?
It was 1986 and the disease was rife in the area. Certainly more lofts had it than reported it to the MAFF. Anyway, I'd actually injected the old birds but not the youngsters and I got it in my young bird team. I had six or seven with twisted necks so I culled all those except one that I experimented with. I fed it myself to try and help it through, but the first time I let it out of the loft it flew round in circles and crashed, so I had to kill it also.

Did all your youngsters have it?
Yes, and it was the fittest pigeons, the ones that were winning, that had it the worst. I don't know why they were more susceptible, but I've known other fanciers suffer and they said exactly the same. I'd be interested to know why this should be.

How did you try to stop the spread?
Although I realised that the disease travels through the air I tried to eliminate everything. I isolated the ones that had it the worst, sterilised the water for a month, cleaned and disinfected the loft every day and fed them on the best food I could buy, but all to no avail.

What happened to those youngsters that pulled through?
I had about twelve left. None displayed any signs of having had the disease, there were no fret marks or anything like that, and I thought they'd do okay. Anyway, I kept them until they were two and they flew quite well, winning minor club prizes, but I never had an actual win out of any of them.

Do you get many sick pigeons generally?
No, although I do think there is a time in a young bird's life when it is susceptible to most things. That time is early autumn, when the damp, cold weather is new to them. My loft isn't to my liking in so much as I'd prefer it to be warmer and dryer, and this problem manifests itself in the form of a poorer moult.

Does it also cause dirty wattles?
No. I never get those because they bath twice a week all year round with permanganate of potash in the water. An old London north road flyer told me about the benefits of it many years ago. I don't mind that it stains the feathers a little. I also put one or two grains in the young birds' water for a week when they're just weaned. You'll notice that the first time youngsters see water they want to get in it, so I leave the top off the fountain and let them splash about.

Do you normally give sick pigeons a chance?
No. If they get coccidiosis for example, I cull them. As for canker, well I've never had a pigeon suffer from it.

Do you spray the loft?
Yes, once a week with *Duramitex* and *Jeyes' Fluid* mixed together. I add half a fluid ounce of both to two pints of water.

Is it necessary to do it every week?
I do it for my own convenience as well as for the birds' benefit. I've got a bit of a chest problem and I find it helps to keep the dust down. And it smells nice; in fact, I love the smell of *Jeyes' Fluid*.

Do you sterilise your drinkers?
No. As I use plastic drinkers I find that a sponge and clean water is adequate. This allows the pigeon to build up some degree of immunity.

How do you combat lice?
I dip all my pigeons in *Duramitex* twice a year, just before pairing up and again when they've grown most of their new body feathers. I fill a washing up bowl and add just enough *Duramitex* to colour the water. I occasionally see lice just before I'm about to dip them again, but by dipping my pigeons and spraying the loft at the same time, I'm totally clear of lice for most of the year. Dipping is the only way to keep on top of lice because it destroys the eggs.

Would dipping during the racing season affect the webbing of the flights and stop them acquiring bloom?
I wouldn't have thought so.

Do lice prevent a bird reaching tip-top condition?
It depends on the type of lice. I've had pigeons win for me in the past that had the long tic sort, but quill mite are a different thing altogether. They spread like an explosion, are bad for the feathers and drain a bird's resources.

You read of lofts that don't treat their birds systematically but still win. Do you accept that the lengths you go to aren't always necessary?
I accept that, from what one reads, some fanciers get away with not treating for one thing or another, but personally I've never been in a winning loft that didn't take preventive measures.

When you do visit other fanciers, are you able to pick out their best pigeons?
Yes, though not necessarily their very best bird. One thing I would add is this: when you go elsewhere you always see something you think you haven't got. You know, the grass is always greener. But it isn't necessarily so, they might just keep their birds in a better way than you do.

Describe your approach to the sport?
Very laid back. I'm definitely not a fanatic. No, definitely not. There are more things in life than pigeons.

Would you say you've embraced modern racing methods?
Yes, but not with both arms.

What are your thoughts on eye-sign?
I'm very interested in it and I've got my own thoughts on what is a good eye. Vitality. An eye has to speak vitality and has to be pronounced in colour. It's very difficult, though, to put into words what I look for.

Try anyway?
Okay, let's say that I like an eye that looks like a full moon on a cold winter's night.

Please go on.
I've never had a good pigeon that had eyes like two domes stuck on its head. I don't like to see bulging eyes, but then again, I don't like to see flat eyes either. For breeding, I like a full circle with a serrated edge all the way round, but the colour of the sign depends on the colour of the eye. With a pearl eye it should not be as dark as the pupil. I prefer gravel eyes and, indeed, most of my birds have them. This means I have to pair the same eye colour together quite often, so if I find the eye getting weaker I try to pair to a nut brown in the next generation to bring back the vitality. I also like small pupils, but the most important thing, in my opinion, is the outer ring of the eye. It should look like a bicycle tyre. I can't say I've ever had a good breeder that didn't have this.

What about egg-shaped pupils?
I think that if you looked more closely, you'd find that, although they looked egg-shaped, they are in fact round. Remember, the eye is the pigeon's telescope and, as we all know, telescopes are round.

What do you look for in a racing eye?
There are so many different sorts of eye for racing, so I go for vitality above all else. Yellow eyes, for example, I find very deceiving. I had one particular pigeon that showed absolutely nothing in its eye and yet it won a couple of races. Whether racing or breeding, though, I've never had a pigeon that had good feather, good bone, strong constitution and a good clean throat, that didn't also have a good eye.

Do you breed from birds that haven't won?
Yes, because I don't subscribe to the view that you should only breed from winners. I'm always trying a pair I fancy. In my lifetime, I've had three pigeons that were completely useless as racers, but which turned out to be absolute goldmines when it came to breed-

ing. If I'd judged them on performance, I'd have culled them. Knowing which to breed from is where stockmanship comes in.

If you had to give yourself a score out of ten as a stockman, what would it be?
Nine.

And as a racing man?
Eight.

What stops you from scoring a ten in either instance?
I never have sufficient time and, because I don't visit many lofts, I don't handle enough good pigeons.

You mentioned the throat earlier. Can you say a little more?
Yes, Frank Tasker's throat theory is right. I never keep a bird with a dark grey tongue because they are no good. Don't ask me the reason why, all I know is that I've never had a good one. Also, a pigeon with a good constitution should have a pink to red throat. If it's pale pink, it just means the bird is out of condition. You can bring a pigeon round that has a white or grey throat, but a dark grey throat never changes and a bird with such is no good.

What about the cleft in the throat?
I've watched this. I've always found that a narrow slit that tapers away towards nothing at the back shows a bird in peak form. I don't like to see the cleft wide open as, to me, it means the bird is overweight and gasping for air.

What else don't you like to see?
I hate flat-headed pigeons and I've never had a good one. They don't have any brains.

What else shows condition?
The skin around the keel should be clean, sticky and scale-free. For most of the year, pigeons have scale on the skin and the only way to get rid of it is by bringing them into condition.

How often do you pick the right pool pigeon?
Because you can't predict the conditions on race day, about fifty per cent of the time. I'd say I manage to have my pool pigeon in the first three arrivals about eighty per cent of the time. You have to know your pigeons.

How do you condition a bird?
I fly mostly natural and treat the birds as a team. Each comes into condition in its own time. This year, for a change, I switched the birds onto widowhood half-way through

the season, with good results. I thought the pigeons were sent fitter, did the distance better and came back fitter. This year, I also flagged my old birds for the first time. I flagged for thirty minutes at a time and supplemented this with a thirty mile chuck in mid-week whenever it was possible.

What do you feed your old birds?
A high protein mix for rearing and leading into the first two races. Then I gradually switch over on a weekly basis, working from Sunday to Friday. On Sunday they get a breakdown mix, more or less all the way through the season. Monday and Tuesday I feed a high protein mix, and Wednesday to Friday a high carbohydrate one. I use *Natural* grains; *Depurative* Sunday, *Liège* Monday to Tuesday and *Widowhood Natural* Wednesday and Thursday.

Do you measure the feed?
Yes. They get a good ounce on Sunday, fed through the day, a good ounce on Monday and Tuesday, fed morning and evening, a dead ounce on Wednesday and Thursday and, on Friday, half an ounce only, fed at 8.00 am. Throughout the week, I also feed a very small amount of *Hormoform*. A 15lb bag lasts me six weeks. And for trapping only I use a canary seed mix.

What do you add to the water?
I've used *Johnson's Tonic* on a Tuesday for thirty years, following the recommended dosage. They also have molasses when they come back from a race.

What do you feed them on return from a race?
A very light feed of depurative. They stay on that until Monday.

Describe your feeding methods for youngsters?
When rearing, I feed the old birds as much as they can eat twice a day. I don't use the hopper and never leave food in the loft overnight because it encourages vermin. Once weaned, they are fed peas until they start to fly out morning and night. Then they have depurative in the morning and I restrict the peas at night to make sure I can get them in next day before I go to work. I feed until one or two start going to the drinker. I've never had a greedy pigeon that was any good. They are fed like this until the second race, by which time they know what their job is. Then I feed them the same as the old birds.

Can you see any drawbacks to the way you feed?
Yes, I'm too generous, if anything. Pigeons can be very deceiving, making you think they're hungry when they're not. It's critical to get the balance right.

What do you look for as regards young bird performances?

Consistency and real triers. It doesn't matter if they don't win. If they're four or five hours behind I don't mind, as long as they've tried. I let them make as many mistakes as they want, but one type I won't tolerate is the pigeon that repeatedly goes over the top and comes back on Sunday. My young birds are taught to race from a very early age. For the first few chucks, they go up with the old birds and that way they don't wander too much. I want them to get used to homing quickly, not roaming the countryside, and when they return it's a case of 'down and in'. They are trained to race and, consequently, they race to win. I don't think they ever forget this lesson.

Do you add anything else to the young bird diet?
I like to play with my youngsters a lot so I tease them with a handful of peanuts every day. They have to fight for them out of my hand on the floor of the loft. I don't feed them on their perches because I haven't got the patience.

How many of the birds you breed make the grade?
I rear about twenty-four youngsters and expect three or four of those to make up into good, winning pigeons.

What sort of pigeon succeeds in the Northampton Town and District Fed?
For the distance, an individual. The short races can be a bit of a lottery because, being such a big, well-spread fed, the wind plays an important part.

How would you describe the sport in Northamptonshire?
It's a very hard area to fly to whether you race north or south. Many fanciers who have left and raced elsewhere have done well, but fanciers coming in from other areas have often struggled. I regret the lack of opportunities to compete in other programmes. There are no two-bird or mid-week clubs and only a couple of open races. As far as racing with the NRCC or the MCC, I think if more fanciers from this area competed we'd do better. At the moment we send only a few and our birds are having to break very early to stand any chance of success.

Do you buy pigeons?
Rarely. The most I've paid is £50 and the best pigeon I've ever bought was a blue pied Warrington cock that cost just £3. He bred a lot of winners.

Do you sell pigeons?
No. I'd rather give them away. I don't believe in selling and I think it's killing the sport.

Have you ever worked out what it costs you to keep pigeons?
Does it really matter?

Who do you rate as the best local fanciers?
In the club, our secretary, Graham Groom, and in the Northants Fed, Barry Andrews.
They are two very dedicated fanciers.

Of the fanciers you've visited, whose set-up struck you as the best?
I was particularly impressed by Alan Corbett's loft in St Helens. Alan struck me as a
genuine, working man's pigeon fancier and his pigeons were so contented that after a
couple of minutes they acted as if there was no one in the loft.

What strains do you keep?
A sprinkling of Barkers from the late H Manning of Brixworth, but mostly Janssens
and Busschaerts. The Janssens are Pickering Janssens through Graham Groom and the
Busschaerts are the very best of Jimmy Hampson's Billy Parkes pigeons.

Which is the best bird you have raced?
A blue pied hen, '999', which won Thurso three years on the trot.

And the best bird you have bred?
'Barmy', raced by my good friend Graham Groom. In all, he won twenty-four individual firsts.

Which book or video have you learnt most from?
I've learnt little from the books on the market, and I would say the video I've learnt
most from is the *Best of British* one featuring Frank Tasker and Geoff Kirkland.

What are your short and long-term ambitions?
In the short term, to do better. In the long term, to stay in the sport. It's becoming
harder because of cost and time. I'm concerned, too, about the diminishing number of
fanciers.

Which aspects of the sport do you most enjoy?
The social side and the friendship, and seeing a bird home from the distance. When
you get a lump in your throat, or tears in your eyes even, that, to me, is the beginning
and end of pigeon racing. It's why I race.

BARCELONA INTERNATIONAL 1995

20,900 birds liberated July 7th at 07.20 hrs

BICC Result
58 members sent 197 birds

Pos	Name	Location	Dist	Vel
1	W Aherne	Neasden	709	911
2	M/M WJ Bradford	Sutton	696	908
3	M/M K Hine	Hayes	709	759
4	Lyden Bros	Sandwich	681	563
5	D Coulter	Worthing	633	540
6	G Townsend & Son	St Mary Cray	695	538
7	S&D Jordan	Canterbury	684	505
8	S&W Knox	Canterbury	685	503
9	G Hunt & Son	Westmarsh	684	501
10	G Hunt & Son	Westmarsh	684	486
11	G Hunt & Son	Westmarsh	684	475
12	P Delea	Rainham	703	442
13	J Emerton	York	879	435
14	G Hunt & Son	Westmarsh	684	355
15	G Hunt & Son	Westmarsh	684	321
16	G Hunt & Son	Westmarsh	684	318
17	B Williams	Westmarsh	684	286
18	Lyden Bros	Sandwich	681	277
19	R Clarke	Clyffe Pypard	721	264
20	R Clarke	Clyffe Pypard	721	246
21	Shepherd & Buckley	Chichester	667	236
22	P Stone	West Drayton	707	225
23	P Delea	Rainham	703	224
24	R Clarke	Clyffe Pypard	721	223
25	R Clarke	Clyffe Pypard	721	222

JOE BRADFORD

Back in the autumn of 1978, when his birds were heavy in the moult, Joe Bradford would come out of his loft and feel a pain in the centre of his chest for half an hour or so. Fearing he was suffering from pigeon lung, he made a concerted effort to cut down his numbers and so occurred the disbandment of a quite exceptional team of distance birds. Today, with his problem having eased to next to nothing - he now only needs to wear a mask when cleaning out - he has begun to wonder if that was what the problem really was. The last few years have seen him trying to rebuild a team on a par with his performers of yesteryear. By all accounts, he has not found it easy, but then, when your sole aim is 700-mile racing, you are restarting virtually from scratch and only keep twelve pairs, it is never going to be anything but difficult. The following conversation took place prior to the Barcelona International of 1995, in which he was to take 2nd British section with his gallant four-year-old chequer hen, now named 'Little Conchita'.

What got you interested in distance racing?
A wonderful hen, Skone and Everall's 'Champion Jendy'. When I was in the Army in Germany in 1957 my mother would send me copies of *The Racing Pigeon* and I read of 'Jendy's' exploits from Pau. From an early liberation and flying 660 miles up into Shrewsbury, she beat the second bird, which was flying 140 miles less, out of sight. And, in winning, she beat two of the best pigeons I think ever to fly in the national, 'Cosham Success', who scored five times and 'Twilight', the Pau National winner who scored four times. 'Jendy' was, in my opinion, the best Pau National winner, and she converted me to 700-mile racing. On being demobbed I set my stall out for the long ones from Palamos and Barcelona with the British Barcelona Club and the British International Championship Club. And today, I also race from Pau. Not with the National Flying Club, but the London and South East Classic as they have an early lib and get birds back on the day.

Why don't you fly Pau with the National Flying Club?
Because no one will convince me that a mid-day lib leads to a fair race. It plays into the hands of the widowhood men and the sprinting-type pigeon. After all, most pigeons should be able to fly seven to eight hours and, with a rest, fly another seven or more. How many pigeons, though, can fly fourteen or more hours? Like me, I bet most fanciers can count them on one hand. With a mid-day lib the best bird does not necessarily win. After all, they don't go down together and I'm damn sure they don't all get up at the same time. Plus you lose time with the hours of darkness, with our clocks being one hour different to the French. It doesn't stay light till 10 o'clock in France. If they had

asked Red Rum to run two miles of the Grand National one day and two miles the next, he would never have won three nationals. No, the only way to find a true winner is with an early morning lib as then the best pigeon, put down in the best condition, will win.

Do you think there is any danger of birds being caught in the channel at nightfall?
No. I don't think they are that silly. If they don't get there early enough they won't cross.

I know one or two people are put off joining the LSECC because for Pau they mark Wednesday for a Friday lib. Where do you stand?
I must admit that I would sooner they had another day in the basket because I think one of the things which causes most problems is not giving birds time to rest and orientate. I know that when I've been training in a hurry and I've let my birds go after two minutes they've taken an age to strike for home, but when I've given them twenty minutes to orientate I haven't seen them. They don't even circle. The LSECC has managed a number of day birds from Pau, but even so I remain sceptical.

In your experience, is success at the distance more down to the pigeon or the man?
A bad fancier can muck up a good pigeon, so the man plays his part, but I would put it at seventy-five per cent the pigeon and its *origin*. I don't care how good the man is, without the right pigeon he won't win.

With placing such emphasis on origin where did you go to obtain what became the base of your old Barcelona and Palamos team?
Mainly to Joe E Shore of Northwich and to Frank Cheetham of Pontefract. I bought eight from Mr Shore and six from Mr Cheetham, with the pair that bred nearly all my best pigeons coming from the former. I paired them together because when I looked at their pedigrees I noticed they both had the same outstanding blue hen close up. Her ring number was NU66P47506 and she had won 13th and 251st open NFC Nantes. The sire of my Spanish Diploma winner, 'Jubilee Lady', 1st, 21st and 141st open Palamos, was all Joe Shore as was my four-times Palamos cock, 'Lucky Lad'. He also won a Spanish Diploma and got his name because he was twice shot and once came home from Palamos with his rump torn open. The nestmate to the sire of 'Jubilee Lady' was herself 2nd and 4th Barcelona with the BICC. You wouldn't have given tuppence for her, but a son out of her when paired to a daughter of Frank Cheetham's 'Blue Pearl', four times Pau, 708 miles, produced a lot of good birds. A little later I also bought a son of Tom Gilbertson's 'Boney M', 1st Anglo-Scottish Border Amal 1979, sixteen hours on the wing. This cock bred a cock to fly Lerwick for me at my first attempt, flying 609 miles on the day after fourteen hours and forty minutes on the wing. His nestmate, paired to a daughter of the 2nd and 4th Barcelona hen, produced a blue cock I sold to Tony Tyerman which figured prominently in the breeding of his Barcelona winner. My red cock, which was 2nd open Palamos, was bred by the late Ernie Parker of Sutton,

from his good Clayton Gits family, which flew from Palamos in the south and Lerwick in the north.

How much of this blood remains in your loft today?
I still have a grandson of 'Lucky Lad', but he is the only surviving link. 'Lucky Lad' had a tumour on his leg and I put him down, and the others I sold or gave away in an effort to cut my numbers down, including all the best ones. I didn't want to part with anything but the best just in case people didn't like the birds I sent them. And to this day, I don't like selling pigeons because I don't want to upset people.

You say that you have struggled to find birds as good as your old family. Do you think that is because there are fewer good distance pigeons around today?
Yes.

Why might that be?
Two reasons. Firstly, because of all the rubbish that goes into pigeons these days - it has weakened their constitution. And secondly, because we have imported too many birds. For years we brought in Belgian birds and then, when we began to get fed up with them, we turned to the Dutch. You only have to look at those countries to see that they are as flat as a pancake so they should be able to get birds at 700 miles. I remember Maurice Henrotin of Belgium writing in *Squills* as long ago as 1970 of how the Belgians were paying for their widowhood system, racing youngsters on it and breeding from untried hens that had been locked up for eight months of the year. They go 'rustic'. And I fully agree with what he said. I'm sure all this breaking pigeons down must weaken their constitution - one hard race and they are finished. Frank Cheetham and Joe Shore used to have pigeons that had flown 700 miles three and four times, but there are not many pigeons or fanciers about who can do that today. Indeed, nowadays three out of four pigeons only have to hit one hard race and they go down. You only have to look what happened the last time the NFC had an early lib at Pau - only 260 birds made it on the day.

I assume you haven't considered flying widowhood, then?
Not at all. I only know one way - natural. For me, hens are too valuable to waste. They are the ones that often come late at night because it is they who would normally be sitting at that time.

Which birds are you now trying to climb back with?
Mainly 'Misty Lady' and 'Workman' lines. I've had one or two pigeons from Tony Tyerman, including a daughter of 'Misty Lady', and two daughters of the late Ernie Parker of Sutton's 'Double Dax Hen'. The interesting story about these pigeons is that when the dam of my four-times Palamos cock went on her legs I asked Ernie to kill her for me. He asked if he could try and get a pair of youngsters out of her first. Anyway,

he paired her to a Clayton Gits cock and they produced a mealy hen which became the grandam of his 'Double Dax Hen'.

In your search for those elusive 700 milers, what sort of bird are you looking for?
I think the only way to produce 700 milers is to breed off pigeons which have flown fourteen or fifteen hours on the day, not two-day pigeons. Beyond this I'm looking for an individual. A pigeon that can get away and fly on its own.

Does singling up make a pigeon into an individual?
I believe it certainly helps, so if they are flying freely round home I will single up my youngsters from twenty miles on the first toss. If you take them far enough they won't mess about and you'll soon get rid of the duffers. I don't agree with people who say that single tossing slows pigeons down.

How many good birds do you expect to breed?
I remember the racehorse trainer, Cecil Boyd-Rochford, saying that, for every 2,000 horses bred, perhaps as few as 200 ever reached a racecourse. In the same vein, the late, great TA Warrington reckoned that if you bred a hundred young birds and got five good ones you would have done well and I think he was spot on. I breed twenty young birds so if I get one or two I am happy, even though I am careful what I take youngsters out of. I only breed off old pigeons so long as their youngsters are robust, and then I rear their offspring under younger pigeons, and I don't breed off prisoners. To increase my chances further, I like to see winners in the pedigree no more than two away from the champion. If I have an outstanding bird, I use it as my stud pigeon and breed around it. If it's a cock I pair it to several hens and then mate the resulting half-brothers and half-sisters (this was how my 2nd open Palamos cock was bred), testing them all the time. At the third generation I like to pair back to the grandparent.

How many youngsters do you take off your race birds?
In the years I was doing particularly well, only two a year off any pair, including my Palamos winner, but nowadays I float the first round eggs from my best performers. Although I only keep twelve pairs, I don't breed off everything because I believe there are only a limited number of pigeons capable of producing winners. Most can't, including plenty of those that have won themselves. The best pigeon I have ever owned was bred from yearlings so I also like to take a pair out of yearlings if I have any good ones. This way I find my breeders early.

Do you feed any supplements when breeding?
Only groats, of which I use a lot. First, I soak them in molasses, dry them off with glucose powder, then add cod liver oil and dry this off with *Old Hand*'s *Calcium Powder*, which I swear by. I keep it in the fridge as I've found that in the summer it goes off.

What do you regard as the single most important grain for distance racing?
The bean, because if you want to build a pigeon up for 700 miles it must have protein.
When it comes to the crunch it is beans that count. For this reason, I always feed beans
only, by the hopper, with groats soaked in cod liver oil plus a little wheat and linseed
given by hand. I know some people say beans make their birds sluggish, but mine
exercise very well.

Why don't you hopper feed this mix?
Because pigeons eat to their individual taste and they wouldn't be getting what I wanted
them to have. This is one reason why I don't feed maize. The other reason is that you
have to be careful with maize. With being a germ corn it can become 'mustardy' and
knock them off form. Incidentally, as long as corn is sound I am not bothered if it is
polished or not.

Do you put anything in the water?
The only thing I use is *Johnson's Tonic*, which I swear by, every Sunday. I have tried
garlic as well, but basically I like to keep as close to nature as I can. For that reason I've
never treated my pigeons for canker, coccidiosis, worms or respiratory disease. It even
grieves me having to vaccinate and I do so only under protest. There are not enough
hours in the day to give your pigeons all the things people say they are supposed to have
and, anyway, if you play around with Mother Nature you are sure to get your fingers
burnt.

Have you ever had birds with canker or cocci?
I've had occasional young birds with cocci, but it is a minor thing to my way of think-
ing. And as for canker, well, I've never had it in the loft so it really surprised me when
I read that all pigeons carry it.

Do you have your birds tested?
No.

If you did and they were showing a high canker count, would you then treat?
No, I would clear out any bird with canker.

Do you ever treat sick pigeons?
No. If one is off colour and doesn't pick up within forty-eight hours I dispose of it. If
you want to win at 700 miles, which is all I do want to win at, you can't doctor pigeons.
None of my 700-mile birds ever had a day's illness in their lives.

With being on 'open hole', do sparrows cause you any problems?
No, because I have overcome any potential problems by using a plastic bucket as my
drinker. I was told years ago that sparrows will not drink out of anything which they

can't see behind and it's true. The bucket I use has six two-inch square holes around the side, five inches from the base. With putting a lid on it as well, it not only keeps the sparrows out but the dust and dirt, too. In my opinion, nearly all disease starts through the drinker so I change the water as often as possible, perhaps up to five times a day when I am breeding.

Is it really necessary to keep sparrows out, as many successful lofts on 'open hole' are host to them?
If they've got just normal drinking fountains perhaps that's why they have to treat!

What happens, then, when your birds are exposed to foul water and pigeons which are sickening in the race-basket?
I find it hard to believe that you will find a sick pigeon when you mark for Barcelona or Palamos, and likewise the members in the LSECC know what they are about, too. This is one of the reasons why I race almost solely in specialist clubs. It cuts down the risk.

As your aim is to get birds to 700 miles with the requisite experience behind them, what do you ask of your youngsters and yearlings?
Although I do like to send a few to Guernsey with the LSECC, in the last few years, since there have been a lot of losses, I have mainly only trained my young birds to the coast, with quite a few single-up tosses. I like to train off the line of flight. It makes them think and puts them right mentally. My yearlings are also nursed along, but all must fly my local club's longest race, which at the moment is Bordeaux, 450 miles. They have one short channel race four or five weeks before this, and ideally I like them to fly between eight and ten hours as I've found it puts them right both physically and mentally.

How much training do your yearlings have before their first race which, as you said, is a channel race?
Not a lot because I don't believe basket experience is that important, really. I pair up in the middle of March and, after my yearlings have finished rearing their young birds, I like to give them a week's rest before I start to train them. I have a grilled front to my young bird loft and I find that some are still trying to feed their youngsters. Their minds are not on the job and you can sometimes lose them. I prefer to wait for them to be sitting properly again and for the sun to be on their backs and I won't train them if there is a cold north-east wind blowing. I go carefully with them and then, a fortnight before Nantes, I give them some coastal tosses. With having an open loft they are reasonably fit anyway and I don't work them any harder because I don't want them to be ready in early June. I'm not really worried about being behind, I am more concerned with hours on the wing. When they return from Nantes I then leave them to go down on eggs again and give them some more coastal tosses, the last one being on the Sunday before the big race to put them right. Using this method I had ten out of twelve on the

day from a hard Nantes and then had four of them on the result from La Reole, including one on the day flying fourteen hours. Most of my best pigeons have flown the longest channel race as yearlings. In fact, 'Lucky Lad' did so with a velocity of 641ypm.

When do your birds first go to Palamos or Barcelona?
Usually when they are three, although 'Lucky Lad' went for the first time as a two-year-old. I believe he was the first pigeon to fly Palamos three times on the winning day. (Up Friday, home Saturday, winning 41st, 33rd and 3rd open and a Spanish Diploma).

And is one long race per bird per season sufficient for you?
Yes. If you go to the well once too often and the pigeon has a hard knock its constitution takes a whacking. Not only can it be spoilt for racing, but also for breeding.

Is that equally true of cocks?
It's especially true of cocks as I believe it makes them become sterile more quickly. I remember a chap saying to me after I had a cock take four and a half days from Palamos at my first attempt that it would breed me nothing the following year, and he was right. I lost both his youngsters off the loft and he never bred me a light after that. Some birds just don't make up again.

What do you feed on return from a race?
Small corn, consisting of coarse oatmeal, groats soaked in cod liver oil and a little wheat.

Do you also lightly race your Palamos and Barcelona candidates?
Yes. I never over-work any of my pigeons. As with my yearlings, I like my long distance birds to have a race four or five weeks before the big one, again, ideally a fly of between eight and ten hours. I train them after that according to how hard a fly they have had. I do not want my birds on form for this prep race as, in my experience, June winners never go on to win at 700 miles in July, but the interesting thing is, you can tell within two or three days of their returning from this prep race whether or not they will do any good in the long one. My Palamos winner had a night out from a hard Rennes race so I shut her up in her nest box for four days to rest her and build her up again. She had two tosses from the coast and then went on to win Palamos by over four hours.

Do you ever flag them?
When I raced with my father in the fifties and early sixties we flagged our pigeons for about two and a half hours a day and we won more than our fair share at the distance. Nowadays I have an open loft and train them if I think they need it. Incidentally, although I have an open loft my birds have never gone fielding.

How much weight should they be carrying for 700 miles?

I recall a good flyer once saying that the trouble with a lot of fanciers is that they send their pigeons with too much meat on them, thinking they'll fly it off, and he was right. You have only to compare a marathon runner to a sprinter to see his point. It is the same with pigeons. I used to send them heavy and indeed it wasn't until I was 2nd open Palamos that I realised the error of my ways. He was sent very light and came home exactly the same.

Won't they put on weight in the basket?
People may say that but I don't think a fit pigeon will eat much. It will just pick at a little bit.

How should a bird handle?
The best thing I can compare it to is the feel of a tennis ball in your hand - if you can imagine it with a head and tail. Not only should they be like that when they go but also when they come back, as fit pigeons don't lose much weight - even at 700 miles.

Do you play any tricks?
For the longer channel races I may put either a chicken egg or a cluster of eggs under a pair. It works, but only once. You can't repeat it.

How do you know when a bird is right?
To recognise form you must study your birds. I spend a lot of time just watching them and they tell me in different ways. For example, when I took 'Lucky Lad' training he would clap his wings four or five times on release, whereas, when he was right, my 2nd open Palamos cock would dart out of his nest box whenever I walked into the shed. He was not alone in having this trait either, as, when paired, my pigeons always keep a watch on me and this is something I like. When unpaired, they also go away from me - even the hens (I've never had one that's shown to me) - so you can see they are not tame pigeons. But they are not wild either.

Have you tried making them tamer?
No, as I think tame pigeons are more liable to go in when tired. I don't even talk to my pigeons other than to call them in.

Do you look at the state of the wing?
No. As long as a pigeon is moulting normally I never worry. I think you can get bogged down in too many theories. It's not theories that win races, but good pigeons.

What is your ideal type?
All my best racers have been different types, either small, long cast, pin-headed or whatever. Consequently, I don't condemn pigeons on type, although I would say that I prefer small to medium sized cocks to large ones because they recover better from a

knock. Many big pigeons will only take one hard race.

Is there any type of bird you won't tolerate?
Yes, grunters and wet feeders. Neither have any place in my loft. Grunters are always on edge and unsettle the others and wet feeding is a sign of weakness.

Are you a good judge of a pigeon?
I wouldn't say I was brilliant but I'd be confident that, given a choice of birds, I'd choose the right one. I've picked out some good birds in my time.

What do you think of eye-sign?
To me it's a farce. The hen that bred 'Lucky Lad', the sire of my Palamos winner, my hen that was 2nd and 4th Barcelona (who was not very good-looking either) and a few others, had just a plain yellow eye.

Would you let an eye-sign man come into your loft and take away what he thought was your best pigeon?
I've already had one come, and if I'd listened to him I would have killed all my pigeons. I handed him a bird that had bred winners from Poitiers and Bordeaux. He looked at its eye and told me it was no good and then, after I told him what it had bred, he said it must have been paired with a good hen.

Have you any quirks?
Well, I always powder the tips of their tails with *Johnson's Insect Powder* when they go to a race, as I was once told that most lice get from bird to bird via the tail. I actually think the lice problem is one of the most important aspects of pigeon racing. Lousy pigeons won't win as they can never rest properly. I check them for lice once a week and, when they're sitting, I spray *Duramitex* round the nest bowls. I also use powder in the nest bowl, mixing it with a bed of shavings.

What do you use for nesting material?
I do as the wood pigeon does, I use birch twigs. They make the nest more airy and give the youngsters something to grip. I don't like straw because it gets damp and soggy.

Do you put disinfectant or anything else in the bath water?
No, as I don't want them drinking anything. I like to use rain water if I can.

That's interesting. I heard a fancier saying only recently that rain water, because it contains impurities, knocks pigeons off form.
Well, all I can tell you is that there's a chap near here who has always flown well and his birds have never seen tap water in their lives. He collects rain water in a bucket which has a filter on top and gives them that instead.

When do you give the bath?
On Sundays, when racing. In the close season they bath inside the loft as I don't let my birds out from the end of September until the following January.

Why not?
Because I had such a good season after doing it for the first time I thought I'd better make a practice of it. I believe it stops winter form. Incidentally, although my birds are hopper fed throughout this time I don't seem to have much trouble keeping the fat off them. Indeed, six days after I let them out the following January they fly for forty-five minutes.

Would you describe your loft?
Firstly, I built it myself. It is L-shaped in design, has louvres at the front, back and sides, a grill front to keep the sparrows out when it is closed and two windows in the roof for more light to get in. I also have a twelve-foot high fence on one side, with a door in it, with hanging wire around the shed so no cats can get in. It is very open, with plenty of air flowing through and sometimes it gets a bit wet. I think the deep-litter system is very good, but I'm a scraper man myself. If there is any trouble, you see it more quickly.

Are there any dos and don'ts that you would say to a novice?
Yes. Never send a hen training or to a race when in egg or for three days afterwards. A hen will only lay so many eggs and by abusing her, she will lay even fewer. Never over-race your birds. Don't overcrowd your loft - I have twenty-one nest boxes but only keep twelve pairs. Don't keep chopping and changing your methods because pigeons are creatures of habit. Try to keep as near to Mother Nature as you can and always give the bird the benefit of the doubt.

Has the sport changed for the worse over the years you've been involved?
Yes. There is now too much infighting, causing a 'them and us' situation. The comradeship has gone.

Do you like having visitors in your loft?
Not really. When I won Palamos I had loads of people in the loft and I sometimes wonder if that was one of the reasons for my downfall.

'Jubilee Lady'
1st club, 2nd fed Seaton
467th open NFC Pau
143rd open Palamos vel 277
21st open Palamos vel 544
1st open Palamos vel 843
RNHU Gold Medal and
Spanish Diploma winner.

Red Cock
2nd section, 2nd open Palamos vel 856
Bred by E Parker, Sutton.
Raced by Mr & Mrs WJ Bradford.

'Lucky Lad'
4th club Bergerac vel 644
19th section, 169th open Palamos
4th section, 44th open Palamos vel 836
11th section, 33rd open Palamos vel 731
1st section, 3rd open Palamos vel 679
RNHU Gold Medal and
Spanish Diploma winner.

Bobby Adair and his son, Martin.

BOBBY ADAIR

Bobby Adair and his sons, Martin and David, keep in their home a replica of what is known, simply, as the Big Cup. The original, which is solid silver, is valued at £22,000 and stays in a bank vault. It is awarded to the winners of the Derwent Valley Federation's Combined Averages and in its entire history only three fanciers have won it twice. Adair and Sons have won it nine times and, what's more, they have been runners-up on two other occasions. They have done this with a team which, for many years, seldom numbered more than twenty-eight old birds and thirty youngsters. And they have done it with their own, enduring family of birds, flying to what has often been described as one of the last outposts of England.

Bobby, yours is clearly a loft of all rounders, so would you give me an idea of the programme your birds face?
We race our birds with Flimby Homing Society which is affiliated to the Derwent Valley Fed and the Cumbria Combine, and also compete in the Cumberland Social Circle, a specialist club. The federation programme consists of nine old bird inland races of between 65 and 288 miles, along with five channel races of between 425 and 525 miles, and for the young birds, nine inland races up to 200 miles. All these races count for club and fed averages, whereas the combine races are the longer old bird and young bird races only. These usually form the CSC programme, too.

Do you fly natural or widowhood and which races do you concentrate on?
I race entirely natural and, although I win my share from all distances, I mainly concentrate on the long ones.

What breed do you fly?
I'm often asked that - it's a fashionable question - and I always reply with the same answer - 'Loxleys', explaining that is from whom I purchased my baskets. I keep putting the pigeons into them and those that return the quickest, I keep. If pressed further, I say Vandy and Dr Anderson Bricoux. I have blended both these breeds into my own family, and they have gone on for more years than I care to remember.

From where did they originate?
The former are the bloodlines of Bill Heatley and Alf Robinson, mainly from my life-long friend George Gorley, and the Bricoux came via Dr Anderson and Tommy Buck.

Which were the key pigeons?

Two mealy cocks, both bred in the same year, 1972.

Could you tell me a little more about them?
They were both Vandy/Bricoux, although unrelated. One of them won an RNHU award as a young bird, scored again as a yearling and was then 5th fed at Avranches as a two-year-old. The interesting thing about him was that when he was 'right' he used to dance, prance might be a better word, on his perch. He did this the week before Avranches, so I took the risk of sending him to Lymington and he topped the fed. Three weeks after Avranches I sent him to Rennes with the Cumberland Social Circle and he won that, too. In all, he won twelve races and I bred out of him until a peregrine took him when he was sixteen years old. The other mealy cock flew the channel fourteen times. Although he never actually won the fed, he was on the fed sheet thirteen times and the only time he didn't score, he came back shot.

How important did these two mealy cocks prove to be?
Very. They formed the two branches of my present-day team. I built a family around both, keeping the line separate, and then used descendants of each as a cross for the other. To this day, each time I breed a really good bird, I start the process all over again, inbreeding and line-breeding round it. The first thing I do, if it's a hen, is put it to two different cocks in the same season. The following year, I mate together half-brother and half-sister (my favourite mating) and then pair the best cock from these back to the original hen.

One of the original mealy cocks referred to in the text.

Do you race these birds just the same?
Oh yes. All my birds race, with the exception of the odd cross I bring in. I am ruthless when it comes to testing pigeons. You have to be.

What do you expect of your birds?
Always providing they are fit, my youngsters fly 200 miles, my yearlings fly the coast, 288 miles, and my two-year-olds fly the channel. Sometimes they go over the water twice and if they have not scored at this age they are not retained. I should say that unless a bird is particularly fit, it never goes to the coast again after the yearling stage because a 300-mile race is just too far prior to the channel.

How many youngsters do you have left at the end of the programme?
Last year, I started with twenty-nine and ended up with twenty. I've done better than that in previous years, but we had a couple of particularly hard races.

At what age does your family peak?
They should be at their best at three. And I expect them to prove it by performing well in the longer channel races.

Have you introduced any outside crosses?
Only in latter years and then only one or two. From 1965 to 1981 I didn't have another breed in the loft at all. Each time I bring in a cross I go to another closely-bred family but then, having used it for a while for a bit of hybrid vigour, I prefer to breed it out again.

Why did you seek a cross?
I thought one or two of my cocks were showing the first sign of looking a little henny, which indicated to me that a slight deterioration was beginning to set in.

Which pigeons have you introduced?
At the moment, I am trying a double-granddaughter of 'Scottish Lady' from my friend, Michael Spencer, of Barnoldswick. Both the youngsters to have come off her scored well as young birds and if they continue to do okay, they'll stay. And I've also exchanged a pigeon with Alfons Bauwens, whom I met at the Blackpool Show. I have two off it, one of which came from Rennes last year to take 3rd fed. The important thing when bringing in a cross is only to use birds bred from pigeons that have won at your required distance and the nearer you can get to the original performers, the better. Of course, there are exceptions to all rules, but don't rely too much on them.

Are these introductions similar in type to your own family?
If anything they are a little shorter cast than mine. Other than that it's difficult to say how else they differ, but people who come to my loft do tend to notice them as being different.

Have these crosses altered your type?
No. In both instances, they are breeding to my type. It's just as well because if they weren't, I'd be a little bit bothered.

How many birds do you house?
I've now crept up to about forty, but most of my success has been achieved when keeping only twenty-eight pigeons. I might add, though, that even forty is approximately half, or in some cases, much less than half, of the number kept by many of my rivals.

What do you take into consideration when selecting your matings?
I use my natural instincts and pair together those pigeons which I visualise will breed the type I am always looking for. Having said that, as most of my birds are related, it doesn't matter too much what I pair with what.

How many good pigeons do you expect to breed?
Not many, perhaps two each season. If you can do that you will always be at the top.

Is there any benefit in single rearing youngsters?
I wouldn't say so. The only difference I've noticed is that, whereas double-reared youngsters often have creases on the their first two primaries, single-reared youngsters don't. But it doesn't matter, as they moult them out.

Cheq Cock
1st Cumbria Combine Rennes

Why do youngsters have these creases?
I think it's probably because the parents don't cover two as tightly as they cover one.

Do you sell any youngsters?
Usually only about six late-breds each year. I could sell many more, but I do not believe in sapping my birds' strength by overbreeding.

Are you happy breeding off old pigeons?
Yes, but their offspring must be reared under young feeders. Actually, the best pigeon I have had in recent years was bred from a twelve-year-old hen. I'm not keen on prisoners, though, but then, as I haven't got the facilities, I haven't made a practice of keeping them.

Has a bird to win before you'll breed from it?
No, most of my birds are bred from. My criterion being that if they are not good enough to breed from, they are not good enough to keep.

Turning to diet, what do you feed during the winter?
Once the birds have grown their end flights, which is about Christmas-time, I put them on one hundred per cent barley, which I get from a local brewery. I must emphasise that the barley I use is really good and not like some of the stuff you see, which is all husk. If you were to feed one hundred per cent of that you'd end up starving your birds.

Do you give them as much as they want?
No. I like to get them really lean, so I restrict the amount, only allowing them extra if the weather happens to be really cold. It means I have to harden my heart and shut the door quickly before they come looking for more. I then steadily put them on the main mix in the three weeks before pairing up and, with this treatment, they are raring to mate.

What does your main mix consist of?
Four parts peas, four parts maize and two parts beans.

Is this any particular brand?
No. I buy it all locally, getting the merchant to mix it for me.

Is any of this corn polished?
No, but it's of no consequence. I don't think it makes much difference to the goodness of the feed whether it's polished or not. I admit it looks better to sell, but one must beware that it is not mouldy or contaminated corn that has been polished to make it saleable.

And they rear, race and moult on this mix?
Yes, although for years and years I fed just peas and maize and no beans at all. I prefer peas to beans because they are more palatable to the pigeon and easier for them to digest.

Why did you introduce beans, then?
Because I once lent a pigeon to my good friend, Ken Gardiner. Two years later I paid him a visit and the pigeon had more body on it than it had ever had when it was with me, even though it had been a good pigeon when it was here all the same. I asked him what he was feeding and he said one hundred per cent beans.

Having introduced beans yourself, do your pigeons now have more body on them?
No.

Whether you've fed just peas, or both peas and beans, have your performances differed in any way?
No. They have remained just the same.

Do you add anything to the corn?
Yes. If I consider my birds need a little more weight, which is usually only when they are rearing youngsters, for the four days following a hard or long race and for building pigeons up for channel events, I use a light dressing of *De Scheemaecker Natural Yeast*, adding it to a cod liver oil base. I mix it fresh for every feed, adding just enough drops of oil to make sure the yeast sticks to the corn. Conversely, to help get rid of internal fat and surplus weight or to make sure they don't put on any more weight, I use sunflower or safflower oil.

What else do you add to the diet?
Peanuts, but only when we are coming up to the water races. I believe I was one of the very first fanciers to feed peanuts. I give them four to six every night in the nest box and the pigeons come looking for them. I also give each bird a wheatgerm capsule every night for three weeks before its main channel race.

Why?
Because the germ in the corn has gone dead and wheatgerm puts back what they can't get out of their normal diet.

Do you feed any seed?
Very, very little, otherwise they become too advanced in the moult. Once they get past their fourth flight, they start to moult their body feathers which is obviously something you want to avoid.

How do you feed?
I hand feed twice a day when racing, giving them as much as they want.

Do you feed pellets when rearing?
I was recently asked this question on a quiz panel. A chap wanted to know what was in the little purple tin I take down to my loft twice a week. The answer is pellets. For years I didn't feed any at all, but my late friend, Bill Heatley, got me onto them. At the time he was feeding turkey grower pellets and he said 'try them and just see the difference in your youngsters'. I did, and it was as he said, so I have used them ever since.

Have you tried any pellets specifically designed for pigeons?
Yes, one or two sorts, but my preference is still for turkey pellets - the ones which have had the antibiotics removed.

What do you wean on?
One hundred per cent maple peas, twice a day in the hopper for a month. After that my youngsters go on my normal mix of peas, beans and maize.

Do you breed many late-breds?
Not many and then only off good pigeons. For example, if I am sending a really good bird over the channel, I will occasionally keep the eggs it is sitting when it goes, to compensate if I happen to lose it. I did this last year when I lost a very good bird in a disaster from Nantes.

Dark w/f Cock
1st Cumbria Combine Nantes

Have you had much success with them?
Yes.

Do you race them along with the rest of your yearlings?
No. They are trained with the following year's young birds before being put on the road as two-year-olds. I don't start them any earlier because I find that if they get a very cold north-east wind, even in training, I lose them.

Why do you think that is?
Lack of experience. Flying into this area, with its hills and fells, causes great problems for inexperienced birds. You see, although we race the south road, invariably our birds can be seen to arrive from the west and occasionally from the east. The deciding factor being the route they have taken through the Cumbrian fells, which is ruled by the wind. The nature of racing at the home end is very difficult, as the last forty miles is through the Lakeland fells. If we get a stray in here from the south, it's usually here to stay because this is a difficult area to get out of. They set off home going south, but turn around and come back when they hit the fells.

Since you're not in a rush with late-breds, do you allow them longer to prove them-selves?
Yes. Whereas I eliminate everything else that does not score by the time it is two, I wait for late-breds until they are three. Providing, of course, they have shown promise.

Dark w/f Hen
1st Derwent Valley Fed Avranches

If they fail at three, do you eliminate any offspring they may have bred?
No. I judge my pigeons on individual performance, not on what they are bred off.

Turning to hygiene and health, what are the most important factors in a well-designed loft?
To begin with dryness is a must. So is correct ventilation, although you don't want a gale blowing through. Apart from that, though, I think too much emphasis is placed on loft design. Many are built more to please the human eye. Pigeons are not proud creatures. I have seen them fly to all sorts of structures and they will continue to do so if the right environment has been created.

How do you keep on top of disease?
I regularly use my own microscope, and when I require a second opinion I call on the services of a local man who specialises in pigeon ailments.

If a bird falls ill, do you try and cure it?
That depends on what the sickness is. I don't recommend many treatments, though, as you can think they have worked, only to find later the bird will break down in times of stress.

Which products do you use?
For canker I obtain tablets from my local vet. They have the same formula as a well-known brand that sells at approximately £15 for forty, but the tablets I purchase cost ten pence each, and one tablet treats four birds. I believe this is called commercialism. For coccidiosis, I think *Sulphamethazine* is as good as anything I know of. And for worming, the new *Hoechst Panacur* tablets cause no vomiting and are most effective. Whatever the treatment, though, it is only given if and when necessary.

Do you agree with vaccination?
To a degree. Having witnessed infected lofts I simply would not take the risk of not doing it so I have had a fully-vaccinated team from day one in 1983, with no ill-effects at all. However, I would add that possibly too much importance is currently being placed on vaccination as it now seems that paramyxo is not the killer disease we once thought. It appears pretty obvious the threat to the poultry industry is nowhere near as great as was suggested originally and, consequently, their interest in the matter seems to have waned somewhat. This being so, the powers that be should endeavour on our behalf to hound the MAFF to get fewer restrictions of adherence. I think one could be forgiven for saying that too much advertising to sell the vaccine - in other words, commercialism - is milking the fancier dry and causing friction within our sport.

Is it important to eliminate lice?
Yes, and credit where credit is due, there are some good commercial products available.

Having lice is absolutely unforgivable in this day and age.

Do you treat for anything else?
Yes. If I have any respiratory problems I use *Sliepsanol* from *Malibu Grains*. This is a natural product which shows instant proof of success.

Which other products do you use?
Basically herbs, recommended to me by a chap who specialises in pigeon healthcare. On a Sunday I give a product called *Anti-Microbial Sinus Expectorant*, which helps with bronchial problems, on a Tuesday I use a nervine relaxant for stress-related conditions, and on Thursdays I use a general tonic. I also use garlic - one clove crushed in a fountain - on return from a race to guard against infection.

Do these products benefit the birds?
I don't know, although I am sure they don't do them any harm.

Changing subject, would you take me through the typical preparation you give your channel candidates?
Their preparation begins when I pair up in the middle of March. They are then trained with the rest of my team whilst on their first round of eggs and I aim for them to fly three races, the distances of which, when added together, are more or less the same as the distance of the channel event they are being prepared for. For example, they may have one race at 100 miles, another at 150 miles the week after, then a rest until being given a 250-mile race three weeks before the 500-mile race.

What nesting condition do you look for?
For the big event, I usually aim for my birds to be sitting ten to fourteen-day eggs.

When do you set them down so that they'll be in this condition?
As early as possible because it's no use breaking the cycle just three weeks before the big race. I firmly believe that birds come into form by going through the natural cycle so I take the eggs away six weeks before the big race, or even earlier if possible. That is the difference between fitness and form. You can make a pigeon fit but form comes in cycles.

What flight do you aim to get them on?
My preference is for the second flight to be half-way up. Having said that, I don't mind if it hasn't been thrown and indeed, I've even won the fed with pigeons that hadn't cast at all.

How much exercise do your birds take round home?
They are worked for up to one hour, morning and evening. I don't need to force them as

I trap to an open door and they learn when they are little to fly when the door is shut.

Do your birds field?
No, and they never have, despite the fact that I live in the open countryside. But then they have never been on 'open hole' which may contribute to the habit. I think fielding is something which they learn from one another. For example, all the pigeons at Flimby in years gone by made a habit of going to the nearby shore, but in recent years they have stopped. Could this be, one may wonder, because they know more about the emissions into the Irish Sea from Sellafield than we do?

How much muscle do your distance birds carry?
As much as I can put on them. I never prepare my pigeons for a fast race, always a hard one, and because of this I usually know I'll be thereabouts if we get a north or north-west wind on channel days.

Do you tend to be behind if it's an easy race?
No. I usually get a good one if it turns out fast, too.

Will a pigeon that has had a particularly hard channel race recover to score again?
Perhaps not in the same season, and if it had had a fifteen or sixteen hour fly I wouldn't send it again, but providing it's got the constitution, it should be as good as ever the following year. Constitution is the one big factor you can't see.

Cheq Hen
1st Derwent Valley Fed Dorchester

You can't see constitution, but what do you make of the things you can see, such as the eye, the wing and the throat?
Well, I believe that pigeons use their eye-sign to navigate to some extent, but I don't believe one type of eye is any better than another. Whilst we're on the subject, I recently had my cataracts removed. The surgeon happened to be a talkative chap so I told him about eye-sign in pigeons and the various theories put forward.

What did he make of it all?
He said there were fairies down the bottom of his garden, too!

Do you look for anything in the wing?
Yes I do. A fad of mine is that the end flight should be of equal length to the ninth. And it is also my belief that with distance pigeons, one usually finds a step from the secondaries to the primaries and up to the last four flights.

And the throat?
Let me tell you a little story. I once put a young bird in a charity sale. The purchaser, after arriving home, phoned me to say 'it has some teeth missing' (throat theory). I told him to bring it back and he could pick himself a replacement, which he did. The next day a friend visited my loft and took a fancy to the returned youngster, so I told him he could take it home with him as a gift from me. My friend had a good laugh over the charity sale incident, but not as good a laugh as when the pigeon won the fed for him as a young bird and later flew Pau to Cumbria, featuring on the result.

Red Cheq Hen
1st Derwent Valley Fed Nantes

How do you select your pool pigeons?
Actually, I must admit that recognising form and choosing pool pigeons is not my strong point. Too many pigeons have proved me wrong over the years.

Do you look at the skin around the keel to determine a bird's condition?
No, never.

What keeps a bird on the wing for fifteen hours?
The love of home and the bond with the owner, plus fitness and form. I think if you provide all these you will then get the right birds from the distance. Talking of birds flying all day, I don't know why it is but we aren't able to time as late at night now as we once could. In the past I've timed pigeons - invariably hens - up to 11.00 pm, which is when the hours of darkness rule comes into operation, but it's too dark to clock at that time nowadays.

What do you feed after a particularly hard race?
A light feed of grains and pellets, although a tired pigeon will not gorge itself whatever the food put in front of it. The most important thing is for it to rest in peace.

When do you know a pigeon has had enough and is better retired?
When it doesn't want to fly around home as fast or for as long as the others. It can be very difficult to know the right time, though, and like everybody else, I've lost good pigeons by sending them once too often.

What other mistakes have you made?
I don't know if you can call them mistakes, but I've lost some good inland pigeons, including some that had won four or five races, by sending them over the channel. You see, a lot of people around here won't send a good inland pigeon over the channel, but my policy has always been to send over anything which is two years old. My philosophy being that you will only win by sending your best pigeons.

Have you thought of having a go at the Nantes National?
Unfortunately I am situated too far north. Added to which, of course, the geography of the area into which I fly would put the birds at a disadvantage. There are too many bends. How I wish, though, that I was twenty miles further north still. That would take me over the border into Scotland, enabling me to compete in the Scottish National races.

Does the geography of your area not make inland racing something of a lottery?
To a degree, but we are allowed to use breaking points. We select a place where we know our pigeons break from and measure the distance from there to our lofts. In effect, we are measured from the racepoint to the breaking point, and from the breaking

point to the loft. It leads to a fairer race than it would otherwise, although it does mean that you can win your fed without necessarily winning your club.

What would happen if a pigeon flew over the fells rather than following the breaking points?
It wouldn't happen. Pigeons don't get above the fells.

What do you consider are the major causes of losses?
Lost pigeons are usually the rubbish that are bred from generations of untried pigeons with costly pedigrees. There are other reasons, of course, such as keeping too many pigeons in the available space within the loft, unfit pigeons for the task being asked of them, overcrowding in the transporter and the odd day when there are elements in the atmosphere we either don't know are there or don't understand. I fear widowhood, too, may play a part in losses in the distant future. At the moment, we are trading on years and years of domestic bliss which may eventually be bred out.

I notice you haven't put clashing forward as one of the reasons for losses. Why?
Because although clashing may be a problem with young birds, it's not the major one. And if the old birds are lost through clashing, then good luck to them. More of a problem is the peregrine. Indeed, they are probably our biggest problem and I would go so far as to say that, if they are allowed to increase in the manner they have been doing over the years, it will be the end of pigeon racing in areas like Cumbria, sooner rather than later. Fanciers from outside the infested areas, so to speak, may think they do not have a problem, but let me assure them they have. One has only to witness a flock racing through an area such as ours, being attacked by these killers. The flock immediately scatters in all directions, diving into or onto anything that may be of protection to them. The pigeons are absolutely terrified, sitting in a proper daze, trembling and prey for any predator looking for an easy meal. One might even argue that the birds which get caught are the first flocks of the day for that race. The question that then comes to mind is 'what value could have been put on the real winners?'.

The problem is that serious?
Yes, make no mistake about it. Our sport, under present legislation, is doomed. The do-gooders of this and other countries are making quite sure of that. We have no teeth.

Apart from the increasing threat of peregrines, how else has the sport changed?
Well, there is certainly not the comradeship today that there was years ago and the sport is also more political now. I was a region delegate for quite a number of years, but I'm afraid that I have become very disillusioned of late and am trying ever so hard to keep at arm's length. There is now more money involved, too. Read the adverts in the pigeon weeklies. They lead us to believe one must be a millionaire to compete these days. Clever advertising is brainwashing many fanciers into purchasing products they know

absolutely nothing about. They do the pigeon no good at all in many instances - and they may even do them harm. In my opinion, commercialism must be avoided like the plague.

Which fanciers from your area do you have the utmost regard for?
Hargreaves and Gates.

How important is the role of the fancier?
It's all part of the equation. The good fancier will get the best out of a good pigeon and may even make it into a champion, whereas some people will never race pigeons - they just keep them.

Blue Pied Hen
3rd fed, 10th combine Rennes 1988
14th fed Rennes 1989
1st fed Niort by 1° hours 1989
14th fed Rennes 1990
1st fed Niort by 3° hours 1990

RICHARD HOWEY

Richard Howey is a member of that rare breed of fancier absorbed by the breeding side of the sport who has maintained a winning family of pigeons over a long period of time. Chopping and changing to meet each new fashion is not for him. He has stuck with his family of Carmichael pigeons for thirty years and, through his own selective breeding and rigorous testing at the distance, has produced a family which he could, if he wished, now justifiably call his own. After many years as a highly-successful club racer on two routes, he is now motivated almost solely by winning races at the distance. Above all, his attention has switched to Pau, his overriding passion.

While John Carmichael pigeons have proven to be the backbone of many a good fancier's loft, I have spoken to a number of flyers who have struggled in vain with the same family. Do you think these differing fortunes are simply the result of not possessing the right Carmichael pigeons?
You'd need to ask those who struggled firstly, how patient were they and, secondly, how far did they send them. I acquired my first birds from the master in 1963 but my first real success only came three or four years later when one won 1st club, 10th fed Thurso. It took me quite some time to get to the bottom of them. They repeatedly made mistakes but, as they matured, their performances improved. As my friendship with John Carmichael blossomed I kept adding to my team with pigeons off his very best, and eventually I was sending birds back to him.

How have you managed to maintain the quality of your family?
Through constant testing, with all race birds going to the extreme distance, and selective breeding. Although mine is an inbred family, I only go as close as half-brother and half-sister when I want something for stock. For racing purposes, cousins are as close as I go.

Are you looking to introduce any crosses?
Yes. If you talk to people who have a family of pigeons you come to appreciate that you need hybrid vigour now and again. Up to now, I've only used a cross very sparingly, but I now think that my pigeons would benefit from the right one. I've heard it said that bringing in birds of similar bloodlines from a different fancier acts like a cross, and for that reason I believe the pigeons I have from my good friend, John Tyerman, will be as good as a cross for me. I've also recently brought in a Bricoux hen from Horace Baker of Bridgwater, a fancier with an excellent record from Palamos.

I notice your team is mostly made up of mealies and reds, with plenty of black splashes on the cock birds. Have you a preference for that colour?
Yes, I do actually have a soft spot for reds, partly because in my family many of my best birds have been reds with black splashes. I've always been disappointed that my section winner was a blue hen, but you need to have a number of blue hens in order to put the black splashes on the red cocks.

What are your views on eye-sign?
I've spent an awful lot of time studying eyes and believe that there's certainly something in it. I have never handled a classic winner from 500 to 600 miles without excellent eye-sign. I like a pigeon to have more sign towards the back of the eye, with thicker eye-sign for breeding than racing. As well as using performance and pedigree to match my pairs I also go by eye colour, pairing gravel or violets to nut browns or yellows wherever possible. I sometimes wonder, though, whether I haven't got too many good-eyed pigeons now.

Did John Carmichael consider the eye when pairing?
Yes. He was a master breeder who took everything into consideration, even the colour of a bird's toenails and beak.

What do you think of egg-shaped pupils?
I've never had a pigeon with an egg-shaped pupil.

How many of the youngsters you breed each year make the grade?
If I'm telling the truth, and a lot of people don't, about three or four out of forty. It's amazing how a lot of fanciers only have one bird missing when you speak to them on a Saturday night. After what I cull and what I lose only a small percentage make up into decent pigeons. For example, I've only got two 1988-bred pigeons left in the loft now. If you keep sending them to Pau, 600 miles, you soon sort the wheat from the chaff.

Why did you switch from north road to south road racing after the 1981 season?
By the late seventies I had a tremendous team of Carmichael's and I simply became fed up with winning the same races year after year.

Did success come automatically on the south road?
No. South road flying into Northamptonshire is different to north road and my performances were up and down in the mid-eighties.

Can you account for the difference?
There are a lot of rural clubs with lofts well spread over a large radius. Often the result isn't a true reflection of a pigeon's merit because a lot of pigeons are what I call 'back flying'. The races tend not to be fair because the result is often influenced by the wind.

This is one of the reasons why I became interested in national flying. National pigeons have to sort themselves out much earlier in a race and, for that reason, I believe you usually get a fair result.

Are you suggesting that it takes different pigeons to win in the nationals than it does to win in club racing?
Yes, but I'm not sure why there is a difference. It could be because national birds are taking a different route from the one they're used to and are competing against a greater number of pigeons. There comes a time when they realise it's time to break for home.

Have you found that a pigeon which puts up its first performance of any note in a national continues to score when returned to the club scene?
No. They can be relied upon to do well in other nationals but they don't seem to shape any better at club racing.

At what age do your candidates first go to Pau?
I'm a very patient man and believe that you need three-year-olds to go to Pau with. By then they have plenty of experience under their belts and can look after themselves.

In order that they gain the necessary experience, what do you ask of young birds, yearlings and two-year-olds?
I like my youngsters to have several races and, if I have time, I double them up or let them go in small batches from forty or fifty miles on the line of flight. I have now given up sending to the Young Bird National because it can be a waste of good pigeons. If they hit a nose-ender you're throwing them away. I've learnt with yearlings not to start them off too early because everything is new to them - mate, eggs and youngsters - and they don't know where they are at the beginning of the season. As a rule, my yearlings have just three or four inland races, but I occasionally prepare one or two for the Saintes National if I think they're ready for it. When they reach two they all have to go over the water. I don't hold anything back at this stage because they've had all the grounding I can give them and I also have younger pigeons coming through all the time.

Do you practise roundabout, widowhood or natural?
A combination of natural and roundabout, with the emphasis on roundabout for most of the season, including for Pau if the birds are still flying well.

Can you describe your roundabout system?
I pair up early in March and allow them to rear one or two youngsters in the first nest, usually from the stock birds. It makes no difference whether they rear two or one. I don't mind if I miss the first race if the birds aren't ready. Once the youngsters are weaned, I part the cocks and hens and they go on a straightforward roundabout system. Both sexes do about forty minutes in the morning and an hour at night, with the hens

going out first. If they don't fly freely I flag them, but that isn't usually necessary because the hens in particular run like youngsters, disappearing for twenty minutes at a time.

What are the advantages and disadvantages of the roundabout system?
It takes about four hours' work a day to do it properly, hence I rise at 5.30 am, but on the plus side, the birds are easier to get fit, stay fitter longer and, because they aren't going through the nesting cycle, can be sent more often.

Do you send both the cock and the hen to the same race?
No. I always like one of the pair to be there when the other one arrives home. I like to pair the older birds to yearlings and I don't race yearlings until the weather improves anyway. Yearlings take a while to learn the system, so if you're not careful you can lose even the best. I've noticed that many crack widowhood men have a separate loft for yearlings. Over the last two or three seasons, since I've held them back, my yearling losses have been negligible.

How long do the sexes stay together on return from a race?
Sometimes I part them the same evening and sometimes on the Sunday after they've had a bath. I've found that it makes no difference how long they are together.

Do you put anything in the bath water?
Yes, very occasionally I add one or two potassium permanganate crystals.

Which products do you use for canker, coccidiosis and worms?
Harkers' for canker and cocci and either *Spartakon* tablets or *Inversol* from the vet for worming.

Do you treat your birds for respiratory problems?
No. I've never done so because I've never had respiratory trouble. On a similar theme, though, I do use *Sliepsanol* when racing - once when I part the birds after the first nest and again four days before a race.

Does the *Sliepsanol* have any effect?
It's difficult to know. The birds are coming into top condition before a race anyway, so you can't tell if it's that or just natural condition that makes them look so well.

What other products do you use?
I believe that pigeons win races through natural health so I use very little else. I do, however, like to experiment with foodstuffs, and last season I took a jar of extract of malt, added flour to make balls the size of beans and fed my Pau candidates one per night in the week leading up to the race.

How do you maintain a healthy loft?
Apart from having grilled floors and ionisers in each compartment, I spray with *Jeyes' Fluid* and *Duramitex*.

How many birds do you send to Pau and what are your returns like?
I had six out of seven in 1992 and last year six out of nine. Nine is the most I've ever sent.

Have you found that pigeons usually improve on their first effort at Pau at the second or third time of asking?
Yes, even though flying Pau slows them down. They get to know the game and because of this, two-day racing pigeons are a type of their own.

At what stage do you choose your Pau candidates and what races do they have beforehand?
I earmark them before the start of the season and like them to have only two or three races before they all go to the Nantes National. Hopefully one of those races will be a nose-ender from either Plymouth of Exeter. I've learnt through experience that the last thing they want after Nantes is another race. I prefer to let them rest, so after Nantes they go on 'open hole' if I decide to pair up. My practice now is to give them a good toss, perhaps from the coast, ten days before Pau and send them sitting up to time. ·

Why do you sometimes let them pair up before Pau?
To give them that extra incentive. I've scored with pigeons at Pau on roundabout but it's difficult to keep them right.

Why do you like your candidates to have a stiff fly at least once before they go to Nantes?
Time on the wing helps to bring a bird into condition. One year I won Exeter with a pigeon I named '2003' because its velocity was 2003ypm, but my other two entries were six or seven hours behind. The following Thursday, I put them in the basket for Nantes and the two that had been behind came to take 2nd and 3rd section, whereas '2003' was hours behind. Unlike the other two, she hadn't had the necessary time on the wing.

Are you troubled by cats when you leave the birds on 'open hole'?
No, because I have an electric fence in front of the loft. Sometimes I hear the birds clapping around at four in the morning.

Do you revert to roundabout after Pau?
Pau is the last race of the year for those that go, as I think too much of my pigeons to ask them to race again after that, but yes, the rest of the team go back onto roundabout in preparation for the Saintes National.

Would you like to see an early liberation from Pau?
Yes, mainly because of the unpredictability of the weather. When you liberate at dinner time you don't know what the next day's weather will be like. The mid-day heat must be extremely uncomfortable even for fit pigeons.

Would different pigeons score given an early liberation?
Yes, because not many pigeons will fly twelve plus hours and continue the next morning, but an awful lot will fly for half a day and then get up and have another go.

Would you favour a switch to a racepoint other than Pau?
Yes. Pau is the wrong point from which to hold a national because it's often shrouded in mist and the heat can be tremendous. I would favour a coastal point - somewhere like Dax would be worth a try.

Would you be against a more central route?
No, although you would be asking the birds to negotiate some tricky terrain.

What else could the National Flying Club do to give the birds a better chance?
I think transporting the pigeons by air would be a step in the right direction. That way they could be race-marked as late as Thursday. Air conditioned transporters would also be of benefit, as would ensuring the birds are kept in the shade instead of in the mid-day sun at Pau airfield.

Is 500 plus miles equally difficult whatever the route?
No. I've found it much harder to time pigeons out of Pau than I ever did from Lerwick. Lerwick pigeons are crossing water when they're fresh, whereas distance pigeons on the south are tiring when they reach the channel. A lot of channel pigeons go along the coast and cross at the narrowest point. Whichever route, though, I'm sure pigeons don't like going over water. One year my wife and I liberated a basket of experienced channel pigeons on the beach at Milford-on-Sea. Although there was a promise of thunder in the air, it was a clear enough day that you could see the Isle of Wight. They refused to fly above the water and circled along the beach edge instead.

Have you found that it takes a different sort of pigeon to score from Lerwick than Pau?
No. The best and most consistent pigeons score from either. Physically you need a strong-backed bird for both, one with the shape to build on. I try to put as much weight on my candidates as possible. After an eight to ten hour fly from Nantes they are in flying condition so they just want building up. In the last few days before Pau I feed more maize and a few peanuts because the birds lose weight through being in a basket for three and a half days. My first pigeon last year was the heaviest one I sent.

Why do you prefer distance racing?
Because you don't get many pigeons that will do the distance and I like to think that a bird has given its heart and soul to get home. 'Noble Attempt' put up one of my best performances when I clocked him at 8.20 pm after a 5.40 am lib, flying into a head wind out of Angouleme. I've no interest in sprint racing anymore. On those occasions when I do have my clock set, I still might not bother to time in - it depends where I am in the garden when a bird drops.

What velocity best suits your birds?
I know I'm in with a chance when the birds are doing 1200ypm or less.

Do you sell many pigeons?
I'm not swamped but I do receive a steady demand, usually from people who are look-ing for a cross. I suppose I sell about sixteen from my first round so I'd like to think that distance racing is coming back into vogue.

Do you like people visiting your lofts?
No. I try to discourage people from coming, especially in the lead up to Pau, and by the same token, I don't visit many lofts either.

What brand of corn do you feed?
De Scheemaecker Concord for my race team, and when they're rearing *De Scheemaecker Young Bird*, to which I add 50 per cent peas. This year for the first time I also fed *Spillers Breeding Pellets* ad lib. Youngsters' droppings should be like marbles coming over the edge of the nest bowl. I also usually use *Hormoform*, although I have to be careful not to overdo it as I find it brings the birds into form too quickly. Young birds are fed 50 per cent *Young Bird* and 50 per cent peas. For a conditioner, I use either *De Scheemaecker Green Label* or *Haith's Red Band*. The *Concord* mix is made up of 37 per cent maize, 24 per cent peas, 12 per cent wheat, 10 per cent dari, 8 per cent cardi, 5 per cent tares and 4 per cent mungbeans. The *Young Bird* mix consists of 48 per cent peas, 25 per cent wheat, 12 per cent dari, 10 per cent cardi and 5 per cent tares.

What supplements do you use?
De Scheemaecker pickstones, standard black minerals and red minerals called *Stablemate,* produced by Frank Wright of Ashbourne which I get from a farming sup-plies outlet in Towcester. They eat no end of these when feeding youngsters.

What do you add to the water?
I split a garlic clove and leave it in the drinker for a couple of days each week, and after a hard fly I sometimes use honey. Don't dissolve it in boiling water, though, as it kills the goodness. That's all I add because I believe in drug-free health.

What do you feed after a hard fly?
Red Band on the same day and the normal diet the day after. The birds are out flying again after a couple of days.

Are you in a good position in the Midlands National?
No. The Midlands National races tend to be very one-sided in favour of the western members, at least until we reach Bergerac, because we lack the numbers here in the east. We can't compete with the West Midlands unless we have an exceptionally favourable wind and so a lot of fanciers around here don't enter. That, in itself, makes it more difficult for those who do to stand a chance. I would like to see more national marking stations around the country, as I'm sure this would increase the birdage.

Did you top the section with the national, flying roundabout?
Yes, but it was partly through chance. I was going to put the blue hen in question back with her mate after tea, as she was due to go at six the next morning, but I only found time to do so just before dark. She didn't know whether to pair to her cock or me. It was a very hard race, with an east wind over the channel and rain all evening, and she was the only bird in the clock station on the day. My red pied hen that took 3rd section couldn't have been more different, though. Not only was she sitting her own eggs, but also the eggs in the box above where another hen had lost her cock. I remember being quite worried because I couldn't find her.

What other nesting conditions have you had success with?
You don't often read of this, but a hen sat chipping whose cock has been removed on the morning of basketing, often does well. I also like a cock feeding a large youngster and starting to drive his hen again.

Have you had much success with late-breds?
It depends how you define late-breds. I think birds only beginning to fly out in October have no chance because they need to be trained. My 3rd section hen was latish-bred but was still trained.

Would fanciers lose fewer youngsters if they just trained rather than raced them in their year of birth?
Not in this county. Losses are tremendous amongst pigeons that haven't been raced as youngsters.

Why are south road returns so bad into Northamptonshire?
I think the Chilterns have a lot to do with it. Years ago we flew with the Inter Counties Fed and losses were horrendous. Pigeons coming on a line also meet the Vale of Evesham and end up in the West Midlands. Inland racing into the south-east is different to here because those pigeons are able to hug the coast. If I had the time I would go to the coast

as often as possible and single up.

Can you think of an oft-written theory that you have shown to be unfounded?
Yes. People told me that the old English breeds wouldn't perform on a widowhood-type system, but they obviously will.

What would you like to read more about?
The different ways of getting the best out of individual pigeons.

If you could give one piece of advice to other fanciers, what would it be?
Always make sure you wear a mask when cleaning your loft.

'Romance Expected'
1st section, 65th open NFC Nantes, 10,591 birds
& 17th section NFC Young Bird Guernsey.
A granddaughter of 'Lauderdale Marathon', 3rd, 10th & 45th
SNFC in the same season for the late John Carmichael.

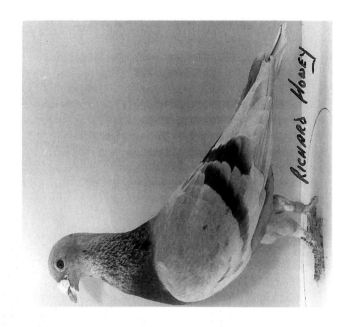

'Noble Producer'
1st Lerwick, 1st Thurso, 1st Thurso, 3rd Thurso
& 4th Morpeth. Sire of 'Noble Attempt'.

'Noble Attempt'
10th section, 34th open MNFC Angouleme,
14 hrs & 11 mins on the wing.

'Romance Expected'

SU85SB06314
Direct John Carmichael
Always stock. Dam of
Romance Expected &
several other good birds

Red Cheq Blk-Splashed cock
GB85Z26919
Carmichael
Violet eye. Sire of winners,
including Romance Expected
1st sect H, 65th open NFC
Nantes 10,591 birds

Red Cheq hen SU80S5841
Lauderdale Marathon
1st sect, 3rd open Hastings
10th open Sartilly
45th open Rennes

Red Cheq Blk-Splashed cock
GB84J00958
Carmichael
4th club, 18th fed Rennes
Flown Pau, 614 miles

Red Cheq hen *The Big Hen*
GB83F19762
46th sect Nantes, then stock
Outstanding producer

SU80S5877 *Carmichael*
31st sect, 91st open
SNFC Dorchester &
6th sect, 7th open
SNFC Dorchester

Red Cheq hen SU80S5841
Lauderdale Marathon
1st sect, 3rd open Hastings
10th open Sartilly
45th open Rennes

SU74S5828
Direct Carmichael. Always stock
Grandson of No Surprise

SU82S7699
Direct Carmichael. Daughter
of 338 Twice 1st Avranches

SU82S7679
Direct Carmichael. From 2610 x 2504
Grandson of SB18 & 338

SU82S7676
Direct Carmichael. From 1895 X 2899,
Grandson of 2302/338 & 2854/4

SU78S2861
Bred by John Carmichael
Always stock

SU77S1871 *Carmichael*
Lauderdale Princess,
1st sect, 33rd open SNFC Rennes

SU79S2633 *Carmichael*
Flown Sartilly

SU72SB338 *Carmichael*
1st fed Cheltenham, 6th fed Avranches,
10th fed Avranches

JOHN BOSWORTH

John Bosworth puts maximum effort into races of 500 miles plus and applies what he terms the 'Law of the Jungle'. In a nutshell, this means only the fittest, best and luckiest birds survive. This approach has yielded, in the last fifteen years alone, one hundred and forty-three Scottish National Flying Club diplomas, numerous averages, including twice Best Average All SNFC races, two Dewar Trophies, given for the best dual performance by a pigeon into Scotland and, in 1993, a Gold Award. He is a member of Elphinstone RPC, a club renowned for being a hotbed of competition.

What bloodlines do you fly?
The origin of my stock isn't clear, other than that it's based on gift pigeons from some local fanciers in the Musselburgh and Whitecraig areas and the capture of a Fife racing stray belonging to D Murdoch & Sons of Leslie. The Whitecraig source came by way of my grandfather and one of his workmates, a Mr Greig senior. These pigeons were collected together in about 1964 and became the foundation stones. They were tested almost from the outset from 500 miles, as every year I sent the whole lot, about twelve in total, including yearling late-breds, to the Vaux Usher race from Beauvais, 498 miles. Therefore the foundation strain was a proven 500-mile one. In the thirty years I've kept pigeons I've brought in very few crosses. Indeed, I never brought in any for at least the first ten years and in that period I developed a team of mealies and reds that topped the Midlothian Fed on three occasions from Beauvais, featuring in the top ten in the open. My first good pigeon was a mealy hen, SURP66ML9109, which won four times from Beauvais and produced two sons which won twice each from the same racepoint, one as a yearling late-bred in his fourth race, which I named 'Super Mealy'. These three pigeons became the source of the 'Bosworth' strain.

What were your losses like in the longer races in those early years?
Not great. I was very lucky in that I obtained good birds from the outset. I probably got nine or ten back out of the twelve or so I sent but I never worried about returns. Back then I was at college studying to be a quantity surveyor and I was more bothered about my fortnight's holiday with the boys in July.

What did the older generation of fancier have to say about your methods?
I don't know because I was not in regular contact with the local fanciers and therefore always did my own thing. I do know some were amazed that I regularly got birds home from 500 miles and I think one or two even thought I must have been at the racepoint. Many of them were still at the stage when to get one from 350 miles was thought of as

a good result, whereas I considered that young, fit pigeons must be able to fly 500 miles and in my ignorance I sent the lot. Ignorance is bliss.

From where did you bring in crosses?
The first one came from Donaldson Brothers of Dunbar. This cross boasted the genes of a severely inbred team of fourteen pigeons and within two years it produced the winner of the Scottish Young Bird National, as well as 6th open and 8th open Sartilly. Thereafter, other important crosses came from good friends such as John Ellis and the late Jimmy Little of Port Seton. These blended well and have been responsible for keeping my strain freshly injected with new 'blood'. In fact a gift pigeon from Jimmy Little - a direct son off his 'Five Times a Lady', 1st Scottish National Nantes - has won four times over 600 miles, including 7th open Nantes. It is now named 'Big Little'. I also tried, with great success, a Ko Nipius crossed with an Orr of Peebles pigeon. The Ko Nipius was a gift pigeon from D Steel of Musselburgh which he had purchased from Mr & Mrs Kippax direct off their 'Border Chief'. From these pigeons I evolved a team of gay pieds which scored from Stafford through to Nantes on the day, but they were eventually either lost off the loft or from training tosses - perhaps the target of an amateur shot or hawks. I've always fancied getting more of the Kippax pigeons but I suspect direct stock from the 'Border Chief' line are no longer obtainable. These were direct Ko Nipius, not pigeons with watered down pedigrees.

Are you trying any other pigeons at present?
Yes. More recently I've made some introductions from Willie Montgomery, Eddie McWilliams, John Cosgrove and Gunn & Cherrie. I'm watching these with interest at present and the signs are promising. As you can see, I go to fanciers with a record of success, not one-year wonders, and I'm looking for proven stock bred direct off winning pigeons at national level, flying into a similar environment to my own. The pigeon must be similar to mine, having good feather quality and so on, but paper pedigrees going back generations do not impress me. However, I don't intend to introduce any more crosses for at least the next five years, so as not to allow my own basic strain to be thinned too much.

Do you breed from introductions straight away?
No, I use as my guideline proven winning 500 milers and for that reason no cross is bred from until it has endured the same regime as my own pigeons. With this method I'm left with the most robust and mentally alert types to base a strain on. And winners breed winners.

How many birds do you house?
At the start of the breeding season I aim to have no more than sixty pigeons in all, including late-breds and the lucky pensioner. I started this year with sixty-four pigeons, consisting of twenty-seven two-year-olds or older, twenty-three yearlings (all of which

had flown to a maximum of 220 miles as youngsters), nine late-breds and five pensioners. I don't like to keep a large team as I find it tends to hide untested pigeons which one is tempted to breed from.

Do you breed off old pigeons?
Yes, but I try not to too often. Better to breed from those members of my racing team which have recorded an open performance in national races. These are full of vitality and at their peak performance level.

Do you breed off prisoner stock?
I may on a short-term basis if they have already proved themselves, but they are few and far between and are never kept in a section of the racing loft.

Do you sell pigeons?
A limited number, yes, either a few late-breds or older pigeons approaching retirement. My preference is for the selling of eggs, for a number of reasons. It restricts the transfer of viruses and infections, it's more economical for the fancier and it puts less strain on my racing stock - I really do not keep enough pigeons to rear stock for sale during the old bird season. And lastly, I believe pigeons should be reared in the environment in which they are to reside. If I want a cross I much prefer eggs reared in my own racing loft.

What is your preferred type?
Pigeons which survive my method up to two years old. These tend to be medium sized - give or take a little - with good feather quality, strong backs, good pectoral muscles, and buoyant and full-bodied when fit. I make every effort to retain pigeons of a similar size, muscle and bone structure, in other words light and buoyant, and pair like with like. I also try to avoid broad outer flights, preferring a step in the wing with the outer flights being like fingers. I also like to see pigeons demonstrate a desperate love of the loft and nest box. I do *not* like close-coupled, heavy-framed or long-legged pigeons, and nor do I like mature pigeons which have a tendency to fan their tail upwards. Some of my birds tend to be long cast so it takes a wee while for the hump at the base of the tail to fill out, but the tendency is still for them to push the tail down.

Of all the distance pigeons you've won with, have any of them had weak backs or rumps?
No, because I just won't keep such pigeons.

Can you tell at the young bird stage which will be your best channel birds of the future?
Sometimes. There are always one or two you can pick out - the sort that are always 'clean' looking.

Are you a good judge of a pigeon?
That's for others to decide, not me.

Do you think sprinters can be made into distance pigeons?
I don't know enough about that to say for sure, but I wouldn't have thought so. I suppose diet might come into it, but basically I think distance pigeons fly more conservatively. The bird which flies the longest distance in one hop is the cuckoo. When fuelled up it will fly 700 miles without stopping and the thing to note is that it has a very slow wing beat. It is the same with distance pigeons.

Are pigeons getting faster?
Sprinters, yes, but distance pigeons, no. I recently researched a piece for the Scottish National Flying Club's centenary publication and I was looking back over the results for the past 100 years. The winning velocities were just as good in years gone by as they are now.

So you don't think modern methods have improved performance?
No. You still only get out what you put in and the successful boys from the past were doing what we do now - they just had to go about it in a different way. They still set their pigeons down in the same condition and worked them just as hard as we do, but they had to make use of the excellent railway network or flag more because they didn't have cars.

What sort of pigeon do you need for the longest races on your programme, Nantes and Niort?
Real tough ones that won't win at the shorter points unless it's hard. Most of my Nantes pigeons have never won at 500 miles. They are pigeons that would be there next morning saying, 'give me another 200'. You are looking for a different constitution for Nantes and Niort - pigeons which have a slightly slower wing beat and burn off energy more slowly. Having said that, I also think there may be something in the idea that, once you get to the real distance, some pigeons are just unable to navigate because they are too far from home. And another factor may be the timing of the longest race. I'm sure some pigeons, like racehorses, are seasonal, meaning they come into form at the same time each year.

Are your Sartilly pigeons of a more racy type than your Nantes birds?
Yes, if that's the right word. More athletic, perhaps. They are what I describe as 'sporty', fourteen hours on the wing pigeons. I don't send them further, which is perhaps just as well because lately our 600-mile events have been very hard and I doubt if some of them would have been able to do it. Time and distance kills.

Have you any theories?

No. A pigeon that can fly all day and win at 500 miles plus is the only thing that counts.

So you don't take any notice of eye-sign?
What is eye-sign? Surely we are looking for good, healthy eyes that are strong in colour rather than wishy-washy, and beyond that there is more to be learnt by watching what comes out the other end.

Do you look at the throat?
Only to make a general observation, looking to see it is pink and healthy. Otherwise I've no fads.

On a more general theme, what is the sport like in your area?
The main emphasis is on long distance racing. There are a few clubs which enjoy the shorter races but it is safe to say that the members of my own club, Elphinstone RPC, are mainly concerned with the Scottish National events. Indeed every one of us flies with the national and between the eight of us we have perhaps as many as eighty birds away at a time. As far as club racing goes, we send 200 to 300 birds a week, with club racing being a build up for the longer races.

Does widowhood work into your area at the distance?
I don't have enough knowledge of the system to comment. There are those who are successful as far as the coast, 350 miles, and some have tried it at the distance, but not enough to give a fair indication. Personally, I only race natural and have never considered other methods for distance racing or middle distance racing into this Scottish terrain as I've had a fairly even spread of success with cocks and hens in both fast and slow races at 500 miles plus.

Do you see yourself trying widowhood in the future?
I suppose I might if the widowhood men started to beat me at the distance but it would be very difficult because I don't work regular hours.

Do you find your natural birds ever become stale?
In the main, no. It usually only happens if you go hammer and tongs to begin with. I prefer to compete in the longer distance federation races and the nationals so I don't want condition/form until June and July. This means early training and breeding is limited and I don't pursue acceleration systems of early conditioning. As a result an enclosed loft isn't necessary, and small seeds and early season carbohydrates are not required either.

So how fit are your channel birds early on in the season?
Pretty fit but not honed to compete against the speedsters. Consequently, I don't expect to be within ten minutes of the winners and I'm just as happy to see them take a longer

time and look as though they've enjoyed it.

How often do your birds go across the water in the course of a season?
Rennes and Nantes pigeons - proven birds and ones I particularly fancy - go only once, whereas the others generally go to both Sartillys. This is ideal as the two races are a month apart and so fall bang on the natural cycle. This hasn't always been my way, though. In the past I've clocked pigeons on a Friday from the channel, and sent them back to Nantes the following Tuesday and timed them again.

Why don't you still do that?
Because I'm now of the opinion that it takes a wee while to get over a 500-mile race.

How do you prepare your national birds?
They have about four races up to and including a 200-mile plus event, after which they are set up on their preferred nesting condition to suit the night of basketing and there-after given continuous training for about eight days at a distance of forty or fifty miles. I train on a general line of flight, meaning from south-east to south-west, before con-centrating on a direct line at the final preparation stage. Because we are now getting our share of hawk problems, I am normally down the road before 5.30 am to have the birds back before the hawks take advantage of the thermals. They are then rested for two or three days and sent to the race I've chosen for them. During the period after they've laid and the concentrated training period takes place I begin feeding a high protein and fat diet, with carbohydrates being added towards the end of the training period and during the rest period. I've adopted this method for a considerable number of years, therefore the type of pigeon which I now race either responds to this system and comes into timed condition or falls by the wayside.

Do your birds take much additional exercise around home?
No, they probably do more walking than flying. I operate an 'open hole', anti-cat system and my pigeons spend a lot of time fielding. They are constantly on the move, taking off all the while, and I think this is vital to build up stamina.

How much weight do you like to have on your distance birds?
I don't go on weight, I go on buoyancy. They handle big but it means they are buoyant, not heavy. Their muscles pump up, their air sacs fill out and they are like feather dusters.

And are they like this for Nantes and Niort, too?
Yes, but with a bit more body.

How much weight do they lose during a race?
It depends on the race, but even then you can't generalise. If it's a buoyant flying day,

they'll fly off perhaps fifteen per cent of their bodyweight but when it's a smash you wonder how they've got back. Pigeons must have body to work and I think that's where widowhood falls down - they are too fit. If I flew widowhood I'd race on thirty per cent peanuts. As it is, mine select their own diet and they have as many peanuts as they want. They know themselves what they need.

How do you pick your poolers?
It's hard to describe. You just get a feeling about them when they're right. I know my family type and their best condition and I look to see how much pleasure they take from tosses and the races two or three weeks before the big one. More specifically, I like to see cocks roosting next to their nest bowl, as if on sentry duty. They will stand there puffed up and, given half a chance, push their hen out. When right, some of my cocks will be in the nest bowl at five in the morning. I also like to see bloom lying between the shoulder blades. Bloom lubricates the feathers and makes them more efficient in flight so if you haven't got it, you are struggling for condition. Choosing the right one is not easy and I wish I could pick them more often.

Which nesting conditions have you had most success with?
Cocks, and hens of two and three years of age, sitting twelve to fifteen days, and older hens flying to two or three-day-old babies. Condition is the best form in which your pigeons can be on *the night* of basketing.

Can you get your distance birds back on eggs after a race?
It really depends on how long they've been away. If I give them a youngster they'll usually plop on top of it, but if they've had a really hard fly they've not been flying for anything but love of the loft.

Would you say love of the loft is the single most important motivating factor?
It is for the real long ones, but for 500 miles they need to be super-fit and have an edge brought about by nesting condition. Having said that, I used to send all my spare hens to the longest race, hoping to lose a few, but I found they could win it, too.

Are those pigeons which come late at night invariably hens?
No, I wouldn't say so. A mixture of each. Anyway, I don't want them late at night, I want them at 8 o'clock.

What care do you give to particularly tired pigeons?
I give them the basic mixture and additional fortifications of peanuts and rice. The day after they can pick as much salt block as they want and have a bath and then they are given complete rest until their body shape is up to the standard of the trained flock.

Do you become anxious before a national?

Anxious! When I know they are right - when I've been down the loft and seen the shine on them and the way they've been floating about in the days prior to basketing - I can't sleep the night before the race. I get a tingle and the adrenaline's really pumping. Of course, nobody can say for sure that they'll do well, but if I don't get that feeling, I know I'll probably be behind.

With having to give distance away to fanciers in the Borders, would you like to see a late lib for the nationals?
No. The only pedigree of a long distance pigeon is time on the wing without a rest, flying from early morning to dusk or arriving early next day (depending on weather conditions). I remember the comedian, Charlie Drake, telling his audience that he would do the splits - half tonight and half tomorrow night. Very few of us could do it in one go and long distance pigeon racing is much the same. The only time I would agree with a mid-day or afternoon liberation would be to avoid a holdover and to let the race-control team take advantage of a window in the weather, but even then they would have to ensure that no pigeons could arrive on the day of liberation to the shorter flying lofts.

Is it your ambition to win another national?
No, it's to continue to be consistent. I rate a fancier who is there in every race more highly than one who has peaks and troughs.

With that in mind, whom do you rate as the best national flyers in Scotland?
The fanciers in my own club are as good as anybody but beyond that I'm not prepared to say. There are a good number of decent fanciers, maybe a dozen or more who do consistently well and, of these, who is to say who is the best?

You apply what you describe as the 'Law of The Jungle' approach to pigeon racing. Specifically, what do you ask of youngsters and yearlings?
Those youngsters bred early enough must complete the whole of the federation programme up to 240 miles and, if they have not cast their second last flight, they are then sent to the Young Bird National, 270 miles. All go down the road irrespective of breeding. As for yearlings, I send them to as many of the club races as possible through to the south coast, 365 miles, and then prepare them for Sartilly if the moult allows.

Do you think you run the risk of burning your youngsters out?
No, because my pigeons are not hammered, they are *sent* and there is a difference. Unlike some, I don't toss on Monday, Tuesday, Wednesday and Thursday and then send. Pigeons can become sickened of basket work, so I'd rather go once a week to forty miles. Distance is not a problem, as in my experience more young pigeons are lost within 100 miles of home than in the longer races. One year, although I don't recommend it, the fourth time my youngsters were in a basket they were at 185 miles. I got about sixty per cent home and half of those went on to score in the nationals.

Why don't you adopt a more patient approach?
Because I believe pigeons must be stretched and tested and taught to work early in life. My method means my pigeons are thoroughly tested and educated by the time they are two so I can then set them up for specific national events with a degree of confidence.

Do you single your youngsters up?
No, nor old birds. Pigeons are naturally gregarious and I do not believe they enjoy or feel safe flying solo. I start mine at twenty miles and they always go up in a batch. The fitter pigeons will pull up the less fit pigeons and they will eventually tighten up and compete against each other.

How do you educate late-breds?
Those which are paired to my national-winning pigeons as 'safe mates' are tossed with the young pigeons after the old bird season, while those which are not paired as 'safe mates' are raced with the old birds through to the south coast, 365 miles. As two-year-olds they are then treated like any other old pigeon and expected to compete in the 500-mile plus events. I breed about twelve out of my best winning pigeons every season and they have given me some excellent results, both as breeding yearlings and racers. For example, I was 1st east section, 3rd open Sartilly, 500 miles, with a two-year-old late-bred and, when I lived in Musselburgh, 69th open Beauvais with a late-bred yearling having only its fourth race.

How many of the pigeons you breed come through the two-year-old stage with success?
On average, about fifteen per cent of the initial crop will have recorded a federation position at 200 miles plus or a national position.

How long will you wait for a pigeon to prove itself?
Until it's three. If it hasn't either won at old bird open or national level or bred a winner by then it is not kept.

As a matter of interest, how many youngsters do you lose off the loft?
Not many, perhaps about ten to fifteen per cent. One or two because they fly into pylons or because they can't get the hang of my anti-cat trap. Perhaps the reason I don't lose many is because they live and run with the old birds until the old bird season is complete, so they are slower on the wing and the old birds steady them.

What are racing losses like in your area?
It does not seem to be a great problem. Many of the fanciers have retained Scottish, or should I say UK blood, and these pigeons seem to survive the difficult races much better than the fashionable continental types, which are not suited to the UK environment. Also, we have as early as possible liberations from all distances. In other words,

liberations to suit the pigeons rather than arrival times to suit the fancier. Often this means our pigeons are home before other organisations liberate.

Aside from those factors, what are the other causes of losses?
I think there are a number of points to consider. For example, do we liberate young pigeons too close to home too often; do organisations persist in liberating from areas of bad clearance; do people really basket train young pigeons to drink; and do we crowd young pigeons into the race panniers? To my mind, twenty-eight pigeons maximum would be best in a Catterall's-type pannier for the shorter races. I note with interest that the same organisations have more disasters than others. Some tend to hammer down the road and often don't give sufficient time at the racepoint for watering and rest. I'm sure that if transporters departed immediately after basketing and arrived with ample time to spare at the racepoint it would reduce the stress-factor and reduce losses, especially with young pigeons. Further, if pigeons are heading in a similar direction I believe organisations should liberate together for reasons of economy and strength of convoy. What's the advantage in liberating at fifteen-minute intervals, having the unliberated pigeons frustrated and stressed?

Turning to general management, where do you stand on treating sick pigeons?
I use as my maxim 'if in doubt cast it out' so any pigeon with a minor ailment which is not on the mend within seven days of treatment from a broad-based antibiotic is quickly dealt with - permanently. The immune system must cope with 'life in the wild', which is where people who give them a spoonful of something every Sunday go wrong. I never put anything in the water after a race and only use antibiotics as a cure rather than just for the sake of it. With being on 'open hole' and not being able to keep sparrows out, my pigeons are exposed to cross-infection so they build up a natural immunity to many things. I don't change the water in my drinkers, but just top them up daily with fresh water, cleaning them out at weekends only.

Does that not invite problems?
No. The pigeons can't dirty the water because I use lengths of guttering kept in special enclosures which they drink through as if in a basket. What's more, this guttering sits on a mesh base so there are no damp patches where cocci can survive. Incidentally, I never keep grit or minerals in the loft. I keep them outside. I also provide a pink cattle-lick containing such things as cobalt, magnesium, iodine and much else besides, all year round. It's very good for them, but you have to watch they don't use it to excess when feeding youngsters because the salt can cause watery droppings.

What does go in your drinkers?
Other than multivitamins, which I give after each treatment, nothing.

What do you treat against?

Canker, coccidiosis and worms, and I do this seasonally: pre-breeding, early summer, pre-young bird racing and pre-Young Bird National. I use *Emtryl* for canker and water treatments also for cocci and worms, with every pigeon being subjected to the full dosage. The only time I avoid treatment is during egg-laying and when youngsters are in the nest but I'm happy to do it at other times because modern products are kinder to the pigeon. In the case of worms, for example, the vet tells me that many modern wormers don't purge the pigeon, which was the old-fashioned way, rather they anaesthetise the worm and the pigeon's own system digests it. That's why what you see now is not worms in the droppings but just good, firm droppings. The old purges did not necessarily remove all the worm, either. A tapeworm, for example, may have had its body knocked off, but its head may have remained and so the worm grew again.

How long have you been treating as you do?
About ten or fifteen years.

Is it necessary to treat at all?
It's vital. Any pigeon can catch disease and parasites - it only has to pick at infected corn in the basket when it's hungry. I'm not prepared to take the risk. What would you rather do: take preventive measures or suffer the consequences?

Do you give any respiratory treatment prior to racing?
No, because I don't believe respiratory disease can be cured. Suspect stock could not stand my management and would be culled. If you have a loft like mine that gets natural sunlight and plenty of fresh air it's unlikely you'll have many respiratory problems anyway.

What other thought should be given to loft design?
It depends on your garden or allotment size. My pigeon loft in the early days was a six foot by four garden shed, but my birds still raced to it, lawnmowers and all. Whatever your circumstances, it should be easily managed, of simple design, damp-free and well ventilated with an obvious movement of air and your pigeons must feel safe and secure. A good loft design is only part of the equation, though. Good management, good pigeons and the avoidance of overcrowding are other essential components all year round.

What do you use on the loft floor?
Up to 1991 I operated a deep-shavings system which I changed every six to eight weeks. The only flaw was the mess to the garden and the trail of shavings into the house. For those reasons I now operate a grid system with absorbent material 150mm below the grid. I've found no difference in the performances of my pigeons and I feel a lot better myself in the dust-free environment.

Which aspects of the sport do you most enjoy reading about?

I find good, short, informative articles on dietary methods of great interest, but other than that, I don't read much. A lot of what is written is very repetitive. Consequently, I now feel any free time is better spent in the garden.

Could you recommend any of the books you have read?
I forget the title, but one of the better ones, which was easy to digest, was written by Ken Kippax. Another handy one is *Healthy Pigeons* by Dr L Schrag.

Having given a lot of thought to dietary methods, which brand of corn do you feed?
It wouldn't be fair to mention a specific one as I obtain my feed from various manufacturers via a local supplier and then mix the various grains to suit my requirements. The basis of my feeding is peas - maple, green and dun - with *small* quantities of maize and smaller grains such as wheat and dari. My pigeons never get beans because they don't seem to enjoy them and they are not keen on maize either, therefore carbohydrates are sourced from rice. I hopper feed the following throughout the year with no restrictions at any time:

Oct-Feb: 75 per cent moulting mix, 25 per cent peas
Feb-May: 75 per cent peas (various), 25 per cent wheat, dari, maize
May-Sept: 50 per cent peas, 25 per cent peanuts, 25 per cent made up of wheat, dari, maize (with rice used for carbo-loading towards the end of the training programme and during the rest period)

Do you prefer polished corn?
No. There is no advantage in it and it is done purely for presentation to the ill-informed punter.

What are your views on commercialism in general?
With me, pigeon racing is a private affair and not about marketing a product. However, if someone can make a living out of the various elements of the sport by creating a service at a fair price then I see no harm in it.

What about pigeon politics?
I think opinions are best stated openly at the relevant AGM of the club concerned. I certainly do not wish to enter into politics subject to scrutiny in the fancy press.

What do you think the future holds for the fancy?
I believe membership will level out to a hardcore of fanciers who will have become more professional in their approach. These fanciers will be those with older council housing with large gardens without restrictions, private homeowners who can afford property without the restrictions set down by today's developers and those with access to allotments provided by local authorities in certain areas where pigeon racing is rec-

ognised as a traditional sport.

To sum up, what do you think are the key factors in success?
A combination of good pigeons and good management. For consistent performances over the years, all aspects of your management must be kept to the highest standard, whilst a successful fancier is one who *never stops testing* his stock, learns from his mistakes and knows his pigeons. He finds those which like to be teased and those that want to be left alone. I also believe that a pessimist will not be successful with any animal. If you're down in the mouth, your pigeons will be too, whereas if you have a spring in your step it will rub off on them.

Scottish National Positions 1979-1993

Racepoint & Distance	Positions	Total
Sartilly 500 mls	2nd, 3rd, 4th, 7th & 8th Open plus 44 other positions	49
Rennes 542 mls	8th & 9th Open plus 17 other positions	19
Nantes 603 mls	3rd & 7th Open plus 11 other positions	13
Niort 672 mls	7 Open positions	7
Avranches 505 mls	6th & 8th Open plus 4 other positions	6
Falaise 500 mls	2 Open positions	2
Inland Nationals 365+ mls	4th & 6th Open plus 11 other positions	13
Young Bird Nationals 255-281 mls	1st Open plus 33 other positions	34
	Total positions	**143**

Blue Cheq Hen 77E4432
Dam of 1st open Scottish YB National
Daughter of Mealy Hen SU66ML9109,
John Bosworth's foundation hen.

Dark Cheq Hen
1st open Scottish YB National

Dark Cheq Cock
A typical example of John Bosworth's 500 mile plus family.

Max Hinde.

Top 3 Positions Won from Scottish Racepoints

	Perth/Arbroath 305 miles	Lerwick 545 miles	Thurso 451 miles	Fraserburgh 370 miles
1982	1st	2nd	2nd	1st
1983	1st & 2nd	1st	-	1st*
1984	2nd	-	1st	3rd
1985	-	1st & 2nd	-	3rd
1986	1st	-	-	2nd
1987	-	-	-	1st, 2nd & 3rd
1988	1st	1st & 3rd	-	1st & 3rd
1989	1st	1st	1st & 2nd	1st
1990	3rd	-	3rd	-
1991	2nd	1st & 2nd	3rd	1st
1992	1st & 3rd	-	3rd	1st & 2nd
1993	1st	1st & 2nd	1st	1st, 2nd & 3rd
1994	1st	1st	-	-
1995	1st	2nd	1st	-

Total 27 firsts, 14 seconds & 11 thirds (*clock stopped)

MAX HINDE

There is one thing which nearly all successful pigeon fanciers are agreed upon and that is the need for regularity. Here we focus on a fancier with over thirty years of success behind him whose work as a courier cum chauffeur makes that impractical - Max Hinde of Wellingborough. His job takes him all over the country and during the summer months it is not uncommon for him to be away from home from dawn till dusk. Most of his success has been gained on the natural system, but recently he has tried his hand at roundabout, with excellent results. His birds spend much of their time in a small box and it is eye-opening to see how eager they are to get in it, how contented they are once inside and the condition in which they come out of it.

What have you found to be the chief advantages of roundabout?
For a start, it means less training. Whereas you've got to put the work into naturals, I soon found that on roundabout those pigeons which had had no training would come and beat those which had and come in good enough time to win the race. Consequently, I now only train once a fortnight, and if I'm not going anywhere for some other reason, my pigeons don't go anywhere either. Roundabout pigeons are definitely fitter than those on natural and easier to keep fit, too.

How much exercise do they take around home?
I let the cocks out morning and evening and then I leave the traps open and the hens are out most of the day. The cocks will fly on and off for about half to three-quarters of an hour in the morning, whilst at night they have an open loft for a couple of hours and some will be going off on their own and flying all the time. As for the hens, when I first let them out they fly like youngsters and it gets to the point where they will even clap off after strays. The rest of the time they do as they please and some will take a little more exercise by going off to the fields across the village. That doesn't worry me at all as some of the best seasons I've had have been when they've gone fielding.

Where do you keep your cocks during the day, and your hens at night?
In a little box about two feet by five feet which is built into the loft. It has a double door on the front, one made of wood and the other of mesh, so if it becomes too hot, I slide back the wooden door for extra ventilation. It holds fifteen pigeons and I've never had one pecked an inch, partly I think because they are on a bed of sand and the box is eighty per cent darkness. When I slide the door back they are so contented that most will be lying down like pigeons in a race-basket.

Do you have difficulty stopping your hens from laying?
No. The most I've had lay in a season is two lots of hens paired together. I don't bother about it. I just take the eggs away when it's the cocks' turn to go in the box, and then make a bit of a nest again and put the eggs back when the hens go back in.

Did those hens which had laid go off form?
No, it didn't make any difference to how well they raced, it was just harder to exercise them. All it meant was that they weren't as keen for their cocks. They flew to the box instead.

Did your older hens, who had only ever been flown natural previously, take to the system?
Yes, they did really. The first season I tried roundabout I only switched them onto the system after four races and I then won seven on the trot. The first one to win was an older hen and the cocks only beat the hens once in those seven races.

Which raced better in your second season on roundabout, cocks or hens?
The cocks.

Why might that have been?
I don't know for sure, but I think it was probably because for some reason the cocks exercised better than the hens and I didn't make up for it by giving the hens more training.

When do you put your birds on the system?
The first time I tried it I only parted them after the fourth race, and the second time I took the hens away when they'd all been sitting their second round roughly ten days.

How long can you keep a roundabout pigeon going?
Ten weeks, easily.

Ten weeks would bring you into the longer races on the programme. Generally speaking, do you think a roundabout pigeon will continue to beat a natural pigeon when it comes to the distance?
It would probably depend on the conditions prevailing in the races, but I'd need another couple of years on the system to prove that one way or the other. Last year I didn't pair them for the distance events and they continued to fly well, but that was only one season.

This year you decided to re-pair for the longer races. Did your birds go off form when you did so?
No. I found they continued to exercise better than they would normally have done had

they been on natural all along and both sexes still flew well.

Although you like to win them all, your greatest love is for the longer races. So how forward are your birds early in the season?
Not very, unless it's an exceptional year and we have a warm spell. I used to win the early races at one time, but nowadays I usually start off finishing last. Then I'm half-way up in the second race and after that I'm pushing hard to get in the first four. The reason for this is that I always pair up in March and I never like to do anything with my birds until the youngsters are at least twenty-one days old. My pigeons have an open loft but there are a lot of east winds early in the year and I won't work even established racers, let alone yearlings, until the wind turns. East winds affect everything - humans, animals and birds - and if you work your pigeons in them it doesn't give them a fair chance. Generally, I don't bother with my yearlings too much anyway and I don't mind if all they have is four races. I work them hard as two-year-olds instead, when I send them to anything up to 500 miles. Those that then don't score are given one last chance as three-year-olds.

Have you any pigeons which you won't send to the distance?
Odd ones, but they are very rare. Most have to do it in the end.

How much food do your race birds have, be they on roundabout or natural?
Too much at times. I tend to overfeed a bit and sometimes that can be my downfall. They have as much as they want twice a day - old birds in their boxes and youngsters directly on a bone-dry deep litter of thirty per cent sand and seventy per cent sawdust which I sieve once a week - and they always have a full crop. I feed *Teurlings Sport No 1* throughout the year, which consists of 31 per cent plate and French maize, 21 per cent yellow, green, maple and dun peas, 9 per cent safflower, 9 per cent milo, 8 per cent wheat, 7 per cent dari, 5 per cent tares, 4 per cent seed mix, 2 per cent tic beans and 1 per cent each of rice, groats, sunflower seed and hemp. To this I add some extra maize and a few more beans when I start racing, and an extra ten per cent peas when we come to the longer races. Years ago I used to feed a lot of beans and peas but I think pigeons seem happier on a good mixture, so nowadays I never buy my corn separately and they never have just one grain.

Do you feed a breakdown mixture?
I've tried it, but not as most fanciers do. Instead, on a Sunday and Monday I've given them beans only. All it did really was stop them eating as much, which was what I was after, and it now means I've got pigeons that like beans that didn't like them before.

Which is the most important grain?
Peas really. A pigeon fed on beans will always come on a hard day, but I prefer peas because they make them less sluggish. Basically, though, I'll feed anything but barley.

I know it produces lean meat but I don't like slimy droppings.

How important is it to adopt the right feeding methods?
It's half the battle. I always think if you give them good food you can make them do the other things. I don't believe you need to put anything on the food, though. Just natural corn and that's it.

Do you prefer cleaned corn?
Cleaned, yes, but not too clean. Somebody once said to me if you don't feed a bit of muck, they'll go and find it and I think that's right.

How often do you pick the right pool bird and what do you base your choice on?
I'd say I pick the right pigeon about seventy-five per cent of the time. I look for a super-fit one - if there is one! - and, if it's a natural bird, the right sitting condition, usually ten to fifteen days at the time of basketing. I want to see flashy, bright eyes, nice white wattles and feel plenty of muscle. A fraction more and a fraction harder muscle for the shorter races than for the distance because I think if you send them with too much muscle they can become muscle-bound after spending three or four days in a basket.

Do you play any tricks?
Sometimes, yes, if I feel I need to try something different to get a pigeon keyed up. Occasionally, for example, if I'm flying natural, I will take the cock away and let his hen sit all day before basketing.

How much weight do your distance pigeons carry?
It depends on the pigeon. I prefer them to be on the heavy rather than light side, but I send both, just in case it's an easy race when a light one will come up. That said, a pigeon that's right in every way is the one that comes.

Do you take any notice of the wing when basketing?
Yes. I like to see flights in the first half of coming up and if I thought they'd drop a flight in the basket I wouldn't send them. I also think they've gone past their best when they get to their fourth or fifth primary because it puts a gap in the wing. It doesn't matter with young birds, though. If they're fit, they go.

Do you look at the slit in the throat when picking a pooler?
Well, let's just say by using that as a final guide, I've picked the right pigeon to pool out of a team of twenty more than a few times over the years. Of course, they'll win when it's not open as well, but it's not as likely.

Does the colour of the skin around the keel reflect a bird's condition?
I don't know. That's a bit of a debatable one really. I wonder if skin colour has some-

thing to do with pigeons being on widowhood and therefore not being paired. I've noticed the skin on the ones of mine that are unpaired has been whiter than on birds that are sitting, so I don't pay particular attention to it. Basically, if the pigeon handles right and all the other things are right I let the skin go by.

Does a fit pigeon have warm feet?
That theory has worked sometimes and, there again, sometimes it hasn't, so I've no firm opinion about it. Some I've sent with burning feet have come really well, but others have done no good at all.

Do you look for anything else?
Yes, I like to see mascara really start to show up around the eye-cere after the first two or three races, and I also go by how they exercise. If they are still flying at a quarter to nine at night all the better and I look for a pigeon that is turning and keeping in the front four or five of the batch all the time. I also want to hear a crack in the wings when a pigeon flies from my hand and if something startles the batch it should sound like a gunshot when they take off.

Do pigeons come into better form once they've cast their first flight?
Yes, I think they do, but I'm sure it's to do with the time of year as much as anything else. It's usually getting warmer by the time they cast so they're naturally easier to condition anyway.

When all is said and done, how important are these factors compared to wind and drag?
It depends on the fed. In ours, unless the wind is out of the ordinary, the wind and the drag don't make a lot of difference. For example, I'm on the east side but in a west wind I've been beaten by those on the west many times. The drag of big clubs can make a difference and is definitely more important than wind, but if your pigeons are flying well you'll take a lot of beating, whatever.

Are you a good judge of a pigeon?
Average, I would say.

What do you look for?
An abundance of nice silky feathering, width in the flights, a good body and a decent head - one that looks as though it's got something in it.

What do you dislike?
Flat-headed pigeons and pigeons with pale eyes, although I've had pigeons with the latter win.

Would you condemn a pigeon that stuck its tail up?
No, definitely not. I once had one of the most terrible cocks with eleven flights in each wing and a tail that used to stick right up in the air, yet he won five or six races from 150 miles through to Fraserburgh, 370 miles. I'm frequently surprised by pigeons, young birds especially. I've one at the moment, a dark cock which I didn't like because I thought he was too narrow. He's filled out and is actually quite a nice pigeon now, but he flew better when he handled horribly.

Do you take any notice of vents?
Only as a guide to condition. The fitter the pigeon the tighter its vents.

Do you prefer narrow or broad flights for the distance?
I'm not particular. I've had pigeons do well with either.

Do you breed off unproven pigeons?
Yes, because I've found that pigeons which don't win breed winners.

Which bloodlines do you fly?
Westcotts mainly, which I got from Sid Dillingham of Peterborough around about 1964 to 1965, and the old black pied Gonderies which go back to a chap named George Dickens of Wellingborough who raced them in the forties. Sid Dillingham had some lovely deep pencilled Westcott cocks and I remember the first time I went to his loft, his young birds had just cleaned up and he had seventeen left out of seventeen after the programme. My father had some originally and the ones I had from him were all good pigeons. I've also had other birds over the years from friends and since 1987 I've added some Pickering Janssens from my cousin, John Munns of Retford. These are mostly schailies and, pure or crossed, they have won through to Thurso for me. As well as these, I have the odd Busschaert or Imbrecht, again from my cousin.

Which have been your most important breeding pigeons in recent years?
A pigeon I called my 'One-Eyed Hen', and an old black pied cock. The 'One-Eyed Hen' was out of a Westcott cock and a stray Belgian hen which I had given to me when I reported it, and the black pied cock was out of a hen from a direct pair of Gonderies. The little dark hen I won Lerwick with last year is his granddaughter and he has bred me numerous other winners over the years, quite a few when paired to a silver pied granddaughter of George Gorley's 'Pioneer'.

Are your pigeons as good today as in years gone by?
I suppose so, yes. I always class myself as an average flyer so if I win some races every year I've not done so badly. I have years when I win out of turn but I don't think it means my pigeons are any better, just that I'm doing my job a bit better.

Do you buy many pigeons?
I've only bought two in my life and they were thirty-two years apart. The first one was back in 1960 and the other was a show pigeon I bought at the Old Comrades in 1992. To my way of thinking, there must be quite a bit of show pigeon blood behind some of the modern Belgian breeds, which would explain where some of the funny colouring comes from, and I fancied experimenting myself. I've crossed it this year with one of my racers and I've bred a nice chequer out of them which I've just started training.

Do you think it will go on to score?
Definitely. It's just the type. In actual fact it seems more of a racing type than some of my others.

How many birds do you house?
I winter eighteen pairs and breed, on average, about twenty-five youngsters.

Of those twenty-five, how many would you expect to lose off the loft?
Normally, none. Over the years I've kept a pair of tumblers for the sole purpose of dropping the youngsters when they go a bit mad and they usually do the trick. I had an old tumbler cock who came in handy for another reason, as well. He would sit on the corner of the loft until late on race nights and then fly up in the air and do a somersault to let you know you had one coming. He could tell from half a mile away if it was a pigeon for me or not. You could guarantee it.

How many of your youngsters make it through the programme?
On average about fifteen to eighteen, but in exceptionally bad years about six.

Does a good youngster make a good old bird?
It depends. If you get a good, keen, young hen then you've got a good future old bird that you can rely on for the distance, but cocks in general are always a bit hit and miss. Hens are more reliable all round. A good one will usually go on until she is six, but you can't say the same about cocks. I've had some very good ones which have won up to three years of age and never had a hard race in their life. Then, just when I thought I would have another good season with them, I couldn't get them to win.

Have you any theories?
Not really. Only that you need good food, clean water, and plenty of mixed grit and minerals all year round. I'm a strong believer in plenty of mixed grit because I think it has a lot to do with pigeons keeping in good respiratory and digestive condition. Pigeons which don't digest their food properly tend to get other problems as well, but if you give plenty of grit they won't have food in their crops for too long. It doesn't matter what kind of grit. Last time I went for some, I picked up the wrong bag and it was pheasant grit. It's a bit big but they love it and this year I've not had a single youngster

with the slightest greasy wattle.

Do you get many respiratory problems?
No. I'm a believer in plenty of fresh air so I have pretty open lofts. The wind blows through at times, but it doesn't matter.

If a pigeon does become sick how do you treat it?
It depends on what's wrong with it. If one is just generally off colour, I remove it and give it a *Beechams* pill. If one has canker in the mouth I take the canker out, and if one is rattling I give it plenty of grit because, as I said before, it's probably got a digestive, not a respiratory problem.

Do you give preventive treatments against canker or coccidiosis?
No, not normally, and I can't say that I've ever wormed them either. I might try it sometime if the droppings aren't right, but basically if the pigeons seem right and their wattles are nice and white I don't give them anything.

What does go in your drinkers?
Just plenty of fresh water.

Anything else?
No. Actually, I tell a lie. I did try a sterilising agent once. I've still got the rest of the packet somewhere, but I've never used it since because I don't think there's any need for it.

How do you keep on top of lice and other parasites?
I creosote the floor of the nest boxes before I pair up and after that I spray the loft with *Duramitex* at least once a month, or even more often in warm weather or when I've got youngsters in the nest. I also use *Johnson's Insect Powder*.

How often do your birds have a bath?
It's in front of them all the time. I just add clean water and brush the bloom off once a week. A word of advice, though. If you do leave a bath out all the time, always remember to empty it before a race and not after!

You say you haven't any theories, but from your own obervations have you found there to be anything in eye-sign?
Half and half, I suppose. In some cases it does seem there is something in it, but there again, I've had pigeons which have won themselves and also bred winners, yet one or two people have told me they've had nothing in the eye at all.

Do you take the eye into account when pairing up?

Yes, but only in so much as I won't pair two yellows or two pearls together. There's probably nothing at all wrong in doing so, but I'd just rather have more colour.

Have you found your best pigeons to be those with the smallest pupil?
No I can't say that I have as the only time I take any notice of the pupil is when I'm getting them ready for a race. The more work you give them and the fitter they get, the smaller the pupil.

Is the size of a pigeon an important consideration when you select your pairings?
Yes. Basically I like medium-sized pigeons, so I try to breed to that, pairing small with medium to increase the size of the smaller one and big with big as you usually find such pairings produce a smaller type than both parents. I don't like to have too many very small pigeons, even though I would have to say that, on average, those which I have had have been good ones capable of winning at all distances. Pigeons are a bit like race-horses, aren't they? Sprinters have big backsides and powerful fronts, whereas a nice, well-proportioned racehorse is better at the distance.

Which is the most important motivating factor for a pigeon?
A happy environment mainly. Get that right and they'll want to come back quickly. Mine are so contented that some of my cocks sleep in other nest boxes.

Do you like to see a strong love of the nest?
Yes I do. When mine are sitting they tend not to take any notice of me or anyone else, not even my granddaughter, who's always going in and stirring them up. Normally they won't come off their eggs for anything, except occasionally when I've had a spot of cat trouble.

Are your birds tame?
More semi-tame than tame. That's the way I prefer them, but really, so long as they are happy, it doesn't worry me what they are like.

Do you talk to your birds?
No, not a lot. The most I might do is swear at one if it won't trap on a Saturday.

Do you make many mistakes?
Tons and according to my wife, Pat, one of them is that I spend too much time with the pigeons. My biggest fault, though, is knowing I've a good pigeon and over-racing it. I'm frequently guilty of thinking that, just because it's a good pigeon and it looks well and handles well, one more race will make no difference. That's wrong. If a pigeon has a bad race from 300 miles, it puts it out for the year and really it wants a winter to get over it.

Given a rest, will such a pigeon be as right as rain the following year?
You can't be certain, but you hope so.

Is it just a case of sending it and seeing?
No. You can usually tell whether or not it's come back to itself by the way it exercises around home. If it hasn't, it never shows that zip and it's unable to turn in the sky with the others.

Will you condemn a pigeon for making a mistake?
No. In fact one thing I do like is a pigeon that comes back with threadbare flights after twelve months away. I've had two or three like that over time which have gone on to do well. I remember once I got accused of cruelty for sending a yearling to Berwick, 250 miles, with threadbare flights.

Did it win?
Yes, by fifteen minutes, and it was only just pipped for 1st fed.

Will you give a bird another chance if you have it reported?
Yes, always, unless the loft to where it went is too much on the line of flight. I had one sent back only last year and it went on to take a first and two seconds. If I get a stray in here I'll always give it a chance as well, but I can't weigh them up. It seems that with some of them the last feed they have is the most important one. I've tossed strays twenty miles away next day, yet they've come back, and I bet some have come right over their home loft to do so.

How seriously do you take pigeon racing?
Well, I enjoy it, I'll say that. Enough that I want to win over the average - or at least see them come in good time.

Which is more important, the fancier or the pigeon?
I'd put it at fifty-fifty, for all distances.

How important is regularity?
Fairly, and that's one thing mine don't get because unfortunately my job makes it difficult for me to stick to a routine nowadays. I would say time is more important than regularity, though. Not necessarily time to muck about cleaning them out, but time to see how they exercise and to study their habits. That is very important.

Why aren't some fanciers successful?
They're too fussy, cleaning out, messing about and handling their pigeons all the while - that sort of thing. You need to let pigeons get on with their own lives and for that reason I don't handle mine much. I always think back to some of the best long distance

fanciers I've come across and they were people who just left their birds to it. I've an old book somewhere about a woman fancier who let her pigeons live like wild ones all year round and she won without doing anything with them.

Has the sport not moved on and become more competitive since then, though?
No, it's food and natural training that you win good races with really, or at least the more natural they are, the more chance you have of getting them to come back in all conditions. You can do things like widowhood and roundabout to improve trapping and get them like athletes, living and training like soldiers, and you can probably improve their times. But nearly every time the weather's cold, the natural pigeons will beat the widowers. You know yourself, if it's a funny race nine times out of ten a natural man wins and the men with 'super' pigeons have a bad race. It seems to me widowhood pigeons need the sun on their backs.

Who have been the best local fanciers over the years?
For consistency in the fed for quite a lot of years, the late Harold Thompson. He was a very hard man to beat. It was very rare he would send a yearling to a long race, but when he did pick one out, it was there for only one reason - to win. His motto was every time you go in your loft look for an excuse to cull one and I suppose he was right in a way.

Which racing moments stand out in your memory?
Timing birds on the day from Lerwick, 545 miles. But, above all, clocking a hen from Thurso in twelve hours to win 1st section in the Midlands Championship Club in 1989.

Do you still get the same enjoyment out of your birds today as you did when you first started?
I suppose I do, yes. I work long hours and pigeons to me are a relaxation. I can forget everything when I go to my birds.

ALAN CORBETT

Alan Corbett of St Helens assumes no knowledge of pigeons. He would tell you that he is a poor judge, that pigeons make fools of us all, and that success, more often than not, is down to luck. Perhaps, though, he understands pigeons better than most, for his way is based on simplicity. Feed them well, keep them healthy, make sure you send them fit enough to face the worst kind of day and, if the constitution is there, you will get them. There is also one other factor, and it is the love of home. He has certainly got the environment right and developed a bond between himself and his birds.

Which clubs do you compete in?
My local clubs are Thatto Heath Homing Society and Rainhill Two-Bird, and in recent years I have also flown with the National Flying Club. I regard Thatto Heath as one of the strongest clubs in the North West Combine. Its members have topped the combine on numerous occasions, one has won the North West Classic twice and another, Dave Harrison, has won National Flying Club Nantes.

How many birds do you winter?
About forty.

Do you sell any surplus to get down to that number?
No, I never sell any, although I see no harm in it.

And how many youngsters do you breed?
This year I've ordered twenty-five rings, although I shan't use them all. I only take one round off selected pairs and three rounds off my Number One Pair. I haven't the room for any more.

Do you breed any late-breds?
Yes. Some of my best pigeons have been late-breds. Indeed, in one race from Rennes, when there were only two birds on the day, I won it by an hour and a half with a yearling that still had seven nest flights. I don't breed many, but percentage-wise, I think that if I was to breed as many late-breds as first-rounders, I'd have more good pigeons. The only reason I can think of why they should be better is the obvious fact that they are bred at the best time of year.

Do you train them in their year of their birth?
No, because I can't be bothered charging about in the car. I'm too lazy. I hope they go

missing from the loft for a few hours, but of course that doesn't happen very often. I don't think it's vital to train young birds. They are growing so I let them grow. I've always been involved with livestock and I had it drummed into me from an early age that you should let things grow.

As you don't think education is essential, do you race any young birds?
Yes. I give them three or four races up to 130 miles. I have no interest in young bird racing, however, and just expect them to come home in reasonable time. I don't lose many.

What about yearlings?
It is at the yearling stage that I look for my birds to start showing promise. All must cross the channel twice and home in good time.

And after the yearling stage?
Two and three-year-olds go to 500 miles, and I may send one or two older birds to Pau if I think they are good enough.

Are you a natural or widowhood flyer?
I race natural and concentrate on the middle to long distance events.

What do you treat for?
Canker, coccidiosis, worms, paramyxo and respiratory problems.

Do you agree with vaccination?
Yes, and if everyone had vaccinated from the start it wouldn't now be necessary.

When do you treat?
I try to leave it as late as possible because in the winter, when it's cold, a pigeon will drink hardly anything at all. So how can it be getting what it is supposed to have?

Why do you treat?
I do it out of habit and because I'm frightened not to. I don't think they always need it.

Have you always treated?
No, it was only when I started reading books and comics.

Do you use the services of a vet?
Occasionally, if I'm after a particular product. I prefer to keep away, though, because vets can bleed you. What's more, some town vets haven't a clue when it comes to pigeons.

Which products do you use?
Harkers' because theirs are the cheapest. I have also tried *Tylan* for respiratory treatment, although I was told by my vet that it's meant for pigs, not pigeons. This year I used a German product, but I shan't again because it's too expensive.

Do you ever treat during the racing season?
No. I'd be afraid of knocking the birds off form.

Have you ever had canker or coccidiosis in your birds?
Never, not even when I wasn't treating. As I said before, though, I felt I should treat after looking at all these videos and books.

Do you treat sick pigeons?
Yes, to the best of my ability.

Treatments aside, if I walked into your loft on any day of the year, what, if anything, could I expect to find in the water?
Garlic. I always have a garlic clove in the water. I leave it in for a few weeks at a time and then replace it with another one. You will see a skimming of oil on the surface of the water and I think that helps to keep things at bay. I don't think garlic does any good other than that.

Do you give them a course of multivitamins after treating?
Not always. If I'm going to get some corn I'll buy some, if not, and I don't have any to hand, I don't bother.

Do you clean out daily?
Yes, in the summer, but I use deep litter in the winter months as I find it more convenient.

How do you control lice?
I use *Duramitex* regularly, and lice are not something that trouble me much.

What criteria do you use when selecting pairs?
I pair best to best.

How many good pigeons do you breed in an average year?
Very few. There are not many pigeons that can win twice across the channel.

Does your loft house any prisoners?
No. I haven't the room for them.

Do you breed off old pigeons?
Yes, providing they have been tried and tested.

Do you attach any importance to the pedigree?
No. The best pedigree is the basket.

Do you inbreed?
Not really. I prefer to line-breed and bring in an occasional cross.

Which strains are your present team based on?
Mostly Van Bruaenes, which I obtained from the late Bobby Mayo of Chester. I got my first ones in 1985 and added to them in subsequent years. More recently, I've introduced Kuypers and Jan Aardens from Dave Hazel and Patrick Brothers of Craven Arms.

Which birds have had the most impact?
My Number One Pair came from Bobby. They were both bred in 1985 and have always been paired together.

How are they bred?
I can't tell you much because I didn't want a pedigree for them, but I do know that the hen is a granddaughter of 'Scaramouche' and the cock is a grandson of Bobby's 'Nightwatchman' when paired to the 'Delbar Hen', Belge 4693596, which WV Troughton of Portadown, Northern Ireland, sent over especially as a mate.

Did you race them?
No. The cock wasn't raced because he hit the wires as a youngster, being so badly hurt that I had to climb on the shed to get him down, and the hen was never raced because she was paired to him as early as the yearling stage and I could see the youngsters they were producing were going to be good.

Are they still breeding as well as ever?
I don't know if their youngsters are as good now, as I'm losing one or two round home. They're doing daft things. I had one reported in Sheffield and one in Chorley in Lancashire. When I went to fetch it, I was amazed it had gone in because, with all respect to the fancier, I was surprised his own pigeons could find the loft. It was like going down a chimney. There again, last year we had a bad Sartilly and I timed one in off the pair when some clubs didn't get any on the day. At Nantes the year before, which was another bad race with very, very few birds home, I timed four: two children and two grandchildren. I also timed in a late-bred cock off them over the channel that had thrown two flights at once, including the next to end one.

Why do you think you are now losing one or two, and have you thought of splitting

them up?

I was talking to a friend about it recently and one theory that came up was that pigeons that are bred off parents which have been in a loft for a lengthy period of time seem to want to break away and start a family of their own elsewhere. As to your second question, yes, I have thought of splitting them up, but to be honest they have been such a good pair that I'm scared too.

Many fanciers believe the Van Bruaenes to be late developers, and indeed Van Bruaene himself adopts a patient approach, but what have you found?

My birds are a slow-maturing family which peak at two years old.

Have you tried crossing your Van Bruaenes?

Yes, I've recently crossed one or two with Jan Aardens. Three grandchildren all did well over 500 miles last year, one yearling and two two-year-olds. The farther they go, the better they seem to come. They are never tired and I can't condemn them in any way.

Why did you decide to bring in a cross?

Because, although my Van Bruaenes have been reliable pigeons over the years, I felt they could do with being a little faster. The second reason is that I currently have eight off the Number One Pair and, as I keep a small team, I would have been breeding too closely.

How will you use this cross at the second generation?

They'll go back into the Van Bruaenes rather than into more of the Jan Aardens.

When do you pair up?

Half-way through March. My pairing date is governed by channel plans. I don't want pigeons coming into form until the end of May, but mine is an old-fashioned method.

What do you feed when rearing?

When I mate up they are on an equal measure of peas, beans and maize, but I give them a few more peas and plenty of *Homon Pellets* when there are youngsters in the nest. *Homon Pellets* are a balanced feed.

How do you adapt this diet when they are racing?

I don't. I believe this diet is sufficient for racing. I give them as much as they can eat twice a day, but as you know yourself, a pigeon does not eat the same food from one day to the next.

Don't you feed any differently even for the channel races?

No, I don't change it at all.

Do you add anything to their staple diet apart from *Homon Pellets*?
Yes, I also feed *Hormoform* all year round. Normally they stop eating it before Christmas after their new feathers are grown and they themselves think they don't need it, but this year, for some reason, they kept eating it until the end of January.

Which brand of corn do you feed?
I rarely feed a commercial mix. Most of my feed comes straight from the farm. As a consequence, very little of my corn is polished. Farm corn is no worse, and it's cheaper.

Your sole aim is to do well in the channel races, so how do you hold their form until June?
I do nothing different when it comes to the channel races. Hopefully they'll come into form through the natural cycle and all of them must then go.

When does your channel preparation begin?
Once the young birds are weaned. They are trained up to 40 miles on the line of flight and I also begin flagging for between forty-five minutes and an hour, morning and night.

Do you take the hens off the nest?
Always. In fact everything goes up, stock pigeons and all. The old Number One cock does ten minutes, limps around and is let in through the bob-hole so he doesn't attract the others.

What groundwork do they get?
I don't over-race them and they are usually only given three land races.

Do you send channel pigeons carrying plenty of weight?
No. Pigeons don't want a lot of weight for the distance, and if they're worked hard they won't carry any excess.

When is a pigeon in form?
When its eyes are shining extra-brightly, its wattles are as white as snow and it looks as though it is cut out of marble.

Do you take the wing into consideration?
No, if they're sitting ten days they go regardless.

Even if they were going to cast in the basket?
That isn't usually a problem because I make sure my pigeons always have a good wing.

Ten days is the condition you favour?

Yes. Mind you, I've had pigeons sitting ten days that looked immaculate, but I've known they weren't right and when I've sent them, I've lost them. Pigeons sitting ten days are like a pregnant woman, they bloom, but they can look like this even if they aren't fit and haven't had the work.

What type of day do your pigeons excel on?
Hard ones. If it's an easy day mine haven't got a cat-in-hell's chance.

Do you lose many over the channel?
No, but I've lost a few good ones at Pau. A funny place is that. I've sent twice, timing on the winning day once, but in the bad race of 1992 I sent four and I didn't see a feather. I never send anything less than four years old, as, by then, they've had plenty of experience and aren't going to get any better. A four-year-old in my loft will have crossed the channel eight times. *(In the very hard Pau race of 1995, in which only twenty-two birds were clocked in Section L, Alan timed one of his two entries to take 3rd section, 132nd open. This pigeon was a grandson of his Number One Pair.)*

I assume the four you lost were all good birds?
Yes, in fact they had all scored at Nantes and Niort. One pied cock who had won Niort was never a bit knocked about. He would come home and bounce around no matter how hard the race.

Why do you think they failed?
They could all do the hours, I know that, so I think it might be something to do with the fact that at 700 miles a lot of pigeons can't tune in to their loft. Having said that, two of them had been timed from Pau the year before.

How have you fared in the Nantes National?
I've sent in each of the last six years and had three in the first twelve of the section. My average team is three or four, and out of the twenty I've sent, ten have scored. One year I had four out of four, two off the Number One Pair and two Workman crossed Van Bruaenes.

What type of bird does it take to score in national competition?
Something special.

When is the time to stop a pigeon?
When it stops coming.

What keeps a pigeon going late at night?
Constitution and fitness. As to what motivates it the most, I don't know. It's very rare they'll come and go straight back on the nest, although when I topped the North West

Combine easily, the hen almost knocked me down to get in and went straight on the nest.

Was she sitting ten days as is the norm for your birds?
No, more by accident than design, she went on a four-day-old youngster.

Have you tried others in that condition since?
Yes, but with no joy.

What breed was she?
An old Barker. I used to have a number of them, but they were coming back from the fields shot, so I ousted them and brought in new pigeons that hadn't developed the habit. Apart from being shot, of course, I don't think fielding does pigeons much harm, providing they are not picking at treated food.

What do you give them on their return from a race?
I put glucose in the water and feed *Homon Pellets*. If pigeons are any good, I like to see them flying next morning if they've done ten to twelve hours. Some fanciers reckon that if you don't get them out, they stiffen up. I've had Niort pigeons be the first up next morning.

Do you keep them on the short side in the close season?
No, they get as much as they want. They fly out all winter and don't put any weight on. In fact, they put more on in the summer, especially when sitting.

Do you feed barley after the moult?
A very small amount and also a very small amount of wheat. I'm not tempted to feed more barley, as I've not got much faith in it. I remember an old chap once telling me that rats leave it till last, so it couldn't be much good. I can't believe that myself, but nevertheless I'm not a great fan of it.

Which is more important, the fancier or the pigeon?
In my opinion it's eighty per cent pigeon, twenty per cent man.

Have you a good eye for a pigeon?
I'm a very poor judge of a pigeon. I think there's a lot of luck involved in finding good birds. If my Number One cock had not hit the wires, I might never have tried him at stock. I might even have lost him racing. He isn't the only such example. The worst pigeon in Bobby Mayo's loft, not just in my opinion, but in that of many others who saw him, was 'Champion Nightwatchman', but what an outstanding racer and breeder he was. Bobby would never kill anything, so he was given his chance, but a lot of people would have. I myself have a pigeon I call the 'Kuyper Cock', which came from Dave

Hazel. He said I wouldn't like him when he sent him and he was right, I didn't.

What happened with him?
I bred off him to begin with and he didn't see a basket until he was two years old. Anyway, I thought, 'look, I still don't like you, so you'll have to race'. Well, he started coming well, so I sent both him and a yearling cock off him to Sartilly. His son won it, topping the fed and finishing 9th combine with over 7,000 birds, and he was third. Then, the week after, another son scored from across the channel. I thought, 'hey up, I've got something here,' so I stopped him again. Meanwhile, I sent his son, who had won Sartilly, over again, this time to Nantes. He topped the fed a second time, taking 3rd combine and finished up 9th open Catterall's Championship Race against more than 10,000 pigeons. They were both hard races with just the odd bird home on the day in most clubs.

Do you follow any theories?
None. I think there must be something in eye-sign, but I don't know what it is. Recently I watched the video *Thru' the Looking Glass*, featuring Brian May. I played it so often it was steaming hot by the time I'd finished. I told my wife she should try drying the washing on it. Anyway, I went out and bought an eye-glass. I looked at about twelve pigeons before I gave up. They all looked the same to me.

Even the eyes of your Number One Pair?
Yes. Mind you, they all had what you're supposed to see in a good eye.

Have you seen any other videos?
A few. I like to watch them, just as I like to read about the sport, but in the end, success is down to common sense.

You are a small team flyer and every bird must earn its perch, so what do you think of studs?
I think that places like *Louella Pigeon World* have had a good effect, allowing the working man to acquire stock he might not otherwise be able to afford.

How important is loft design?
I don't think it matters for my way of flying as I'm more interested in channel racing, but with widowhood, I'm sure it's important.

Is membership falling in your area?
Yes, and it's quite understandable with so many people out of work. In our club of approximately twenty-five members, there are only about five in work.

How hard do you find pigeon racing?

It's not hard, but there's a lot of luck.

What is your biggest mistake?
Keeping too many pigeons.

What do you think is the biggest factor in your success?
The matter of not destroying pigeons when they are still youngsters. I let them grow and mature, giving them the best of everything.

Blue Cock
1st club, 1st fed, 8th North West Combine Sartilly, 6,729 birds, 328 miles
1st club, 1st fed, 3rd North West Combine Nantes, 3,329 birds, 431 miles
9th open Chris Catterall Championship Nantes, same race, 9,913 birds
Both these performances as a yearling.

The Kuyper Cock - Sire of Blue Cock (see photo opposite)

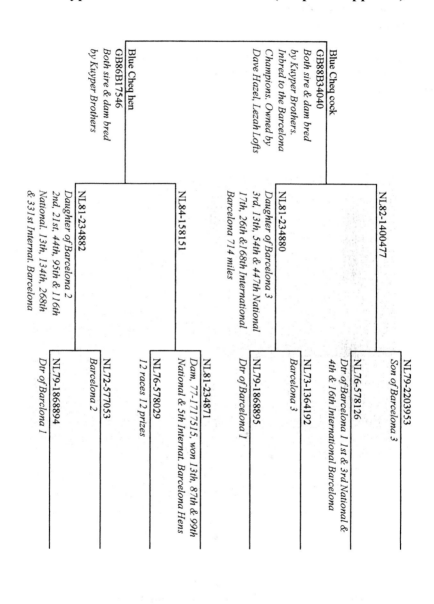

Blue Cheq cock
GB88B34040
Both sire & dam bred
by Kuyper Brothers.
Inbred to the Barcelona
Champions. Owned by
Dave Hazel, Lezah Lofts

NL82-1400477

NL81-234880
Daughter of Barcelona 3
3rd, 13th, 54th & 447th National
17th, 26th &168th International
Barcelona 714 miles

NL79-2203953
Son of Barcelona 3

NL76-578126
Dtr of Barcelona 1 1st & 3rd National &
4th & 16th International Barcelona

NL73-1364192
Barcelona 3

NL79-1868895
Dtr of Barcelona 1

Blue Cheq hen
GB86B17546
Both sire & dam bred
by Kuyper Brothers

NL84-158151

NL81-234882
Daughter of Barcelona 2
2nd, 21st, 44th, 95th & 116th
National. 13th, 134th, 268th
& 331st Internat. Barcelona

NL81-234871
Dam, 77-1717515, won 13th, 87th & 99th
National & 5th Internat. Barcelona Hens

NL76-578029
12 races 12 prizes

NL72-577053
Barcelona 2

NL79-1868894
Dtr of Barcelona 1

Bobby Mayo's *Champion Nightwatchman*
One of the grandsires to Alan Corbett's Number One Pair

Sire   Blue Cock *40744*, son of *Scaramouche*, *Belge 71/3344006* and *71670*, a grand-daughter of *Blue Mist*, Wescott x Van Bruaene, 1st Welsh National Lerwick for Derek Alcock, Abercynon. Sire of *Blue Mist* was *3711*, grandson of *Andre*, *Belge 51/3532356* & *Belge 51/3532355*, daughter of *Le Coppi Hen*, *Belge 51/3532355*

Dam   Blue Hen *Belge 3452631*, daughter of *Belge 3377884* & *Belge 3447301* pure Van Bruaenes imported direct

Flew channel twenty-three times including Nantes, 411 miles, ten times and Niort, 483 miles, five times, winning 1st, 1st, 1st, 2nd and 10th. Flew over 15,000 miles in racing alone, always on widowhood. RPRA Meritorious Award winner, outright winner of Lancashire Social Circle's Diamond Jubilee Trophy, and qualified for the British Team at both the Blackpool and Amsterdam Olympiads

1974   All stages to Penzance as a young bird

1975   All inland stages, winning minor positions
Nantes with NFC, 6th pigeon to the loft on the day
11th Club Rennes, 99 birds
13th Club Nantes, 56 birds

1976   Nantes with NFC, second bird to loft
1st Championship, 2nd Club, 4th Fed, 15th Combine Rennes, 3,502 birds

1977   4th Club, 12th Fed Weymouth, 2,754 birds
7th Club Weymouth, 246 birds
35th Beeston Castle 2B Club Nantes, 204 members sent 379 birds
2nd Lancashire Social Circle, 2nd* South Lancashire Combine Nantes, 1,886 birds
1st Lancashire Social Circle, 13th* South Lancashire Combine Niort, 1,235 birds

1978   4th Club, 23rd Fed Chepstow, 2,293 birds
8th Club, 44th Fed Chepstow, 2,451 birds
125th Section L, 724th Open NFC Nantes
3rd Club, 8th Championship, 18th Fed Nantes, 703 birds
1st Lancashire Social Circle, 36th* South Lancashire Combine Niort, 1,310 birds

1979   1st Club, 1st Championship, 3rd Fed, 3rd Combine Avranches, 6,126 birds
2nd Club, 5th Championship, 15th Fed, 48th Combine Rennes, 4,918 birds
8th Club Nantes, 96 birds

1980   12th Audlem 600 Mile Club, 170th Sect L, 526th Open NFC Nantes, 10,557 birds
2nd Lancashire Social Circle, 29th* South Lancashire Combine Niort, 784 birds

1981   7th Club, 9th Championship, 35th Fed Sartilly, 1,298 birds
10th Lancashire Social Circle Niort   *denotes equal*
Details taken from the late Bobby Mayo's 1985 stud list

DAVID WEBBER

David Webber of Norwich is a fancier of the old school and proud of it. His basic approach to pigeon racing was formed back in the nineteen-twenties and thirties and he has seen little since to make him alter his ways. Indeed, he laments the passing of what he regards as the halcyon days of the sport. He is of the firm belief that pigeons win in spite of what we do with them and so he keeps things simple. In other words, his method is pigeon racing without the frills attached, one which has suited his family of Brutons over several decades.

How much racing do you do nowadays?
I now only compete in the odd national race due to age and deteriorating health, but before my retirement I regularly competed in the nationals as well as two local clubs.

What is the nature of racing in your area?
The majority of racing in Norfolk is north road up to Lerwick, which is 540 miles to me. A minority fly south-west to Truro and Penzance, and then jump into the south road nationals, and a few south road specialist clubs also exist. In my heyday I also flew south with the East of England Continental Flying Club, but this was open to the whole of the east and south of England, and was a mini-national.

Which is the hardest route?
I used to think the north was twice as hard as the south, but after getting sixteen birds on the day from Lerwick I'm now not so sure. After all, it's still considered an achievement to time a bird in after two or three days from Pau.

I know that you have maintained a family of Brutons for many years. When did you obtain your first ones and what birds did you fly prior to that?
From the late twenties until the outbreak of World War 2, I flew Bryant Grooters, most of which were obtained from Turney of Seven Kings. Indeed, even my first race after the war was won by a Grooter. I still believe that that old strain was unbeatable for the circumstances at the time, such as train travel and the lengthy periods spent on boats for distance races. I won San Sebastian twice in 1935 and 1936 with a Bryant Grooter, but times have now changed, what with motor transport flying up the M1 at seventy miles an hour, and I suppose you need a different type of bird to suit today's environmental hazards. Post war, I have flown the Brutons to this very day. Mostly they were obtained at Bruton's dispersal sale of 1960, when I was the largest purchaser. Prior to the sale, I had been introduced to the family by FWS Hall. The strain has been kept pure since, with no other family having been introduced, and this has resulted in a very close-bred

family with all the weeds bred out. The original Brutons originated at the turn of the century from Servais and Stanhope, who, in turn, in around 1892/93, were influenced by the Grooters of Carvill of Lewes in Sussex. So it is possible that there is a little Grooter influence even now. In 1992, I sent two pigeons to the World Championship Race in Bangkok, and one of these won 2nd Great Britain team and an International Gold Medal, so the courage and stamina are still there after a century.

Which pigeon has had the most influence on your loft?
Going back to the fifties and sixties, Bruton's 'Lerwick Hen'. Three of her sons passed through my hands including one rung '5913'. He never flew anywhere, but excelled at stock and his line is still very, very strong in my loft today.

What system do you race and what distance do you concentrate on?
I race natural only and concentrate on the distance races. I can't abide widowhood and I'm sure that if I tried it I wouldn't be able to do it properly.

What corn do you feed?
I feed a sound mixture of grains purchased from Peter Titmuss of Wheathampstead, who is not only an excellent corn merchant but also an excellent fancier of many years' standing. I vary the mixture throughout the year, but I am not a great believer in beans.

Why don't you like beans?
It's not that I think there is anything wrong with them, in fact I'd like to feed them because they are cheaper. It's just that I can't get my pigeons to take them properly - they leave them and flick them about. If I were to shut them up and leave them without food for a couple of days, then I'm sure they'd eat them, but I wouldn't have the heart to do it.

What is the best food for rearing healthy, robust youngsters?
It depends on the time of year and, ideally, one should adapt the diet to suit the weather and the hours of darkness. Perhaps it is the dying scientist in me, but I prefer to feed a varied mixture because of the wonderful spread of amino acids and micro-elements this ensures.

How many rounds do you allow your birds to rear?
I like them to rear as few as possible. I've fought with myself over the years about letting hens over-lay, but I now think it better to let them complete their normal cycle - they seem to live longer and breed longer. When you start messing about, they lay and lay and before you know it they have big vents.

You sometimes hear it said that third round youngsters resemble their parents more than preceding rounds. Have you found this to be true?

I've never heard that before and wouldn't like to comment. One thing I have heard many times, though, is that the first round from yearlings often seems to be top notch, and I would certainly agree.

Do you use any antibiotics?
I abhor drugs and other concoctions that seem to make the fancier feel good rather than the pigeon, but I do use TLC throughout the year.

What is that?
Tender Loving Care.

I assume, therefore, you do not treat very often, if at all?
My birds never have canker or coccidiosis and all I do is worm them once a year. At one time I used to exhibit carrier pigeons, and they used to get a little canker in their mouths, but it was never serious and soon went again.

Do you think that treatment can be harmful?
No, it can be helpful if you've got a problem, but I just feel that canker and cocci must show that a pigeon has a weakness and I prefer my birds to build up their own resistance.

Do you treat any pigeons if they do become sick?
Rarely, unless they have an injury. I have a motto: 'Even the best are not good enough'. A repaired pigeon is probably only worth saving from a breeding point of view. For long distance racing you have to have every little bit of stamina possible, not patched-up pigeons.

Vaccination against paramyxo-virus is a subject close to your heart. Where do you stand on this?
'When the blind lead the blind, they both fall into the ditch' - so says the Good Book, and never has it been more true than in the case of vaccination. Less than one per cent of fanciers have any veterinary or scientific knowledge, and yet they babble on about something they don't understand. Vaccination was introduced by the Ministry of Agriculture to protect the poultry industry, with absolutely no regard given to pigeons. Even today there is no published research on vaccination and, most importantly, its *effect* on pigeons. Bernard Matthews is probably more interested in it than the pigeon fancier. I say this as an ex-Personal Adviser to Christopher Soames, Minister of Agriculture at the time of the awful outbreaks of Fowl Pest in the early sixties. My experience and research was offered to the RPRA in 1984, 1985 and again in 1986, but each time it was rejected out of hand. Obviously I could write a book on the subject!

What are your thoughts on pigeon politics?

They will be the ultimate death of the sport as it is now. But this is perhaps a good thing, as a new beginning, embracing the old principles, is a must if the sport as sport is to survive.

What about the increase in commercialism in recent years?
Commercialism obviously goes hand in hand with pigeon politics. Pigeon racing was originally the sport and pleasure of the working man. Now it is used as an attempt at finance and business.

What programme do you map out for your race birds?
I like young birds to have plenty of basket experience and they race perhaps up to 200 miles. The main objective is to get lots of basket work into them at this stage, as they never forget what they are taught as babies. Yearlings go to 300-350 miles and I like to see some sort of winning form start to show. I once sent eight yearlings to Lerwick, 540 miles, and timed six on the day, but I do not recommend this. Two and three-year-olds should go all the way. In fact, I have found birds of this age fly faster than when older. They seem to possess a little extra keenness.

What roadwork do you give your distance pigeons?
I like to concentrate on getting them into peak physical fitness but I do not necessarily send them any distance, unless I want to sharpen the odd bird. I like them to be extremely happy and showing their well-being about home.

How do you select which birds to send?
Recognising form and choosing pool pigeons is a matter of knowing your team or family of birds. When you get to know them, some will just 'shout' at you to go, whilst others will give you the thumbs down. It is more important to recognise those that don't want to go than those that do.

Have you noticed any common characteristics in your best pigeons?
I have always found the outstanding racer to have a very quiet and friendly nature. It has a sort of bond with me, as if it had a little bit of 'human' in it. Nervous, flighty, racy types never make good long distance racers, although they may occasionally win a sprint or shorter race.

How do you determine your matings?
I obviously breed from pairs that have already bred winners and if a pair is successful I keep them together. Having a family that has been closely line-bred for many years, I occasionally experiment with a mating to throw back to certain individuals, but if it is not successful I do not persevere.

What's the average size of your birds?

The cocks tend to be medium to just over, and the hens medium to small.

How long does it take them to mature?
Three years. Some fanciers see a yearling of mine and when it reaches three, refuse to believe it's the same pigeon.

Have many of the older families died out because fanciers do not have the patience to wait for them to mature?
I'm sure, and it's the same with many things in life.

How do you combat lice?
I occasionally powder the birds, but I seldom see any lice. Years ago I used to dip them in fluoride. It was wonderful as far as lice were concerned, but I don't think it did the pigeons any good because fluoride damages the nervous system.

Some fanciers who are good racing men seem unable to preserve a family of pigeons over a number of years, which suggests they are unable to breed good pigeons. Why do you think this is?
The qualities needed to be a successful breeder are, I feel, inborn and cannot be taught. Some fanciers are born breeders, good stockmen, but others just have no idea.

Having a family which you know must increase the number of good pigeons you breed. How many actually make the grade?
It depends on what you mean by 'make the grade'. There can only be one winner of a race, while perhaps a hundred good birds close up will win when weather conditions are more favourable to them. I sent twenty-two birds to my last Lerwick race and had sixteen on the day. I won the race, but I am quite sure that there were some superior birds close up. As long as they race, not just home, I consider them to be of equal value to the winner. In this race I had a little hen that was 5th open, which the previous year had won the Championship race from Berwick, 300 miles, and was a prizewinner in the NRCC. This pigeon is probably superior to the outright winner, although she took a slightly less impressive position. Five hundred miles is about the most a bird can be expected to do on a fine day, but I regard many next-day birds as far superior if the weather has been against them.

What special attention do you give tired race birds?
On their return from a race I always make glucosed water available, plus a little seed, and then they have perfect rest and quiet. This way they have almost completely recovered by the next day. In the case of hens that have been sent in a nesting condition, I like to see that they are back with nest and eggs, or at least in a position to see their family surroundings, even if they do not incubate for some hours. It helps them recover their peace of mind. Quietness is the salvation of many an exhausted pigeon.

How many birds do you winter?
About twenty pairs, give or take a few.

Do you sell many?
I sell a few, but I give away more than I sell. But I find that fanciers who pay good money for birds seem to value them more highly than gift birds. I particularly like fanciers to notify me of any good results that they may have achieved with my birds. So often I am happy to read in the press of a good performance by a bird of my breeding, but the owner neglects to notify me of its success. Being told is a little thing that is worth a lot.

Do you breed from old pigeons or prisoners?
Yes. There is nothing wrong with doing so providing they are well fortified with vitamins and micro-elements through their diet, and that their eggs are transferred to feeders, preferably yearlings, for rearing. I still have my old five-times Pau cock and another grandson of Bruton's 'Lerwick Hen', both bred in 1976, and they both bred very well last season. They are obviously sires of winners, and have had careful treatment, and hopefully they will breed well again this year.

Are the youngsters from these old pigeons still as good?
Yes, I would say so. The five-times Pau cock has bred a good pigeon every year and continues to do so.

Do you believe in any theories?
No, all theories, be they eye-sign, wing, throat or any other, are absolute rubbish. However, theories are all part of what makes the sport.

Having a family, have you noticed any traits which indicate a pigeon will be good?
I occasionally get pigeons with a tiny horseshoe on their backs, which is a throwback to good pigeons of the past, and they are always good themselves. Having said that, if they don't have the horseshoe it doesn't mean they won't be any good.

How have you maintained the quality of your Bruton family?
Obviously, I am a great believer in both line-breeding and inbreeding, providing that you always, and I stress always, discard anything that shows the slightest weakness. All my pigeons are Brutons, but I have maintained distinct lines within my family and use these as a form of cross. For example, my '555 ' line comes down from a bird called 'Lofty', a pigeon which Doug Went introduced from Bruton and which was responsible for his Steptoe family, 'Steptoe' being an inbred grandson of 'Lofty'. 'Lofty' was given as a gift to a fancier called Hollis and its offspring made him almost unbeatable. Hollis only raced about fourteen pigeons and when he gave up the sport, I bought them all. It may sound silly, but when I introduced the 'Lofty' line it proved more successful than I

actually wanted it to be. I wanted to have a more even spread of winning lines. I also have a very distinct line of reds which go back to the 'Bruton Supreme' line, and it is from these that the 'Pink Panther' comes. If I was turning south and going to 700 miles, then I think the 'Lofty' line would do the better of the two, but that is only based on a funny feeling.

In effect then, you have used Brutons from different environments as a form of cross?
Yes, and this has enabled me to maintain the quality of my family without having to use a complete outcross to gain hybrid vigour.

Can you tell me a little about the 'Pink Panther'?
If I'd had a publicity agent he would have become a very great pigeon. He was never beaten from Orleans. One year he won Orleans twice, which meant he was leading on points for the top pigeon of the year award. To make sure of winning it, I sent him to Nevers. The weather was so bad they brought the pigeons back to Orleans and he won it again, this time by seventy yards a minute.

Why are losses so high?
I think I have heard moans about clashing and losses for the last fifty or sixty years. I think both are due to the enormous number of useless birds which appear to be bred nowadays.

Do you like late-breds for racing purposes?
No. In sixty years, I have never had any success with them.

Is it advisable to train birds on the their line of flight?
I don't believe that it is entirely necessary to do so and I have never considered it to be of very great importance. I think the experience of the basket and the fly home educates the bird whilst helping to get it fit. The homing faculty remains the beautiful mystery of our hobby, and although we probably aim at training along their race path, it is not always possible. Many fanciers have to use the facilities that are available to them, such as a friendly lorry driver. He is not necessarily going on the line of flight, but the exercise and experience gained by the pigeon is just as valuable.

Is there any advantage in feeding polished corn?
No, in fact I believe that in some cases the polishing of corn results in vitamin loss - it certainly does with rice - and, in general, polishing is carried out to please the purchaser rather than the pigeon.

Have you had any experience of birds fielding?
Yes. It is sometimes a problem during the breeding season when parent birds seem to

search for something different to feed the squabs. In my own case, I know by the mud on their feet that the birds rush off to the marshes. I have overcome the problem by scattering sheep minerals in numerous little piles in my surrounding meadow and orchard. The birds come upon these and seem delighted at what they have found. My biggest worry over birds fielding is the constant use of toxic pesticides and herbicides, which can totally disrupt your season.

What are your views on deep litter?
There are many deep-litter systems I have seen which seem to work admirably, providing they are not an excuse for laziness, and I have tried several myself. These include a sand and lime mixture, which is good but inclined to be drying and dusty, proprietary floor covering, which is excellent, but beyond the means of my pocket, and chopped straw which I found excellent if handled properly.

Have you found any books or videos to be particularly informative?
I have not been impressed by the videos I have seen, as most of them show a routine and method which is not really possible for the ordinary fancier to carry out. Some just go to the ridiculous. They are really an extension of the commercialism we discussed earlier. If people really believe that all these European fanciers are so far ahead of us in the UK that we have to watch their videos, then it's time to stop. Pigeon racing in Belgium and Holland is quite different from our own. The very numbers kept and finance involved differs from the old-established English way. Perhaps I'm too old fashioned. Undoubtedly the best books on racing pigeons are those written by Dr Leon Whitney. He had sound scientific knowledge together with practical experience in the fancy.

Can you account for the declining number of pigeon fanciers?
Falling membership is a great subject. When people talk of falling membership do they mean of the RPRA or the number of fanciers in general? I suspect the former. I am not in the least surprised that membership of the RPRA is falling fast. Fanciers joined the sport to breed and enjoy their pigeons, not to be regimented and ordered around by a self-appointed body. I don't believe that the number of fanciers is falling, it may even be increasing. The yardstick is *not* the RPRA or its magazine.

What are the prerequisites of a well-designed loft?
When I first started, loft design was influenced by Tate & Lyle sugar boxes, wire netting, and staples and nails. Nowadays many lofts are better than retirement bungalows for the old and disabled. This again has distorted the image of a happy, peaceful sport, mainly for the working class, making it a toy of the very rich. The difference has, I'm sure, caused rifts in the sport. My early successful years were spent flying to an old granary over a cart shed. Wonderful days, I wish I could return to them. I know the pigeons were happy and so was I. Whatever your situation, keep the birds happy and

dry, and they will do their best.

Which is more important, the fancier or the pigeon?

I think that success is ninety-five per cent down to the pigeon and five per cent the man. The majority of pigeons win or fly well *in spite of* their owners. The ring number of the bird on the prize card is far more important than the fancier's name.

Do good south roaders make good north roaders?

Yes, good pigeons can be turned around. Years ago I flew south, but I decided that, where I lived, the better opposition was on the north, so I switched direction. All those pigeons which won at Lerwick and Thurso were pigeons which had crossed the channel as many as five times. In fact, my only pigeon on the day out of Thurso had crossed the channel, as far as Angouleme, six times. He had never been outstanding on the south and I think he won Thurso because he had a very good day. This raises the question of why pigeons which have won nothing before suddenly put up a top-class performance, and the answer, I'm sure, is that they are the right pigeon for the right day.

After all your years in the sport, which moment most stands out?

I suppose the time when my daughter was four or five months old. My wife went shopping on a race day and left me to change the nappy. I had a mouthful of pins when a race bird arrived and I had to decide in that moment whether to drop the baby, or finish the nappy and then time in. I know what ninety-five per cent of fanciers would have done. I opted for the latter and finished second.

'5059', bred by JW Bruton.
Last son of Bruton's 'Champion Lerwick Hen'. '5059' was sold at
Bruton's dispersal sale and bought by Mr Devito of Cardiff. Sire of
the last two birds bred by Bruton, 'Silver Supreme', bought by David
Webber, and 'Jimmy', purchased by FWS Hall. Both outstanding
stock pigeons which figure prominently in the ancestry of Mr
Purcell's Faroes winner and of the 'Pink Panther'.

'Pink Panther'. Bred and raced by David Webber.
1st Fareham, equal 1st Plymouth, 4th Weymouth, 1st
Tonbridge, 1st Orleans & twice 2nd Chichester. Then, as
a 2 year old, 1st Beauvais & twice 1st Orleans,
winning the Ace Pigeon of the Year title.

TOM GILBERTSON

The Gilbertson loft in Carlisle is home to one of the most enduring long distance families in the British Isles. When the late Frank Gilbertson visited the lofts of Dr Buckley during the war years and decided that he'd found what he wanted, little could he have imagined that half a century later his son, Tom, would still be winning with them. The birds in the loft today are, of course, no longer pure Buckleys, but it is these pigeons which remain the base and very few introductions over the years have left a lasting mark. Like his father before him, Tom Gilbertson is absorbed by the breeding side of the sport, and this has been the key to the loft's longevity. Great planning has gone into the matings and, in due course, the race birds have been judged on their performances in the races for which they were bred to succeed. And for this loft the all important races have always been the channel events, the shortest of which is 431 miles. In an era in which many of the better long distance families have gone by the wayside, to be replaced by more fashionable foreign imports, the value of this approach will not be lost on those fanciers who now look upon empty perches after a hard race.

What is the ideal type of pigeon for the distance?
I don't think you can really define a particular type. I've seen and had winners in all shapes and sizes, so providing a pigeon is physically strong and never ails, I much prefer to go by whether or not it's got years and years of breeding behind it. Of course, I have my preferences. In my own breed, I prefer them to be not too deep, yet with plenty of scope, and the hens to be above medium. I like cocks to be medium to large, and to look like cocks, with a bold head. However, it wouldn't matter if I thought a pigeon was too big or too small. Not every one is the same, so you've got to keep an open mind and allow for something.

But, broadly speaking, what other qualities do you prefer to see?
Well, I go on balance and strength of back quite a bit. I have won the odd channel race with a weak-backed pigeon, but only in an absolute blow home so if I'm left with a choice of young birds at the end of the season I eliminate those with a tendency to push their tail up. Some pigeons have rock hard backs and tails that sink right down, but they don't all have to be quite like that so long as they are at least bordering on it.

Do you think you can tell if a pigeon is good just by handling it?
It seems you can sometimes, yes. A lot of it is feel - instinct more than anything - and when you get hold of a really good pigeon, a champion, something just clicks inside you.

What are your thoughts on such features as bone and vents?
What you want is a pigeon which is physically strong but has a lightness of feeling. You can, for example, get pigeons with bone which is too 'good'. By that I mean when you handle them, rather than feeling buoyant, it feels as if their bones are filled up with something. A pigeon like that is not necessarily a bad pigeon, but it will have difficulty keeping in the air and you would need to put a tremendous amount of work into it. As for vents, they should be quite firm and tight and the distance between the end of the keel and the vents should be about the width of two fingers. For breeding purposes a hen's vents can be slightly apart but they need to be much the same as the cocks' for racing.

Are there particular qualities you look for with regard to feather and the wing?
A lot of physical attributes of this kind are to do with the characteristics of particular breeds. For example, my old Buckleys have only a small amount of webbing on the leading edge of the end primaries. That was something you also used to see in the old Lancashire Barkers. My own Bricoux, on the other hand, have much wider flights with more rounded tips but they are just as capable of flying 500, 600 or 700 miles. In general, I look for a longish wing, long flights with steps and prefer the last three primaries to be near enough the same length. But, again, there are exceptions to everything and I've had one or two without those qualities that have won. Similarly, I like the feathering to be as good as possible, but I have had winners where the feathers were slightly coarse. I don't worry too much, as some fanciers do, if a pigeon doesn't have a good covering of feather at the base of the tail. Some of those I've thought could do with a few more have still won.

No doubt those that were exceptions to the rule were still bred off good pigeons?
Yes, which is why I prefer to go by the years of breeding behind a pigeon. Although you're after the nicest-looking pigeons, pigeons have a lot of unseen qualities and, at the end of the day, it's what's in their heart that counts, particularly over a long distance. You've got to race them and find out what they have to offer. 'Fidelity', my Anglo-Scottish Border Amalgamation winner from Sartilly, was nothing to look at compared with my combine winners, 'Frankie' and 'Jay Bee', but she was possibly the more determined of the three. As a young bird and yearling, if I had had to pick her out of a compartment of twenty pigeons I would probably have chosen her about eighteenth or nineteenth.

Do you like a pigeon to be set short on the legs?
Yes, quite short with the legs quite wide apart, but only because I prefer a pigeon to look balanced on the perch, not because I think it has any bearing on a pigeon's ability. You often get a good inbred cock longer on the legs and I've had quite a few Nantes winners that were rather gangling. This is what puts me off a lot of sprinters. Their legs often look too close together and it makes them seem unbalanced.

Have you found a difference in general type between those that win at Sartilly, 431 miles, and those that win at Niort, 604 miles?
No. Different lines are better at one or the other, but physically the pigeons are the same.

You accommodate different types when it comes to racing, but what about for breeding?
No, not as much. For example, I lost two years' breeding from 'Fidelity'. I wouldn't breed off her until she had performed because she was below medium and had quite a narrow head. Even then, I went to special lengths to pick a cock to complement her.

Which are the main points you consider when choosing your pairings?
The people I admire are those who have maintained a family over many years. I read in Wing Commander Lea Rayner's *Creation of a Strain* of how one of Dr Buckley's champions had a common ancestor something like thirty times in its pedigree and that, to me, is the epitome of good breeding. Consequently I give the utmost thought to pedigree and line. During the winter I get out each bird's pedigree and study it and only when I am happy that two birds are suitable on paper do I examine type and see how I think they complement each other. At that stage one of the factors I take into consideration is the position of the eye. I've noticed the eye going further back in the head in a lot of breeds and in the last ten to twelve years it has been tending to go further back in the head of mine, too. This is an old Bricoux trait, but it's not my preference, so I have to allow for it in my pairings. The position of the eye was better in my old Buckleys - near to the top of the head and not so far back.

Have you observed any other changes in the racing pigeon over the years?
One or two. In the olden days racers had quite a lot more eye-cere and bigger wattles than you see now. I don't know why, other than it may have something to do with the type which has been brought into the country in latter years. However, that shouldn't be true in my case and yet I see fewer of the old kind in my own. Perhaps it's got something to do with what we feed them on now.

Your family is becoming increasingly inbred. Is that because you don't think a cross is necessary or because you haven't yet found a good one?
Because I haven't found one I'm sure about. I'm always trying different pigeons but when it comes to the crunch I'm frightened to put them in with my own. If I do and they don't perform I soon get them all out again. I'm always on the look-out for pigeons with a Buckley or Bricoux base, like the ones I already have, but it's becoming more difficult, so really I'd rather cultivate separate families. I think you have got to use a cross at some stage, but I'm fortunate that I can occasionally bring back in pigeons of my own blood that I have let go elsewhere. These are exactly the same way bred as my own, but through living in a different climate, by racing to a different area for a number

of years and through the fancier having paired their offspring as he likes, such things as feather and type change. It's very strange, but nevertheless true that when I reintroduce them it puts more vigour into my own.

How closely will you inbreed?
If I am losing a line I will go to brother and sister, mother to son or father to daughter, then pair the offspring to a cousin. The closer you go the more apt you are to breed the odd funny one that is either exceptionally small or big, but that doesn't worry me. I will breed off them to get back to normal, trying to compensate for any faults over two generations. Likewise, often when I've gone very close, I've got a wing which is more of a sharpish square shape. That's not a good thing for racing, but it's fair enough for breeding.

Is the quality of the first round off a pair indicative of how they will breed thereafter?
Usually, though some pigeons do breed better later on in the year. And I've also noticed that every time I move a pair that have been on the road for five years to the stock loft, it takes them three rounds before they settle down and produce what I expect. I think it's because they can see their old racing loft and the others flying out and they just want to be back there.

As a pair become older do their offspring become slower?
They do in a lot of cases. I've a particular pair at the moment which produced exceptionally good racers for three seasons, but since then, although they've still produced quite nice-looking pigeons, these haven't raced as well. However, their children in turn have bred well. But again, you can't generalise. My Anglo-Scottish Border Amal winner from Niort, 'Jacko', was bred off and reared by two eight-year-olds. He flew the channel six times in two seasons and doesn't lack for anything in vitality, size, or feather quality.

Are those children which most resemble their parents, likely to be the best ones?
They are more likely to be the better breeders, but not necessarily the better racers.

Conversely, is a champion likely to be different in type to the rest of the family?
That's often so, but it may be due more than anything else to the 'man' element. If a pigeon is different you might hammer it more and that might be the making of it.

What do you say to the idea that, as a pair of stock pigeons get older, their children seem to want to strike off and set up home elsewhere?
It's certainly very true. I can think of quite a few such examples. I've also heard it said that, as pigeons get older, nature ensures they leave something behind to carry the line on and I agree with that, too. I often take extra care of the last egg a good pigeon fills at

the end of the season in case it doesn't fill the following year.

In recent years you've kept many of your stock pigeons captive due to hawk losses. Has this affected the quality of their youngsters?
No. I know a lot of people tell you if pigeons are fastened up all the time they deteriorate, but I don't agree - it's the way you look after them that counts. I always test any new products that come on the market on them, give them all they need when they're rearing, try not to be too greedy with the amount of eggs I take off them and during the winter I rotate them so they can fly out with the racers. That way they last just as long.

You have quite a few mealies and reds in your team. Are you happy to pair mealy to mealy or red to red?
Yes, though not too often as I think opposites are probably better. When I do, I make sure I pair the offspring to a darker pigeon in the next generation to avoid losing definition, because poorish markings are regressive. A lot of people draw the line at two mealies but I don't know why. I've paired two together and bred a wonderful pigeon. It can potentially be as detrimental to continue to pair two blues or two chequers together.

You often read that the sons of the best racing hens are better breeders than are the daughters and, likewise, daughters of the best racing cocks are better breeders than are the sons. Is that true in your case?
No, I've found they are about equal.

How many of your best performers breed winners?
Nearly all of them. If they don't win in the first generation, their grandchildren will.

So you don't think the basket is the only way of maintaining a family?
I don't think you could ever just breed off winners. It would be great if you could, but it doesn't allow for the fact that some characteristics definitely do skip a generation. That's one of the reasons why, despite what some people may say to the contrary, you do need to carry a lot of extra pigeons to maintain a distance family. There are so many eventualities, not least quite a lot of luck. It may be three years after you part a pair of pigeons that one off them proves itself a champion.

Taking that a stage further, would you be happy to bring in pigeons from a family which have been unraced for a number of years?
Yes. I don't think it ever really matters, so long as a good stockman has been in control of them, and you know that by whether or not he has kept a type. You will get them to win again within two generations and, in a lot of cases, sooner than that.

Is it possible to pick out your best future performers while they are still in the nest?
I don't think so, but then I don't like to disturb them at all while they are still in the

bowl. The only time I do is when I'm ringing them. I don't even clean the nest box until they are weaned.

So at what age do you start to assess a pigeon?
The average pigeon which is raced as a young bird doesn't have a very good moult so I let them plod along and only really look after the yearling stage. My yearlings only go to the coast, which is nearly 300 miles, so in most cases I can then look at them and assess them at their best. Some pigeons, however, continue to get better with age and it's not until they are two or three that they come more into your expected type. It has a lot to do with line. My Bricoux, in particular, take a while to mature, but then tend to last quite a lot longer than other pigeons. They do reasonably well when they first go across the channel at two and invariably put up their best performance at three. Then they'll go on to five, six or seven if I want them to (although usually I only fly them to six years of age). Last year, one of my seven-year-old cocks, who had always been a consistent pigeon, suddenly came on fire and flew better than ever. Either that or I've lost so many good pigeons to hawks that his performances were just made to look better!

How often are you right in your assessment of a pigeon?
It's not often I'm disappointed now. Having kept the same breeds and knowing the history of the pigeon makes it that bit easier.

How many of your stock pigeons produce the goods every year?
It depends on whether you are talking about actual winners or children, which, in turn, will breed winners. Pigeons which breed a good winner every year are extremely rare. The 'Quiet Man' bred nearly one good pigeon to win across the channel each season but I can only think of a couple of others of my own that have done that. I class as a good stock pigeon one which breeds winners with three or four different mates, or a pair that produce steadily over a number of years. There are not a lot of either. Also, the percentage of good pigeons I can expect to breed has changed over recent years. When you've got the right breed you don't lose many racing, but it's getting to the stage now that unless I breed quite a lot more for the hawks I'm not going to be left with a choice at the end of the season and that's a backward step.

How did the 'Quiet Man' come by his name?
In his later flying years he literally tried to sneak in from a race from different angles and I ended up missing him a couple of times.

Have you ever tried the Bull system?
No. I've always thought I've had better hens than cocks and I like everything to be natural anyway. I suppose there may be a lot of plusses to it, but I wonder what percentage of good pigeons are actually derived from that sort of set-up. To me it means just

using hens as conveyor belts and I would also have thought the cocks are ruined after-wards for normal breeding and racing, as they would never settle to sitting a full round of eggs. I know of a fancier who used two good cocks on the system early on one year and they were both lost at the first channel race they were entered in that season, even though they had flown the channel the season before.

Are you interested in eye-sign?
Yes, quite, but I don't think it is the be all and end all. I look at it for breeding mainly because, if you have a family, you get to know the sort of eye which is going to produce something good. I always look to see if the eyes balance each other and for a variation of colour, but I'm not too fussed if both of a pair have good eyes, so long as there is thickness of sign in one of them (that is definitely important) and I know how the other pigeon is bred. The better the eyes of both parents the better for producing stock pigeons. A good eye to a moderate eye, the better for producing racers. Eight out of ten of my best performance pigeons have what you would loosely term a 'racing' eye, so in a pairing this will invariably be the one that is not as good.

Looking back at the parents of your best racers, has at least one of them had what you would term a very good eye?
Always.

What would you do if the eyes of your birds started to deteriorate?
That's happened to a lot of fanciers over the years and many of them have panicked and thought all they needed was a cross. That's alright if it produces the right spark, but I think you have more chance of spoiling things. I would probably try and solve the problem myself using the birds I already have, although the easiest solution would be to seek the advice of someone with a tremendous knowledge of eyes, like Brian May.

Would you ever introduce sprinters into your family?
No. It makes sense in theory, but it seems to weaken the distance side rather than make a sprinter durable. There have been a lot of good distance lofts ruined by the fancier adding sprinters.

If you were to start with a loft of sprinters, could you eventually turn them into distance pigeons?
Probably if you had enough of them and helping winds. After all, if they win at 500 miles in a tail wind, it qualifies them as distance pigeons. A lot would depend on the particular line of sprinter, how you fed and the terrain over which they had to fly. You could probably extend their range over flat country, but you would struggle with the finish we have through the Cumbrian hills.

Conversely, do you think your pigeons would be too slow if flown to an area with

flatter terrain?
I don't think so, but maybe. I'm sure they would be okay once they'd had the hours on the wing, though. It's a great leveller.

Of all the pigeons you've seen over the years, which have impressed you the most?
There have been quite a lot, but more individual pigeons than families. I was extremely impressed with the late Les Davenport's Cattrysse family just after the height of his fame, but you tend to see a lot of lofts at their peak or when they're just going back and anyone that races will only have a few good pigeons at any one time. This is one of the reasons why I have been very impressed by Mr & Mrs Eric Cannon's performances. They are always consistent and always get a lot of pigeons on the result of the races they are aiming for. In this respect, they can be likened to Dr Buckley. As for individual pigeons, I've been fortunate to handle quite a number of Scottish National winners over the years and the two which really stuck out were 'Solway King' and Jack Wylie's 'Blue Blitz' back in the sixties. I've used them as my yardstick ever since and they are still the two best pigeons I've handled. More recently, Brian Denney's 'Dark Peron' and Geoff Kirkland's 'Pest' are as good a pigeons as I've seen for a number of years.

Do you have any dos or don'ts as regards rearing good, sound youngsters?
I think it's very important to decrease the maize as much as possible. It can cut the mouth of the youngsters and lead to canker. During rearing is the only time there is little or no maize in my mixture. The best food is peas. They will eat them when they won't eat beans so you will get more food into your youngsters. I feed forty per cent. I don't mind a bit of small stuff in the mix, say ten per cent. It keeps it interesting for the old birds and doesn't impair a youngster's development in any way. Then, to ensure they have all they need, I like to feed a cupful of *Hormoform* and a handful of groats to each compartment daily, starting just after hatching. Groats are excellent for pigeons and I give them a handful at all times of the year. You can't overfeed or be too good to the adults when they're rearing youngsters because it takes a lot out of them and it's most important to instil into the adult birds that there will be corn there at all times. Otherwise, if you miss a feed and they start thinking there won't be a continuous supply, they will digest most of it themselves. I don't put anything on the corn, such as cod liver oil, which can soon turn rancid, but I have tried various other things, such as powdered calcium for strong bones. I didn't notice any difference in the youngsters but it may have helped in its own way.

What is your opinion on the use of pellets for rearing youngsters?
I'm not a great lover of them. I don't think they do a lot of good over a lengthy period, as a pigeon must use its bodily functions. Up to now I've not tried them to any great extent, no more than ten per cent, and I haven't noticed much difference. However, it's no good decrying such things until you've used them to the utmost, so next year I thought it might be worth trying up to thirty per cent in one compartment of the stock

birds. I've listened to quite a lot of people over the last twelve months who have used them who say they have never seen better-reared youngsters and whilst I agree, they do seem to come on more quickly, I wonder whether they don't come on almost too much.

What do you wean your youngsters on?
I always have a pot of peas in the nest box so they have learnt how to eat before I wean them at twenty-three to twenty-four days old and then they go onto fifty per cent peas and fifty per cent wheat. I reduce the wheat after about a week - if they're all the same age - and then it's a good month before they go onto a mix of beans, peas and maize and, because it's probably essential to get them used to all grains when young, a small amount of little stuff.

Do you basket train them?
I normally make sure they have at least one night in the basket inside the loft before I start training so they will associate it with home, but some years I haven't bothered to put drinkers on and it hasn't made a great deal of difference to my returns. Basket training always comes at a time when you are most busy with your channel pigeons and to do it properly takes time because whether they drink or not depends on how many you put in the basket. Put too many in and they will just stand their ground and watch each other.

Have you any hard and fast rules about how much racing a youngster should have?
No. I've had just as much success with pigeons that I've taken it steady with and given just one or two races as with pigeons which have been pushed hard. I do think a pigeon has at least to be trained in its year of birth, though. It's rather like learning to drive for people. You pick it up a lot more quickly when you're younger.

Do you tolerate mistakes?
It depends how many they make. I don't mind one and I'm often happy to see a young bird come back after two or three days away because it may have learnt more that way. Two, and it depends on the circumstances, but three and I'm afraid they have to go.

Do you condemn a pigeon that goes into another loft?
I've heard of quite a lot which have gone on to be successful, so it's no good rejecting one automatically. I've tried them again, but in my own case the success rate has not been very high. I think about one in six has turned out to be a reasonable flyer. You've more chance if you're dealing with sprinters, but in distance racing the pigeon will come under stress again at some stage and it will then have to decide if it has the bottle to carry on.

How many different supplements do you provide during the breeding period?
As many as possible and I'm not joking about that, just so they're not tempted to go to

the fields. I didn't used to think fielding was such a bad thing, but with the amount of chemicals used now, it's too risky. For the last five years they have had a *Liverine* block all year round. One year, I think it was around about 1977, the school behind my loft decided to tarmac an extra area of playground and I found that my pigeons started dropping on it and picking at it. I got them off that by putting pots of salt in the loft.

What kind of grit do you use?
I much prefer *Kilpatrick's*. But all kinds are quite good really and in the racing season they have two kinds anyway.

How many youngsters do you let your channel birds rear?
Normally only two. I know a lot of people let them rear at least one in the second round as well because they think it helps with the moult, but I don't believe it makes a lot of difference. I always watch to see how they cope with it. They are pampered all year and should be able to handle two youngsters, but I've found that yearlings will sometimes show distress. If they do, they won't win that year.

I take it you don't presume they are constitutionally flawed?
No. There is always that doubt, but often the next year they've taken it in their stride and gone on to win.

Do you have any hard and fast rules about how much work a channel pigeon needs to have?
No. You've got to treat each pigeon as an individual and find a level it will respond to. I don't automatically put everything in the basket when I go training, but knowing how much work each one needs only comes with having worked with a breed and a bit of trial and error.

Will you train in poor weather?
I'm not really keen on training if the weather's bad on the last three days before basketing for the channel but I don't mind if it's wet half-way through the inland programme. They're bound to hit similar conditions somewhere along the line when racing, so it gets them used to it. However, there's poor weather and poor weather, so you've got to be sensible about it.

Do you single up?
I used to in years gone by, but unfortunately the hawks have put a stop to it. Often, the only way of knowing a pigeon can think for itself is to single it up from forty miles, otherwise it can go through life to four years of age and, in my case, cross the channel four times and still not know what it is doing.

How many inland races do your channel birds have?

It's changing. Three is ideal for most pigeons and in the past I used to jump hens from Redditch, 184 miles, into Nantes four or five weeks later and they would do it with ease. You don't want to put them in the basket too often because of the stress element, but nowadays the hawks have made training more hazardous than racing so I'm inclined to race them more often.

How many channel races can you get out of them in the course of a season?
It depends on the line. Generally, two is enough for my Buckleys, but some of the Bricoux go to three and are only getting fit by the third one.

Do you set pigeons up for specific channel races?
Not often, as I normally have a number of pigeons which will have come into natural condition anyway. I hate robbing pairs of their eggs and try to keep everything as close to nature as possible. If I do want a bird for a particular race, I try to manipulate its cycle by taking advantage of circumstances at the time. I know a lot of people will automatically remove a hen if her cock is away at the races in the hope that they will get the pair to go back on their eggs. Often, however, you're not wanting them to go back on their eggs. It may make more sense if, for example, a cock goes to the first Sartilly, to leave his hen where she is. She will be leaving her eggs by the Friday and nodding to something else on the Saturday (and if she wasn't I would encourage her to do so), therefore she will be coming on to lay again before he comes back and the job is half-started for you.

What nesting condition do you aim to have your pigeons in for the channel?
Again, I don't think you can generalise. It depends on the pigeon. 'Fidelity' was a small hen and was often at her best sitting, due to hatch the day after the race, whereas in latter years I've had more success with big hens. 'Jay Bee' was bigger altogether, and gave her best performance sitting ten days on the day of the race. My reasoning for sending her so early in the cycle was that she put on fat quite quickly once she had laid so I didn't want her to have been sitting too long when I sent her. 'Frankie' was in between - not quite as big as 'Jay Bee' but still bigger than 'Fidelity'. Her best two performances were put up sitting twelve days on the day of the race. A lot of experts say it requires as much effort for a hen to lay as it would to fly 300 miles and consequently she needs to be given time to sit and build up her reserves. I would agree, but you've got to balance this against other factors. There is a fine line and I've had two exceptional performances with hens that hadn't been sitting very long.

Have you had much success racing your channel birds to youngsters?
Not much, but then I've not tried it too often. I usually have good cocks paired to good hens and, as feeding a youngster doesn't really suit a cock, I look for an average condition to suit both sexes. I'm not at all against trying it with an older hen, however. Sometimes when they get older you need to look for something different to motivate them.

How much exercise do your birds take around home?
The cocks are exercised twice a day for one hour and the hens, because generally they don't need as much work, fly once a day for an hour.

Is this forced exercise?
No. I'm fortunate that they learn when young that they must fly whilst the loft doors are shut.

Do you take hens off the nest to exercise?
Not if I can possibly avoid it, but then I'm in a position to let them out at mid-day. If I wasn't, rather than take them off the nest, I would make up for it by giving them extra tosses. You can't beat a half-hour training toss anyway.

Will you work a hen when she is in between eggs?
No, nor for at least three days after she has laid her second egg. Consequently, if I want a hen for the channel, I look for her to lay her first egg no later than the Wednesday the week before basketing. If she lays even a day later I won't send her. This is because I believe being driven and then laying knocks a hen back a bit and you need time to get her wings going again. By the Saturday I let her fly if she wants to, but not for very long. On the Sunday, however, she has her first fly for one hour if at all possible and on the Monday I try to take her for a twenty-five mile toss. On Tuesday she has as much exercise as possible, and she will exercise again on the Wednesday before then being basketed.

Are your best birds the ones that build the biggest nests?
Not necessarily. I've had some which have built sky scrapers yet they have never done any good, whilst others have been just the opposite. It can be a guide as to how certain pigeons will perform in a given season, though. Some years they work harder at it and fly better because they are more contented. I had this happen last year with a seven-year-old cock. He'd always been a steady racer, but after I gave him a new hen - only his third different one in six years - he built a better nest and raced better than ever before.

Can your racers see out of their boxes?
No. They are designed so that half the front is blocked. They feel more at home that way, which I think is important.

Do you think there is anything in love-matings?
Definitely. If I lose the first and second years' youngsters off a pair but the pair themselves are racing well and are happy together, I won't swap them about. It is but a little loss. In a lot of cases I sacrifice three-quarters of a pigeon's breeding lifetime if it isn't paired with something which I think complements it. I might even lose one after five years and have never taken anything off it.

Do you take any notice of the wing moult?
I'm not much fussed which flight they're on, but I like it to be burst. However, it's not something I feel so strongly about that I will put such a pigeon back in the loft, unless, perhaps, it is particularly valuable.

Are you always confident of having pigeons in the clock on channel nights?
Yes, always and whatever the wind, provided the day is reasonable and dry and I've done my job. I'm also lucky that I can rely on my family to do it again and again. It's the breed.

Do you confine your pigeons to the loft the morning after a channel race?
Usually, but if they are anxious to fly I won't disappoint them. Some know when they see the doors open that they don't want to be in the air and make for their boxes, but others, because they have flown out every day of their lives, think it's the natural thing to do and want to be out. Even those that might have looked as if they had given their all the night before.

What's the difference between fitness and form?
Fitness is overall condition. The pigeon looks healthy and is free from disease and form carries on from that. The feathers tighten, the pigeon looks alive and it goes a lighter colour. A lot of people say they go darker, but on a chequer, for example, what actually happens is the chequering goes lighter, which makes them look darker. There is more bloom on the flights. And you can detect a difference in size. Sometimes smaller, but often bigger. In my own breed, the fitter they get, the more excited and easily disturbed they are. The cocks, especially, take off at the slightest thing, whilst a hen will fly that bit longer and more quickly than normal and when she drops after an hour or so she won't look as if she's been in the air. I never really look a great deal at the skin around the keel, as some do, because I prefer not to handle pigeons very much when they're racing. I've seen a few with red spots on the keel, but it has never been a sure-fire indicator of how they would perform. Warm feet, though, is often a good indication of fitness. To me, it suggests the circulation is in order and if you follow that through logically such a pigeon may come on a cold day.

Do you like to see a pigeon sitting its eggs tightly?
Not necessarily. I find hens are usually keener the longer they sit, but the cocks can be quite the opposite. The fitter they get, the more apt they are to jump off the nest.

Does a good pigeon eat less overall than a bad pigeon?
I don't think so, although the fitter they are, the less they eat.

When do your channel candidates have their last bath before a race?
Normally a minimum of five days before. I know some widowhood men say they like to

bath them as close to a race as possible, but for the channel races it is important to build up bloom and the more the better. My father, once the channel programme was reached, would let them bath on a Sunday, but if it was raining on the following three days and they were going to the race, he wouldn't let them out of the loft again. You can tell by the scum on the water how fit they are. If you go to a loft and the bath water is clean then the fancier is a long way from achieving form.

Do you add anything to the bath water?
I've tried various products, looking for something they can drink but that will also clear as many parasites as possible. It's extremely difficult but things are getting better. For the last two years I've used *Bosmolen Bath Salts*, which are excellent and the pigeons seem to drink less. Before that I always used permanganate of potash one week and *Harkers Bloom* the other. I wouldn't just give plain water. Even salt is better than nothing.

Do you add anything to the drinkers during the racing season?
Not a lot. More preventive products than tonics. I use *Gerdon I* on Saturday night and Sunday, substituting it with glucose or multivitamins on the Saturday evening if it has been a cold day or hard race. I have tried other things as well, such as electrolytes. When you read about their properties, it seems to make sense, but I don't think they make a great deal of difference in practice. The birds seem to perform just as well without them. But you mustn't shut your eyes. Try things and then make up your own mind.

Do you use garlic?
I've tried it, but I think it's overrated, not least because a regular fall of down feathers comes about through natural health. I'm quite interested in herbs, in general, though. They will never cure anything, but if they will keep the general level of fitness and resistance that bit higher and so reduce the need for antibiotics, I think they are worth considering.

Are visitors allowed into your loft during the racing season?
No, and especially not when channel racing is on. I work all year for just two or three weeks of performances and so many silly things can go wrong. I can only speak for my own team, but they become more nervous the fitter they are and having people round just disturbs them for nothing. Neither will I let anyone handle my channel team. A person only has to have sweaty palms and they will take all the bloom off. The way I look at it, people have got three-quarters of the year to come to my loft.

Are you better at racing hens or cocks?
I'm probably a better hen fancier. I did a survey of my performances over a five-year period and found that eighty per cent of my best positions were won by hens. I got it

into my head that perhaps my cocks weren't as good, but then looked at it from another angle. Most of my hens over that period were medium to small, suited to sitting well into the cycle, which wouldn't have suited their mate. Since then I've tried even harder to get the maximum from my cocks, pairing two-year-old and proven cocks to yearling hens who won't be going across the channel.

Have you ever been tempted to push your pigeons out to Pau?
I've thought about it on several occasions, but to Carlisle it's 804 miles. My pigeons originate from 700 milers, they have been tested in other areas to 800 miles and very few of them look as if they're on their last legs after Niort, which is 604 miles, so I'd have no fear of getting them (unlike a lot of breeds which, if you don't see in race time, you don't see again at all), but I'd hate to think that, if I kept sending them, I might grind the will to win out of them and turn them into homers. I have flown Nantes with the NFC a few times, though, and I think it provides very good tuition. I've sent two-year-olds, hoping they would get a pull over the channel with experienced southern pigeons, and some of them have gone on to make quite good birds. They have been racing against birds going in all directions and have had to think for themselves.

Is it worth treating sick pigeons?
Up until the last few years I would have said the chances of anything which had been sick going on to race well were extremely low, but I've had cause to reconsider. In 1991 one of my youngsters went thin and he was only cured when I took him to Raymond Ingram's. I put him back on the road and he completed the programme and he then went to the coast as a yearling. As a two-year-old he looked extremely well so I sent him to three channel races. He scored in each of them and he scored again last year.

Do you treat for anything in the lead up to a race?
Not as a matter of course because I've heard of the possible side-effects. My eyes tell me if they are not quite right. I recently decided to have my pigeons tested. I looked at my birds over three days and selected four to take to Raymond Ingram's. Two that looked in exceptional health and two that should have done but whose droppings weren't very good and which had looser feather. The first two were clear, but the other two had crop canker. Like a lot of people, however, I do treat for canker and coccidiosis as a precaution before pairing up.

With pigeons not drinking as much in the early part of the year when the weather's colder, how do you make sure they take the required amount of medication?
I usually leave it in longer. I don't use any more but if the instructions say treat for three days, I just top the drinkers up with fresh water and leave it in for five days.

Is it necessary to treat at all?
I'm not sure. In the past we never bothered and if a pigeon did become sick, nine out of

ten times it could be cured with a dose of Epsom Salts. Nowadays, though, diseases seem to take a bird over more quickly.

Do you prevent sparrows from gaining access to your loft?
I try to, as I think they can be very harmful, but of course it can be a bit difficult when the doors are open on an evening. You should, I suppose, expect your pigeons to develop a natural immunity, but I don't think it is worth taking the risk, especially in the vital part of the season. One infected sparrow can ruin everything. Apparently, snail trails are even worse. It's from these that pigeons get a lot of diseases.

Accordingly, do you prevent your birds from picking about the garden?
No. I do wonder if I should, but I think there's nothing nicer on a summer's night than to let your pigeons walk on the grass after exercise. Some people tell me pigeons should be either in the air or in the loft, but that would take a lot of pleasure out of it for me.

Do you dip your pigeons?
I have done, but I prefer not to because it takes the oil out of the feathers. I remember one year when I dipped them, it rained a week later and they were like rags. It was just coming up to a channel race and it was a case of having to get the prayer mat out!

How often do you spray your loft?
With having an old loft, I try to keep on top of parasites as much as possible, so I spray the nest boxes just before the youngsters are due to hatch with whatever is the flavour of the month, and after that I spray the front of the nest boxes and the perches every week. In the past I have also bought medicated straw for nesting, but for the last five years I've bought half a bale of ordinary straw, put it loosely in bags and sprayed it every time I've gone down the garden, so it's well treated before pairing up. I also creosote the boxes as well - if not the whole of the box, I at least put a blob under where the nest bowl will go. The other thing I use is a *Vapona Bar*.

What's your racing mixture made up of?
To a degree it's influenced by the weather, at least in the early part of the season. I still think beans give a pigeon a bit more to go on when it's cold, so if it's supposedly summer-time and they're over the 100-mile stage they end up with 30 per cent beans, 30 per cent peas, 30 per cent maize and 10 per cent small grains. As the season progresses and providing the weather has warmed up, I increase the peas to about forty per cent instead and reduce the beans accordingly. However, by one week before the channel they have at least forty per cent maize in the mix whether it's still cold or not. I feed a variety because transporters carry a broad mix and it's quite important to be as near to that as you can. One thing I've never been against is changing the actual mixture, that is the brand not the diet, in the middle of the channel races if I think they aren't coming well enough. The ideal method, really, is to use two different brands. That way, if

anything is doubtful at least half of it might be good.

How can you asses the quality of grains?
Because of the scientific methods of processing corn and the way in which a lot of commercial mixes are presented, you haven't any way of telling until you've fed it. Much of it is highly polished and soaked in something to make it more presentable. But it isn't as good as it should be and you have to be very, very careful. One of the biggest difficulties is in knowing whether the corn has become damp at any stage. Maize is the most difficult to assess. I don't know how they transport it now, but in the past it used to come in from abroad in open-topped lorries and if it had become wet, it could be very dangerous.

Is it better to hand feed or hopper feed for the distance?
I don't think it makes a lot of difference. I used to hand feed, but for the last three years I've hopper fed a mixture and the birds have flown just as well. The only difference is they seem to recover from a hard race more quickly on the hopper. People say they will become too heavy given a hopper, but I haven't found that to be so at all.

If you hand feed, how can you gauge how much they need?
That's the problem, really. I don't think you can assume they've all eaten sufficient as soon as the first few make their way to the drinker, but then again the amount you can get into them in three feeds can be too much. It's difficult and the only real guide is the weight each bird is carrying.

How much weight do your channel birds carry?
I know some fanciers say they should be slightly heavy to see them through their time in the transporter, but I like to put them in the basket how I'd like them to come out. It feels as though there is plenty of weight on them but they are buoyant, as opposed to a dead weight. You don't want a dead weight because after they've eaten in the basket they will struggle to fly.

Can pigeons be kept in too good a condition in the close season?
I've thought about this a lot. Some people think that because the pigeons are just sitting in all day, they can feed rubbish and then the boost of good corn the following spring will bring them into condition. Others have gone a step further. I know of two guys in Scotland who open the loft doors once the moult is through and let the pigeons fend for themselves. The idea is that their pigeons will be able to look after themselves during a hard race. I can see the merit in both those methods, but personally I try to do what's best for the pigeons at all times. They need a certain amount of fat in the winter months, so I provide plenty of variety and enough for sustenance and refuelling. Over the last few years I've also used plenty of linseed and *Hormoform* both during and after the moult to try and get as much oil as possible into the feathers. I used to give the

linseed every three days but now I put it in the mix so that when they walk away for a drink they have eaten everything bar the linseed and barley which they will then go back and pick at for the rest of the day.

Does this mean your birds become overweight?
Yes, but it just means I have to work them a bit harder at the start of the season. Anyway, it's all action from mid-February onwards, so there's plenty of time to get them into condition.

Being overweight does birds no harm, then?
No. Better that way than on the lean side.

You mentioned barley. How much do you give?
Nowadays, not more than fifty per cent. I know successful fanciers who feed as much as ninety per cent and I've tried it myself, but it's a grain which dries the feather too much. Consequently, if a flight takes a knock it may crack and break off, whereas if you get plenty of oil into the feathers they may just bend. Old Fred Marriott used to be very hot on that.

Is the sport on the decline in Cumbria?
I would say so. I could name twenty fanciers who have given up in the last three years alone. Mostly they have done so either because of the hawk problems or because they feel that let down by the RPRA. There's a great deal of bitterness and disappointment among flyers, who feel that the RPRA should do an awful lot more on fanciers' behalf. The amount of funds generated at Blackpool is a commendable feat, but people in this area think, probably rightly, that we shouldn't give any more to charities. It's not a question of generosity, as the lads around here wouldn't think twice before organising a charity sale for a sick friend, rather that we have our own problems to sort out. I'm sure if we explained to the beneficiaries of the Blackpool Show that we needed the money for a year or two, they would get behind us and strengthen our lobby.

Where do you stand on vaccination?
I'm totally convinced now there has been a deterioration in pigeons since it was introduced. I know a lot of people blame it for their cocks ceasing to fill their eggs and indeed it has happened to my own in a few cases, too. In some areas, I think it could also be causing epidemics of things such as wet droppings and young bird sickness. At first I blamed losses and disease on the influx of pigeons from abroad because I don't close my ears to the way they dope pigeons. I still think that's a part of the problem, but over the years we've been lowering the level of resistance of all our pigeons. We never got diseases on the present scale even five years ago, yet pigeons mixed just the same.

What effect have the hawks had on your own loft?

I'm losing, on average, eighteen to twenty pigeons a year to the hawk, and that's just old birds. That's quite a lot in my book and I must say the hawks should be commended for their choice of pigeons. I've lost two that had won 2nd fed at Niort in the last three seasons and numerous others which had scored in the first ten of the combine. How long does it take some fanciers to find such pigeons? It would probably take some all their lives to get just one to perform to that level. I was fortunate that I got into a capable team of pigeons and my breed is sufficiently well-established to keep producing good birds despite these setbacks, but it still makes it no easier to accept.

Which side of the sport do you prefer, the breeding or the racing?
The breeding side. I'm absorbed by it. Nowadays, because of the number of good pigeons that have been wasted as hawk meat, as far as racing goes I would have to get annoyed with someone or something to get motivated again. I've even considered in the last six months stopping racing altogether, or at least until the situation improves. I would miss it because there is no feeling in the world to compare with the one you get inside you when you see a pigeon coming from 500 miles. I don't get a better feeling than that from anything. But I think too much of my pigeons to throw them away. This is one of the reasons why in the last few years I've taken a particular interest in people who have scored regularly with my blood. It is the supreme accolade and I feel really honoured. It softens the blow of hawks and has given me a boost, if you would. Because of the hawks I am not getting a true reflection of my birds, but with other people trying them it at least keeps me abreast of my pairings.

Do you see yourself trying widowhood?
I thought I might have a go next year. I don't want to, but I may have either to change my methods or pack in racing altogether. I'm told you don't have to train widowhood pigeons and, if that's so, it may be my only hope of having a little bit of enjoyment.

Have you any golden rules?
One in particular. Always give a pigeon the benefit of the doubt. If I race something hard from the word go and it has a bad time which shows up in the moult, I will often leave it for twelve months, with good results. That is not to say, though, that a pigeon will not win carrying bad frets. I remember a blue hen which won Nantes carrying a very severe fret on her sixth flight.

What causes lofts to have ups and downs?
Good and bad years result from an accumulation of many things, as with any performing athlete. You may feed exactly the same and do all the other things the same, but there are a lot of internal things with regard to the pigeons which you don't see. Also, the human element comes into it. Two or three good pigeons are enough to carry a loft for three years, especially over the channel. But when that fancier comes to pair up, he is either unlucky, doesn't think about it enough or he uses a poor outcross.

Can you win races in today's competition with just food and water?
I'm still naive enough to think it's possible, yes. To be quite honest, I think stock birds are more in need of pick-me-up products than racers.

Pigeon or man, which contributes more to a loft's success?
For shorter distances, loft location is the most important factor. For the distance, I would say it's sixty per cent pigeon and forty per cent man, or perhaps nearer fifty-fifty. The man plays his part by getting a pigeon fit and in the right frame of mind, but I firmly believe the pigeon needs years and years of breeding behind it, too.

'The Show Hen'
1st club, 1st fed, 2nd Combine Nantes 1971
5th club Nantes 1972
1st club, 2nd fed, 6th Combine Nantes 1973
1st club, 2nd fed Nantes 1974

'Johnny'
1st club, 1st fed, 2nd combine Rennes

'Frankie'
1st club, 1st fed, 4th combine Nantes
4th club, 1st fed, 1st combine Nantes

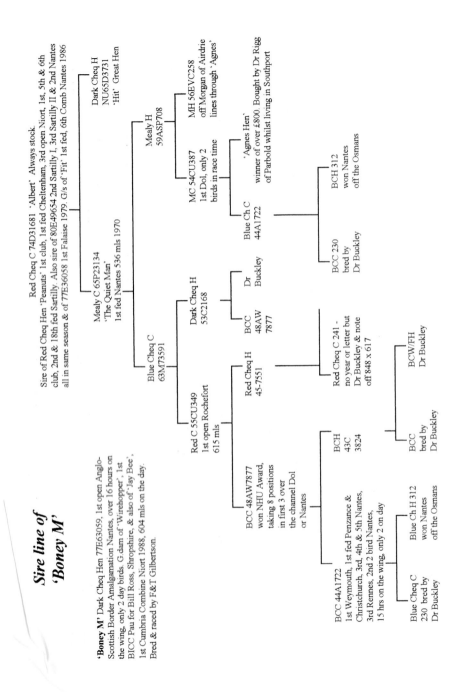

Sire line of 'Boney M'

'Boney M' Dark Cheq Hen 77E63059, 1st open Anglo-Scottish Border Amalgamation Nantes, over 16 hours on the wing, only 2 day birds. G dam of 'Wirehopper', 1st BICC Pau for Bill Ross, Shropshire, & also of 'Jay Bee', 1st Cumbria Combine Niort 1988, 604 mls on the day. Bred & raced by F&T Gilbertson.

Red Cheq C 74D31681 'Albert' Always stock.
Sire of Red Cheq Hen 'Peanuts' 1st club, 1st fed Cheltenham, 3rd open Niort, 1st, 5th & 6th club, 2nd & 18th fed Nantes. Also sire of 80E49654 2nd Sartilly I, 3rd Sartilly II & 2nd Nantes all in same season & of 77E36058 1st Falaise 1979. G/s of 'Fit' 1st fed, 6th Comb Nantes 1986

Dark Cheq H NU65D3731 'Hit' Great Hen

Mealy H 59ASP708

Mealy C 65P23134 'The Quiet Man' 1st fed Nantes 536 mls 1970

MC 54CU387 1st Dol, only 2 birds in race time

MH 56EVC258 off Morgan of Airdrie lines through 'Agnes'

'Agnes Hen' winner of over £800. Bought by Dr Rigg of Parbold whilst living in Southport

Blue Cheq C 63M73591

Dark Cheq H 53C2168

Blue Ch C 44A1722

BCH 312 won Nantes off the Osmans

BCC 230 bred by Dr Buckley

Dr Buckley

BCC 48AW7877

Red C 5SCU349 1st open Rochefort 615 mls

Red Cheq H 45-7551

Red Cheq C 241 - no year or letter but Dr Buckley & note off 848 x 617

BCW/FH Dr Buckley

BCH 43C 3824

BCC bred by Dr Buckley

BCC 48AW7877 won NHU Award, taking 8 positions in first 3 over the channel Dol or Nantes

BCC 44A1722 1st Weymouth, 1st fed Penzance & Christchurch, 3rd, 4th & 5th Nantes, 3rd Rennes, 2nd 2 bird Nantes, 15 hrs on the wing, only 2 on day

Blue Ch H 312 won Nantes off the Osmans

Blue Cheq C 230 bred by Dr Buckley

Dam line of 'Boney M'

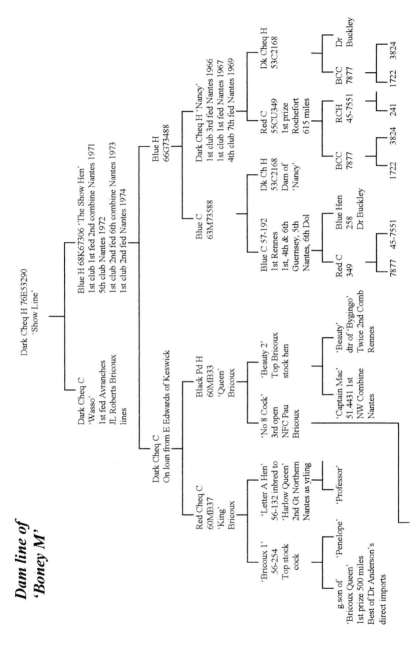

Brian & Thelma Denney celebrating another successful season.

BRIAN DENNEY

Brian Denney lives in the village of Strensall just to the north of York. He is one of the National Flying Club's longer flying members and, despite only sending an average of three birds to each race, also one of its most consistent. He races widowhood and expects a pigeon to win at all times, whether it be racing from 70 or 700 miles plus. In addition to his national record, he has also been many, many times top prizewinner in his local club. Not surprisingly, his lofts house some exceptional pigeons, chief among which are a beautiful black Stichelbaut cock known as 'Dark Peron'. This pigeon, along with his daughter, 'Whitetail', and others such as the 'Bordeaux Cock', '707' and 'Blue 20', has shown that distance and drag need not be insurmountable barriers to success.

Which clubs do you compete in?

My local club is Strensall PRS and I also fly with the Northern Classic, the North East 700 Mile Club and the National Flying Club. I have now also joined the Midlands National Flying Club.

How competitive is racing in the York area?

There are a lot of good club flyers and I would guess that there is a fifty-fifty mix of natural and widowhood practised. Like in a lot of other areas, short, sprint-type racing is popular. I think this is because it is easier to compete in the shorter races than the long ones. Personally, I prefer the distance events. When it comes to Pau, there is only a handful of fanciers who do well. Success in national races, as in all races, depends on where you live and the type of race. Wind and drag count for a lot.

What bloodlines do you fly?

I fly a family that is known as the 'Bry-Den 700-mile' family. This is a family I have developed over the past thirty years. The early base was Derek Smith's (Great Ayton) 'Lolita' blood. 'Lolita', of course, won 1st Up North Combine Bourges at 536 miles, being the only bird on the day. I also had a very good cock of the Burger breed from Holland. This cock won me 1st Bourges, flying 504 miles on the day. Then, in 1974, I bought in the Van Hee's. These were Stichelbaut x Janssen. One cock that I had at stock for ten years bred me a loftful of winners from 80 to 738 miles. He was a grandson of Van Hee's 1st National, 3rd open Barcelona International. These were mixed with the best of my existing birds. In 1981 I fancied some De Baeres, so I bought in six for racing. By the end of the yearling stage four had won at least one first. I have now mixed these in with my other birds, pairing best to best. To complete the Bry-Dens, I bought a Stichelbaut cock in 1986 that I now call 'Dark Peron'. He is not only a great racer, but also a breeder of birds that have won up to 738 miles. This is the makeup of my 700-mile family.

Do you plan to bring in any further crosses?
Yes, I now also have a team of slate Janssens. These are being tested at the moment. They are winning but have still to go to the extreme distance, namely Pau. If they make the grade they will be mixed into my family. These Janssens, like all my pigeons, came from *Louella Lofts*; I go and pick them out, bring them back and race them along with my own young birds.

How important is origin and must a bird be bred for the distance in order to succeed?
A good fancier could turn a sprint-type family into a distance one in three or four years, or five at the maximum, depending on how he goes about racing them and what he feeds. The Janssens aren't renowned for their distance performances, but I see no reason why they won't meet my requirements and I have no doubts about them at all.

So you don't think there is any intrinsic difference in the conformation of sprint and distance pigeons?
No, I don't.

Have you looked ahead to the next stage and brought in another family to follow on from the Janssens?
Yes, but I'm not going to tell you what they are. Let's wait and see how they do first.

Do you fly natural or widowhood?
I race both cocks and hens on widowhood, right out to Pau, although I do occasionally pair up for Pau.

Do you sacrifice success in the shorter club races in order to do well in national competition?
No. Although I prefer the distance races, I try to win the first and last race of the season and as many as I can in between.

Which brands of corn do you feed?
I like to feed a high protein mix from the beginning of the moult proper and through the breeding season until just before racing starts. I believe that good, well-dried beans take some beating. I feed a mix called *Regal* which consists of 40 per cent beans, 40 per cent peas, 10 per cent tares and 10 per cent maize. I also feed a few pellets when rearing. I have found *Sherfin's* corn to be okay and I really like their *Eureka* mix which contains some very good Hungarian red flame maize. The breakdown is 50 per cent maize, 30 per cent peas (New Zealand maples, Australian dun peas, English white and

English green peas), 10 per cent wheat and 10 per cent other small grains made up of tares, safflower, dari and milo. This I use for racing old birds, along with their *Vit-Energy* mix. I hopper feed and my birds are never hungry.

Why don't you feed beans for racing?
I'm not reluctant to feed beans when racing, it's just that I find it difficult to get the right ones. If I could get hold of some I would substitute half beans for half peas, or even all the peas for beans. It doesn't matter whether you feed peas or beans, it's just a matter of maintaining a balanced diet.

Can you describe the *Vit-Energy* mix?
It contains cut cereals and whole linseed, with a high concentrate of wheatgerm oil and liquid mix/vitamins which soak into the cut cereals to give a conditioner high in energy. It also has a good percentage of high quality peanuts, which the birds are very keen on.

When and how do you feed it?
I feed it throughout the racing season. I don't feed it as a tit-bit but give them so much every day in the hopper, increasing the amount gradually so that by the end of the week it is to a depth of half an inch. Therefore they take as much as they want. They won't clean it up in one go, but if, as the week goes on, it is still there, they have to eat it before I fill the hopper up with any more of the racing mix. I try to make sure that my pigeons are never without food, but I like them to eat up the *Vit-Energy* so that it doesn't become stale. My stock pigeons have it ad lib all through the breeding season.

Do you feed or exercise any differently in preparation for Pau?
No, everything is kept just the same.

What do you treat for and when?
I have my birds' droppings and swabs tested by *Northern Hygiene Laboratories* and treat when necessary. For canker I use *Ronidazole*, for coccidiosis *Amprol-Plus*, for worms *Panacur* tablets and *Colombovac PMV* for paramyxo. I used *Ronidazole* for the first time last year after discovering that the product I had been using was only effective against canker of the mouth and throat. *Ronidazole* combats all strains of canker through-out a bird's body.

Many successful fanciers never treat for canker, so why do you think it necessary?
As far as my old birds are concerned I don't think it is, but I treat them to protect against getting it amongst my youngsters later in the season.

Can you tell if a bird has had canker?
Yes. If you look at the frill or curtain that hangs down from the roof at the back of the mouth, it will be eaten away in a bird that has had it. When buying in young bird stock

I always open the mouth and have a look.

If the frill has been eaten away does it mean that the bird will be of no future use either as a racer or breeder?
It might not mean it's finished, but I don't have a canker problem so I wouldn't want to introduce a bird that had suffered from it.

Do you treat any bird that does fall sick?
No. I don't treat sick pigeons. They aren't worth it.

Do you administer any respiratory treatments?
Yes. If I think I have a problem I use *Tiamutin*. If you open the beak and the cleft at the top of the mouth is open, then you don't have a problem, but if it is closed you need to clear out the air sacs and respiratory system.

Do you use any other products?
Yes. *Pego A 700* for race conditioning. It is a high concentrate vit/min liquid which can be given directly down the throat with a dropper for individual treatment.

Do your birds have access to minerals?
Only when rearing and racing. It is not normal for a pigeon to race extreme distances and they have to draw on their reserves, so you need to replace what they lose. I believe that during the winter, when they are not being asked to do anything, they can get all the minerals they need out of the high protein diet. The minerals I use are called *Hy-Rad*.

How demanding are you of your pigeons?
I look for my youngsters to fly the programme through to 220 miles and my yearlings to fly the channel, 365 miles, at least once on the day. The older birds are expected to fly any or all races to 500 miles plus and I think that you can keep them going to seven or eight years of age. I expect those two years and above to win or score at all times. They are flown in any race to get them race-fit as I regard hours on the wing as an important factor in getting birds fit. They have maybe six inland races and are then sent wherever. I never train old birds, since I believe that racing is the finest form of training.

Do you ever put youngsters over the channel?
I have done, but not with much success. If I made the effort, though, I can't see why I wouldn't be more successful in national-type races. They need a lot of work and experience to combat the drag in the NFC Young Bird race, whereas club and fed races are easier.

What criteria do you apply for matching breeders?

I match best to best, meaning the best racers or the best-known breeders. I have no fads with pigeons. Having a family of birds makes it easy to pair up and knowing which have performed well also helps.

Some people say that the first youngsters off yearlings often turn out to be decent. Do you agree?
I've heard it said many times, but I don't know whether or not it's true. From my own experience I've found it makes no difference. I can't see any reason why it might be so.

How many winners do you breed in an average year?
Very few, but more than most lofts!

How many birds do you house?
Usually I winter around thirty pairs of old birds and breed forty to fifty youngsters. I don't have a fixed number as I only keep the best. My loft could easily hold three hundred, but my nest boxes are half-empty at pairing up time.

Do you sell pigeons?
Yes. I always have inquiries for long distance birds, mainly due to my results from Pau.

What are your views on vaccination?
I think it's rubbish.

Do you think prisoners are worth breeding off?
Yes. They're okay if well looked after.

What are your views on pigeon politics and commercialism?
I have no time for pigeon politics and, as for commercialism, I think it has now been carried too far. A lot of people are in the sport just to make a killing.

How much importance do you attach to pedigree?
Pedigree to me means how the bird is bred, that's all. Then it is up to each bird to make its own pedigree as far as performance is concerned. I would not bring a bird into my family without knowing its breeding, then, by racing it, I would soon know its performance.

Do you believe in eye-sign or any other theories?
No, all theories are rubbish. As I said earlier, I have no fads.

Not even a small fad?
I don't like pigeons to stick their tail up - if you can call that a fad. I look at pigeon racing this way: if you don't like the look of a pigeon you have a choice, either cull it or

race it out. By racing them hard I've found that the same type comes through. A type that doesn't have any physical flaws.

Do you not even try to mate birds with opposite eye colours?
No. I cannot see any reason for doing so.

You now have your own family of birds. Do you favour line-breeding, inbreeding or crossing?
All three are very important and must be done to some degree to make a family, based on performance at each stage.

Why are losses so high?
We hear a great deal about the subject. My view is that fanciers are always making excuses for themselves and their birds. Ninety per cent of fanciers don't know what a fit bird is. A lot of pigeons go to the races that just aren't up to it, either in health or condition. If fanciers were to breed and cull, instead of just breeding, there would be a fifty per cent drop in losses straight away. In the races a lot of the so-called clashing would disappear because the rubbish wouldn't be there to cause it.

You mentioned that you don't train old birds, so I imagine your youngsters have a thorough education?
Yes they do and they need to have if you want them to be with you after a hard young bird programme. To gain experience, I think youngsters should be trained from any point, not just on the line of flight, and jumped about to various distances. I start mine at twenty miles, as I think that is about the right distance. Anything less and I've found they mess about. Take them out of their area and they head straight home. Mine beat me back right from the first toss.

How do you combat lice?
I spray the loft with *Duramitex* two or three times a year. This keeps them 'clean' at all times so I don't find it necessary to use anything directly on the birds.

Do you move squabs from under wet feeders?
For a start, I don't like wet feeders so the answer is no. A pair of pigeons would have to be good to stay in my loft if they could not rear a cracking pair of youngsters without stress. I've never had a good pigeon that couldn't rear its own young.

Is there any merit in feeding polished corn?
No, it is no better than corn which is unpolished.

Do you let your birds take advantage of the fact that you live close to some fields?
No. I don't like my birds to field and try to discourage it, as I like to be in total control

of them at all times.

Do you like deep litter?
Yes, I prefer it. I use a form of deep litter made up of straw and chippings and the birds never have dirty feet. It saves a lot of time and, if the loft is well ventilated, the dust is kept down. I don't use it for the widowhood hens, though, as it encourages them to nest.

Do you find it easy to choose your pool pigeons?
No, I find it very difficult because, when I have a loftful of fit birds, they act very much the same. I like a bird that stays up flying on its own, particularly if it goes off for fifteen minutes to half an hour and keeps doing this during the exercise period. I also like the other type that won't leave the nest box except for a clap round before going back in again, never being out of the loft for more than a couple of minutes. This is one of the reasons why I don't close the loft doors at exercise time.

How much weight do your birds carry for the distance races?
They always feel big but are actually very buoyant. They are in race condition.

Do they lose much weight?
Obviously, yes, if it is a particularly hard race, but normally, no, not even from Pau.

Do you lose many birds at Pau?
My birds have been to Pau consistently since 1980 - I've sent perhaps ten times - and I can count on one hand the birds I've lost.

I assume you don't flag your pigeons?
No, and I never have. It's a joy to watch my birds at exercise. They have one hour in the morning and an hour and a half at night and do just what they like.

Have you learnt much from watching pigeon videos?
I have never seen a pigeon video. By the names I see connected with many of them, I assume it's a case of cashing in.

What do you think the future holds for the sport?
The problems facing the sport are very serious. We must all help to keep the sport going, but ours is competing against a lot of pastimes and hobbies which people can become 'good at' more easily in a very short period of time. We don't help our sport as much as we could and more needs to be done at all levels. I liked the ideas put forward by John Wright, organiser of the London Show, which included producing promotional literature.

Your loft is probably unique in that it has an apple tree growing through it. Trees apart, what are your views on loft design?
I think a loft should be as big as you have space for and be kept bone dry with lots of ventilation. It should be made so that nothing can see in and the pigeons can't see out, but still be light and airy.

Which has contributed more to your success, you or your pigeons?
The man is more important than the pigeon because he controls the pigeon one hundred per cent from the day it is born in everything it does. The best fanciers and stockmen get the best results in breeding and racing, whereas the poor fanciers and poor stockmen can't get the results with good, known stock after a year or so on their own.

Would you like to see an early liberation from Pau?
I'm not really bothered. I go by what the convoyer chooses and accept it whatever. It's probably fairer for the longer flyers if it's a late liberation, but I've taken good positions from early and late liberations. From an early lib, I was 1st Section K, 118th open. I do think, though, that all 500-mile races should have an early liberation to give birds every chance to get back on the day.

Do you think you would need different pigeons if you flew a shorter distance and had a chance of getting them on the day?
No, it would make no difference at all.

Do you think you'll ever see the occasion when, given an early liberation, you'll time on the day?
It's not impossible, providing the bird had a helping wind and was capable of flying all day. In 1981 there were about three hundred on the day and some got to six hundred miles.

Does flying Pau slow pigeons down for the future?
No, not at all.

Last year you doubled back Pau pigeons into the Saintes National just three weeks later. Had you planned to?
Yes, if they had had a decent first race. Obviously, if Pau had taken the stuffing out of them it wouldn't have been possible. As it was, they returned from Pau on Sunday and were clapping about again the next day. You don't get many good pigeons, so it's a case of striking whilst the iron is hot.

How do you help them recover from a hard fly?
I do nothing special. The hoppers are full of their normal mix and the drinkers are full of plain water. I very rarely get a bird back that needs special treatment. They get stuck

into what is in the hopper at the time.

Were the pigeons in better shape for Pau or Saintes?
It's hard to say, but I think they were something like equally fit.

When do you know it is time to stop a pigeon?
I'm not qualified to answer that. I race them on or cull them. I retired my old 'Burger Cock' at seven years of age and put him in the stock loft, but he didn't breed anything of note, so I brought him back out when he was nine and put him back on the road. I got another four seasons racing out of him and he actually scored from Angouleme at ten years of age.

Why do you sometimes pair up for Pau?
I do it only for the hens' benefit, as a hen sitting has that little extra incentive to race home after being flown unpaired all season. My good hen, 'Whitetail', 51st open and 234th open NFC Pau, has been to Pau on both widowhood and paired.

You have recently started to house one or two stock pigeons. Why the departure from the tried and trusted method of racing everything out?
In all honesty I'm only now starting to see the light. I want to preserve the line. Some of my best birds are now getting older and I've found that I have very few youngsters off them. If you race widowhood, you can't breed many youngsters off your best birds. Added to that, I sell a few pigeons and naturally people only want them off my best. I end up parting with one from the spring nest and then demand for late-breds means I let some of them go as well. I won't be keeping many youngsters for stock, but they will be off my best and will carry on the strain. I will be pairing sons and daughters of my best-performing birds together and one can't do any more than that.

Of your current race team, which bird has so far proven to be the best breeder?
There's not much in it, but I think 'Dark Peron', the sire of 'Whitetail', has to have the edge.

What preparation do you give your Pau and Saintes candidates?
It differs. Last year, for example, 'Blue 20' had both Sartilly and then NFC Nantes, '707' went only as far as Rennes as he is more of an inland pigeon, and the 'Bordeaux Cock's' last race was Sartilly five weeks before. After that he was just flying round home. At Pau, the 'Bordeaux Cock' took 109th open, and 'Blue 20' 170th, whilst at Saintes '707' was my first bird at 84th open, the 'Bordeaux Cock' took 133rd open and 'Blue 20' was 337th open.

Did you send 'Dark Peron' to Pau?
No, he has never been. There's no reason why, other than the fact he scores consistently

from 500 miles. His programme consisted of Sartilly, 365 miles, Rennes, 410 miles, taking 3rd open Northern Classic, then Niort, 533 miles, again with the Northern Classic, where he took 15th open, fourteen hours on the wing. He followed this by going to the Saintes National, 573 miles, where he was my third pigeon on the day, taking 247th open.

What is your greatest ambition?
Above everything, to win Pau at 738 miles.

Do you think you might already have realised that ambition if you'd lived further south?
It would have helped, but I'd rather win it against all the odds.

What advice do you have for novices?
Don't be afraid to throw your birds in at the deep end. Remember, a bird in the loft which isn't winning anything is a bird in the loft which isn't worth anything. Get to know the best fancier in the area, then follow his methods. Use your brain and work out how to beat him, then go for it.

NFC Record from Pau since 1986 & Saintes/Bordeaux since 1991
(sending an average of 3 birds per race)

	Section	Open	Birdage	Racepoint
1986	8th	439th	4,585	Pau
1987	7th	174th	5,333	Pau
1987	18th	546th	5,333	Pau
1987	19th	548th	5,333	Pau
1989	3rd	62nd	5,465	Pau
1990	4th	51st	6,213	Pau
1990	9th	104th	6,213	Pau
1991	5th	234th	4,992	Pau
1991	8th	452nd	3,776	Bordeaux
1992	3rd	33rd	5,070	Saintes
1992	6th	137th	5,070	Saintes
1993	7th	109th	5,423	Pau
1993	8th	170th	5,423	Pau
1993	5th	84th	5,273	Saintes
1993	7th	132nd	5,273	Saintes
1993	15th	246th	5,273	Saintes
1993	18th	337th	5,273	Saintes
1994	20th	419th	5,976	Pau

Bry-Den Blue 20 GB85 S35520

4th Fareham 220 miles, 3rd Wallingford 168 miles, 2nd Basingstoke 193 miles, 2nd Basingstoke, 4th Rennes 410 miles, 3rd Nantes 469 miles, 4th Wallingford, 4th Basingstoke, 3rd Nantes, 4th Rennes, 3rd Nantes, 3rd Sartilly 365 miles, 19th Section K, 709th Open NFC Nantes, 12,027 birds, 8th Section K, 170th Open NFC Pau 738 miles, 5,423 birds & 19th Section K, 337th Open NFC Saintes, 573 miles, 5,273 birds. These last three performances as an eight-year-old.

Pedigree:

GB84S43002 — 1st fed Sartilly 365 miles, 1st Nantes 469 miles, 1st Rennes, 2nd fed 410 miles, 12th sect, 345th open NFC Nantes, 6th sect, 137th open NFC Santes 573 miles, Winner of another five firsts inland etc

- **Dangerman GB79V56351** — Winner of eight 1sts etc. Only flew three seasons due to losing an eye
  - **BELGE75-3105749** Van Hee
    - BELGE73-3104092 Napoleon
    - BELGE73-3104166 Madam Motta
  - **BELGE75-3105428** Van Hee
    - BELGE73-3104144 Jean Pierre
    - BELGE73-3104122
- **GB77N3818** Van Hee
  - **NEHU74E9075**
    - Spleidine BELGE74-3204643
    - Constable BELGE74-3204675
  - **GB79V30165** Van Hee — This pair filled my loft with winners / The Super Van Hee NU74V68045
    - Benedictine NU74V68045
    - The Super Van Hee NEHU74E9075

GB84S43068 — Stock. Sister to the dam of Whitetail, winner of 51st & 234th open NFC Pau, 738 miles. Sire of Whitetail is Dark Peron, 33rd open NFC Saintes 573 miles

- **Darkman GB81S17027** — 1st fed Montlucon 555 miles, Clocked from Pau 738 miles twice
  - **GB77N3818** Van Hee
    - GB77N3704 Son of The Super Van Hee
    - GB77N3829 Dtr of Continental Queen
  - **GB78N20634** Pau Hen
    - GB71E 60847
    - Derek Smith's blood
- **GB79N09474** Pau Hen — 1st North East 700 Mile Club, 1st sect K, 118th open NFC Pau 738 miles
  - **GB78S47387** — Full-sister to Continental Queen
    - NU73H73611 Cheq Lady
    - Dtr of Old Burger x D Smith

ALAN PARKER

Alan Parker has reached the top of the tree not once, but twice, first flying into Clitheroe, and latterly to Downham. When he moved to Downham in 1982 he sold off his entire team of stock and race birds. These were Ken Kippax and Ponderosa Jan Aarden x Ko Nipius and had been responsible for many outstanding birds through to national level. The main birds went to Clwyd Lofts, including 'Kipo', 'Bronzy', 'Dutchman', 'Maggie May', the 'Spencer Hen' and 'Champion Scruffy', a pigeon he describes as a fantastic racing machine. Many a fancier would have struggled to re-establish himself. However, he soon unearthed pigeons to take their place and his current team of mainly Delbars and Busschaerts have kept him to the forefront in an area noted for being ultra-competitive.

Do you pay any attention to the eye?
Yes, and I think most good fanciers do, regardless of what they may say. Many are just too embarrassed to admit to it or talk about it, but the eye is the first thing they look at. Personally, I have been interested in eye-sign for twenty-five years. During that time, I have travelled thousands of miles, not to buy pigeons, but just to see the top birds, so as to gain an idea of what I should be looking to breed. I've always looked to see whether they had a good eye and I have many memories of the champion racers and breeders and their eyes. In 1972, when I was a young lad, a couple of friends and I went to Louis Massarella's. We camped outside his place, which was then at Kirby Muxloe, and I knocked on his door and asked him if we could handle the champions. He agreed, so we went to the lofts every day for three days and I handled them all: 'Townfoot Goodboy', 'Gladys', 'Pauline', 'Solway King', 'Whitehaven King'. All of them. And they were all the same. They had fantastic eyes, and their conformation and feather was fantastic, too. On the same trip we went to see George & Webb's loft in Wellingborough. There I handled 'Pandora', 'The Flying Dutchman' and 'Fechan Lass' and they, too, were just the same. You could spot all these pigeons a mile away. Anyway, what I saw stuck in my mind and I made a habit thereafter of going to see big winners. I would just ring a chap up and ask him if I could go and have a look at his pigeon.

What do you look for in the eye?
It's hard to describe but first of all, I love family eyes and, within that, I like to see an eye with plenty of colour and not too big a pupil. I don't understand correlations, but I want to see a build-up of colour in the iris as I have found that a dominant-coloured eye always goes hand in hand with very good feather quality.

Have the eyes of your best birds anything in common?
For breeding, yes. They all have fantastic multicoloured eyes.

What about your best racers?
No, the same isn't true with some of them. Actually I judged the eye-sign classes at Blackpool in 1994. The breeding class turned out to have plenty of good-eyed pigeons, but when I got to the racing class, I struggled. Talking of Blackpool, I once entered a hen there in a Flown-Pau class. In one season, she flew Niort, 530 miles, twice on the day, winning 1st Blackburn Fed, 2nd amal and, a week later, 10th Pennine 2 Bird, both very hard races with velocities of 1108 and 1107ypm. I didn't enter her to win, but just to see what the judges thought she would be like for breeding. Anyway, she didn't get a card, so I went over and asked the judges what they'd faulted her on. They told me her tail stuck up in the air and that she wasn't balanced properly.

What did that tell you?
That you can't see a pigeon's heart and you can't see its brain either and that constitution is everything. For that reason I now don't criticise anybody's pigeons. I have seen so many that I haven't liked, which have won races.

What is your preferred type?
I like the wing to be long, with a good step between the seventh flight and the last three and also between the primaries and secondaries. I have found that my best distance birds have wings like this. I also like a one-tailed pigeon with balance - not deep keeled - and with good vents. Vents should be very strong and you should just be able to fit your finger between the end of the keel and the vent bone. To avoid them becoming looser I try not to let my hens get too fat. The other danger with fat hens, of course, is that they can become egg-bound.

Can you help such a hen?
Yes. I use castor oil and a syringe for lubrication and, putting my finger inside, work the egg round.

Does this mean she is finished for breeding?
It depends on whether or not you pull her egg sac out. I had an egg-bound hen only recently, but I rested her for a year and she laid as normal last season.

What criteria do you use when selecting your pairings?
I like to pair my birds up on eye-sign and I have produced many excellent birds this way. As I said before, I believe that the best breeders have top-class eye-sign and, when paired to a mate with an ideally-matched eye, they will produce top-class birds. Providing, of course, the balance and shape is right, too.

Alan Parker

Do you pair two dominant-eyed birds together?
No.

Is pedigree important to you?
Only if it gives racing details of a family. I attach no value to just a list of ring numbers.

Since you have a number of different strains, do you practise widespread crossing?
No, but I am going to try it, as I see that many top birds are the product of a cross. In the main, though, I try to build a family around good birds, line-breeding and inbreeding to my best. I have a particular liking for half-brother and half-sister matings.

Which strains do you fly?
Mainly Delbars. The hen of my Number One Pair won 1st Preston 2 Bird Nantes in 1989 for Wilf Orritt of Chorley. When Wilf retired from the sport at the end of that year I purchased quite a lot of his birds, including my Number One Pair. They were both bred by JR Sutton of Congleton and exchanged with Wilf via the Lancashire Social Circle. This pair are of the old Delbar lines and have bred four different direct Nantes winners at 460 miles (the cock bred a fifth Nantes winner when paired with another hen). They have bred oceans of winners and their grandchildren are winning too. Last year I timed a yearling hen, a granddaughter of my Number One Pair, at 8.34 pm out of Niort, fourteen hours and thirty four minutes on the wing to win 1st club, only three birds on the day, and 1st fed. I also have a very good Delbar cock from Jack Roberts of Marple. Paired to '35', a hen out of my Number One Pair who won three channel races as a yearling, he bred a pigeon to win £1,200 in the 1993 Young Bird National. I also have a number of Busschaerts, my main pair being 'Larco' and 'Downham Lass', both of which came from Tom Larkins in the early eighties. Last year a hen out of a grandson of 'Larco' won 1st East Lancs Amal, 2nd Lancashire Combine Nantes for T Norgrove of Chatburn. My good Busschaert cock, 'Downham Lad', bred a hen which bred the Queen's Cup winner from Lerwick for Tom Swiers of Summerbridge in North Yorkshire. I have one or two other strains as well, including a Wildemeersch cock called 'Toe' which has won nine firsts and an RPRA Award and, in turn, has bred a hen called '32', which has also won an RPRA Award. Her seven firsts have included 1st Pennine 2 Bird and 1st Border Amal.

Is 'Larco' still breeding?
Yes, although he had a bad time of it for a while when I changed the loft. He gave over filling his eggs until I gave him a course of pills from *Gerdon*. I believe that racers keep themselves fit but stock birds are different, especially as they get older, so I now give them plenty of iron in the form of tablets or crystals from the chemist, and watercress. It is worth the effort, as I have produced some of my best birds out of old pigeons, and likewise out of pigeons which have been kept prisoner for years.

What's the competition like in north-east Lancashire?
Very, very strong. A lot of money is spent each year on improving stock and there are many fanatics who would go without meals so as to purchase either good corn or pigeons. The best club for many years in Blackburn Fed, has, in my opinion, been Clitheroe HS, whether inland or across the channel. Most of its members race natural. The Barnoldswick PFC is just the opposite, being mainly widowhood. The Lancashire & Yorkshire Border Championship Club, a four-bird specialist club, is particularly competitive. Indeed, all the best long distance flyers compete in it, duplicating their birds back from the National Flying Club. You would hear a lot more about quite a few of them if they were in a better location for the nationals, meaning if they were further south, and if we had as many good scribes as they do in the Blackpool area, which have made all the winners there household names.

Which races do you concentrate on?
I try to win every week, whether from 70 or 730 miles, although in the last two seasons I have put more effort into the channel races, at 350 miles plus. This is the direction I will continue to go in the future, and all my birds now have to be able either to produce outstanding birds or score from the distance themselves.

Do you chase averages?
I used to, but not anymore. Actually, I never set out to, but somebody would say something to spur me into action and I would empty the cabin. I won't be doing it again.

Why the change of approach?
I want to get out into the big, wide world. When you win a lot locally you can get a lot of stick and, to be honest, I can do without the hassle. I try not to get involved in pigeon politics anymore and do not like all this 'we do not want him in because he's in a good position' mentality. If a fancier applies to a club and is in the radius he should be allowed in.

How has this changed your management?
I now pair up later - at the beginning of March - because to do well in the channel races you don't want to be starting too soon. I have had success in the distance events when racing from start to finish, such as winning Section L in the Pau National at 730 miles, but on occasions it was more through luck than good management.

Which system do you practise?
Mainly widowhood. Over the last few years I've raced twenty cocks on the system, although I increased that number to thirty in 1994. I also keep a few naturals, racing some of my best channel hens to young cocks. As they are kept with the young birds they only pair up when the cocks are old enough and I have won many long distance races using this method. I have never tried roundabout, but would love to fly a team of

hens on it if I had more room and time. My brother, David, has been very successful with hens on both roundabout and widowhood and I can see a lot of advantages in the system.

Do you always show the hen?
No. Pigeon racing is all about knowing what motivates an individual and adapting accordingly, so I work different methods at different times for different pigeons. For example, a lot of my cocks only see the nest bowl for three or four races. I don't leave the bowl in the box, as some do, but re-introduce it before basketing. For the distance races, however, I believe you have to motivate a lot more. You've got to get into their brain what there is to come home to. I've had some good wins from 460 and 500 miles with widowhood cocks in the last few years, but I've always put their hens in with them for the two days before basketing. For example, in 1993 I won NE Lancs 2B with a yearling cock that had been allowed to re-pair with his hen. He shadowed her all over the sky and built a nest in a day and a half so I knew he would do well if he crossed into this country.

Have you had much success at Pau with widowers?
I've had three section positions, but nothing of any substance. And I've sent good pigeons so it's possibly me who is at fault. I always like to have a go at Pau, but I think for 700 miles you want to be basically natural. Certainly, I've done better with natural hens. And you need a pigeon that can fly 700 miles in around twenty hours, which is not necessarily a pigeon that wins at 500 miles on the day but rather one that comes next morning. Birds that can fly 400 miles the first day and 300 the next are very few and far between. Many turn up about two weeks later, having been in the fields. Incidentally, in the very hard Pau race of 1992, when Section L was won on the Thursday, I actually had a hen reported in South Wales the day before. She hadn't gone in, the chap had caught her on the top of his aviary, but needless to say, if I'd been less than honest I could have gone and fetched her and clocked her. As it was, I let her make her own way back and she eventually turned up just after the close of the race.

How do your widowers trap?
Straight to the nest box. I always have a tit-bit of *Red Band* or peanuts waiting for them so they know to expect it. People tell me I shouldn't use peanuts because they contain harmful toxins, but, to me, if it says they are for human consumption, you can't get a better guarantee than that. The pigeons love them and they do the pigeons a lot of good if given in small quantities.

When do you first introduce your cocks to the widowhood system?
This year, with changing my approach, I raced my yearlings on natural just to get them to home, but my normal practice is to teach them the widowhood system as early as possible. Widowhood is easy, but they must be taught the system so, starting in the

November of their young bird year, I take them up the field to teach them what it is all about.

Do you flag your pigeons?
Flagging is my obsession. When racing I flag both old birds and young birds morning and night. All I have to do is put plastic bags on a pole and, after a week, they know they have to exercise.

Are your channel hens raced prior to mating with the young cocks?
No. I am a big believer in private tossing so they are just sent training, perhaps as far as Cheltenham. Their first race is over the channel and, as they invariably only pair to the young cocks at the beginning of June, this normally coincides with their first nest of the year. Using this system I can get perhaps as many as three channel races out of them in a year.

Do you train from anywhere?
I do now, although when I was only keen on sprinting, I just took them twenty miles to a breaking point on the line of flight.

Turning to diet, what do you feed during the winter months?
Two parts beans, one part best milling wheat and a pinch of rape, all of which comes from the farm. (I leave polished corn alone.) To this I add cod liver oil and leave it to stand in the house for a day. At this time of year I only feed once a day, at mid-day in hoppers, and they have as much as they can eat, although I have found that, since they don't go out much, they can miss a feed and benefit from it. Their droppings are loose, but I know it does them no harm. Indeed, it cleans their system out and keeps them very fit and, once put back on a high protein breeding mixture, they fly for hours. All they get apart from this is clean water or mollases, of which I use a lot. When I pair up they have beans in hoppers, and this is supplemented by a high protein breeding mixture once the squeakers appear in the nest. I give little, but often, so that the old birds continually go and feed the squeakers and I always produce good youngsters this way.

Why feed beans?
Because they are cheap and because they are an excellent protein feed for building muscle.

And rape?
Again, only because the farmer brings it to me and it, too, is cheap.

Do you clean your farm beans?
No, they've still got the black husk and all sorts on. Incidentally, the best four flyers in my area all fly on these same farm beans.

What do you wean on?
I don't give them any maize. They are hopper fed beans and hand fed a high protein mix - as much as they want - until I start training. As you can see there is always food there if they want it, as I don't believe in limiting them at this time.

Don't they get on the heavy side?
They are overweight, yes, but this lets me control them. They won't fly until I get their bodyweight down, so the week before I start training, I feed them depurative for a few days.

Are you a good young bird flyer?
Not anymore because I now think for the future. There is no doubt in my mind that if you want to win young bird races they've got to go training every day and be fed a restricted diet. I used to do this, feeding them only an ounce a day but, looking back, not many of those youngsters went on to do fourteen or more hours on the wing.

How many good pigeons do you breed?
I would say about ten per cent make it as racers. I am sure, though, that within a true family you should be able to get something like ninety per cent capable of breeding winners.

How many birds do you keep?
About a hundred.

Do you part with any?
Yes. I sell a number of young birds each year to help pay for my hobby, and to give others the chance of trying my birds.

Turning to your old birds' racing diet, what do your naturals race on?
Fifty per cent beans and fifty per cent maize throughout the season.

Is that all?
Yes, apart from what I call my 'treat'.

Which is what?
Twelve eggs mixed in a bucketful of groats. I put it on a board to dry out in the sun and give one or two handfuls to twenty pigeons daily. I've always been a fan of groats. Only recently I went to a talk on pigeon food given by *Spillers*. It was brilliant. They weren't just interested in selling their corn, they took the time to explain all about the nutritional value of grains and one of the things that came out was how good groats are for pigeons.

Do you feed your widowers fifty per cent beans, too?
No, far from it. I use a commercial widowhood mix. I wouldn't expect to win sprints if I was feeding beans as they make the birds too sluggish. They are fed *Spillers Depurative* and *Spillers Widowhood* with extra maize, always fed on the floor in hoppers. On Thursday night, I add peanuts and maples - as much as they will eat. I feed for about ten minutes, giving it to them in the hopper until they have bursting crops. On Friday they are fed at about 10 o'clock by my wife on a mixture of three types of maize - cinquetina, plate and the big dog-tooth. I don't feed popcorn maize as I don't think it would give me what I want. I give them this as it is speed-food, full of carbohydrates and I have found they don't look to drink as much water. By the way, once on this system, my widowhood cocks never go out to exercise on a Friday.

Do you break your widowers down?
I used to when I was keener on land races, breaking them down until Wednesday morning, but I now give depurative only on a Saturday when they come back or, if it has been an easy race, until Sunday night.

Do you treat for canker?
Yes, but not all my pigeons to the same degree. My stock birds are done only once, after they have reared a round of squeakers, as the cause of a lot of problems is not letting the birds' own system fight the disease. But with the racers it is a different matter. If you don't treat, it can stop them from reaching peak form and if you want them to win the big ones and be consistent, the birds have to be fit.

So how often do you treat your racers?
In the last couple of years once a fortnight when racing - on the Sunday - and I have found they have kept in top condition. I use *Ridzol S* one year and *Emtryl* another.

Is fortnightly cankering not excessive?
No. They are only treated for one day and then only at half-dose.

Is it necessary to treat for canker at all?
I think you've got to be aware that it's always a potential problem. I'll tell you a story. About three years ago my pigeons weren't doing as well as they might. A couple of good birds had what I thought were respiratory problems, so I treated them and they got no better. Anyway, I took them to the most knowledgeable pigeon fancier you'll ever meet, Raymond Ingram of Workington. He took swabs and was able to tell me within five minutes that they were both riddled with canker. The point is, you couldn't tell just by looking, as the canker wasn't visible.

Do you now have your birds regularly tested?
Not as such. I went out and bought my own microscope, so I can now see for myself if

there are any problems. If there is anything I still don't understand, I then get on the phone to either Raymond or Rod Adams. I don't use local vets, as most, since they don't specialise in pigeons, haven't a clue.

Do you give them multivitamins each time?
I give vitamins the day after and then they have two days on herbs. One day for the nervous system and one for depurative. These are from Raymond who, using herbs, has perfected the keeping of birds in a healthy state.

Do you think such regular treatment against canker will have any adverse long-term effect on your birds?
Like you, I've asked that question too and all the experts have said no, it won't harm them. I'll tell you what I think may be harmful - the traditional way of treating. I listen to people when I'm on panels and they invariably treat for everything at the start of the season in the space of a few weeks. I'm sure that doesn't do the pigeon any good.

Do you worm your birds?
Only when I think it necessary. If the droppings are small, and my birds are producing healthy youngsters and racing well, I leave well alone.

How do you treat sick pigeons?
I use my own experience. For example, if I see one 'hitched up' I use *Sesqui*, which I have found to be great, and if one has a gut problem or poisoning, I use charcoal tablets. Generally, I put sick pigeons in a wire-floored aviary - which is particularly good for solving respiratory problems - and if I have any other problems I put treatments in the water.

Which product do you use for vaccination?
A different one each year, to make sure it has the full effect.

Have your birds had any other health problems?
Although I don't seem to have much trouble, last year my youngsters couldn't fly off the floor. Their throats were inflamed and they started vomiting so I asked about in order to find out what the problem was and a local partnership said they'd had the same trouble. It turned out to be thrush, caused either by an airborne oral virus or mildew on the corn. I treated them with a product containing bicarbonate of soda, called *Nystan*, and it was fantastic.

Did this thrush have any lasting effect on the youngsters?
No. One of them went on to win 92nd open and £1,200 in the Young Bird National and 1st Lancs & Yorks BCC at 362 miles on the day in a north-east wind.

Do you place any store in young bird performances?
Yes, as I have found the best ones for the future are those which fly consistently well. All my young birds have to fly 225 miles at least twice and quite a few go to the 300 to 365-mile races. Those which are timed on the day from these two longer events usually go on to become my best channel birds. They are rested as yearlings, having just the odd race, and then they go to 500 miles as two-year-olds.

How far do you send the rest of your yearlings?
If I see something special, it will only go as far as the coast, but the rest, including those which I am trying out, have at least three channel races, one of which is at least 500 miles.

Have you had much success with late-breds?
Yes, they have proven to be some of my best birds. Indeed, my top racer, 'Lone Ranger', a winner of ten firsts and over £1,000, was a late-bred. They have been bred out of my best racers after the racing season, pairing best to best.

Do you race them along with the rest of your yearlings?
No, I train them with the following year's young birds.

What preparation do you give your distance birds?
They all get different preparation. Some have every race inland, whilst others have only a few. I train them on the wagon from any distance and direction, although having said that, my best pigeon in 1993 was a red cock who had no training. He started off by winning 10th fed Stafford, scored twice more inland and then had four channel races. He won 169th open MNFC St Malo, 216th open NFC Nantes, 6th 2B Nantes and 5th fed Niort, 530 miles. He was so fit, he was doing somersaults all season.

How else can you tell when a pigeon is on song?
You have to watch your birds every day and they will tell you in different ways. Generally, the cocks can't keep still. They are up and down all the time, either on the loft or in the air. I also know a hen is on form when I see her in the fields picking straw and reeds. She will pick it up, set off over the countryside, deposit it in the loft and go straight back out for more. Incidentally, to keep them busy I put nesting material and food down in the fields and they travel round looking for it. I have also found that some of my best hens would not come off the nest when it was the cock's turn to sit, or they have gone into other nest boxes and taken over the eggs or squeakers of another pair. And I would add the observation that when pigeons are indifferent to food, they are right. I take notes on their keenness and how they shape in training. Once you find out a bird's favourite condition - the condition in which it is keenest - you have got a good bird.

Do you take any notice of a pigeon's throat?
I only look to see that everywhere is clear. From time to time, they are prone to having dry mucus in their nostrils, and if this is the case I clear it using *Golden Oil.*

What goes in your drinkers after a race?
Either five or six drops of *PLG* or a similar such product, or *Colombine Tea* mixed with Glauber's Salts. I make up a bucketful and put some in their boxes for an hour after every race as they return. Then for the rest of the day I give them tea and vitamins. Unless a bird is very tired, in which case I add glucose to lukewarm water and put it in its nest box for a couple of days. I'm no vet, but I know that there are many things now that pigeons can pick up in the basket, so you must do everything you can to stop cross-infection. As soon as they go in that pannier you have no control over them. The water can be awful and you can tell, when you look in the baskets, that a lot of birds are not in good condition. Many have respiratory trouble caused by fanciers having too many birds in their loft. I have an aviary attached to mine and it is ideal. I am sure this is one of the chief causes of losses, particularly amongst youngsters. That, and the fact that many panic through insufficient schooling. If you just train your own and lift them into the third or fourth race you will find that it is not the distances which lose youngsters but the fact that so many have not been educated properly. In my area, we have a 75-mile race on Sunday morning each week which gives the young birds an excellent start to their education.

What else goes in your drinkers?
You name it, I've tried it, so usually something. As I mentioned earlier, I've always used a lot of molasses and they have that on most days. This year, I've used *Aviform*, but only because my daughter won a bottle of it. There are no magic potions, though, and I judge a product's worth simply by the effect it has on the birds. If you can see a change for the better then it's got to be good.

What are the main requirements of a well-designed loft?
Dryness and ventilation. I have many different types of loft but the main thing they have in common is that they are all dry and well ventilated. You can tell your ventilation is right if the droppings are dry. Whilst on the subject of loft design, I regard the fields as my natural loft and when I first moved here, my plan was to house my birds in a barn and have them on 'open hole' for twenty-four hours a day. However, it was so cold up there that they only came into form for one week a year. If I'd stuck with it, I'd still be a novice.

What do you use on the loft floor?
My youngsters are on grills, my stock loft has a deep litter of straw, which I like very much, and the racing lofts are cleaned out every day. I also use loft white in the boxes when racing. It makes the pigeons look better.

Why not use straw throughout?
Because I tried it and it got everywhere, as my wife would testify. Anyway, my widowers stand on blocks, so it doesn't take five minutes to clean out.

How do you control parasites?
I'm a big disinfectant fan. I eradicate lice by dipping in *Ectofen* and using lice powder and I also spray my loft every week with pine disinfectant. If you do not keep lice off your birds they burrow into the quill stem and consequently it becomes very brittle and splits. Whilst breeding I use newspaper in the nest boxes, soaking a little in creosote before putting it under the nest bowls, and I also put a small washer under the bowl just to lift it off the wooden nest box so that damp and condensation do not occur and cause other problems. Once racing has finished, I thoroughly clean and creosote my nest boxes and perches again.

Have you watched any pigeon videos?
Many, but I prefer books as they have many useful tips. You can and will always learn something from others.

Why is the fancy in decline?
Cost, which is an aspect I think the RPRA could do something about. They could do a lot to make racing cheaper. For example, paramyxo vaccines should be bought and sold at cost price. In other respects, commercialism does not bother me, except that some of the big studs are after making money, not producing winners. Some of their birds are way distant from actual winning stock.

Pigeon or man: which contributes more to success?
I think that if you get the birds fit, the main thing is the pigeon. Once you have a good one, it will come week after week. In today's competition you need something special. Pigeons which do not follow others. That's why I give them a lot of private single tosses, even as young birds. You will soon lose the duffers.

Who is the best fancier you've met?
Ken Kippax. I was brought up in his area and, in my opinion, he was the best. He was a master when it came to matching pigeons and he taught me a lot with his training technique. Over 700 miles, he also owned the best pigeon that will possibly ever fly into this area, 'Maggie Ada', nine times Pau and seven times a prizewinner. She was out of Louis Massarella's Five-Star family which we talked about earlier.

Alan Parker (left) with Vin Donnelly.

Alan Parker's *Number One Pair*

Principal progeny

Scalpy Blue hen 91N06717

1991 8th Lancs & Yorks Border Championship Club Weymouth, 225 miles
4th Lancs & Yorks Border CC, 38th Section L, 1,158 birds, 343rd Open NFC
Young Bird Sartilly, 357 miles, 9,681 birds. 11 hours & 11 minutes on the wing
in a north-east wind. Velocity 949ypm
1992 4th Barnoldswick PFC Rennes, 400 miles, 1st NE Lancs 3 Bird, 4th Border
Amal, 6th NE Lancs Fed Championship, 20th Lancashire Combine. Velocity
970 ypm
1993 1st Bacup Clock Station National Flying Club Nantes, 1st Lancs & Yorks Border
CC, 17th Section L, 1,293 birds, 126th Open, 12,027 birds. Velocity 1130ypm.
Hard race - north-east wind
2nd Clitheroe HS, 4th Fed, 10th Amal, 50th Lancs Combine, 105th Open Chris
Catterall's Nantes, 9,466 birds. Velocity 1116ypm. Another hard race. Lost to
hawk 1994

Wilfy Blue cock

1990 13th Section, 55th Open North West Classic Young Bird Picauville, over 300
miles
1991 2nd Barnoldswick PFC Niort, 3rd NE Lancs Fed, 7th Amal, 24th Lancs Combine
1,641 birds. 530 miles on the day (only 20 on the day in fed)
1992 1st East Lancs Fed Championship Nantes, 460 miles, 1st Barnoldswick PFC
(only 2 on the day in club), 2nd NE Lancs Fed, 4th Amal, 12th Combine, 2,390
birds, 44th Chris Catterall Open, 9,913 birds. Velocity 998ypm. Hard race. 13
hours, 32 minutes on the wing. Now stock & sire of a yearling in 1994 to take
8th Fed Sartilly, 356 miles & 20th Fed Rennes, 400 miles

Blue hen GB88

Winner of three channel races & now one of my best stock hens
Dam of **Nystan**, 1st Lancs & Yorks Border C/C, 92nd Open YB National, 9,368 birds

N Berry's son of the Number One Pair

1991 1st Padiham Young bird Breeder/Buyer race
1992 1st Burnley Central HS Nantes (only 2 on the day), 64th Combine, 2,390 birds.
Velocity 862ypm

Alan Parker's Number One Pair

Young Duke   Delbar
Blue cock   GB87143439
3rd Preston 2 Bird Nantes
450 miles then stock.
Bred by JR Sutton, Congleton
& raced by Wilf Orritt of
Chorley. This pair bred
channel winners for Wilf
before I bought them &
since 1990 they have bred
together 4 different Nantes
winners.
The cock has bred 5 Nantes
winners

Classic   Delbar
Blue hen   GB87133151
7th Eccles 2 Bird Bergerac
velocity 766. 23 hrs, 58 mins
on wing, 610 miles.
1st Preston 2 Bird Nantes
Now stock. The best hen I
have ever owned.

The Duke
Cheq cock   GB83Z38362
9th sect 20th open Mid Nat.
Rennes. 1st Lancs Soc Circle
Rennes. 9th & 20th Great
Northern Saintes, 4th Saintes
Minshull Open, 12th Rennes
Cheshire 2B, 3rd club Nantes

GB84Z30478   Delbar

GB86J52545   Delbar

GB84J32327   Delbar

GB80J59708   Delbar
4th sect NFC Sennen Cove
62nd sect NFC Pau

GB81W24430
Bred by T Thorley

GB82N95236
95th open NFC Nantes

GB83Z38368
4th club Cheltenham

GB83J53933   Delbar
2nd club Sartilly

GB77N95536   Delbar
1st LSCircle Nantes

GB82N95245   Delbar
60th sect NFC YB Guernsey,
2nd Rennes, 12th fed & &
2nd Great Northern Saintes

GB81W09711   Delbar
1st club Penzance
5th club Rennes

NU74N30451   Delbar

BELGE74-452822   Delbar

GB82Z70535   Delbar

GB81N46749   Delbar

GB80R85254   Delbar

GB80R85244   Delbar

GB80J59735   Delbar

GB80R85241   3rd Sartilly,
18th & 34th sect NFC Pau

GB80J59729   4th fed Sartilly
36th Gt Northern Saintes

NU73V94836   Delbar

NU71125065   Delbar

GB80J59722   3rd Nantes,
3rd Avranches & 3rd Saintes

GB80J59727
2nd Mangotsfield

GB80R85244   Delbar

GB80J59729   4th fed Sartilly
36th Gt Northern Saintes

NEIL BUSH

Mr & Mrs Neil Bush and their daughters live in Amcotts, a South Humberside village perched at the northern end of the River Trent. It is a location which you might term off the beaten track as far as national racing goes and it is also a long way away from Pau, their favourite racepoint. In recent years, however, their birds have put up some wonderful performances. Significantly, they have shown their versatility by scoring whatever the prevailing conditions. When the weather has allowed, they have raced all of 709 miles, and when it has not, they have stuck at it with an iron will. The Bush pigeons have few equals when it comes to the extreme distance.

How much interest is there in national racing in your locality?
I live in a sparsely-populated area and most of the clubs are small. Very few fanciers compete in national races, probably due to the distances involved in travelling to marking and clock stations. This means there are very few pigeons coming into the area from the nationals, so you invariably need an individual that is prepared to travel long distances on its own.

Which races do you set your stall out for?
Only the long distance ones. Prior to 1981 this meant races up to 500 miles, but since then I've concentrated on Pau, which is 709 miles to Amcotts. I fly in one local club, but inland I use it for training only. I have no clock set. I also use it to give yearlings education over the channel and for getting older birds, two-year-olds and above, fit. I concentrate on the National Flying Club and the Midlands National, duplicating into the North East 700 Mile Club and the East Midlands 650 Mile Club. I joined the Midlands National in 1992 specifically to fly Bergerac, 608 miles. I scored in both 1992 and 1993, but am now losing interest again due to their going to Saintes, which is a shorter distance.

Saintes may be a shorter distance, but it's still 500 miles, so why aren't you keen on it?
There's a sixty mile difference compared with Bergerac and that means the shorter flying southerly members are only racing 400 miles. I can hold my own against widowhood cocks once it gets beyond 450 miles, but would struggle at anything less.

Have you achieved your success on natural or widowhood?
Natural. I keep my pigeons as natural as possible. They are on 'open hole' all summer and race in a variety of nesting conditions.

How many birds do you winter?
Forty pairs or more.

What is the origin of your Pau birds?
I fly my father, Ned Bush's, Old King's Cup-winning family. They are Osman-based and have had various crosses over the years. I started with them in 1976, with birds coming from my father and my brothers, Alfred and Keith. The main bird, namely the 'Nantes Hen', came from Keith as a squeaker in 1978. Her blood runs through most of my best pigeons.

Have you any other birds bred the same way as the 'Nantes Hen'?
No. I never asked until a couple of years after I got her how she was bred, and by that time Keith had culled her sire.

Could you give me some idea of the impact she has had?
I called her the 'Nantes Hen' because she was 37th open NFC Nantes, beating over 12,000 birds. Her daughter, the 'Mealy Hen', was 4th and 13th section NFC Nantes, and the 'Mealy Hen's' daughter, 'Betty', in turn, was 3rd club Nevers, 9th section NFC Bordeaux, and 2nd and 4th section Pau. That makes three generations of good pigeons and obviously she is responsible for many other winners besides.

How many good pigeons did she breed?
One a year.

Have you introduced any crosses since 1976?
Yes. A useful cross came from Frank Cheetham of Pontefract in 1978/79 via a postal auction in aid of TRPA funds. More recently, in 1989 I brought in a good hen of Ernie Deacon blood from D O'Brien of Swindon. She was an exchange youngster. Other crosses have been tried but have not survived. I like to try a new cross but these are then tested through to Pau before any further interbreeding with my family is carried out. I don't want the genes throughout the loft until they have proved themselves.

What do you look for when bringing in a cross?
I always buy from good, long distance stock with a good record over a number of years, preferably flying to an unfavourable position in national competition.

How much importance do you attach to pedigree?
Paper pedigrees are of no use to me, but it is essential that the pigeon is closely related to winning stock at *all four corners* of its pedigree. By that I mean all its grandparents must have been good pigeons. I am quite happy to buy a youngster out of two yearlings provided all its grandparents have scored well at my required distance, but I need to be confident that the person I am dealing with is sincere. That is very important. I hate

writing out paper pedigrees and see no point going past grandparents because it's no use living in the past. If I see an extended pedigree, it makes me wonder why they had to go back so far. Is it to find a good pigeon? The apples don't fall far from the tree, as they say.

Would you consider buying in stock from a commercial stud?
The problem with commercial studs is that they don't always buy the best pigeons. They are more interested in the publicity a pigeon has attracted or will attract than its performances. More importantly, though, there is not enough progeny testing. Pigeons must be tested at every generation to prevent deterioration. At the studs you find generations of untested pigeons which means a greater percentage of second-rate pigeons compared with the proportion you would find in the loft of a good racing man or woman. Even the best racers and breeders produce a lot of rubbish and it is only through testing - natural selection - that these can be removed. Otherwise the 'family' or loft as a whole degenerates.

What has a pigeon got to have achieved before you will breed from it?
I breed from all birds that have scored from over the channel, and from one or two children directly out of my best pigeons. As I don't work my youngsters hard, I have to carry a lot of yearlings that are not good enough, and that is why I don't breed out of many yearlings.

What criteria do you use when choosing your matings?
I pair best to best. I never look at the eyes for pairing, regarding the eye purely as a useful indicator of fitness and health. If I feel a pigeon is a bit on the large size, I look for a small mate to complement it. I don't mind them being on the small side, in fact I prefer a small to medium pigeon.

How many good birds do you breed?
I don't breed enough good pigeons. If I did, I would not rear forty or fifty youngsters each year. I get two or three good pigeons in a good year. About five per cent go on to score from Pau, but I would probably double that to ten per cent if we're talking about those which will score at 500 miles. Any idiot can race pigeons, it's breeding them so you keep winning that's hard. Once you've got good bloodlines, breed a lot out of them and race them.

How many birds do you sell?
I don't like selling, so very few, perhaps two or three a year. I haven't a stock loft in which to breed loads of youngsters and any old birds that aren't good enough for me aren't good enough to sell. I don't kill many because I'm not a killing man, but I'd sooner kill one than sell it.

How closely do you inbreed?
I tend to line-breed to my base hen, favouring half-brother to half-sister, mother to grandson and so on. I don't like to go as close as mother to son or full brother and sister. I am always looking for a *good* cross but have had a lot of disappointments. I will then breed this in and gradually dilute it into my own in the hope that it will invigorate and add new, beneficial genes. I also find it interesting to compare how others' stock does under my basic management.

And do you race the youngsters out of half-brother and half-sister matings rather than put them to stock?
Oh yes. They all go.

When does your preparation for Pau begin?
When I pair up, which is on the nearest Saturday to March 7th. I allow them to sit for seven to ten days before drifting their eggs under feeders. They are allowed to go to nest again and rear the second round themselves and this gives me two pairs off the best racers and holds back both their form and their moult.

Do you flag your pigeons?
I can't flag my pigeons in the summer as they are not at home. They are sitting in the fields all day. My pigeons field persistently throughout the breeding and racing season. They don't even fly round once, they go straight to the fields. They are coming and going in dribs and drabs all day and I often have to wait for them to come home before I can basket for a race.

Are you happy about your birds fielding?
I don't mind what they pick up, as it doesn't seem to hurt them, but I would prefer they did not go to the fields, as I regularly lose one or two. Presumably they are shot. I have told them not to go, but they take no notice.

Would your performances suffer if they didn't field?
No, I don't think so. I'm not sure how much exercise they actually take. I don't think it's much because they're walking around for the most part.

Is 'open hole' the best way to fly distance pigeons?
I'm not sure. I think more than anything 'open hole' breeds contentment, and that is very important.

What roadwork do you give them?
They are given one or two inland races then, five weeks before Pau, the eggs are taken away and they go down to nest again. After having two or three more inland races plus three or four forty mile tosses, they are allowed a full week's rest before they are basketed

for Pau.

What is your preferred nesting condition?
They are usually sent sitting up to time or on a small youngster.

Do you always use this preparation?
This is my general method, but I have varied it to suit the individuals concerned. In 1992, when I was 2nd, 3rd, 4th and 7th section Pau, I sent them to Fareham, 200 miles, as their first race, with no training, then the next week to St Malo, 340 miles. I then let them go down to nest again and gave them a couple of short races and two or three tosses at 40 miles. All except one candidate, that is. She didn't go over the channel and guess what? She was the hen that took 2nd section.

Having been so successful with this approach in 1992, did you try and repeat it in 1993?
No, in 1993 none went over the channel before Pau. I sent seven and had all home in race time, clocking five to finish 4th, 6th, 13th, 15th and 17th section.

What does that say about the ideal preparation for Pau?
If there is a moral to this, I am not sure what it is, except that you need good pigeons in good condition and it doesn't matter how you get them fit.

Have you tried any other approach?
Yes, I've also sent them to the Nantes National, 440 miles, before Pau and scored well with them, but it is not my usual method. As they say, many roads lead to Rome. Talking of Rome, when they flew from there the other year my brother, Alfred, had the second bird back over a thousand miles with a bird he could trace back to 'King of Rome', winner of the Rome race in the 1920s.

What preparation have you given your other channel candidates?
The pigeons that have scored from Bordeaux, Saintes and Bergerac in nationals over the last three seasons all went over the channel prior to scoring, mostly using NFC Nantes as the pipe-opener. They performed much better the second time over the channel, showing that the work of the previous race had tuned them up.

How many do you send to Pau?
I've sent seven, twelve and thirteen on the occasions I can remember off the top of my head. The most I've ever sent was twenty-one in 1989. I got eighteen, although not all in race time.

How do you recognise form and select pool pigeons?
I pool my pigeons very little as I don't think you should put on what you can't afford to

lose. Since I have three growing daughters, I don't have a lot of cash spare. Back to the main question of recognising form, though. Different individuals show form in different ways. The eye colour deepens, they moult two flights close together, the cocks bounce about, the pectoral muscles tighten so they are like a rubber ball, and they come well in previous races. Along with this, I look at how they performed the previous year from the same racepoint. You have to be observant and notice any changes in the behaviour of the bird, and you can't do this in an armchair or propping up the bar.

How much does Pau take out of them?
I've found that when a pigeon does well, it doesn't look tired when it drops, but give it an hour and it does. They pull round after twenty-four or forty-eight hours if they're any good.

Do you lock them in their boxes to make sure they rest?
Oh no, I don't do anything like that. Mind, I don't force them out either.

Do you think you could get Pau pigeons back into condition to fly the Saintes National three weeks later?
I don't think so, especially not hens. Give me a month, though, and I would say yes. Even if I could get them right I wouldn't send them because I don't believe in flogging a good pigeon. I send the others that still have something to prove, and we've all got plenty of those.

Why do you consistently do better from Pau than Nantes?
Because my birds don't get sufficient preparation for the Nantes National. It comes too early in the season for them. By the time Nantes is flown, they have only had two or three inland races and three or four forty mile tosses. I was beginning to think my birds weren't fast enough, but I am now sure it's lack of work that makes them a bit slow as, when it comes to Saintes later in the season, the same pigeons are usually there or thereabouts. Also, my brother Keith scores well from Lerwick, 500 miles, with the same family of pigeons.

Have you thought of having a really good go at Nantes?
I haven't got the time or enthusiasm to pair up earlier and work them for it. Pau is my only serious race. Bordeaux or Saintes with the National Flying Club come before Nantes and even they are a distant second.

Sometimes fanciers with a poor record do well at Pau. Why is that?
Pau is like any other racepoint. They have a good pigeon on the right day. It's often one which has made a mistake somewhere along the line earlier in the season, causing it to put in some work to get back on the right track. If a pigeon scores at Pau, it doesn't necessarily mean it's good. I've scored with some myself that I didn't think were good

birds, and sure enough, I've lost them the next time.

Despite all your good performances, topping the section has so far eluded you. Is that your ambition?
Not really, I just want to keep being consistent. I think my pigeons would need more work to win it. I send them prepared for a grueller and therefore they aren't quite fine enough. I'm quite happy to continue sending them to face the hardest of days, as I wouldn't forgive myself if I got them ready for an 'easy' Pau and they hit a hard one.

Aren't you tempted to pick out just one bird and give it a go?
I have done it once with a hen. She scored, but it knocked the stuffing out of her. *(Neil was subsequently to top the section in the very hard Pau race of 1995.)*

So how much weight do they carry for Pau?
They need a bit of extra weight for two-day racing, but I wouldn't call them fat. Rather, they are well-fleshed with plenty of muscle.

What is the ideal type for Pau?
I've had good pigeons of all shapes and sizes, but they must be robust, as any weakness will be found out at 700 miles. If it is really difficult, as in 1992, I find my hens are more reliable. They seem more determined to get home than the cocks. Whatever the type, they must have long distance bloodlines throughout their pedigree. Occasionally sprint pigeons will prove me wrong, but they are only a flash in the pan. They must also be able to use their heads. It's no good their following pigeons all over the country. I think lots of pigeons can fly 500 miles or more, but many do it in the wrong direction.

Does flying Pau spoil hens for breeding?
I wouldn't like to say, although if I think they are breeding well, I'm prepared to stop them. It's not always the best racers that make the best breeders, and if they aren't breeding me anything I keep them going.

Do birds deteriorate as breeders with age?
In general I think younger pigeons breed best. If I am breeding from an old pigeon I find it a young mate. My best stock hen, though, the 'Nantes Hen', bred good pigeons all her life, but then, she was an exceptional pigeon. At twelve years old she was paired to a red cock out of my brother, Keith's, 'Rocky' and they bred one of my best pigeons, my good 'Dark Hen'. She won 4th section, 53rd open NFC Saintes in 1992 as a two-year-old and 7th section, 24th open MNFC Bergerac, velocity 738ypm - a very hard race - in 1993. Obviously she is of sound constitution. I think whether they are old or young, they need to be fit for breeding and this becomes more of a problem as pigeons get older. This is one reason why I have no prisoners. If I buy an old pigeon, I breed two rounds off it and then try and settle it. If I lose it, so what? It's odds-on it will have

bred nothing and if it does leave something behind, I have more than my money's worth. It is also a bind to keep shutting them up and seeing them trying to get out. I now usually buy youngsters straight from the nest.

Which is the harder, 500 miles on the day or timing from Pau on the second and winning day?
I enjoy flying both 500 miles on the day and 700 miles in two days, if I can get them. It's never enjoyable if you don't time in. I know which is the harder, and I think the people who knock two-day racing are generally those who are struggling to time in.

Does it require a different type of pigeon for one than the other?
I've never had a 700 miler that wouldn't score at 500 miles, but I've had lots of 500 milers that couldn't do 700 miles. In the NFC Pau race the 700-mile pigeon has to be up with the 500 milers on the south coast, or how can it score in the open result? They don't get faster over the last 200 miles! The 700-mile fancier has to be single-minded and send his best. It's no good sending the also-rans. They get slower still or, more usually, don't come at all.

Are there any drawbacks in consistently sending to Pau?
The main problem with 700-mile racing is that it is very demanding on the pigeon and I think it probably slows them down for the future. Consequently, when they have been to 700 miles I never bring them back to 500 miles.

Would you like to see an early lib from Pau?
No, we do better up here if they liberate later so I'm a mid-day man. Early liberations worry me. If it's a hard race, they'll hit the channel at nightfall.

Have you thought of flying Barcelona?
Yes, but I'm not interested. It's not that I think it's too far - mine would fly it - it's because I think the best competition is to be found in the National Flying Club.

When do you first send them to Pau?
I may send one or two two-year-olds, particularly those which are the product of a cross I'm trying, but normally I wait until they are three years of age or older. Most of my three-year-olds go to Pau, although I might keep one or two back for NFC Saintes, or Bergerac with the Midlands National.

How far do you generally send two-year-olds?
My two-year-olds go to NFC Nantes, followed by NFC Saintes. They must be showing promise by then, or else!

What do you ask of your yearlings?

They have two channel races up to 400 miles. I expect them to home on the day if conditions are reasonable, but give them another chance if they don't. I have put up some good performances with yearlings over the channel, topping the fed, for example. Whatever its age, if I send a pigeon over the channel, it should be able to face any type of day without distress.

What education do you give your young birds?
They have two or three races up to 180 or 200 miles. They are raced to the perch and only have to home to ensure a perch for the winter.

Does it matter which direction you train from?
I always train youngsters on the line of flight, but for old birds I think training off line is a good idea. It takes the pigeons a lot longer in terms of flying time, so it gets them fitter and makes them think for themselves. As they invariably get split up, it gets rid of some of the slow-learners as well. It's not for the faint-hearted and if you start to worry if your pigeons are a bit late or have a night out, then training off the line of flight is not for you. Liberating in poor conditions also has the same effect.

Aren't you tempted to send some youngsters over the water?
No. I think the channel, which is 340 miles to me, is too far if they get a hard day. I liken it to sending a boy to do a man's job, especially as my youngsters are hatched in April and May. They are still growing and are even more immature than most people's. It would be okay if you could guarantee a fair, easy day, but I don't think you can risk young stock on that premise.

Would a hard channel race finish a youngster off?
Yes. Once you have knocked the stuffing out of them, you can't put it back no matter how much tender loving care you give them.

What are your youngsters fed?
Youngsters are hand fed in troughs, with the basic mix of peas, wheat and maize in the morning, and a beans-only feed at night.

What are your thoughts on late-breds?
Some of my best racers and breeders have been late-breds so I think they are alright. I always breed some. They are out of my best pigeons when they are at their peak of fitness, so how can they be anything but the best? They are easier to lose than early-breds, as they have not been tested as youngsters and lack experience. But, with a little patience, I find they are worth waiting for. I like to train them a little in their year of birth to ten or fifteen miles and I will even train in November and December if the sun shines.

Do you give them any special treatment?
Yes. I keep them separate from the older birds, as I feel they need plenty of food because they are still growing and moulting. They are fed the same as the others except in January and February, when they have a mix of 80 per cent barley and 20 per cent beans in the morning and just beans at night.

When do you first race them?
They tend to be slow starting as yearlings and are better left to races in May or June. Mine usually go over the channel as yearlings in late July. I send them in the last channel race with the fed, which is 322 miles, and they have even scored while double moulting.

What is your basic feeding system?
From January 1st until February 28th I give them one feed a day, keeping them on the short side. This is made up of 80 per cent barley and 20 per cent beans. From March 1st to December 31st they are given beans ad lib and have a mix of one third wheat, one third dog-tooth maize and one third green peas. The basic mix is hand fed morning and evening and they get as much as they want.

What brand of corn do you use?
None. All my corn comes straight from the farm. I never feed polished corn because I can't afford it.

Do you feed it as it comes out of the bag?
Yes, it's all uncleaned except the maize and any food left is returned to the corn bin.

Which are the best grains for pigeons?
For breeding I would say beans, but perhaps that's because I can't afford maple peas. I don't know which is the single most important grain for racing. They need a variety: protein for muscle and carbohydrates for energy. It doesn't really matter from which grains they get this balance or from where you get your corn, it's just important that they do get a balance.

Do you buy new beans?
I prefer to as beans don't get any better with age. New corn germinates better, so there must surely be more goodness in it.

How do you alter your feeding as you approach the channel races?
I add to the basic mix 5 per cent dari and 5 per cent safflower and also increase the percentage of maize. The amount is dictated by the birds: if they want it they get it. I observe what is left in the trough and feed accordingly.

As you only add a mix to the hopper morning and night, how do you make sure the hens, who will be sitting both times, eat the same as the cocks?
I don't worry about it. They have to eat what's there. I'm sure we worry too much about pigeons.

What else do you feed?
I give each bird three or four peanuts a night as channel racing approaches, but I only use about two stone a year. They really look forward to these and it helps me to develop a good relationship with them. Over the last two years I have also fed a little oil seed rape to the old birds whilst they are racing and moulting. Once again, this comes straight from the farm.

Why did you introduce rape into the diet?
Only because I had it given to me. I shan't bother with it when my supply runs out. I'm not a great fad feeder, not for 500 miles.

What are your birds fed on their return from a race?
My hoppers are full of beans as usual, but I also give them a light feed of 50 per cent barley and 50 per cent of the basic mix through to Sunday evening. On Monday they go back on the normal feed. If they haven't recovered after two days they are no good to me. By recover, I mean looking fresh, as they may still handle light.

Do you put anything in the water after a channel race?
Yes, I dissolve a dessertspoon of honey to a four-pint drinker. I'm not convinced it does them any good, but it doesn't do them any harm. My father always used honey and he won two King's Cups. Old habits die hard.

How do you account for losses?
The thing which I think is responsible for most losses amongst youngsters is ill-health. I think young pigeons are like young children going to school. They catch all the childhood illnesses and gradually build up their immunity. Just like children, they are as fit as fiddles one day, very ill the next and right as rain again the day after. Pigeons may look well when you send them, but may be in the incubation stage of an illness. If so, then by the time they are liberated they could be very ill and so never return, as young pigeons soon become skin and bone.

You don't automatically cull a sick pigeon, then?
I would not condemn a young pigeon for being ill provided it made a quick recovery, and I would never train or race them if I knew they were ill. This is where you need time to observe your birds carefully. Old birds are different. I am very suspicious of those that show any sign of illness.

How do you treat sick pigeons?
I isolate them and give them a pot of barley and clean water. If they show no sign of recovery in two or three days I suppress them.

Does clashing cause many pigeons to be lost?
I am sure it does, but surely if they have not got the sense either not to follow others or find their own way back, then are they the type of pigeons we want anyway? I don't think they would compete successfully in NFC racing to my area, where they have to come alone for long distances. Survival of the fittest, in this instance, means survival of the most intelligent.

Have you had experience of pigeons which have made mistakes going on to be good birds?
Plenty. The 'Nantes Hen' made no end of mistakes. One season she nighted-out three or four times inland, but she was the first in the clock when I put her over the channel. Another good cock I had, who scored at Pau, was lost off the loft as a late-bred and went missing for twelve months. I don't take any notice of mistakes like that.

When do you vaccinate?
I vaccinate my young birds as they leave the nest, and all the birds in early January, using *Nobi-vac.*

Are you happy about doing it?
Yes. I have never had any adverse effects from vaccination. I always use the cheapest product on the market and would continue to vaccinate even if it wasn't compulsory.

What else do you treat for?
I normally worm my old birds three times a year: before pairing, after rearing and again just before the first channel race, although this year I didn't bother. I never treat for cocci as I haven't had it for donkey's years, and normally only treat for canker if I see any sign of it in my youngsters. In the past I dosed the whole flock with *Emtryl Soluble,* but this year I used *Ronidazole.*

Do you give a course of multivitamins after a treatment?
No.

Why didn't you treat for worms this year?
I had my birds tested for the first time by a vet. I took a pigeon from each section, a cock, a hen and a late-bred and the only thing he found was a touch of canker in the late-bred.

What have you used for worming in the past?

All sorts. Normally animal worming treatments.

What supplements do you provide?
I use chicken grit (oyster shell) ad lib all year round, various brands of pickstones and pink and black minerals.

Do they always have access to minerals?
No, I don't give them in winter as they absorb moisture from the atmosphere and become a sticky mess.

What consideration should be given to loft design?
A loft should be designed more to suit the fancier than the pigeons but, having said that, it needs to be dry, well ventilated and vermin free. I like my loft enclosed around the bottom so that cats and pests can't look in and disturb the birds. Contentment is important and they must feel secure. On this point, I like a good lurcher prowling around the garden. The birds soon get used to it and it keeps away all unwanted visitors.

Do you use a deep litter or clean out daily?
I now scrape out daily, but I've tried a deep litter of straw and droppings mixed together. They flew well on it in 1989 out of Pau, taking 5th, 8th, 12th, 13th, 18th, 21st and 26th section on a hard day, but my scraper lad (father-in-law) did not like it. He said it was too dusty, so he cleaned it all out, otherwise it would probably still be there. I don't see scraping out as a chore, as I like to be amongst the pigeons. I don't think it makes any difference to the pigeons what you do, although they are certainly content on straw and nest all over the floor.

How do you combat lice?
My old birds usually have a few lice on them and I don't think it does them harm. My youngsters seem to get quite a lot so I powder them with a louse powder made for farm animals. I once dipped my pigeons in a solution of insecticide commonly used for spraying pigeon lofts and killed eight or nine pigeons, some of which had scored at Pau the previous year. It affected their nervous and respiratory systems and they died within four to eight hours. Never again! I'd rather see a few lice. Apart from that, if it can be absorbed through a pigeon's skin, can it also be absorbed through mine?

How could we improve the sport?
I think local clubs should fly for prize cards only. Less money means less bickering. If people want to fly for money, they should do it through pools. We also need to create a more friendly, caring atmosphere, particularly towards the novice, whether young or old. Young members, those below sixteen, should pay reduced membership and birdage fees. They should also have their own section of the club. We must make it easier for them to have success in order to encourage them to stay in the sport. Special plaques,

cups and diplomas should be given to the novice, as should a sympathetic ear, good advice and plenty of praise and encouragement. I remember the first prize card I ever won. I was 1st club Melun, with the only bird in race time. I was over the moon and my euphoria was enhanced by the congratulations of other members, but I'll always remember a well-known fancier, who hadn't timed in, saying it was only the rubbish that had come - the best birds were missing. It may have been true, but it was no way to encourage a novice.

Do you enjoy pigeon books and videos?

I've only seen two pigeon videos, both on loan some years ago. Though they were both interesting and the two fanciers concerned, Jim Biss and Geoff Kirkland, talked a lot of sense, there were no revelations. But then, I don't think there are any to be made. I enjoy reading anything on pigeons in the winter months, but don't always agree with a lot of it. Too many people are trying to confuse and con people with their secrets. In my opinion, pigeon flying is straightforward. It is more of an art than a science.

Fancier or pigeon: which is more important?

With long distance racers the pigeon is more important than the man. I would estimate it to be 80 per cent pigeon and 20 per cent man. With sprint racing I'm not sure, as I've never had any interest in or success at it. I'm not knocking sprint racing, though, because we should all do what we enjoy.

Are you a good stockman?

I'm better with dogs than pigeons. I would say I'm a good fancier in terms of time and effort, but I'm not an exceptional judge of a pigeon. I would never say I could go somewhere and pick a good pigeon out. Good birds come in all shapes and sizes at Pau and if they're scoring they must be the right type.

Where do many fanciers go wrong?

When they put up a good performance, they look at the rest of their birds through rose-tinted spectacles, thinking they are all good.

Do you believe in any theories?

Only one - the feet theory.

Your best performances have mostly been put up with hens. Is that because you are a better hen fancier?

Although I am definitely a better hen fancier, I'm not sure if that's why I've done better with them. What I'm about to say is all theory, but I think it's a combination of things. Firstly, you only have to look at the results to see hens generally do better on hard days and I always gear mine up for a hard Pau. Secondly, I send hens in better condition. Normally they are sitting up to time, and I think cocks are better if sat ten to twelve days. In effect, with working on the hens, the cocks have to take second best. Thirdly, my brothers and my father have also done better with hens, generally speaking, so it could be that our family of pigeons breeds better hens than cocks.

If that is the case, how do you select which cocks to breed from?
As long as they are robust and all their grandparents were good pigeons, it's enough for me to breed from them.

Which fanciers do you hold in the highest regard?
Excluding my brother, Keith, probably Brian Denney of Strensall. I think Frank Cheetham was probably the best Pau flyer ever into Section K.

Brian Denney has done exceptionally well from the distance, flying widowhood. Do you see yourself trying it?
I don't think so. I wouldn't say never, as it's best not to make rash statements in case you change your mind.

What about trying your hand at sprint racing?
Never. Definitely not. It doesn't appeal to me at all. I can't even work up the enthusiasm to wait for them.

Do you involve yourself in pigeon politics?
No. I have no spare time for it. My time needs to be spent with my pigeons and my family.

What have been your biggest disappointments?
None really.

What about your biggest thrill?
The highlight was Pau 1992, but it was also a great feeling getting all four hens again from Pau in 1993.

Do you think you'll ever do as well again?
I doubt it. I'm lucky to have four good hens at the same time. When they've gone I might have nothing else.

Could you tell me a little about them?
The first one in the clock in 1993 has now been 2nd and 4th section Pau, and 9th section at Bordeaux. She's also scored at 500 miles. She is out of the 'Mealy Hen' I mentioned earlier and a cheq cock which won the club at 500 miles. My second bird is a blue hen that scored at the same Bordeaux race as the above hen. She's now been 7th and 6th section Pau. Keith bred her, but I've no idea what she's out of and neither has he. It

doesn't matter. I could get another twelve out of the same pair and none of them would be any good. My third hen is of Ernie Deacon blood. She has been to Pau three years in succession and been in race time on each occasion, including 3rd section in 1992. The last of the quartet is my 'Little Barren Hen'. She was 4th section in 1992 and has been in the first twenty of the section three years in a row. She is bred in the purple, being out of the 'Nantes Hen' when paired to a grandson of the 'Nantes Hen' which scored at Pau. Incidentally, the 'Nantes Hen' is also the dam of Keith's second Gold Award winner, three times in the first one hundred out of Lerwick with the NRCC.

Will the 'Little Barren Hen' be given an honourable retirement when the time comes?
No, she will have to keep going.

You're not sentimental about your birds, then?
No. To stay in the loft, a pigeon has got to be able to do me some good.

How you view your season is dependent on success or failure at Pau, so what are your feelings in the weeks leading up to the big race?
I don't think I become unduly anxious. Perhaps I do. You'd really have to ask my wife.

Do you get excited when you learn the birds are up?
Oh yes. I'm with them all the way.

Do you try and learn of early times?
Yes, because I like to know when to expect them. I leave it to my brother, Alfred, to find them out for me. He is brilliant at estimating what time they'll be in, whereas I'm not, so I take his word as gospel.

Do you feel a sense of expectation fulfilled when your first bird arrives?
I like that description. I'll write that down and use it myself. No, perhaps I feel a tinge of relief because I'm never one hundred per cent sure or confident at Pau. I know what it can be like. I always see Pau as a challenge and I'm always a little doubtful. When a bird does arrive, I don't go silly. I just get up out of my chair and wander across.

Do you think it can be won where you fly to?
It's possible. There have been three outstanding performances up here in recent years.

What would you do if you won Pau?
Probably sell up.

The present day pigeons of both Keith and Neil Bush have their origins in stock raced by their father, Ned Bush, whose original stock was obtained locally and were predominantly Osmans. To these were added Osmans from the King's Cup winning lofts of Perry Morgan and Headman Bros, exchange birds from AR Hill of St Just, and more Osmans from AH Cornes of Stockton Brook. A half-sister to George Breuninger's King's Cup winner was later introduced, as was a dark cock from R&M Venner of Street. This pigeon was half Trueman Dicken and a grandson of 'Barcy Boy'.

'Barcy Boy'
NU59 N 10747
(Bred & raced by L J Clack of Fareham
and later sold to R Trueman Dicken)

1st Nantes	2nd Pau	2nd Rennes
1st Bordeaux	2nd St Malo	3rd Marennes
1st Guernsey	2nd Guernsey	4th St Malo

1965 3rd Section, 5th Open Barcelona, 674 miles
1966 6th Section, 10th Open Barcelona
1967 8th Section, 16th Open Palamos, 647 miles

Grandsire of **'Ramona'** 1st British Section Barcelona 1972 & 2nd Open Palamos

Mr & Mrs Bush's Section K Record from Pau	
1982	15th
1983	No channel racing
1984	17th
1985	15th & 22nd
1986	5th
1987	9th, 22nd, 23rd & 24th
1988	31st & 34th
1989	5th, 8th, 12th, 13th, 18th, 21st & 26th
1990	24th & 26th
1991	11th & 19th
1992	2nd, 3rd, 4th & 7th
1993	4th & 6th
1994	5th, 6th, 12th, 13th, 15th & 18th
1995	1st, 3rd & 12th

'Betty'

'Betty'

3rd club Nevers, 500 miles, 1989
1st EM 650 Mile Club, 2nd NE 700 Mile Club, 9th section NFC Bordeaux, 607 miles, 1991
1st EM 650 Mile Club, 2nd NE 700 Mile Club, 2nd section NFC Pau, 709 miles, 1992
1st EM 650 Mile Club, 4th NE 700 Mile Club, 4th section NFC Pau, 1993

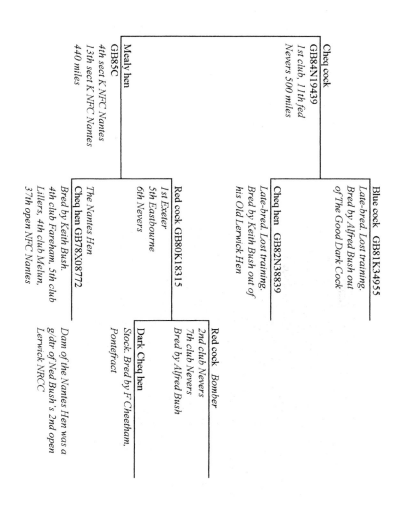

Mealy hen
GB85C
4th sect K NFC Nantes
13th sect K NFC Nantes
440 miles

Cheq cock
GB84N19439
1st club, 11th fed
Nevers 500 miles

Blue cock GB81K34955
Late-bred. Lost training.
Bred by Alfred Bush out
of The Good Dark Cock

Cheq hen GB82N38839
Late-bred. Lost training.
Bred by Keith Bush out of
his Old Lerwick Hen

Red cock Bomber
2nd club Nevers
7th club Nevers
Bred by Alfred Bush

Dark Cheq hen
Stock. Bred by F Cheetham,
Pontefract

Red cock GB80K18315
1st Exeter
5th Eastbourne
6th Nevers

The Nantes Hen
Cheq hen GB78X08772
Bred by Keith Bush.
4th club Fareham, 5th club
Lillers, 4th club Melun,
37th open NFC Nantes

Dam of the Nantes Hen was a
g/dtr of Ned Bush's 2nd open
Lerwick NRCC

NFC PAU
1992-1995

Average position of first bird for those fanciers who have
recorded at least one open position in each of the last four years

	Member	Location	Dist	Sect	Average
1	M/M Cannon	Godalming	538	A	29
2	Puddephatt Bros	Crawley	535	A	52
3	A Holdoway	Portsmouth	519	B	89
4	King Bros	Bristol	570	G	90
5=	Fear Bros	Clandown	557	G	99
5=	Shepherd & Buckley	Chichester	519	A	99
7	J&R Wills	Frimley	550	E	100
8	B Sheppard	Trowbridge	558	G	102
9	A&T Deacon	Waterlooville	521	B	107
10	M/M Hine	Hayes	565	E	115
11	S Biss	Brundall	645	H	122
12	L Painter	Southampton	523	B	129
13=	S&V Miles	Peasedown St John	558	G	131
13=	G Burgess	Wraysbury	560	E	131
13=	P Stone	West Drayton	562	E	131
16	M/M Bush	Amcotts	709	K	132
17	W Bainton & Son	Wimborne	519	B	141
18	G Baker	Bridgnorth	641	J	143
19	P Whitelegg	Liss	532	A	144
20	J Jones	Dymock	604	J	149
21=	G&E Rann	Ventnor	502	B	155
21=	A Cottrell	Wimborne	520	B	155
23	D Delea	Rainham	565	E	161
24	J&T Ellis	Whitchurch	565	G	162
25	M/M Mauger	Aylesbury	582	E	165
26	P Lovell & Son	Shaftesbury	536	C	173
27	Kinnersley Bros	Hayes	563	E	180
28	J Rawlings	Southampton	523	B	183
29	L Brazier	Sparkford	540	G	184
30=	G Wood	Ventnor	502	B	203

Neil Bush

NFC Pau 1992-1995 continued

	Member	Location	Dist	Sect	Average
30=	J Horler	Reading	562	E	203
30=	J Townsend	New Addington	551	E	203
33	L&R Hodges	Ryde	509	B	213
34	M/M Furlonger	Guildford	546	E	214
35	M/M Peters	Hornchurch	569	E	216
36	T Glover	Coalville	649	I	218
37	M/M Bunney	Portsmouth	519	B	222
38	D Brain	Portsmouth	518	B	229
39	M/M Stovin	Didcot	571	F	231
40	N Bishop	Ringwood	521	B	244
41	K Otton	Keinton Mandeville	544	G	246
42	Bowden & Auger	Southampton	524	B	254
43	Wyatt & Gray	Bristol	570	G	268
44	G Deacon	Newport	510	B	278
45	G Inkley	Hillingdon	566	E	279
46	Miss D Reed	Emsworth	519	A	282
47	M Lupo	Eastleigh	527	B	283
48	D Callard	Wantage	571	F	284
49	D Farr	Bognor Regis	514	A	296
50	J Newell & Son	Feltham	559	E	303
51=	R&R Wilton	Street	548	G	319
51=	A Mullholland	Bristol	570	G	319
53	J Kitching & Dtr	Brighton	519	A	348
54	M/M Kulpa	Reading	558	E	349
55	Mark & Peart	Sanderstead	551	E	359
56	M/M Lewis	Worcester	613	J	381
57	J Reading & Son	Morden	555	E	400
58	J Bates	Wednesfield	644	J	411
59	F Griffin	Chippenham	567	G	421
60	J Dixon & Sons	York	735	K	474

JOHN GOODWIN

As chief convoyer for the National Flying Club, John Goodwin was the man entrusted with the welfare of some of the country's most valued pigeons. A heavy burden, but one which rested comfortably on his shoulders, as he brought to the job a knowledge of weather-reading gained as an RAF navigator and many years of experience acquired on the road. These qualifications, allied to a rare passion for getting it 'right', meant he stepped down from the position with a record second to none. This conversation took place shortly prior to his retirement.

Do you race pigeons yourself?
I've never raced on my own, but many years ago I raced with my father in Catford as Goodwin & Son.

What led you into convoying?
My father became a convoyer and you could say I followed suit, as my first recollection of being on the road was as a six-year-old in Bournemouth. In the old days when we went by train, I remember we used to leave Waterloo with fourteen coaches for the pigeons, one for us, and the engine. Formerly, I convoyed for the London South Road Combine and the Surrey, Middlesex and Three Borders Combine (SMT).

How long have you been convoying with the NFC?
I joined in 1978 and convoyed without a break until 1989. I took a rest from 1990 to 1992 because of illness, but was back in 1993.

Which aspect of the job do you most enjoy?
Getting it right. I like to think I go about it in a very professional way. Any fool can liberate pigeons on a good day and any fool can hold them back on a bad day. They are the black and white of the job but in between there are a million and one greys - the marginal days - from high risk to low risk. They need skilful handling in which experience and knowledge play a large part. The kudos comes from having a grey day and producing a good race, albeit one more favourable to some than others. But that is the essence of what pigeon racing is all about - wind on the day.

What experience did you bring to the job?

I am an ex-Air Force navigator, having joined the RAF in early 1942. I always wanted to be a pilot. Indeed I went solo in a Tiger Moth after only eight and a half hours' tuition, but after I took a simulation aptitude test in navigation, they decided I would make a better navigator. I was brilliantly taught in meteorology, amongst other things, learning how to observe, record and point out the rights and wrongs at debriefings. It was wonderful training for pigeon convoying.

Is there any fundamental difference in convoying for the national compared with combines?
Combines are a lot easier because the birds are racing to a small wedge, whereas with the nationals I have to sit down and think about it a lot more. I have to keep in mind that if a fancier from Cumbria has prepared a bird he expects a fair race just as much as any other flyer, so that's what I try to give him. The committee and the national members pick the venue and the date so it is of paramount importance that I produce a race on that day if I can. The wind assists if racing into a wedge like the Home Counties and, on this matter, it is little different with the national. Those that have the good fortune to fly the wind are, of course, assisted.

What other differences are there?
The weight of responsibility is greater with the nationals. Sometimes you say to yourself, 'that was pretty good', but you can't make a silk purse out of a sow's ear. You benefit some and not others. I don't let it worry me, though, as I'm concerned with what I think, not what others think, excepting, of course, the assistance given to me by the president and race advisors.

Do you get it right more often than you get it wrong?
I've got a pretty good record and I like to think that, if the weather is readable, I can read it. Obviously, I've had my disasters where things have gone wrong, but that will always happen when you are dealing with a maritime climate with its rapid rate of change and its many variables and possibilities.

When does your preparation for Pau begin?
On the Monday. I ordinarily go to the London Weather Centre to talk through, for half an hour to an hour, the week's forecast, analysing the weather charts through to race day. I go to Reading the next day, armed with the charts and thereafter I listen to the shipping forecast. People ask me 'why bother, what use can the charts be?', and I tell them it's essential for me to build up a picture. It gives me confidence. In the old days I used to update the charts with coloured pens, but I don't need to any more because I can now build up a picture in my mind's eye. In 1993 the forecast wasn't brilliant, indeed it was very average, but a liberation was on nevertheless. We arrived at Pau at 1.15 pm on Thursday and immediately set about getting the transporters into position. At Pau this is straightforward as there are very rarely any other organisations there.

Perhaps just a tiny French wagon.

Do you make use of the airport met office at Pau?
Today it has been updated with all the latest technology, satellite information and the like, so we'd be fools not to. Each year I quickly make myself known and in 1993 it proved invaluable. The duty officer told me that Friday looked like being bad news, as there was a broken front across central France that would trace back into Pau, and this proved to be right. As you may know, fronts break and spin round, which can create a secondary front more vicious than the main one. The important point about this is that, despite having charts from London and having listened to the shipping forecasts, this was my first inkling that this would happen. Thursday evening promised rain - you know how you can feel it in the air - and sure enough, it was wet on Friday. The duty met officer said there would be no change until he updated the forecast on Friday evening, so Friday was a 'no go' day. He said we would get some more rain early on Saturday but that the day would improve, and he was dead right again. I looked at the TV monitor and it promised one of those dead and lifeless days. I was wondering if it was worth liberating, but it improved rapidly and the information for the rest of the route was pretty good, so there was no point keeping them on the ground. I said 'they won't fly more than 400 miles in this weather' and I don't think they did, although people said afterwards that we'd liberated two hours too soon. The pigeon which, I think, proved my point was Les Painter's of Southampton. It was clocked at 9.45 next morning, which, counting back, meant it was about four and three-quarter hours, roughly 150 miles, from its loft on the first day. This meant it was on line and hadn't gone to the east as a lot of the others did To my mind, this was an excellent pigeon because it had faced conditions early and stayed on line.

If you had, say, a twenty-five mile per hour westerly, would you liberate?
How precise you are depends on the distance, but generally I wouldn't worry too much about it, as long as they didn't have it all the way. Fortunately I've never been presented with a roaring westerly at Nantes or Pau, although at Pau in 1993 it became westerly for the last third of the race. For some reason, Saintes often becomes north-westerly to-wards the home end also. One point worth mentioning about wind is that, if it is light and variable, it generally means there is a little bit of 'north' in it.

Are you obliged to liberate at a particular time?
I can liberate at my discretion - early or late. When I started in 1978 I was more or less mandated to liberate at mid-day, but I didn't think that was right, so I put my cards on the table and said 'trust me, leave it to my judgement'. I look at what is in the best interests of the birds and so far I have managed three early libs. The pigeons have already been in the basket for a long time, so I liberate at the first opportunity. My attitude has also been moulded by the fact that I was once at Niort when we could have liberated before 4.30 in the morning. To miss such an opportunity if it ever arises again

would, to my mind, be criminal.

How hot can it get at Pau?
Very. You often see the heat shimmering on the tarmac and the temperature is rising all the time. That's why I'm against mid-day libs. They are just not on in such heat. To my mind, it is not intelligent race-controlling to keep the birds in the baskets and liberate in the heat of the day.

What effect does being kept in the baskets till mid-day have on the pigeons?
Like us humans, they feel more lackadaisical the hotter it gets. In the morning you can tell by the noise they make that they are raring to go, but by 2 o'clock they are not too clever. They go quiet. They have no zest. No gusto.

Would you liberate Pau birds at 4.30 am?
The earliest you could ever get them up at Pau is 5.00 am, or a quarter to if you were really pushing it, because the light is not as good there as at some racepoints. The mountains and high ground make sure of that. At that time of day you are looking for light, combined with a brilliant atmosphere without haze. This may be something we never see again now that we are pumping so much into the air, but I am ever the optimist.

A 5.00 am lib would give pigeons the chance to fly for over sixteen hours on the first day but still not reach home. I just wonder if that would leave them without the resources to carry on the next day.
There are those who think distance racing is all about hours on the day, but, even so, I would only liberate that early if I could give the birds every assistance. They would need it if they were up that early.

Out of the three early libs you've managed, what's the greatest number of birds to have been clocked on the day?
629. Pau requires a particular type of pigeon and there aren't that many birds around that can do it. We haven't had a day-race from Pau since 1988, when there were 260 clocked. They were up at 6.15 am and, if my memory serves me right, the winner, George Burgess of Wraysbury, timed at 7.15 pm for a velocity of 1245ypm. Charlie Miller of Wrexham did a little projection on the times of the early birds next day and worked out that approximately 900 must have been in the country on the first day. Out of a total convoy of 4,569, that is not such a huge percentage, especially when you consider that 1988 was a year when everything went the birds' way. They had a southerly component for the first 150 miles and, as the velocities showed, the result sheet was filled pretty rapidly. The conclusion I came to from this was that a lot of pigeons aren't good enough.

Wouldn't it have been possible to liberate early in some of the other years?
People ask why can't we do it more often if the CSCFC can, but they don't think it through. We need to have a southerly component in the wind for the first 150 miles to get a day race - without it, it becomes marginal - and we need to get birds up country. If we can only get a bird or two into the Isle of Wight then, to me, the race has been a failure. This almost happened in 1986. We got one into the Isle of Wight and one into Alton in Hampshire, but Lol Green of Runcorn came to our assistance with the wonderful performance of 'Lol's Pride'.

Do the birds behave any differently when liberated at Pau?
Yes, it's as though they know they have a long way to go. It's difficult to say if they sort themselves into groups going east or west, but it does look to me as if they do begin to do so right away. At Pau they are very rarely in a rush. The field can almost spread to an angle of 130 to 140 degrees, whereas at Nantes they use an angle of less than 90 degrees. They get up much higher and are in your view longer at Pau, but at Nantes it is a different matter. Whatever the weather is like there, when you liberate it's a case of crash, bang, wallop and they're gone.

You said that at Pau it's as if they know how far they've got to go, so do you think it is possible that some pigeons are lost at Pau, not because they can't do the hours, but because they can't get a 'fix' on their loft location?
I take your point, but I'd hesitate to say they can't 'lock on' to their loft location. I'm more inclined to think that at that distance many pigeons just can't do the hours. Distance kills in my opinion. There are not many that can do 500 miles and, when you get to 600 and 700 miles, there are even less. In 1991 there was a pigeon of H Searle's of Ormskirk that took 64th open after flying for twenty hours. There are other examples I could quote, of course, but I think that performance backs up my point that you are looking for special pigeons.

Have you handled many pigeons?
Sufficient, I reckon, to know that many are not good enough. When marking, you sometimes get a pigeon in your hands and, in your own opinion, it shouldn't go. I've also done counter marking in France and I do sometimes think of a particular pigeon that, if it had been mine, I wouldn't have sent it. There's not enough weight on them. I think a pigeon has got to have something to 'spend' when it gets beyond 400 miles.

What's the latest you would liberate?
Two o'clock is the cut off point. I wouldn't liberate later than that. People argue, and rightly so in my opinion, that pigeons would still be full of fly in failing light and would run the risk of injury. There is a relatively new phenomenon now, though. What we see when we are coming back is the northern horizon lit up by road and town lights. Pigeons are still flying around at 1 o'clock in the morning in Trafalgar Square, which

suggests to me that, these days, if a pigeon wants to keep going, it can.

Will birds actually tackle the channel in failing light?
It all depends on the day and the point of crossing. From Cherbourg you can see the English mainland lit up and I think some, those with courage, will have a go. I speak to people who work on the channel and they tell me they see pigeons still churning away in the twilight.

When and how much do you feed?
We feed once per day, generally at four in the afternoon. Over the years I've found that an ounce per bird is about right, but when I know the day in front of them will be testing like last year, I now give them a light feed over the odds. We have twenty in a basket for Pau and I use a dog food tin which holds twenty-four ounces, so I fill it an inch from the top. Last year I fed the full tin, which works out at one fifth of an ounce of additional food.

How much time is there between the final feed and liberation?
Obviously it depends on whether they go up early or late next day, but fourteen hours is the least amount of time. Because we don't know the liberation time in advance when we come to give the last feed, we have to compromise. Extra food might be a handicap if they go early morning but it will turn out to be an asset if they hit a hard day. It is compromise which leads us to sprinkle some food - about one third of an ounce per bird - in the baskets at the marking stations. It's not necessarily the best thing to do as most birds will have been well prepared at home, having eaten before being marked, but it's better than their being fed late in the evening, just prior to being shipped, particularly if the crossing is going to be rough. The food will at least tide them over until we reach France. As you can see, because we are dealing with the unknowns of the weather, we can't plan things perfectly.

What is fed in the baskets?
It can vary from year to year, and is often dependent on whether a corn company is sponsoring the race. The National committee is always having samples sent to it. In any case, we always use a top quality racing mix containing various sorts of pea, plenty of maize, some small stuff - hemp and rape - and a small proportion of beans.

Could you put a percentage on the amount of beans?
I wouldn't like to guess, but it's not much.

Is there a rule to cover what is and isn't fed in the baskets?
I wouldn't have thought so. The subject has been spoken about at length by the committee and fanciers, especially by the widowhood men, but as far as I know, there's no hard and fast rule so long as it's a top quality racing mix.

What basket dressing do you use?

We always use wood chips and there is no better material, especially in long holdovers. In my opinion you can't have too many of them as they wrap around the droppings and dry them off.

Is the way we feed birds - putting the corn into a soiled basket - the best method?

Feeding on the floor of the baskets is also a matter of compromise. After two or three days the baskets are getting a bit mucky and, of course, this can affect a bird which may be a little delicate to begin with. But what are the options? Troughs create a problem because the pigeons hear the corn going into them and go barmy and, remember, we're trying to work in there. A feeding mechanism in the centre of the basket would require freshly-designed panniers, and baskets which allow a pigeon to put its head out of the sides create as many problems as they solve: I've seen pigeons decapitated when loading and unloading takes place. Trays are also a compromise because dominant pigeons will take more than their share.

Do they eat up the full ounce?

By Wednesday afternoon they are beginning to look for grub, but really it depends on how you go about your feeding. If you pull the crates out slightly before you feed, the pigeons get lively and this activity is good for them - it gives them something to do. We take our time and this period is effectively the same as shouting 'food's up, lads'. We feed down all four corners and put a bit down the middle and they eat up better, with all birds having the opportunity to get at their fair share.

Would you explain your watering procedure?

The Catterall's watering system is ideal. The drinkers are made of stainless steel and we have a little squeegee with orthopaedic felt on it, which we run through to clean the drinkers. When we pull the crates out to feed, we don't get them too near the troughs because if they are any nearer than nine inches, it creates too much work. If you do your job properly and don't put the water in until all the activity has died down, you don't get too many chips in the troughs.

Have they access to water at all times when the transporters are stationary?

On the journey to Pau we have to water whenever we stop because of the heat that builds up. Once at the site, water is in front of the birds for the maximum number of hours each day and again on race day.

What's the most days you can successfully hold birds in a basket?

It differs. Youngsters shouldn't be more than two days in a basket, as they soon deteriorate. You can manage old birds better, especially in Catterall's transporters, but, even so, with Pau I would be thinking by Monday about bringing them back to a shorter racepoint.

How long does it take before all birds are airborne?
In all, about twenty seconds. Catterall's transporters are divided into three tiers and we let the bottom one go first as they have less air space and therefore less margin for manoeuvre. I give the command 'go first - clear; go second - clear; go third'. All we are trying to do is get as many as possible out of the line of other birds. I'm not in favour of instantaneous libs because if you let 5,000 birds go at *exactly* the same moment you are asking for trouble. No pigeon's chance from any distance is enhanced by first being beaten to the ground on take off. Pigeons are heavily wing-loaded and it takes them a considerable effort and time to become airborne.

Is Pau a good liberation site?
Satisfactory. It's not as good as it was when we could liberate on a playing field. Nowadays, with 5,000 birds, it requires some intelligent placing of the transporters. You have to be careful to line them up so that the birds don't clash.

What about Nantes and Saintes?
Saintes is okay and Nantes is absolutely first class, being in the centre of a sports complex. It can take twenty or thirty transporters and even a howling wind wouldn't worry you.

Is St Malo a good spot for young birds?
I would say it is as good as you can get from the pigeons' point of view, and it's good for us because we can get there early and sort things out. There's no need to go further inland because when the birds pitch out to sea they are able to use the Cherbourg peninsula as a steadier. If they've got any sense at all, they will fly low over the sea, using the benefit of the cliffs. We once used Lamballe but it's no good because you are tipping straight into the bay

What about Guernsey, which the national also used to use?
We have had a couple of cracking races from Guernsey, but the weather has to be particularly good. You want no wind with young birds because they are already confused. If there's no wind, it gives them time to 'well', otherwise the very well-trained youngsters can drag a lot with them that shouldn't be going their way. Once we had a classic day at Guernsey. They dwelt before drifting off in groups away from the site. After milling about some broke away and struck off in what I took to be the right direction at 120 degrees. The times bore this out. Pigeons were clocked at roughly the same time in Devon and Cornwall as in Kent and Sussex.

Was this untypical?
In a sense. The point with young birds is that they generally don't tackle wind head first - they fly with it. You've got to be careful at Guernsey, as there's often more than a moderate wind.

Could you give me your opinion on some of the other sites we use?
I've seen some dreadful sites. One, close to Dorchester, was next to a clay pigeon range. They were banging away all day. Even then, people tried to say it was okay, but I'm afraid I can't even talk to people like that. Rennes was okay until we moved away from the centre of town, but it's no good now, no matter what anybody says. It can be lethal. It's by a factory entrance and there are articulated trucks coming in and out all the time. There is also a wire fence on one side, and trees and hills on one fringe. It is diabolical and I don't know why we don't use the enormous car park at the football ground. Le Mans is diabolical, too, and they tell me so is Chartres, but I've never liberated there. Sartilly suits the national if it's there alone, but I can imagine it gets a bit naughty if there are seventeen or eighteen thousand birds on site. People moan about Niort because there are cars coming in, but it's okay if you can liberate at the crack of dawn. Lamballe was dreadful, too. It was right in the centre of town and the traffic had to be stopped to allow us to liberate. Avranches can be alright if you're there on your own. It's home to the premier garden in France and a great cathedral, so on marginal days it can be a problem. Bergerac was difficult, but I understand that the site has now been moved to a swimming pool area that is quite satisfactory.

If some sites are so bad, how come they are still used?
The reason is partly that, when combine delegations go over, they see the site in a narrow light. It may be alright for their organisation, but they don't ask themselves what happens when ten or twenty transporters turn up. The problem with some French sites is that they are okay for liberating 900 pigeons, which is as many as some French transporters hold, but they're not okay if you've got 15,000 birds. To my mind, it needs sorting out. An official delegation, which speaks fluent French, should go over and seek out alternative sites. At the moment what we get is governed by what the French fancy wants.

Couldn't we simply use farmland?
I don't see why not. So long as there is a considerable hard standing area available, all we need additionally is a phone and a water supply and these wouldn't present a problem, really.

What's the secret of a good race?
Getting the birds to leave the racepoint quickly. On some days there will be a dark patch out at sea and, from a liberation, a batch of 200 or 300 birds will head straight for it. Consequently, the number milling around grows bigger and bigger with each subsequent liberation. Pigeons will fly directly towards storm clouds, there's no question about it in my mind. I can only think the static electricity spins the old compass a bit. I'm not at all certain that we know enough about what goes on.

Does the sun have to be fully over the horizon before you'll liberate?

I like to see the sun rising just above the horizon as you'll get a snappier lib. Again, though, I've got to qualify this. It is totally different with the nationals than the combines. National birds are special pigeons in prime condition and already know a bit about the game. You can tell by listening that those pigeons know what it is all about. The quality drops with the combines. They are not as eager and never so snappy. You can get a good lib with the national on marginal days, but not with combines so additional care is needed. Unless you're an idiot, your mind catches onto these things.

Whatever the time of day, does the sun need to be clear of cloud to ensure a good start to a race?
For the nationals I like to see the actual sun, but you've got to know a bit about cloud. I've liberated in hazy sunshine and had a good race, but I've known that the cloud would break. The important thing is the strike. Given a good start, pigeons will tolerate quite poor conditions, dog-legging if need be.

Will mist stop a pigeon?
Not necessarily. On a misty day you can get 400 to 600 feet above the ground and see for miles because the angle is different. Pigeons aren't silly and they'll go up higher, especially given a favourable wind.

Do odd pigeons leave the transporter and head straight for home, whilst the others are still circling?
I'm certain they do, although you'll never prove it. Once, at Dorchester, I watched a liberation from a nearby tower. Three or four pigeons from different parts of the batch peeled away from the main group, buzzed together and went.

What is a pigeon's natural flying speed?
All throughout my career I've believed that a pigeon's still air speed is 33mph, but I'm inclined to increase that now. In adverse winds, they can still clock 40mph. Ninety-nine per cent of pigeons will fly better into an adverse wind than on a dead day.

Do pigeons fly in a straight line?
You can't prove it, but I believe they edge the wind. In an aircraft, for example, if you are flying north into an easterly wind, you would point the aircraft further east and crab along the route you want to make good. At Blandford, which is on a platform quite high up, one year the wind was north-north-east and pigeons liberated down country and on their way back to the home counties and London area came over not 15 inches off the ground. They went round and between the transporters and when they got to some trees at the edge of the site they didn't go up, but went round the side of them. Pigeons are brilliant hedge-hoppers.

What do you attribute losses to?

With the best will in the world, to my mind, the majority of fanciers rely on inexperienced weather readers to liberate their pigeons. There are some weekends when, if you were to ask me about the weather the day before, I'd say the birds were better left in the loft. There is also the problem of co-operation. At Weymouth I've seen pigeons from the east of England liberated with those from the west and it has been disgraceful - disgusting. Fortunately, matters are better there now that there is a marshall. I once saw a bloke arrive and immediately set about feeding the birds, even though they were going up that day. When I asked him what he was doing, he said he'd been told to feed them once a day. He didn't realise that that only applied if there was a holdover. He knew nothing about pigeons and it was obvious the organisation had just given him the pigeons, told him to drive down to the racepoint and provide them with a race.

Should more time be allowed between liberations?
At Weymouth on a marginal day ten minute intervals are insufficient. Ten minutes is not long enough with young birds unless it is an exceptionally good day. They need fifteen minutes plus.

Do you get many poorly basket-trained youngsters?
Yes, but it is easier to make up for it with the national because you can make a fuss when you are watering them. It is less easy with some of the combines because they use long, narrow crates and it is harder to draw the young birds forward.

Who should the final decision to liberate rest with?
The convoyer. I'm strongly against control from the home end because the colour of the race is decided at the start. Lots of convoyers are pushed and shoved from the home end and this shouldn't happen.

Since some fanciers are put off sending with the national because of the distances involved with marking, couldn't we have more basketing centres?
The difficulty comes in trying to co-ordinate everything. Even having three marking stations creates a problem. Nothing must travel unaccompanied and the more quickly I've got everything under my control, the less worrying it is.

Could the Pau birds not be marked a day later?
I don't think it would benefit them. To me it is rubbish to rush it, driving all through the night just so as you can have them up as soon as possible. At Pau we arrive at 1 or 2 o'clock, feed the birds at four and it's lovely. It gives the pigeons time to orientate before the next day and us time to sort everything out.

Is air transport the answer?
I've travelled with birds on aircraft - the London South Road Combine experimented for a couple of seasons many years ago - and it has its problems. Non-uniformity of

crates meant they were criss-crossed when loaded so it was difficult to look after the birds, and holdovers are another problem. Invariably the birds are unloaded in a hangar, so on a marginal day you have a situation where, unless you can cover the baskets, you're taking them outside and bringing them back in again. What also happens is that only one aircraft is hired, not a fleet, so if it can't accommodate all the birds it takes one lot and comes back for another. To me, that means treating birds unfairly. For a start, when would you feed?

Can you foresee us making use of the Channel Tunnel?
I don't think it will happen and I'm not absolutely sure where the authorities stand on livestock.

Does any race stick in your memory?
There was the Jacques Chirac incident. One year we turned up at the gate at Pau airfield only to find it shut. There was a little man in a sentry box who, alarmed at seeing our wagons, started muttering 'Non, non, non!'. He got onto his walkie-talkie and consulted some officials. Anyway, down came a couple of high-ranking gendarmes and one or two soldiers, and you've never seen anything so funny in all your life. It was like Laurel and Hardy. In what was meant to be a tight-security area, our two wagons had suddenly presented themselves. We phoned the liberation agent and eventually there were a dozen of us discussing what to do. When they realised on top of everything that we were tied to a mid-day liberation the next day, you should have seen the blood drain out of their faces. Little did we know, that was when Monsieur Chirac's plane was due in. We ended up going to an area belonging to a municipal company and we are still there today.

Do you still get a buzz when you cut the strings?
It does pump the adrenaline, yes, even though I've been doing it so long.

Are you only as good as your last race?
Strictly speaking, yes. You get very few accolades if things go right - not many people will come over to you and say 'thanks, you gave us a good race', but you'll soon get called over the coals if things go wrong. If a race doesn't work out as I imagined it would, I go back to the met office and get the *actual* weather charts to see where I might have gone wrong.

I take it you do the job for love, not money?
Oh crikey, yes, it's never been that well paid! Last year I think the committee suddenly realised they were paying me the same rate as when I left to take a break in 1990 and so they gave me an increase.

PAU
Top Tens

A section-by-section look at some of the best birds & fanciers competing in the National Flying Club Pau race 1992-1995

PAU *Top Tens*

SECTION A

1992 (123 sent 623)	1993 (118 sent 623)	1994 (138 sent 735)	1995 (116 sent 615)
1. Cannon	1. Puddephatt Bros	1. Cannon	1. Lilliott
2. Wynn	2. Jukes	2. Cannon	2. Lilliott
3. Harding	3. Wynn	3. Puddephatt Bros	3. Cannon
4. Kingwell	4. Shepherd/Buckley	4. White W&A	4. Reed
5. Cannon	5. Shepherd/Buckley	5. Shepherd/Buckley	5. Lilliott
6. Cannon	6. Wynn	6. Kitching & Dtr	6. Puddephatt Bros
7. Whitelegg	7. Jackson	7. McGee	7. Cannon
8. Morter	8. Everett	8. Puddephatt Bros	8. Newman
9. Shepherd/Buckley	9. Cannon	9. Cannon	9. Farr
10. Cannon	10. Cannon	10. Cannon	10. Whitelegg

MULTIPLE PERFORMERS

Cannon's 10th Section, 83rd Open 1993 & 10th Section, 111th Open 1994 same bird

Cannon's 5th Section, 62nd Open 1992 subsequently 42nd Section, 303rd Open NFC Pau 1995

Cannon's 9th Section, 70th Open 1993 previously 300th Open NFC Bordeaux 1991. Subsequently 27th Section, 298th Open NFC Pau 1994

Puddephatt's 8th Section, 68th Open 1994 previously 13th Section, 122nd Open NFC Pau 1992 & 50th Section, 410th Open NFC Pau 1993. Subsequently 13th Section, 360th Open NFC Saintes 1994

Cannon's 9th Section, 98th Open 1994 & 3rd Section, 29th Open 1995 same bird

Lilliott's 1st Section, 3rd Open 1995 previously 27th Section NFC Saintes 1994

Cannon's 1st Section, 14th Open 1994 subsequently 12th Section, 123rd Open NFC Pau 1995

Cannon's 2nd Section, 22nd Open 1994 subsequently 28th Section, 231st Open NFC Pau 1995

Puddephatt's 6th Section, 47th Open 1995 previously 18th Section, 226th Open NFC Pau 1994. Subsequently 6th Section, 95th Open BBC Bordeaux less than a month later

Cannon's 7th Section, 58th Open 1995 previously 10th Section, 348th Open NFC Saintes 1994

Farr's 9th Section, 92nd Open 1995 previously 7th Section, 255th Open NFC Nantes 1995

*(not in table) Blake's 11th Section, 90th Open 1993 subsequently 6th Open BICC Perpignan 1994

PAU *Top Tens*

SECTION B

1992 (184 sent 886)	1993 (191 sent 847)	1994 (181 sent 833)	1995 (170 sent 799)
1. Ayling	1. Painter	1. Stanley	1. Stanley
2. Lupo	2. Deacon E	2. Holdoway	2. Stanley
3. Painter	3. Stanley	3. White	3. Harris A
4. Gregory	4. Sparshott	4. Wood	4. Holdaway
5. Cottrell	5. Cox	5. Holdaway	5. Rawlings
6. Squibb	6. Corbin	6. Smith P&F	6. Bunney
7. Monnery	7. Wright	7. Bakes	7. Holdaway
8. Deacon A&T	8. Corbin	8. Attrill	8. Deacon A&T
9. Rann	9. Bunney	9. Holdaway	9. Gordon
10. Thorn	10. Bainton	10. Willis	10. Attrill

MULTIPLE PERFORMERS

Ayling's 1st Section, 11th Open 1992 subsequently 27thSection, 172nd Open NFC Pau 1994

Cottrell's 5th Section, 34th Open 1992 subsequently 33rd Open CSCFC Pau 1994

Monnery's 7th Section, 65th Open 1992 previously 23rd Open BICC Perpignan 1991

Thorn's 10th Section, 79th Open 1992 subsequently 74th Open BBC Palamos 1993

Painter's 1st Section, 4th Open 1993 subsequently 36th Section, 158th Open NFC Pau 1995

Deacon's 2nd Section, 19th Open 1993 subsequently 36th Section, 217th Open NFC Pau 1994

Stanley's 3rd Section, 32nd Open 1993 subsequently 18th Section, 108th Open NFC Pau 1994

Corbin's 6th Section, 66th Open 1993 previously 17th Section, 70th Open CSCFC Pau 1992 & 92nd Open CSCFC Rennes 1993. Subsequently 318th Open NFC Saintes 1994, 8th Open BICC Pau 1995, 55th Open BBC Bordeaux 1995 & 1st BICC Dax 1995

Corbin's 8th Section, 82nd Open 1993 subsequently 83rd Open BBC Nantes 1994, 27th Section, 158th Open CSCFC Nantes 1994, 32nd Section, 198th Open

NFC Pau 1994, 68th Section, 310th Open NFC Pau 1995 & 79th Open BBC Bordeaux 1995

Bainton's 10th Section, 114th Open 1993 subsequently 344th Open NFC Nantes 1994 & 45th Section, 210th Open NFC Pau 1995

Stanley's 1st Section, 11th Open 1994 subsequently 20th Section, 196th Open NFC Saintes 1994 & 74th Section, 468th Open NFC Nantes 1995

Wood's 4th Section, 33rd Open 1994 previously 10th Section, 25th Open CSCFC Pau 1993. Subsequently 89th Section, 484th Open NFC Pau 1995

Smith's 6th Section, 43rd Open 1994 subsequently 67th Section, 308th Open NFC Pau 1995

Attrill's 8th Section, 46th Open 1994 & 10th Section, 31st Open 1995 same bird

Willis's 10th Section, 63rd Open 1994 subsequently 21st Section, 72nd Open NFC Pau 1995

Harris's 3rd Section, 11th Open 1995 previously 53rd Section, 338th Open NFC Nantes 1995

PAU *Top Tens*

SECTION C

1992 (56 sent 206)	**1993** (51 sent 178)	**1994** (48 sent 182)	**1995** (40 sent 152)
1. Lovell	1. Mills	1. Woods	1. Haydon
2. Snell & Fursey	2. Hustler	2. Staddon Bros	2. Hustler
3. Pitney	3. Whitbread	3. Lovell & Son	3. James
4. Russell	4. Whitbread	4. Haydon	4. Jack
5. Walters	5. Stoodley	5. Jack	5. Hemburrow
6. Staddon Bros	6. Stagg	6. Lovell & Son	6. Lovell & Son
7. Bond	7. Churchill	7. Lovell & Son	7. Woods
8. Whitefield	8. Whitbread	8. Jack	8. Bond
9. Stephenson	9. Wellen	9. Thomas	9. Ford
10. Phillips	10. Woods	10. King	10. Stephenson

MULTIPLE PERFORMERS

Staddon's 6th Section, 94th Open 1992 previously 3rd Section, 77th Open NFC Bordeaux 1991

Whitefield's 8th Section, 115th Open 1992 subsequently 35th Open BICC Perpignan 1994

Mills's 1st Section, 120th Open 1993 previously 25th Section, 67th Open CSCFC Pau 1992 & 16th Section, 367th Open NFC Bordeaux 1991

Whitbread's 3rd Section, 131st Open 1993 previously 21st Section, 395th Open NFC Bordeaux 1991

Stagg's 6th Section, 312th Open 1993 previously 138th Open CSCFC Pau 1992

Churchill's 7th Section, 353rd Open 1993 previously 323rd Open CSCFC Rennes 1993

Woods's 10th Section, 415th Open 1993 subsequently 170th Open CSCFC Pau 1994

Lovell's 6th Section, 178th Open 1994 & 6th Section, 91st Open 1995 same bird

Lovell's 7th Section, 188th Open 1994 previously 49th Section NFC Saintes 1993

King's 10th Section 1994 previously 16th Section, 506th Open NFC Pau 1993

Jack's 4th Section, 66th Open 1995 previously 14th Section, 439th Open NFC Pau 1994

Woods's 7th Section, 291st Open 1995 previously 20th Open CSCFC Pau 1992 & 13th Section, 318th Open NFC Bordeaux 1991

PAU *Top Tens*

SECTION D

1992 (106 sent 260)	**1993** (96 sent 254)	**1994** (97 sent 262)	**1995** (80 sent 246)
1. Watson	1. Stout	1. Stanford	1. Underhill & Watts
2. Grose	2. Pym	2. Carpenter	2. Parker D&S
3. Jenkin	3. Randell	3. Steere	3. Buck
4. Carpenter	4. Bacon	4. Naum	4. Carter
5. Steere	5. Sanders	5. Gullon	5. Steere
6. Jordain	6. Plowman	6. Wellington	6. Andrews/Goddard
7. Stout	7. Davis	7. Wellington	7. Buck
8. Bowden	8. Randell	8. Randell	8. Pring
9. Cox	9. Dicks	9. Dart	9. Anthony
10. Tozer	10. Portshouse	10. Wilkinson & Son	10. End

MULTIPLE PERFORMERS

Grose's 2nd Section, 9th Open 1992 subsequently 23rd Open BICC Perpignan 1994

Jenkin's 3rd Section, 19th Open 1992 subsequently 7th Section, 86th Open NFC Nantes 1993

Carpenter's 4th Section, 28th Open 1992 & 2nd Section, 268th Open 1994 same bird

Steere's 5th Section, 41st Open 1992 & 3rd Section, 486th Open 1994 same bird. Also 34th Section NFC Saintes 1993 & 15th Section, 468th Open NFC Pau 1995

Cox's 9th Section, 54th Open 1992 previously 10th Section NFC Bordeaux 1991

Randell's 3rd Section, 587th Open 1993 & 8th Section 1994 same bird. Previously 5th Section, 408th Open NFC Bordeaux 1991

Bacon's 4th Section, 605th Open 1993 previously 4th Section, 155th Open NFC Saintes 1992

Randell's 8th Section, 780th Open 1993 previously 10th Section NFC Saintes 1992

Naum's 4th Section 1994 previously 21st Section, 423rd Open NFC Nantes 1993, 3rd Section NFC Saintes 1993 & 18th Section, 96th Open CSCFC Pau 1993

Dart's 9th Section 1994 subsequently 16th Section, 485th Open NFC Pau 1995

Buck's 7th Section, 236th Open 1995 previously 22nd Section NFC Saintes 1993

Anthony's 9th Section, 418th Open 1995 previously 17th Section, 246th Open NFC Saintes 1994

PAU *Top Tens*

SECTION E

1992 (344 sent 1438)	1993 (307 sent 1418)	1994 (324 sent 1620)	1995 (289 sent 1362)
1. Berry	1. Lyons	1. Brunt & Son	1. Mauger
2. Entwistle	2. Bacon	2. Pisani	2. Dickinson
3. King	3. Hayward	3. O'Connor P&A	3. May K
4. Muir	4. Pisani	4. Ball	4. Freeman
5. Sando	5. Mark & Peart	5. Barrable	5. Gartshore
6. Townsend R	6. Besant	6. Thompson	6. Lane/Broadbridge
7. Delea	7. Cadden & Pussey	7. Stone	7. Flint
8. Kinnersley	8. Besant	8. Birch & Son	8. Archibald H&P
9. Taylor & Ramsey	9. Roper	9. Morris	9. Wills J&R
10. Still	10. Redfern	10. Roper	10. Burgess

MULTIPLE PERFORMERS

Delea's 7th Section, 35th Open 1992 subsequently 83rd Open L&SECC Le Mans 1993 & 7th Open BICC Perpignan 1994

Lyons's 1st Section, 3rd Open 1993 previously 8th East Section EECC Beauvais 1993

Hayward's 3rd Section, 8th Open 1993 subsequently 96th Section, 344th Open NFC Pau 1994

Pisani's 4th Section, 9th Open 1993 previously 17th Section, 104th Open NFC Saintes 1992

Besant's 6th Section, 11th Open 1993 subsequently 12th Section, 36th Open NFC Saintes 1993, 39th Section, 158th Open NFC Pau 1994 & 39th Section, 368th Open NFC Saintes 1994

Cadden & Pussey's 7th Section, 12th Open 1993 previously 8th West Section EECC Falaise 1993

Brunt's 1st Section, 2nd Open 1994 previously 53rd Section, 119th Open NFC Nantes 1994

Thompson's 6th Section, 21st Open 1994 subsequently 17th Section, 96th Open NFC Pau 1995

Stone's 7th Section, 23rd Open 1994 previously 82nd Section, 395th Open NFC Saintes 1992

Morris's 9th Section, 30th Open 1994 previously 72nd Section, 193rd Open NFC Pau 1993

Mauger's 1st Section, 5th Open 1995 previously 27th Section, 175th Open NFC Saintes 1992, 125th Section, 479th Open NFC Saintes 1993 & 24th Section, 277th Open NFC Saintes 1994

Wills's 9th Section, 67th Open 1995 previously 13th Section, 42nd Open NFC Pau 1994

Burgess's 10th Section, 70th Open 1995 previously 15th Section, 56th Open NFC Pau 1994

PAU *Top Tens*

SECTION F

1992 (78 sent 260)	**1993** (73 sent 213)	**1994** (77 sent 273)	**1995** (76 sent 289)
1. Kendal	1. Wise	1. Clark B&L	1. Biss & Waite
2. Stovin	2. Kimber	2. Rogers	2. Davis
3. Newman	3. Cowley	3. Pitts	3. Kelly
4. Callard	4. Perks	4. Brickell	4. Biss & Waite
5. Ferriman	5. Goddard	5. Flurry	5. Moppett
6. Wise	6. Badnell	6. McCluskey & Keys	6. Biss & Waite
7. Palmer	7. Chupka	7. Callard	7. McCluskey & Keys
8. Stovin	8. Stowell	8. Pitts	8. Biss & Waite
9. Hall	9. Ralph	9. Rogers	9. Biss & Waite
10. Stimpson	10. Merrills	10. Chupka	10. Robinson

MULTIPLE PERFORMERS

Kendal's 1st Section, 1st Open 1992 previously 4th
Section, 86th Open NFC Pau, 2nd Section,
67th Open NFC Nantes 1990, 20th Section,
408th Open NFC Pau 1991 & 6th Section
108th Open CSCFC Nantes 1992

Callard's 4th Section, 43rd Open 1992 & 7th
Section, 146th Open 1994 same bird. Also
22nd Section, 450th Open NFC Pau 1993 &
24th Section, 500th Open NFC Pau 1995

Wise's 1st Section, 25th Open 1993 subsequently
8th Section, 217th Open NFC Saintes 1993

Badnell's 6th Section, 125th Open 1993 also 39th
Open BICC Perpignan 1993

Ralph's 9th Section, 181st Open 1993 previously
8th Section, 74th Open CSCFC Pau 1992

Rogers's 2nd Section, 59th Open 1994 previously
15th Section, 454th Open NFC Nantes
1994, 14th Section NFC Nantes 1993 &
139th Open CSCFC Pau 1992

McCluskey & Keys's 6th Section, 138th Open 1994
& 7th Section, 159th Open 1995 same bird

Biss & Waite's 1st Section, 42nd Open 1995
previously 5th Section, 169th Open NFC
Saintes 1994

Biss & Waite's 4th Section, 129th Open 1995
previously 26th Section NFC Nantes 1994
& 20th Section NFC Nantes 1995

Biss & Waite's 8th Section, 204th Open 1995
previously 4th Section, 151st Open NFC
Saintes 1994

PAU *Top Tens*

SECTION G

1992 (130 sent 481)	**1993** (136 sent 435)	**1994** (135 sent 539)	**1995** (128 sent 506)
1. Miles S&V	1. Selway	1. Harding Bros	1. Slocombe
2. Ellis	2. Newton	2. Fear Bros	2. Nethercott & Son
3. Cooper	3. Harding Bros	3. Reed	3. Brooks Bros
4. Selway	4. Holley	4. Fear Bros	4. Nelmes Bros
5. Fear Bros	5. Allen	5. Cooper	5. Atherton
6. Rivers	6. Wells	6. Allen	6. Nethercott & Son
7. Gardiner	7. Ellis	7. Mullholland	7. Padfield Family
8. Mullholland	8. Rivers	8. Miles S&V	8. Sheppard
9. Sheppard	9. Warden	9. Fear Bros	9. Nethercott & Son
10. Taylor	10. Nurse	10. Bailey	10. Wall

MULTIPLE PERFORMERS

Ellis's 2nd Section, 6th Open 1992 & 7th Section, 115th Open 1993 same bird. Subsequently 25th Section, 200th Open NFC Pau 1994 & 48th Section, 330th Open NFC Pau 1995

Rivers's 6th Section, 12th Open 1992 & 8th Section, 124th Open 1993 same bird

Mullholland's 8th Section, 14th Open 1992 & 7th Section, 31st Open 1994 same bird

Sheppard's 9th Section, 16th Open 1992 subsequently 53rd Section, 469th Open NFC Pau 1993 & 24th Section, 197th Open NFC Pau 1994

Selway's 1st Section, 26th Open 1993 previously 3rd Section, 12th Open NFC Nantes 1993

Harding's 3rd Section, 80th Open 1993 subsequently 51st Section, 438th Open NFC Pau 1994

Holley's 4th Section, 96th Open 1993 previously 30th Section, 314th Open NFC Bordeaux 1991. Subsequently 13th Section, 61st Open NFC Saintes 1994

Allen's 5th Section, 102nd Open 1993 & 6th Section, 29th Open 1994 same bird. Also 21st Section, 86th Open NFC Saintes 1992 & 62nd Section, 407th Open NFC Pau 1995

Nurse's 10th Section, 160th Open 1993 previously 7th Open 31st Open BBC Nantes 1993, 17th Open BICC Perpignan 1992 & 6th Open BICC Perpignan 1991

Cooper's 5th Section, 9th Open 1994 previously 11th Section, 51st Open CSCFC Nantes 1994. Subsequently 24th Section, 95th Open NFC Saintes 1994

Nethercott's 2nd Section, 2nd Open 1995 previously 52nd Section, 467th Open NFC Pau 1993

Nethercott's 6th Section, 27th Open 1995 previously 43rd Section, 331st Open NFC Pau 1994 & 137th Open CSCFC Pau 1992

Padfield's 7th Section, 33rd Open 1995 previously 15th Section, 74th Open NFC Nantes 1993

Sheppard's 8th Section, 34th Open 1995 previously 13th Section, 33rd Open NFC Pau 1992

PAU *Top Tens*

SECTION H

1992 (65 sent 249)	**1993** (81 sent 278)	**1994** (74 sent 265)	**1995** (65 sent 295)
1. Albon	1. Biss	1. Biss	1. Biss
2. Eccles	2. Biss	2. Biss	2. Biss
3. Hakes	3. Biss	3. Mackenzie H&P	3. Long & Cox
4. Hacon	4. Biss	4. Daniels	4. Barber & Wilkinson
5. Biss	5. Biss	5. Biss	5. Rouse
6. Biss	6. Biss	6. Briggs	6. Biss
7. Rix	7. Woodyard	7. Owens	7. Biss
8. Moseley	8. Mackenzie H&P	8. Shaw	8. Shaw
9. Biss	9. Biss	9. Eccles	9. Sharman & Kneller
10. Stow	10. Biss	10. Mason	10. Daniels & Sharman

MULTIPLE PERFORMERS

Biss's 6th Section, 381st Open 1992 subsequently 30th Section, 391st Open NFC Saintes 1993

Biss's 2nd Section, 2nd Open 1993 previously 5th BICC Perpignan, 689 miles, 1990

Biss's 3rd Section, 7th Open 1993 previously 13th Section, 368th Open NFC Pau 1990, 12th Section, 177th Open NFC Pau 1991, 6th Section, 217th Open NFC Bordeaux 1991

Biss's 4th Section, 21st Open 1993 subsequently 14th Section, 319th Open NFC Pau 1994

Biss's 5th Section, 30th Open 1993 subsequently 1st Section, 20th Open NFC Saintes 1993 & 19th Section, 458th Open NFC Pau 1995. Previously 317th Open MNFC St Malo 1992

Biss's 6th Section, 38th Open 1993 previously 2nd Section, 25th Open NFC Bordeaux 1991 & 1st East Section EECC Rouen 1993. Subsequently 11th Section, 202nd Open NFC Pau 1994 & 13th Section NFC Saintes 1994

Mackenzie's 8th Section, 52nd Open 1993 & 3rd Section, 64th Open 1994 same bird. Also 16th Section NFC Nantes 1993 & 15th Section NFC Nantes 1994

Biss's 9th Section, 65th Open 1993 & 6th Section, 311th Open 1995 same bird. Previously 9th Section, 483rd Open NFC Bordeaux 1991

Biss's 10th Section, 74th Open 1993 & 7th Section, 336th Open 1995 same bird. Also 23rd Section, 448th Open NFC Pau 1994

Biss's 2nd Section, 51st Open 1994 previously 32nd Section, 409th Open NFC Saintes 1993. Subsequently 8th Section NFC Saintes 1994 & 12th Section, 392nd Open NFC Pau 1995

Biss's 5th Section, 104th Open 1994 subsequently 2nd Section, 315th Open NFC Saintes 1994. Previously 22nd Section, 293rd Open NFC Saintes 1993

Owens's 7th Section, 125th Open 1994 subsequently 21st Section, 464th Open NFC Pau 1995

Shaw's 8th Section, 136th Open 1994 & 8th Section, 361st Open 1995 same bird. Also 18th Section, 162nd Open NFC Pau 1993, 8th Section, 400th Open NFC Saintes 1992 & 15th Section NFC Saintes 1994

Biss's 1st Section, 73rd Open 1995 previously 13th Section NFC Nantes 1994

Barber & Wilkinson's 4th Section, 140th Open 1995 previously 10th Section NFC Saintes 1994

Daniels & Sharman's 10th Section, 375th Open 1995 previously 16th Section, 149th Open NFC Pau 1993

PAU *Top Tens*

SECTION I

1992 (70 sent 267)	**1993** (97 sent 321)	**1994** (83 sent 308)	**1995** (88 sent 308)
1. Phillips	1. Moore	1. Till Bros	1. Froggatt
2. Edwards	2. Bowley	2. Mole	2. Cooksey & Dtr
3. Glover	3. Whitehurst	3. Bowley	3. Froggatt
4. Glover	4. Cotgrave	4. Potter	4. Glover
5. Glover	5. Page	5. Maud	5. Froggatt
6. Purchas	6. Ashfield	6. Bateman	6. Burden
7. Tranter	7. Moore	7. Stephenson & Allen	7. Oliver
8. White	8. Goddard	8. Froggatt	8. Locke & Son
9. Glover	9. Halstead	9. Oliver	9. Charles
10. Wells	10. Bush	10. Oliver	10. Whitehurst

MULTIPLE PERFORMERS

Glover's 3rd Section, 272nd Open 1992 previously 5th Section, 84th Open NFC Pau 1990 & 44th Open BICC Perpignan, 720 miles, 1991

Purchas's 6th Section 1992 subsequently 12th Section, 208th Open NFC Pau 1995

Cotgrave's 4th Section, 71st Open 1993 previously 30th Section, 76th Open MNFC Bergerac 1992. Subsequently 17th Section, 275th Open NFC Pau 1995

Halstead's 9th Section, 145th Open 1993 previously 35th Section, 86th Open MNFC Bergerac 1992 & 117th Open MNFC Nantes 1992

Bowley's 3rd Section, 65th Open 1994 previously 36th Section, 228th Open MNFC Nantes two weeks earlier

Bateman's 6th Section, 120th Open 1994 previously 21st Section, 210th Open NFC

Saintes 1992 & 28th Section NFC Saintes 1993. Subsequently 17th Section, 214th Open NFC Saintes 1994 & 16th Section, 292nd Open NFC Nantes 1995

Oliver's 9th Section, 205th Open 1994 previously 7th Open BICC Perpignan, 703 miles, 1992

Glover's 4th Section, 348th Open 1992 & 4th Section, 46th Open 1995 same bird. Also 14th Section, 254th Open NFC Pau 1993 & 23rd Section, 475th Open NFC Pau 1994

Froggatt's 5th Section, 54th Open 1995 & 8th Section, 185th Open 1994 same bird. Previously 36th Section, 748th Open NFC Pau 1993

Burden's 6th Section, 68th Open 1995 previously 15th Section, 288th Open NFC Pau 1994

PAU *Top Tens*

SECTION J

1992 (123 sent 316)	**1993** (115 sent 279)	**1994** (133 sent 314)	**1995** (120 sent 316)
1. Jones	1. Shore A	1. Ward Bros & Ptnr	1. Ford
2. Jones	2. Baker	2. Jones & Markham	2. Beech
3. Baker	3. Patrick Bros	3. Shore A	3. Rutty
4. Bennett	4. Rogers	4. Weaver	4. Randell
5. Knowles	5. Lloyd	5. Ellams	5. Patrick Bros
6. Dobson	6. Dobson	6. Whittingham	6. Jones & Markham
7. Kirkland	7. Jones	7. Ford	7. Shore A
8. Lewis	8. Whalley	8. Carter	8. Williams
9. Bates	9. Kirkland	9. Dudley Bros	9. Jones
10. Dobson	10. Davis	10. Patrick Bros	10. Baker

MULTIPLE PERFORMERS

Jones's 1st Section, 24th Open 1992 previously 13th Section, 83rd Open NFC Pau 1987, 7th Section, 244th Open NFC Pau 1988, 4th Section, 81st Open NFC Pau 1989 & 27th Section, 312th Open NFC Pau 1990

Jones's 2nd Section, 46th Open 1992 previously 1st Section, 5th Open NFC Pau 1987, 6th Section, 104th Open NFC Pau 1989 & 54th Section, 788th Open NFC Pau 1990. Sister to 1st Section 1992

Baker's 3rd Section, 171st Open 1992, 2nd Section, 44th Open 1993 & 10th Section, 224th Open 1995 same bird. Also 47th Section, 351st Open NFC Saintes 1993, 74th Open BBC Nantes 1992 & 16th Section, 76th Open NFC Nantes 1993

Knowles's 5th Section, 283rd Open 1992 previously 12th Section, 348th Open NFC Bordeaux 1991

Shore's 1st Section, 33rd Open 1993, 3rd Section, 27th Open 1994 & 7th Section, 150th Open 1995 same bird. Also 39th Section, 131st Open NFC Nantes 1993 & 5th Section, 248th Open BBC Nantes 1994

Patrick's 3rd Section, 73rd Open 1993 subsequently 24th Section, 385th Open NFC Pau 1994

Lloyd's 5th Section, 116th Open 1993 previously 54th Section, 192nd Open NFC Nantes 1993. Subsequently 293rd Open MNFC Nantes 1994 & 54th Section NFC Saintes 1994

Dobson's 6th Section, 352nd Open 1992 & 6th Section, 130th Open 1993 same bird

Jones's 7th Section, 142nd Open 1993 subsequently 58th Section NFC Pau 1994

Kirkland's 9th Section, 156th Open 1993 previously 13th Section, 37th Open MNFC Bergerac 1992. Subsequently 25th Section, 405th Open NFC Pau 1994

Jones & Markham's 2nd Section, 17th Open 1994 & 6th Section, 110th Open 1995 same bird

Ellams's 5th Section, 92nd Open 1994 previously 24th Section, 93rd Open BBC Nantes 1994 & 41st Section, 292nd Open NFC Saintes 1993

Ford's 7th Section, 99th Open 1994 previously 10th Section, 81st Open NFC Saintes 1993. Subsequently 34th Section, 142nd Open NFC Nantes 1995

Carter's 8th Section, 115th Open 1994 previously 424th Open NFC Nantes 1993

Dudley's 9th Section, 118th Open 1994 subsequently 24th Section, 544th Open NFC Pau 1995

Ford's 1st Section, 30th Open 1995 previously 26th Section, 411th Open NFC Pau 1994

Jones's 9th Section, 221st Open 1995 previously 71st Section, 327th Open NFC Nantes 1995 & 16th Section, 210th Open NFC Pau 1994

PAU *Top Tens*

SECTION K

1992 (65 sent 186)	1993 (72 sent 185)	1994 (70 sent 219)	1995 (62 sent 206)
1. Riley	1. Henderson	1. Woollis	1. Bush
2. Bush	2. Gordon	2. Hanby	2. Hinchcliffe & Son
3. Bush	3. Mager	3. Emerton	3. Bush
4. Bush	4. Bush	4. Horsfall	4. Barrett
5. Goacher	5. Hinchcliffe	5. Bush	5. Hinchcliffe & Son
6. Wall & White	6. Bush	6. Bush	6. Henderson
7. Bush	7. Denney	7. Mager	7. Gould
8. Judge	8. Denney	8. Garside	8. Dixon & Sons
9. Hickson	9. Emerton	9. Dixon	9. McGrevy & Co
10. Dixon	10. Littlewood	10. Walker	10. Garside

MULTIPLE PERFORMERS

Riley's 1st Section, 218th Open 1992 subsequently 2nd BICC Barcelona 1993, covering 863 miles at 694ypm. Previously 21st Section, 567th Open NFC Pau

Bush's 2nd Section, 223rd Open 1992 & 4th Section, 75th Open 1993 same bird - 'Betty'. Previously 9th Section, 475th Open NFC Bordeaux 1991

Bush's 7th Section, 480th Open 1992, 6th Section, 86th Open 1993 & 6th Section, 130th Open 1994 same bird. Previously 21st Section, 528th Open NFC Bordeaux 1991

Henderson's 1st Section, 5th Open 1993 & 6th Section, 427th Open 1995 same bird. Also 29th Section NFC Pau 1994

Gordon's 2nd Section, 17th Open 1993 subsequently 19th Section, 367th Open NFC Pau 1994

Mager's 3rd Section, 64th Open 1993 & 7th Section, 154th Open 1994 same bird

Hinchcliffe's 5th Section, 77th Open 1993 previously 22nd Open Northern Classic Rennes two weeks earlier

Denney's 7th Section, 109th Open 1993 - the 'Bordeaux Cock'. Subsequently 7th Section, 132nd Open NFC Saintes 1993 & 3rd Section, 85th Open NFC Nantes 1994. Previously 1st 700 Mile Club, 8th Section, 452nd Open NFC Bordeaux 1991

Denney's 8th Section, 170th Open 1993 subsequently 18th Section, 337th Open NFC Saintes 1993

Emerton's 9th Section, 282nd Open 1993 subsequently 30th Section NFC Pau 1994 & 31st Section NFC Nantes 1993

Hanby's 2nd Section, 52nd Open 1994 previously 1st Section, 14th Open NFC Saintes 1992, 20th Section, 468th Open NFC Saintes 1993 & 30th Section NFC Nantes 1993

Bush's 5th Section, 106th Open 1994 previously 12th Section, 233rd Open NFC Saintes 1993. Subsequently 12th Section, 495th Open NFC Pau 1995

Dixon's 9th Section, 207th Open 1994 previously 8th Section, 161st Open NFC Saintes 1992

Walker's 10th Section, 228th Open 1994 previously 59th Open BICC Perpignan 1992, 776 miles

Bush's 1st Section, 126th Open 1995 previously 21st Section NFC Saintes 1994

Bush's 3rd Section, 334th Open 1995 previously 15th Section, 308th Open NFC Pau 1994

PAU *Top Tens*

SECTION L

1992 (144 sent 379)	**1993** (157 sent 392)	**1994** (161 sent 426)	**1995** (143 sent 388)
1. Pimlott	1. Bradbury	1. Jones D	1. Brough
2. Littlewood	2. Locke	2. Clements P	2. Clements P
3. Little	3. Parkinson/Wilkinson	3. Hulme	3. Corbett
4. Green	4. Fletcher	4. Bellis	4. Lyons
5. Searle	5. Sutton	5. Hibbert	5. Orritt
6. Carson	6. Harrison	6. Allbutt	6. Griffiths & Lloyd
7. Orritt	7. Brough	7. Kay F&M	7. Brough
8. Pogonowski	8. Clements J	8. Croxton	8. Brough
9. Hall	9. Griffiths & Lloyd	9. Marshall	9. Parker
10. Hibbert	10. Allbutt	10. Clements J	10. Richards